HOME RULE

HOME RULE

National Sovereignty
and the
Separation of
Natives and Migrants

NANDITA SHARMA

Duke University Press Durham and London 2020

Printed in the United States of America on acid-free paper ∞
Designed by Drew Sisk
Typeset in Canela Text by Westchester Publishing Services

Library of Congress Cataloging-in-Publication Data
Names: Sharma, Nandita Rani, [date] author.
Title: Home rule : national sovereignty and the separation of
    natives and migrants / Nandita Sharma.
Description: Durham : Duke University Press Books, 2020. |
    Includes bibliographical references and index.
Identifiers: LCCN 2019023958 (print)
LCCN 2019023959 (ebook)
ISBN 9781478000778 (hardcover)
ISBN 9781478000952 (paperback)
ISBN 9781478002451 (ebook)
Subjects: LCSH: Sovereignty. | Self-determination, National. |
    Postcolonialism. | World politics—1945–1989.
Classification: LCC JC327 .S5165 2020 (print) | LCC JC327
    (ebook) | DDC 320.1/509045—DC23
LC record available at https://lccn.loc.gov/2019023958
LC ebook record available at https://lccn.loc.gov/2019023959

Cover art: Pieter Bruegel the Elder, *The Tower of Babel*, 1563.
Oil on panel. Wikimedia Commons/Google Art Project.

For Santosh Rani Sharma and Gaye Chan

CONTENTS

ACKNOWLEDGMENTS   IX

1   Home Rule: The National Politics of Separation   1

2   The Imperial Government of Mobility and Stasis   36

3   The National Government of Mobility and Stasis   62

4   The Jealousy of Nations: Globalizing National   90
     Constraints on Human Mobility

5   The Postcolonial New World Order   117
     and the Containment of Decolonization

6   Developing the Postcolonial New World Order   142

7   Global Lockdown: Postcolonial Expansion of   163
     National Citizenship and Immigration Controls

8   National Autochthonies and the Making of   205
     Postcolonial National-Natives

9   Postseparation: Struggles   268
     for a Decolonized Commons

     NOTES   285

     BIBLIOGRAPHY   299

     INDEX   347

ACKNOWLEDGMENTS

My mother, Santosh Sharma, died while I was working on this book. In many ways I've written it because of—and for—her. Like so many of us, she was continuously refashioned according to the historical changes taking place in state forms, and through an ever-encompassing capitalism. My mother was born a "British subject." As the clock ticked past midnight on the day India achieved home rule, she was made an "Indian national." That same day, she set out for the Delhi railway station to bring food to those forced to flee Pakistan, the other side of partitioned British India. There she encountered people desperate to flee massacres in India and she offered them food as well. Santosh lived the second half of her life in Vancouver, first as an "immigrant" and then as a "Canadian citizen."

Denigrated as a "native" in British India, Santosh and her parents strongly supported M. K. Gandhi's nationalist version of decolonization. My father, Kesho Ram Sharma, was a communist and held a different view of decolonization than my mother, but he was enthralled with modernity. Kesho took Santosh to see her first film: *Mother India*, a classic tale of development. He also forced her to have three abortions in order to comply with India's modernization campaign of two children per (nuclear) family. When my parents immigrated to Canada with my brother and me, we were among the first cohort admitted after Canada's "preferred races and nations" clause was removed. In Canada, Santosh experienced racism day in and day out. Beaten by strangers on the street, harassed on buses for wearing saris and a nose ring, she was only able to find employment at a number of very low-paying jobs, from seasonal farm worker to nanny to dishwasher to short-order cook in fast food hamburger chains. Santosh nonetheless made a life for herself and for those she loved: my brother, Paul Sharma; her mother, Maya Devi Sharma; her sister, Kaushalya Devi Sharma, who was denied entry to Canada; her nephew, Yash Pal Sharma; and me. She even supported my abusive father. She learned Punjabi and made good friends across racialized, nationalized, and sexualized divides. She was never seen as a Canadian in Canada. And she never gave up her fierce anticolonial spirit. In one memorable moment, upon watching the Canadian state send in armed soldiers to put down a revolt by Mohawks in Kanehsatà:ke and Kahnawà:ke in 1992, she commented, "Us and them: same, same." She recognized the violence against Mohawks from her own experiences of colonialism in both India and Canada. "Same, same" was a vow of solidarity to defeat racists, nationalists, capitalists, and anyone who lords their power over us. My mother supported me in all of my own transformations and taught me much. Thank you Mama.

There are so many others to thank for their insights and their material, emotional, and critical support. The first to thank are all the people variously categorized by states as natives, migrants, citizens, or as stateless, whose determined rejection of nations, borders, states, and capital has been fundamental to my thinking about politics and social relations. I'd also like to thank—and remember—my brother, Paul Sharma; Roxana Ng, my PhD supervisor at the Ontario Institute for Studies in Education at the University of Toronto; and my friend Kerry Preibisch, whose unwavering solidarity with migrant farm workers was an inspiration. All three were tremendously influential in shaping my life and work and their passing has left a huge hole in my heart. My partner and comrade, Gaye Chan, has been a balm and a joy. Her support is bottomless and she has helped me to live and love while writing this book. Our work with Eating in Public, an anarchist, rhizomatic project working for the return of our commons, has profoundly shaped this book project (see nomoola.com).

Ideas for this book first took shape in a reading group I joined in Toronto while on faculty at York University. I'd like to thank Gamal Abdel-Shehid, Julia Chinyere Oparah, Rinaldo Walcott, and Cynthia Wright, both for the incredible reading list we put together and for the generosity of their intellectual spirit. As always, I thank my twin brother from a different mother, John Henry Moss, who read and re-read the entire manuscript numerous times. His help with the Tower of Babel story was tremendous. Allison Campbell, my sister from a different mister, is also thanked for always knowing, in true ox form, the value of ploughing on through good times and bad and has shared this with me. Marcus Rediker, an encouraging fellow creature throughout the writing of this book, especially during a memorable lunch at the Cleveland Clinic, is thanked equally for his wisdom, good humor, and singing along. It is truly a pity that I had completed this manuscript before sitting in on his graduate course on "how to write history from below." Sharry Aiken, Bridget Anderson, Deborah Brock, Julia O'Connell Davidson, Tom Dye, Eve Haque, Ruth Hsu, Fiona Jeffries, Renisa Mawani, Pablo Mendez, Dore Minatodani, Radhika Mongia, Caroline Sinavaiana, Andrea Smith, Jacqueline Sanchez Taylor, Sarwat Viqar, Melissa Autumn White, and Cynthia Wright are each thanked for their engaged and animated conversations about the topic of this book, and for their help in honing its content. Alfie Barosso Taylor is thanked for sharing her former school's prayer. In addition to the above (some of whom also offered me venues at which to discuss this work), I would also like to thank Julia Bryan-Wilson, Mel Chen, Martin Geiger, Nicholas De Genova, Steve Gold, Gayatri Gopinath, Vicky Hattam, Katherine McKittrick, Mary Mostafanezhad, Jane Pulkingham, Eberhard Raithelhuber, Wolfgang Schröer, Cornelia Schweppe, Ann Stoler, and Miriam Ticktin for providing important spaces in which much helpful feedback was offered. Ken Wissoker, Duke University Press's editorial director, was the catalyst for my putting these ideas down on paper, and I'd like to thank him for supporting me through the (too) many years it took me to bring this book into the world. The two anonymous reviewers who spent much time making their comments and suggestions have most certainly made this a better book and I'd like to thank them for their very careful readings of it. I'd also like to thank Cathy Hannabach for reining in this book with her initial editing of it, Brian Ostrander for his tireless efforts in its subsequent production, and Paula Durbin-Westby for creating the index. With much love and with a hopeful eye to the future, I'd like to thank my nephew, Addie Campbell, whose sweet heart and sharp mind has made the world a better place. His joyful exhortation, "Maasi, you are writing a book!," kept me going.

And it must be said that although I've gained much from the many conversations and support I've had from the aforementioned about this book, only I am responsible for the words between its covers.

1

HOME RULE

The National Politics
of Separation

Let nothing be called natural.
In an age of bloody confusion,
Ordered disorder, planned caprice,
And dehumanized humanity, lest all things
Be held unalterable!

—Bertolt Brecht, 1937

"CREATION, FALL, FLOOD, NATIONS"

The story of the Deluge comes to us from a time of great antiquity.[1] A divine retribution in the form of a great outpouring of waters flooded the face of the earth. In the aftermath of this catastrophe, the waters gradually subsided to reveal a new world to the remnants of a decimated humanity. In the years that followed, the legend tells us that humanity regenerated itself and set its feet once again on the path of a great collective endeavor: "And the whole earth was of one language, and of one speech. . . . And they said one to another, Go to, let us make brick, and burn them thoroughly. . . . Let us build us a city and a tower, whose top *may reach* unto heaven" (Genesis 11:3–4, King James Version). Thus did they aspire together and so engaged in a great work. The people had a common purpose and a shared vision. They spoke the same language, so to speak.

God was greatly displeased: jealous but also afraid. From his omniscient vantage point, he realized the dire threat the builders of the city and tower of Babel posed to his kingdom. Their city with its "tower whose top assaults the sky" marked humanity's rejection of the border between heaven and earth, the very line he had drawn between his own divine realm and the mundane clay from which he had shaped humanity (Genesis 11:9). He saw that they built not to exalt *his* greatness but their own. Their mutual cooperation demonstrated the builders' "view of heaven as life; not heaven as post-life" (Morrison 1993). Thus, he thundered, "Indeed the people are one and they all have one language, and this is what they begin to do; now nothing that they propose to do will be withheld from them" (11:6).

Thus, God worried, and he fumed. Setting out to undermine the builders' plans, he knew they would not be deterred were he merely to destroy the tower. Had he not just flooded the world in his wrath only to see them striking out boldly without him once again? Therefore, instead of smashing the city and its tower that daily encroached upon his exclusive domain, God set out to confound their collective project. He shouted, "Come let us go down and there confuse their language, that they may not understand one another's speech" (Genesis 11:7). He succeeded. The builders of the great city and the tower of Babel abruptly faltered and ceased working together. Their sense of common purpose, the solidarity that had expressed itself in a grand communal imagining and shared labor, was instantly transmuted into mutual incomprehensibility. In this way did God "scatter them abroad from there over the face of all the earth." By separating people one from the other, God had won. Usurping the creative capacity of the builders, he took the title of *Creator* for himself. Expropriating their productive power for his own aggrandizement, he lorded his sovereign power over them.

The biblical story about the great city and tower of Babel is a very old one. It has been preserved in both written word and oral tradition in many places across the world, well beyond the Judeo-Christian version that is most familiar (Lambert 1969; Dundes 1988). In Genesis 11:9, *Babel* stems from the Hebrew verb *balal*, meaning to confuse or confound and also to mix up. Much as God did when destroying *Babel*, earthbound overlords have separated and disempowered people joined in a collective effort at liberty by placing them in defined and differentiated groups. Done in the name of God, the monarch, the father, the empire, the "race," or the "nation," these separations have had very real and long-lasting effects. The group with which one is identified shapes every aspect, great and small, of our world. Our ability to engage in a common endeavor across—and especially *against*—these differences has become difficult to imagine and even harder to carry out. Separation has indeed been glorified.

God has long since been replaced by the new religion of nationalism. The authority once granted to God (and his earthly representatives) has devolved to the representatives of the "nation," even as religion continues to play a significant part in some ideas of "nationhood." In this book, I examine the emergence of what I call a *Postcolonial New World Order* in which people are defined as part of separated "nations" and ruled through the apparatus of nation-state sovereignty, international bodies, and global capital. Established after the end of World War II (WWII), postcolonialism marks the end of the political legitimacy of imperial-state sovereignty and the beginning of the hegemony of national forms of state sovereignty. After WWII, with astonishing speed, the near-global space of imperialism was mostly nationalized. Between 1945 and 1960 alone, three dozen new nation-states in Asia and Africa were granted either a restricted autonomy or outright independence from empires. In the 1960s, the two most powerful imperial states entering WWII—the British and the French—lost much of their empires and nationalized the sovereignty of their metropoles. For those colonized people who did not get their national sovereignty, the demand for it defines their struggles. For many people identifying as Armenians and Kurds, Mohawks and Hawaiians, Palestinians and Kashmiris, their struggles are seen as one of national liberation. In the Postcolonial New World Order, being a member of a nation in possession of territorial sovereignty is *the* thing to be(come). It is an aspiration, moreover, that cannot be named as such, for, to be convincing, it must not be seen as an invention but an *inheritance*.

By definition, nations are not an inheritance shared by all. As Benedict Anderson pointed out, societies organized as nations always imagine themselves as *limited communities* (Anderson 1991). Because no nation encompasses all the world's people, nor wants to, immigration and citizenship controls become crucial technologies for nation-making (and nation-maintaining) strategies. By limiting entry to national territory and limiting rights within it, these controls "produce the effect of unity by virtue of which the people will appear, in everyone's eyes, 'as a people,' that is, as the basis and origin of political power" (Balibar 1991b, 93–94). The Postcolonial New World Order of nationally sovereign states thus ushers in a new governmentality, one which produces people as Nationals and produces land as territories in control (in the past and sometime in the future if not always the present) of sovereign nation-states (see Foucault 1991).[2] *Territorialization* is a key technology of postcolonial governmentality.

Territoriality, as Robert Sack (1983, 55) usefully defines it, is a "strategy for influence or controls." Territories are never simply the physical lands the state controls; territories are those lands that states successfully abstract as *state space*. National forms of territorialization transform land, water, and air into the territory of a nationally sovereign state and, in the process, forge a naturalized link between a limited group of people and a certain place. As each nation imagines that it has its own place on earth, Nationals come to see themselves as the *"people of a place."* *Postcolonial racism* is the ground upon which national homelands are built. The historical articulation between ideas of race and nation wherein ideas of national soil are racialized and racist ideas of blood are territorialized results in the formation of "neo-racist" practices wherein each nation, seen as comprised of different "types" of people, exists within a supposedly horizontal system of separate and sovereign nation-states (Balibar 1991a, 20). Those excluded from the heaven of national belonging in the actual places they live come to be represented as foreign bodies contaminating the national body politic. They are made into the *"people out of place."*

Hostility to those who move—or who are imagined to have moved—is thus bred in the bone of the Postcolonial New World Order. In a world of nation-states, national sovereigns have the "right" to determine who their members are. By law, only Nationals have the right to enter the territory of a nation-state. Rights within national territory are formally guaranteed only for Citizens. This works to make the Migrant the quintessential Other in postcolonial practices of ruling. Migrants are made to be outside of the nation even as they live on national territory. Migrants are those people whose mobility into nation-states is regulated and restricted. Migrants are those people who are legally denied the rights of national citizenship where they live.

Through the seemingly banal operation of citizenship and immigration controls, the Postcolonial New World Order not only produces but also normalizes a racism in which political separations and segregations are seen as the natural *spatial* order of nationally sovereign states. In the dogma of nationalism, the believers' new sacred duty is to enforce the national borders separating them from Migrants. Much like God's efforts to reinforce his border between heaven and earth, the jealous guarding of the National People of their National Places is seen as a *virtue*, one codified in international law.[3] Nation-states thus mark territorial and affective borders. In so doing, they demand that we choose sides. Thus does nationalism become the *governmentality* of the Postcolonial New World Order, the separation of "national subjects" from Migrants its *biopolitics*, and "national self-determination" its *leitmotif*.

POSTCOLONIAL BIOPOLITICS OF CITIZENSHIP AND IMMIGRATION CONTROLS

The enactment of immigration controls historically distinguishes nation-states from other forms of state power. Imperial states were largely intent on bringing as many people *into* imperial territory as possible. This is captured in the

Roman Empire's maxim of *imperium sine fine*, an empire without end or limit. Limitlessness through the expansion of imperial territory and numbers of imperial subjects was a key part of imperial projects. "Barbarians," people at the edges of imperial-state power, were declared "uncivilized"—and threatening. Empires thus strived to bring these people (and the places they lived) *in*. The more people whose lives imperial states controlled—to labor, pay taxes, soldier—the more power imperial rulers had. For this reason, James Scott (2017) refers to the earliest states in the Near East, formed about five thousand years ago, as "population machines."

Like all states, imperial states also controlled people's mobility. It is not for nothing that an origin of "state" is "stasis," or immobility (Bridget Anderson, Sharma, and Wright 2009). However, imperial states were primarily concerned with preventing people's escape *from* imperial territory. Simultaneously, imperial states also moved people *into* imperial-state spaces across numerous continents and archipelagos, largely to labor or fight for its glory. Indeed, empires developed entire systems of movement, including Atlantic slavery, convict transportation, and the "coolie" system of indentured labor.[4] Imperial-state practices concerning the entry of people into its territories thus operated under what Radhika Mongia (2018) calls a "logic of facilitation."

Nation-states reversed this imperial order by operating under what Mongia (2018) calls a "logic of constraint." Borne from the exigencies of the British imperial state seeking to secure a disciplined labor force in the wake of the successes—and ongoing pressure—of slavery abolitionist movements in the early nineteenth century, by that century's end, immigration controls defined the sovereignty of emergent nation-states, first in the Americas. Indeed, the nationalization of state sovereignty was announced—and institutionalized— by controls limiting both the entry and rights of those who came to be classified as Migrants. Thus, far from a *general* characteristic of state sovereignty, supposedly in place since the 1648 Treaty of Westphalia, immigration controls became a hallmark of state sovereignty only with the advent of the nation form of state power.

vs Schmitt Sov.

The nationalization of state sovereignty profoundly reshaped the imperial imagination of the political community, the space and makeup of society, and, importantly, the relationship between the state and those subjected to its rule. Nationalist discourses, promising a horizontal (and cross-class) *sameness* among Nationals, institutionalized stark *differences* between Nationals and Migrants. This communitarian basis of nationalized sovereignties produced a shift from imperial to postcolonial racist strategies (R. Miles 1993, 117).

Also see P9!!!

The nationalist process of sorting which people were—and were not—the "people of a place" dramatically bifurcated people's freedom of mobility. Nation-states largely eliminated imperial exit controls but increasingly regulated and restricted the entry of people. Nationals not only had the exclusive right to enter the nation-state, but they were the only ones with the right to stay. Migrants, in contrast, came to be defined by their deportability (De Genova 2002). Consequently, Migrants were defined as outsiders to national society and its culture—that is, they were made "people out of place." Importantly, not all people moving across national borders were regarded as Migrants. Nationals of imperial metropoles, and later Rich World states,[5] were not only the most likely to be granted permission to enter other nation-states, but they were often not even seen to be Migrants. They were, instead, "ex-pats," "backpackers," "adventurers," and so on, thus adding to the classed character of the figure of the Migrant.

National borders were not only limits or barriers but also *conduits* for the realization of postcolonial power. Immigration controls created an "environment of life," one that normalized the fragmentation of a global capitalist labor market into national markets (Bigo 2008, 97). Within each nation-state Citizen workers were seen as having a right to jobs, at least the "good" ones. But within every nation-state were also Migrant Workers who came to constitute a distinct labor-market category by virtue of being defined as "people out of place" (Ng 1988; Sharma 2006). One's wages, type of jobs, membership in labor unions, formal workplace protections and rights, as well as access to state benefits and services depended on the citizenship and immigration status one held. Thus, citizenship and immigration controls not only produced National-Natives and Migrants, but they also produced highly competitive labor markets. In so doing, they fundamentally strengthened employers' and states' ability to exploit and control workers.

A world capitalist system in which nation-states ruled gave capital greater leverage. By the late 1960s, the universalization of the nation-state system occurred alongside the start of neoliberalism. With the addition of new nation-states, the number of competing sites for capital investment grew. Each new nation-state came with the enactment of national immigration controls. Citizenship and immigration controls intensified competition between workers within and across nation-states. The result has been greater disparities of all sorts, perhaps the greatest of which is the infinitely greater mobility rights granted by nation-states to capital investments than to Migrants. Far from being a contradiction, this is, instead, an integral feature of the governmentality of the Postcolonial New World Order.[6]

Indeed, national citizenship and immigration controls are, together, the key technologies for the material and cultural realization of postcolonial biopower. Disputes over their scope and application are central to the continuous (re)making of the national body politic. As new nations and new nation-states form and older ones dissolve; the unity needed to keep a nation intact is continually challenged. New national liberation movements arise to remake the borders of nationalized territory and set different limits to national belonging. Centripetal as well as centrifugal forces of nationalist thought take place at various state levels: municipal, regional, state, or federal. People may demand that they be reunited with their fellow Nationals (but not fellow citizens) resident in another nation-state's territory. People may demand more rights for locals over nonlocals in gaining access to property, services, or votes, even when the nonlocals are citizens of the same nation-state. Or they may demand that the nation-state tighten up its immigration controls to better "serve and protect" the nation. Redefining which people are a part of which nation—and which nation should control which territory—secures the body politic as *national*.

Arguably, with every reimagining of the community as national, a hardening of nationalism takes place, one that further restricts membership in the national political community. Increasingly, the discourse of *autochthony* is deployed to do this work. Autochthonous discourses restrict national belonging to those who can show they are Native to the nation. In a way, such discourses define national forms of state membership with its ideas of sovereignty over national territory. Thus, even though the state category of Native—which marked the status of colonial subjects—was thought to have disappeared along with empires as colonized Natives become "independent" Nationals, I argue throughout this book that embedded in each idea of national sovereignty—or home rule—is the notion that "true" Nationals are those who are Natives of its territory. By restricting the making of claims to sovereignty, territory, and rights to those who are *National-Natives*, discourses of autochthony produce borders even more fortified and difficult to cross than those between National and Migrant. I examine one particularly powerful assertion made by those employing a national discourse of autochthony: the assertion that Migrants *colonize* National-Natives.

NATIONAL AUTOCHTHONIES

National autochthonous discourses are a legacy of imperialism. Having constructed a Manichean binary of European/Native, fearful imperial states, beginning with the British Empire's containment of the Indian Rebellion of

Clifford — divide and conquer.

1857, regained control by separating colonized Natives into two, supposedly distinct, groups: "Indigenous-Natives" and "Migrant-Natives," with the former regarded as more native than the latter (Mamdani 2012). The basis of this imperial distinction was the idea that a primordial relationship existed between a certain group of people and a designated place. Indigenous-Natives, not unlike certain flora and fauna, were portrayed as being "*of* the place," further *naturing* them in the process. Migrant-Natives, on the other hand, were portrayed as being subsequent settlers from outside the colony and therefore not *of* it.

Both categories were codified in imperial law so that the two categories of colonized Natives were governed by different laws. These laws, which included differential allocations of land, political rights, and power for people in the two groups, materialized the differences between Indigenous-Natives and Migrant-Natives. Indigenous-Natives were granted formal access to territories and political rights on it through "Native authorities." Migrant-Natives were not. Such imperial distinctions profoundly reshaped politics in the colonies and informed how national liberation movements imagined which people were *the* People of the nation. Nationalists took the imperial idea of indigeneity as a stable and static group and retooled it to fit the nations they were in the process of creating. With "independence," the imperialist meanings attached to both Natives and Migrants were relocated to nationalized territory. When the colonies and, later, imperial metropoles nationalized their sovereignties from the late nineteenth century, claims to *national* status were underpinned by claims to autochthonous belonging. Being Native, once the denigrated Other to the colonizer, has, in the Postcolonial New World Order, become the quintessential criterion for being a member of the nation. Migrants, unable to cross the racialized boundary of Nativeness (at least in the places they actually live) and unable to organize themselves into a nation, remain "out of place."

Placing people into separated categories of National-Natives and Migrants is no trifling matter. People's relationship to nation-states, to national political bodies, and to one another are organized by the rights associated with the category people find themselves in. Across the world system of nation-states, a further *contraction* of the already limited criteria of national belonging has taken place around the figure of the National-Native. At the same time, an *expansion* of the term "colonizer" has occurred, one that encompasses all those seen to be Migrants. Borrowing the imperial meaning of Natives as colonized people, National-Natives see themselves as "colonized" by Migrants. In turn, Migrants' own experience of colonization is seen as unimportant—and unpolitical. Instead Migrants are demonized as destroyers of nations.

Narrative change.

Today, national autochthony is increasingly important to nationalist projects, both from above and from below. Most troubling, the legal and/or social separation of National-Natives and Migrants animates deadly conflicts around the world. A particularly stark example of this is taking place in Myanmar (formerly Burma), where the separation of National-Natives and Migrants is the basis for what has been termed the world's most recent genocide, this time against Rohingya people (International State Crime Initiative, Queen Mary University of London, 2015). Nation-state officials and popular Buddhist monks categorize (mostly) Muslim Rohingya people as "illegal Bengali migrants" and argue that expelling them from both the nation and its sovereign territory is necessary for the defense of national society (see Foucault 1978, 137; Foucault 2003). Over the past four decades, Rohingya people have had their homes and property destroyed; they have been tortured, killed, and placed in camps; their citizenship has been removed; and a growing number have been forced to flee. Having already been socially *constituted* as Migrants, many have been *made* Migrants both in national law and in everyday life.

Treating Rohingya people as deportable people without rights, Myanmar has constructed approximately sixty-seven camps and moved about 140,000 Rohingya people into them since 2012. Many observers regard these camps as nothing less than concentration camps (Motlagh 2014; Fortify Rights 2015; Kristof 2016). Since 2015, violence against Rohingya people has intensified further. From late August 2017 to January 2018, *two-thirds of all Rohingya people in Myanmar*—an estimated 688,000 people—fled to Bangladesh to escape attacks from Myanmar's military (see Ibrahim 2018; UNHCR 2018). Bangladesh, meanwhile, is trying to force them "home." Rohingya people are thus simultaneously victims of both the hardening criteria for national citizenship in Myanmar and the intensification of national immigration controls in Bangladesh and other nation-states, which try to deny them a new life elsewhere. Made stateless, Rohingya people have thus been made subject to the coercive power of *all* nation-states.

Another stark example of the political work done by separating National-Natives from Migrants is the popular "Save Darfur" movement, which has successfully reframed the economic, political, and ecological legacies of European imperialism in the Darfur region of Sudan as a racialized conflict between "Black African" National-Natives and "light-skinned Arab" Migrants. Playing directly into the hands of oil companies, this division has further fueled the Islamophobic U.S.-led war on terror in the region. Probably the best-studied example of the violence ensuing from the separation of National-Natives and Migrants is the 1994 Rwandan Genocide, when those acting in the name of Hutus killed approximately 800,000 Tutsis and those Hutus who opposed this mass murder. Such state-organized killings were evident at least as far back as the first murderous attacks against Tutsis by Hutus in the lead-up to Rwanda's 1961 declaration of national independence. From that time on, the self-identification of Hutus as the National-Natives of Rwanda and the categorization of Tutsis as colonizing Migrants was consistently used to violently expunge Tutsis from the national political body.

A not dissimilar process took place in the 1991–2002 Yugoslav Wars. Ideas of National-Native belonging fueled the claims to Serbian, Croatian, Slovenian, and Bosnian homelands. In each national territory, people targeted for "ethnic cleansing" were said to be Migrants and thus foreign elements in the national homelands of others. A total of 140,000 people were killed, with another two million people displaced. In Myanmar, Sudan, Rwanda, the former Yugoslavia, and elsewhere, women's bodies were abstracted as national symbols. Consequently, rape was a major weapon of war used to define national populations (Chinkin 1994; Agamben 1998; Kesic 2002). No one was spared. Combatants on all sides targeted women for either being Native to the enemy or being the Migrant enemy.

These are only some of the better reported—and most murderous— events where the politics of separating National-Natives from Migrants has been central. Organized through a politics of autochthony, each has employed the politics of home rule to exclude, expel, and even to systematically exterminate those constituted as Migrants. However, autochthonous politics have also been the prime basis for the indigenization of numerous African states, such as Idi Amin's forced expulsion of "Asians" from Uganda in 1972; they are also fundamental to military coup d'états unseating democratically elected "Asian" parliamentary leaders in Fiji; and they are at the core of moral panics over "Migrant invasions" across Europe. *where ice you from?*

The politics of separating Natives from Migrants is also evident in the former "White Settler" colonies. Here there are two very differently situated claimants to National-Native status. *Indigenous National-Natives*, colonized by various European empires, maintain that they are the first inhabitants and "first nations," while *White National-Natives* claim to be the "first improvers" and "first sovereigns" of these territories. Indigenous-Natives maintain that because they are highly subordinated and lack a separate national sovereignty over these territories, they remain colonized. White National-Natives, on the other hand, rely on Hobbesian and Lockean discourses to claim their own standing as National-Natives. The antagonism between White National-Natives and Indigenous-Natives is evident in deadly struggles over who has the sovereign right over na-

Both are anti-migrant. (WNN + INN).

tionally contested territories, a struggle dominated by White Native-Nationals whose claims are often backed by the coercive power of nation-states. Some legal victories have been won by Indigenous-Natives based on national courts' rulings that they hold special constitutionally granted rights. However, for the most part, the long, violent history of their subjugation, first as colonized Natives and now as juridical citizens in these nation-states, but ones who regard themselves as the true sovereigns, continues (see Wiessner 2008).

Much has been written about colonial relations in the former White Settler colonies. My focus is to look at how both White National-Natives and Indigenous-Natives represent Migrants as colonizers. White National-Natives have long seen non-White Migrants as a significant threat. Indeed, the former White Settler colonies, particularly the United States, were among the first to nationalize state sovereignty through their enactment of racist immigration restrictions. What is more novel is how many Indigenous National-Natives, since at least the late 1980s, have come to view all Migrants (White and non-White) as barriers to their own claims to national sovereignty. Indeed, a growing chorus of Indigenous National-Native opinion asserts that *all* Migrants are "settler colonists." Some Indigenous National-Natives have even said that "the label settler is too historically and politically sterile" and that all Migrants are nothing less than "occupiers" (Ward 2016). As the "White" in White Settler colonialism is omitted and replaced by a generic discussion of "settler colonialism," negatively racialized people (i.e., Black, Latinx, or, perhaps especially, Asian people)—each of whom was expressly excluded from the White Settler colonial project—are increasingly depicted as colonizers of Indigenous National-Natives.

Significantly, in each instance of the aforementioned national politics of autochthony, colonization is conflated with migration. In them, real or imagined human migration—today, hundreds, or even thousands of years ago—is seen as nothing less than colonization. Being a "settler/colonist" is synonymous with being defined as a Migrant to national territory. And "colonialism" becomes nothing more than the existence of Migrants in the "nation." This is what makes autochthonous politics uncanny. This is perhaps nowhere more so than when people once categorized as the Natives of various European colonies are now described as colonizers. Sometimes they are said to "colonize" Native-Europeans, at other times, they "colonize" National-Natives in the national liberation states or Indigenous National-Natives seeking a separate national sovereignty.

The conflation of migration with colonialism results from what is a structural aspect of the Postcolonial New World Order. In it, being a Migrant is seen as having no lawful claim to territory, livelihoods, or political membership. Yet being a Migrant is not only a state (juridical) category but also a social one. Consequently, *anyone* placed outside the limits of the nation can be made a Migrant. Indeed, across the world, there is a strong tendency to move people from the political category of Citizen to Migrant. In this sense, the national politics of autochthony is marked by *nativism*. Indeed, it is not a coincidence that nativism, the idea that "some influence originating from abroad threatened the life of the nation from within," arose alongside the influence of nationalism in the mid-nineteenth century (Higham [1955] 2002, 4). Nativism became an important political force when states (starting in the Americas) began the process of nationalizing their sovereignty from the late nineteenth century. Today, turning Migrants into "colonizers" is part of the politics of nativism informed by calls to "make the nation great again." It is not only U.S. President Donald Trump who makes this his central political agenda. Instead, it defines the anti-immigrant politics of both right and left across Europe, Asia, Africa, and the Americas. The Migrant is the figure who, National-Natives believe, prevents the nation from realizing its full glory, a glory that many nationalists worry has become a thing of the past.

At the same time, of course, each instance of autochthonous politics is specific to its own historical and social context and is voiced by people very differently affected by imperialism, racism, and nationalism. White National-Natives within the nation-states in Europe or the former White Settler colonies; Indigenous National-Natives (e.g., "Indians" or "Aborigines") within these latter nation-states; and National-Natives in national liberation states in Asia, Africa, and the Americas each mobilize a discourse of autochthony to make claims to national sovereignty. Yet however much they share in common—and they share much—they are not equivalent.

White people demanding the expulsion of Migrants in the name of being the "indigenous people of Europe," for example, are not the equivalent of various Indian or Aboriginal claims to national sovereignty in the United States, Canada, or Australia. Nor is it my argument that all contemporary discourses of autochthony advocate or mobilize genocidal violence against Migrants. Indeed, discourses of autochthony deployed by some Indigenous National-Natives, for instance, argue that their national sovereignty is essential to taking good care of the planet, each other, and the generations of life to come.

At the same time, however, there are important similarities in the different uses of autochthonous discourses—and these are not merely semantic. All autochthonous discourses portray Nativeness as an essential, unpolitical characteristic of some people. Authochthony is further understood as a concept helping us better understand social relations. However, Nativeness is neither an essence nor an analytic tool. It is, instead, a racialized idea and political category allowing some to make claims against others. All autochthonous discourses are also relational. They *produce* Migrants as the negative others of National-Natives. By articulating Nativeness with "nationness" and claiming that only National-Natives have rightful political claims to power, autochthonous discourses count on the subordination of Migrants. This is the case in far-right autochthonous politics, and it is the case of metaphysical indigeneity in sovereign futures of "decolonial love" (L. Simpson 2013). Each type of autochthonous discourse establishes National-Nativeness as the necessary basis for political action, sets racialized limits to belonging and rights, and valorizes nationally sovereign territory. In doing so, each mobilizes particular philosophical, material, and relational ways of knowing and being that normalize the Postcolonial New World Order with its national forms of political, social, economic, and affective power. By so doing, the enormous disparities and violence of postcolonialism is further entrenched.

Hence, I argue that the deployment of autochthonous discourses reveals a crucial feature of postcolonial power: all nationalisms are fundamentally autochthonous and productive of a hierarchical separation between National-Natives (autochthons) and Migrants (allochthons), Across the political spectrum from far right to hard left, the right of National-Natives is the right to home rule. In the process, Migrants are left without a home in this world. The separation of Natives and Migrants is, I argue, both a legacy of imperialism and constitutive of the hegemony of nation-state power in the Postcolonial New World Order.

Having said this, it is also important to recognize that there are *two* postcolonialisms. The first and more widely known refers to the scholarship that maps the connections forged by imperialism(s) across space and time, exposes its contemporary legacies, and politicizes the postcolonial condition extant in supposedly independent nation-states. The second is the Postcolonial New World Order, which I argue is the *contemporary mode and governmentality of ruling relations*. In this view, postcolonial domination, by normalizing nation-states as self-determinative, produces subjectivities that turn us into National-Natives *of* some place, sometimes places we have never been or places we have left to build new homes elsewhere and with other people. Postcolonial theory is enormously useful to better understand the Postcolonial New World Order.

My use of postcolonial theoretical approaches to understand postcolonialism as also a ruling regime is offered as a corrective to the widely used concept of *neocolonialism*. Examining the Postcolonial New World Order allows us to see not only the legacies of colonialism and the failure of national liberation states to deliver on their promises of decolonization, but also how postcolonialism rearticulates people's dreams of liberation as national dreams *so that they never materialize.* It allows us to see, in other words, that postcolonialism is a *containment* of demands for decolonization. Such a conceptualization is a refusal of the historical amnesia produced by nationalisms. What nationalists willfully forget is that the formation and maintenance of the national form of state power is always already a violent process. People are neither easily excluded nor easily included. The actions used to describe the late-twentieth-century breakup of the former Yugoslavia into several new nation-states—"murder, torture, arbitrary arrest and detention, extra-judicial executions, rape and sexual assaults, confinement of civilian population in ghetto areas, forcible removal, displacement and deportation of civilian population, deliberate military attacks or threats of attacks on civilians and civilian areas, and wanton destruction of property"—are not unique (UN Security Council 1992; also see Shraga and Zacklin 1994). From the start and the world over, elements of these processes are part and parcel of making "nations" and achieving "national self-determination." Partitions, expulsions from nationalized territory through "population transfers," and social and legal exclusion from the nation are par for the course. They are parts of the biopolitical process of creating and separating those constituted as a "people of a place" and those relegated to being a "people out of place."

POSTCOLONIALISM AND THE CONTAINMENT OF DECOLONIZATION

The idea that National-Natives are *colonized* by Migrants is one aspect of the confusion about what exactly postcolonialism is. One of the most commonly expressed complaints—and confusions—about postcolonialism is that the "post" in postcolonialism fails to acknowledge that some people are still colonized, be it politically, economically, and/or socially (Brennan 1997, 2; Dirlik 1999; San Juan 2002; Lazarus 2002; B. Parry 2004, 9). What this usually means is that some people, having organized themselves into a nation, lack sovereignty over claimed territories (e.g., Byrd and Rothberg 2011). This confusion, however, only confirms postcolonialism's hegemony. Embedded in the idea that the "post" in postcolonialism is meaningless is the idea that the end of colonialism occurs when all nations have obtained their national sovereignty. This is a confusion of *decolonization* for postcolonialism.

Postcolonialism, far from ending the violent practices and relationships of colonialism, marks the ascendency of the national form of state power and its reliance on nationalist subjectivities, national forms of exclusion, and kinds of violence that nation-states carry out. Postcolonialism is thus, I argue, a form of ruling that substitutes demands for decolonization with demands for national sovereignty. Postcolonialism has indeed ended the legitimacy of imperial states, but not the practices associated with them. Instead, practices of expropriation and exploitation have expanded and intensified in the Postcolonial New World Order. Far from freeing people, then, postcolonialism has freed up *capital* instead. This is not a coincidence, nor is it a by-product of "neocolonialism" with its web of financial dependencies and military occupations across nationally sovereign states (Sartre [1964] 2001; Nkrumah 1965; Amin 1974; Rodney 1974). Instead, like imperialism, the rule of nation-states is part of a global regime of power. However much each nation-state insists on its separation from others, each operates within an *international* and *interstatal* regime of ruling.

From the start, the United States has dominated the making of the Postcolonial New World Order. Having nationalized its own state sovereignty in the late nineteenth century with the passing of its first immigration controls (the 1875 Page Act), the United States played a pivotal role in ending empires and establishing the global rule of nation-states. Shortly before the end of WWII, the United States insisted on the doctrine of national self-determination as the basis of a restructured global capitalist economy, which it hoped to dominate. After World War I (WWI), the United States was able to enshrine the Wilsonian doctrine of self-rule in the League of Nations. At that time though, this doctrine did not apply to imperial colonies. Empires were willing to reimagine their metropoles as national societies, but they well knew that extending such a status to their colonies would result in the collapse of empire.

By 1941, however, with metropolitan France under Nazi occupation and the British metropole under siege, Britain was desperate for U.S. help in fighting the Axis powers. The United States seized the opportunity to demand a reorganization of the still largely imperial world to its advantage. That year, President Roosevelt succeeded in getting British Prime Minister Winston Churchill to accept the extension of the Wilsonian doctrine of self-rule to the Natives in the colonies. Their agreement was sealed in the 1941 Atlantic Charter. However, the Atlantic Charter was far from an expression of solidarity with the colonized on the part of the United States.

Indeed, the United States could not have been *less* interested in giving up expropriated land (including the lands comprising U.S. national territory). It neither had any intention of ending the exploitation of people's labor power nor in creating a world without hierarchies of worth and disparities in wealth, power, and peace. Instead, the United States understood that imperial-state monopolies over their colonies prevented capitalists based in the United States from exploiting these same territories and the people in them. Empires simply stood in the way of the United States becoming a world hegemon. The basis of U.S. support for expanding the principle of national self-determination to the colonies was the understanding that it would gain from the opening of closed imperial markets for land, labor, and commodities. Such an opening would be achieved by the transformation of both imperial metropoles and colonies into "independent," sovereign nation-states, each enmeshed in an international regime of financial, political, and military ties.

The United States was wildly successful in achieving these goals. The universal principle of self-rule agreed to in the 1941 Atlantic Charter formed the basis for the first major international political institution of postcolonialism—the United Nations (UN). In its 1945 founding charter, the UN enshrined the recognition of the right of national self-determination—or the right to national sovereignty for those people who could successfully claim to being the "people of a place"—as the bedrock of international law.[7] Hostility to Migrants was firmly established in this charter. With its declaration of the rights of nations to self-determination, it would not—nor could it—account for the rights of all those people who were not *the People* of the nation, i.e. those who were "people out of place." The UN Charter thus stood in stark contrast to how many people actually lived, and certainly in stark contrast to the reality of the immediate post-WWII experience of mass migration. As John Torpey (2000, 123) puts it, "With millions of people on the move in response to the transformations that were taking place, and often seeking to escape violent conflict, the limitations of a system that presupposed mutually exclusive citizenries all of whom were distributed uniquely to one state or another became apparent almost immediately."

Hannah Arendt had already understood this in her analysis of the post-WWI efforts of the League of Nations. It was the League's Minority Treaties, she argued, which legitimized the nationalist idea that political rights flowed from membership in a "nation." With the formation of several new nation-states from the dissolution of the German, Austro-Hungarian, Russian, and Ottoman Empires in the interwar period, it was the League and not new nation-states that was charged with protecting the rights of national minorities—that is, those people residing within national territory who could not meet the criteria of national membership. The signing of various Minority Treaties thus institutionalized the communitarian basis of nation-states and led Arendt ([1951] 1973, 275) to declare that the "nation had conquered the state."

CHAPTER 1

Just as the UN Charter of national self-determination organized the *political* order of postcolonialism, the Bretton Woods institutions established its *economic* order. Emerging from the UN's 1944 Monetary and Financial Conference, the International Monetary Fund (IMF), the World Bank, and the (somewhat later) General Agreement on Tariffs and Trade (GATT) together controlled a large part of the international flow of finances. As a result, each sovereign nation-state, while formally holding the financial levers over its economy, also existed within a global field of capitalist power that was far from even. The inequalities of the imperial order were thus far from resolved by the transformation of colonies into nation-states. The sheer weight of past concentrations of wealth meant that nation-states of the former imperial metropoles and the former White Settler colonies reaped most of the benefits. The United States was best positioned to benefit, particularly as it became a global source for finance capital. Its use of $17 billion in Marshall Plan funds allowed it to dominate the devastated economies of Western Europe. Indeed, from 1948 to 1952, the United States was able to extract agreements from various European states to liberalize trade between them, *including their extant colonies*, thus ensuring capital based in the United States entrance into previously closed markets (Scott Jackson 1979).

The political and economic aspects of postcolonialism were enforced by post-WWII military expenditures. Most nation-states, including those containing the most impoverished people, devoted large portions of their budgets to building up the coercive apparatuses of state power, not a small portion of which would be used against people resident in their territories. Again, the United States dominated. Its military-industrial complex grew alongside its power to influence the Bretton Woods institutions. The bifurcated politics of the Cold War, including the nuclear arms race dominated by the United States and the USSR, cast a menacing shadow over life in the Postcolonial New World Order. The United States insisted that it was defending democracy and freedom even as it toppled popularly elected governments and replaced them with dictators who would implement free market policies and follow the U.S. position in global politics. Conversely, the USSR "fought imperialism," all the while extoling the nationalist "socialism in one country" line, expropriating the land and labor of the people in its "socialist republics," and eliminating (politically as well as corporeally) untold numbers of people fighting for socialism (Carlo 1974).

The "alternative" to the Cold War—the "Third World political project," which came into its own with the Afro-Asian Conference in Bandung in 1955 (see Prashad 2007)—also failed to support any real transformation of the social relations of imperialism. While the discourse of "national liberation" mobilized some (but not all) anticolonial movements and oversaw the formation of Third World nation-states, it was also central in turning "classes into masses" (see Arendt [1951] 1973, 460). Speaking for the nation, which was said to unify all classes in a shared project, Third World nation-states tended to support the rural, landed gentry, merchants, and nascent bourgeoisie in their now-nationalized territories. Thus, just as the First, Second, and Third World projects together produced the Postcolonial New World Order, together they also contained the revolutionary forces offering alternatives to it.

Yet in the years after the end of WWII and the dawn of the Postcolonial New World Order, it did not always feel as if one was being contained or conquered by the nation-state. The excitement and sheer joy of living to see the demise of imperial rule was palpable. Postcolonialism, after all, had come about not only through the machinations of the United States but also through the many, many years of anticolonial struggles by millions upon millions of people around the world. For them, the existence of new, seemingly independent nation-states represented the fruition of their dreams of decolonization. The rural peasants and the urban proletariat, without whom the national liberation movements would not have succeeded, imagined that with the end of imperial-state rule and the start of national self-determination, they would finally enjoy the land and liberty long denied them. Their move from the denigrated category of colonized Natives to the exalted category of independent Nationals, they were told, would change everything. Indeed, those who sacrificed much for the national liberation states extended enormous goodwill toward them— and did so for far longer than could have been reasonably expected.

Soon enough, however, the reality of living under nation-state rule failed to live up to the rhetoric of national liberation. Instead, the post-WWII extension of national self-determination to colonized people extended the reach of both capital and states into people's lands and lives. Because of pressure to "develop," land and labor became crucial elements in the glorification of national liberation states. The rubric of "modernization" drove—and depoliticized—these states' emphases on capitalist markets by derogatorily portraying national societies without fully developed markets in land, goods, services, and labor—and without people who had a fully developed sense of either nationalism or possessive individualism—as "traditional." Moreover, national liberation states "grafted" the discourse of national development "onto local class, ethnic, racial, and religious hierarchies" (Shohat 1997, 4). Mega-development projects and the destruction of the rural economy and resultant urbanization, along with import-substitution policies valorizing industrialization, expanded the ranks—and the immiseration—of the proletariat. As more and more land was expropriated, by both states and capital, as more and more of the remaining commons was titled as either public or private property, as more and more aspects of people's lives came under the surveying eye of nation-states, more and more people found that participation in capitalist markets for land, food, shelter, clothing, healthcare, and more had become even more of an imperative than it had been under imperial rule (Wood 2002; Wallerstein 2005). This left most people in the national liberation states with little option but to sell their labor power in exchange for the stuff of life. Thus did the global capitalist system expand under postcolonialism.

Unsurprisingly, a pall of "postcolonial melancholia" soon fell over people's dreams of decolonization (Gilroy 2005). It fell first and hardest over those who had only recently been transformed from the Native subjects of imperial colonies into the National Citizens of "independent" nation-states, those who had actively placed their hopes in the same national liberation states now organizing and exacerbating their impoverishment. But a postcolonial melancholia also enveloped people in the former metropoles that had by the mid-1960s also nationalized their sovereignties. Here the nation was no less an alibi for the expansion of the power of capital and states. The melancholic character of the response to the failures of national liberation meant that in both the former colonies and the former metropoles, it was all things "foreign"—foreign states, foreign corporations, and most especially foreign people—that were held responsible for people's misery (and immiseration). This too was fully in keeping with postcolonial rule.

Many people who became *a People* grossly misidentified their feelings of loss. Rather than question the rhetoric of nationhood or national sovereignty, people in both the former colonies and the former metropoles assumed that their nations did not have *enough* sovereignty. In the national liberation states, postcolonialism was renamed "neocolonialism" in a bid to explain why "national self-determination" felt like imperialism, or worse. In the nation-states of the former metropoles, the recurring (and ever shorter) crises of capital were misread as resulting from the movement of people from the former colonies into now-national territory. Migrants were proffered as an explanation to Nationals for why their nation-states failed to deliver jobs and prosperity for them (and them alone). Both of these deflective discourses only deepened and prolonged the melancholic response. With the nation-state—and nationalism—monopolizing the political, it could not generally be acknowledged that national sovereignty was *bound* to fail people—both National-Natives and Migrants.

The Postcolonial New World Order was not designed to produce an even distribution of wealth, power, peace, or even prestige. Far from it. Indeed, disparities within this system are only worsening. To put the global character of such disparities in clearer perspective, especially between the United States and the rest of the world, it was recently shown that "an American having the average income of the *bottom U.S. decile* [was] better-off than *2/3 of [the] world population*" (Milanovic 2002, 89; emphasis added). Another way of putting it is that the material basis for the Postcolonial New World Order of nation-states has not diverged fundamentally from the previous imperial world order. Unsurprisingly, it is those people who are not recognized as a People—the "subalterns," or those who have had no beneficial part of the nation or its state—who are to be found at the losing end of national hierarchies. National minorities, Tribals, and Migrants are the losers of the UN Charter's declaration on national self-determination. Their struggles are, at best, seen as a thorn in the side of nation-states, and at worst, as targets for military campaigns for national security. This is true in the Rich and Poor World nation-states.

The Postcolonial New World Order is thus not only a particular historical period (the post-WWII era) or the body of scholarship trying to understand it. Postcolonialism is the governmentality of the international system of nation-states and the equally international system of capitalist social relations. While postcolonialism clearly does not work for most of the world's people, the largely melancholic response to postcolonialism sustains it. Support for nationalism and for nation-states remains hegemonic across the political spectrum, as national sovereignty continues to be seen as the last bastion of resistance to "foreign" incursions. This is the hegemony of postcolonialism, and its power is far from spent. Neoliberal restructuring has altered the operation of postcolonial institutions such as the UN, the IMF, the World Bank, the World Trade Organization (WTO, which replaced the GATT in 1995), but it has not altered the fundamental biopolitical foundations of postcolonial power. In fact, the postcolonial politics of separation between National-Natives and Migrants are hardening and expanding in evermore uncanny ways.

A single book cannot say everything about the Postcolonial New World Order with its separation of National-Natives and Migrants, and this one certainly does not aim to be comprehensive. I do not aim to trace the history of postcolonialism and the transformation of imperial states into nation-states—as well as the shift from an imperial world order to a Postcolonial New World Order—through two centuries and through all its various forms and structures in this study. My aim, instead, is to plot the formation of postcolonialism *as* a new world order and to show its biopolitics and governmentality. Thus, I offer an overview of some of the key historical developments in the formation of the Postcolonial New World Order and analyze postcoloniality in its historical and theoretical context. Crucial aspects of this project are a critique of capital that has long been globally operative, a critique of nation-states that usurp people's freedom to move, and a critique of nationalist sub-jectivities increasingly insistent on a partition between National-Natives as a "people of a place" and Migrants as "people out of place."

Before I proceed, however, I find it necessary to state clearly that this book is not against Indigenous people, even if indigeneity is historicized and decon-structed (i.e., repoliticized). There has been a long and infamous list of scholars trying to deny and to depoliticize the violence enacted upon those catego-rized as Natives and to reject their demands for liberty. This book emphati-cally refuses such a project. This book is not "pro-Migrant" either, even as I also historicize and deconstruct the emergence of the category of Migrant to better understand how Migrants became "people out of place." Instead, this book is my effort to contribute to a deepening and strengthening of a collab-orative project of decolonization by making it truly collaborative. By challeng-ing people's placement in the state categories of National-Native or Migrant, what I challenge is the Postcolonial New World Order that contains people's demands for decolonization. In so doing, I challenge the strategy of laying claim to national sovereignty, a claim increasingly limited to those success-fully mobilizing a discourse of autochthony. Historically—and today—there is a much broader collectivity opposed to capitalism than the one that nations can ever hope to represent. Indeed, the existence of this broad, global collec-tive is what must be denied so that nationalist and racist imaginations can exist.

KEY QUESTIONS

In embarking on a critical discourse of how people have come to be Natives or Migrants, I heed Rogers Brubaker's (1996, 15) warning to remain vigilant against utilizing "categories of practice" as "categories of analysis." Native and Migrant are not natural, timeless categories, even if states and people act as if they are. They are *political* categories. I thus begin with the understand-ing that Natives and Migrants have come into being—and continue to exist—within a shared and globally operative field of power. They are therefore best examined by situating them in the same field of analysis. To avoid further reification of Natives and Migrants, I thus de-essentialize these political, state categories by historicizing and repoliticizing their construction.

With this as my basis, a number of questions motivate the following chapters. Why is the separation between Natives (or autochthons) and Migrants (or allochthons) important, and to whom? Historically, how were people separately constituted as Natives or Migrants? How much is the contemporary nationalist discourse of autochthony a legacy of imperialism? Is the privileging of autochthony merely a *defensive* position wherein arguments for essential and incommensurable differences are used (strategically or otherwise) to organize against power (see Spivak 1994)? Or are autochthonous discourses *formative* of power and, if so, what political work do they accomplish? And, perhaps most importantly, what would decolonization look like if we rejected the separation—and the political categories—of Natives and Migrants?

In trying to answer these questions, I examine the construction and separation of Natives and Migrants through a critical analysis of both imperial and national forms of state sovereignty, their specific projects of territorialization, and how each differently constrain people's freedom to move. In particular, I historicize the separation of our world into sovereign nation-states and the immigration controls that establish them as nationally self-determinative structures of power. As all nationalisms attempt to turn classes into masses by promoting ideas of cross-class national solidarity, I also examine how global capitalism has been reorganized—and significantly expanded—by the nation form of state power.

In so doing, I join the many others who have taken "lines of flight" away from essentialist, ahistorical, and reified views of social relations and recognized that difference making is always political (Deleuze and Guattari 1988). Along with the mythical builders of the tower of Babel creating their own heaven on earth, I follow the many, many people who have forged solidarity across—and against—gods, empires, and nations and who have worked for a worldly place that is a home for all. While we have not yet been able to turn right-side up again a world where ideas of race, sex/gender, and nation fundamentally deform our ideas of society and self and allow capitalists to "prowl the globe" (Enloe 1990), this book insists that we can. By "we" I mean all of us who are committed to struggles for decolonization. Claiming this "we-ness" is also a political decision, of course, one that, unlike nationalist autochthonies, is borne out of a shared political project, not a shared genealogy or a shared territory. This book urges us to join the many people over time and place struggling to liberate our land and our labor from expropriators and exploiters. Now, as then, a heaven on earth will only be of our making.

In chapter 2, "The Imperial Government of Mobility and Stasis," I examine how today's growing separation of Natives and Migrants is part of the lasting legacy of imperialism. From the mid-nineteenth century onward, European Empires bifurcated colonized Natives and defined one group—Indigenous-Natives—as both temporally and spatially *static*. Another group of colonized Natives—Migrant-Natives—was defined by their *mobility*. In the aftermath of the British Empire's difficulties in quelling the massive 1857 Indian Rebellion (or "British Mutiny"), a greater emphasis was placed on maintaining imperial rule through biopolitical technologies. Unlike the direct-rule form of colonialism preceding it, indirect-rule colonialism depended on imperial-state practices of surveillance, definition, segregation, protection, and immobilization. Efforts were undertaken to make each and every colonized Native legible as a member of a distinct and discrete group. Employing racialized ideas of "blood," Natives placed in one or another group were said to naturally belong together.

The discursive practice of autochthony was key to the separation of colonized Natives. The imperial distinction between Indigenous-Natives (or autochthons) and Migrant-Natives (or allochthons) rested on—and was productive of—an opposition between the "people of the place" and the "people out of place." Those categorized as Indigenous-Natives were subject to a new imperial regime of "protection," one that worked to enclose them within "custom." Colonialism was now portrayed as necessary, not to *change* Indigenous-Natives (e.g., to "civilize" them), but to *preserve* their (often invented) traditions and customs as they encountered the "modern" world (see Hobsbawm and Ranger 1983). The governance of Indigenous-Natives through appointed "Native authorities" became the new governmentality of imperial states. In contrast, Migrant-Natives, whom imperialists imagined to be more like them than Indigenous-Natives, were seen as better prepared to be modern and, thus, less in need of protection. I discuss these processes, both their similarities and their distinctiveness, across the imperial colonies of Asia and Africa as well as in the White Settler colonies of the British Empire (what is now the United States, Canada, Australia, and New Zealand).

In chapter 2, I show that though the White Settler colonies are often assumed to be distinct from colonies in Africa and Asia, practices of both direct- and indirect-rule colonialism were also implemented there—and within a similar timeframe. From the mid-nineteenth century onward, as processes of nationalizing state sovereignty accelerated in the White Settler colonies, new efforts were made to count, control, and contain Natives. Foremost among them was the creation of "reserved" parcels of land to which Natives were tied. Each existed within broader projects of racist segregation. As with indirect colonialism in Asia and Africa, the system of "reservations" in the United States, Canada, Australia, and New Zealand were created in the name of protecting Natives. Spatially delineated, each "tribe," "band," or "nation" of Indigenous-Natives was nominally ruled by its own Native leaders appointed by the imperial state and, later, nation-state. Recognition as a member of a Native group was controlled by the state through various racialized systems, including that of "blood quantum" to limit their numbers and thus weaken claims to protections upon which the new governmentality of indirect-rule colonialism rested.

This also worked to weaken Indigenous-Natives' competing claims to territories claimed by White people, who came to see themselves as Natives of these colonies (and later nation-states). The autochthonization of Whiteness was an aspect of colonial rule in the White Settler colonies not seen in Asia and Africa. In the White Settler colonies, an amalgamation of the techniques of direct- and indirect-rule colonialism occurred. In the United States, Canada, Australia, and New Zealand, the discourse of "protecting" colonized Natives worked *alongside* discourses of civilization and assimilation. Their coexistence stemmed from the fact that in the rapidly nationalizing White Settler colonies, there were two competing groups of Natives—*White National-Natives* basing their autochthonous claims on being the first "improvers" and sovereigns, and *Indigenous National-Natives* who came to base their own autochthonous claims on having been the first inhabitants and later, as nationalism was widely taken up, the first sovereigns. By the mid to late nineteenth century onward, even as regimes of "protection" were put in place, efforts to forcibly assimilate Indigenous-Natives into the normative practices of White National-Natives intensified. The establishment of Native schools from the mid-nineteenth to the early twentieth centuries was an especially violent part of this practice, as they operated under the guise of both protecting and "civilizing" seized children.

It is important to recognize the significance of Whiteness as a "possessive identity" in the making of these colonies *as* White Settler colonies (see Lipsitz 1995). Inculcating an identity of Whiteness was enormously effective in ending resistance across—and against—ideas of race, resistance evident in numerous instances of joined struggle by those identified as Native, White, Black, and Asian people (see Linebaugh and Rediker, 2000). Institutionalized in the law, racialized separations of Whites, Natives, Blacks, and Asians, along with the relative mercy shown to Whites by states, consolidated the view that all Whites, irrespective of class, formed a community. White people thus came to imagine imperial, and later national, territories as their own. As imperial sovereignties were nationalized in the late nineteenth century, Whites were autochthonized as White National-Natives. Ideas of Whiteness thus allowed the contradiction between practices of colonization and discourses of autochthony to be bridged.

In the rapidly nationalizing White-Settler colonies, however, not only were there White National-Natives and Indigenous National-Natives; there were also people classified as Migrants, a category that by the mid-twentieth century came to include Black people moved there by imperial states as slaves. By the late nineteenth century, a nationalization of the White Settler colonies took place. The process began with the enactment of the first of many immigration controls regulating and restricting people's entrance to state territories. Such controls were racist from the start. Together, the imperial government of stasis and mobility succeeded in planting the seeds of national belonging. Former imperial metropoles along with former colonies would by the mid-twentieth century model themselves on the practices wrought by indirect-rule colonialism, namely, the drawing of a highly consequential separation between Natives and Migrants in the nation-state.

In chapter 3, "The National Government of Mobility and Stasis," I show the centrality of the state category of Migrant to the world-historic shift from imperial states to nation-states. This major shift in ruling relations came on the heels of another consequential shift: the end of the slave trade and the start of the coolie labor system. The first immigration controls implemented against coolies by the British Empire on their colony of Mauritius in 1835 was the imperial state's response to planters' demands for a new system of labor discipline to replace slavery. At the same time, slavery abolitionists demanded that workers moving from British India to Mauritius be protected from new forms of slavery. The contract of indenture along with the enactment of new mobility controls for coolies met both demands.

Significantly, the first mobility controls imposed upon British subjects within the shared space of empire were predicated on the discourse of protection. In this way, the later discourse of indirect-rule colonialism, with its emphasis on "protecting" the "traditional cultures" of those categorized as Indigenous-Natives, was *prefigured* by imperial needs to discipline and contain a labor force freed from the "evil institution" of slavery—but not from the imperative of seeking one's livelihood in capitalist markets. Indeed, the Mauritius Ordinances set the stage for subsequent regimes of immigration controls. Coolieism thus operated as the crucial bridge from what Radhika

Mongia (2018) usefully terms the imperial "logic of facilitation" to the national "logic of constraint."

To demonstrate the significance of the *form* that state power takes—imperial or national—in how states imagine and exercise their sovereignty over stasis and mobility, I compare the first, racist immigration acts of the United States in the late nineteenth century with those of Canada decades later in the early twentieth century. Unlike the United States, Canada, still a formal colony of the British Empire at the time, was beholden to demands by the imperial London Office to not formally restrict entry to negatively racialized but still *British* subjects, in the name of the formal equality among its imperial subjects. I further show how the making of Nationals and Migrants by immigration acts borrowed heavily from imperial discourses of indirect-rule colonialism. From the beginning, Nationals were *National-Natives*. Within ever strengthened nationalisms, claims to nationhood were grounded in claims to autochthonous belonging. Members of nations imagined themselves as the "people of the place." Immigration controls, first implemented under imperial-state rule to discipline and "protect" coolie indentured laborers, were seen, under nation-state rule, as protecting the National Citizen from Migrants.

In chapter 4, "The Jealousy of Nations: Globalizing National Constraints on Human Mobility," I show that while most states in the Americas had nationalized their sovereignties by 1915, a fully developed system of immigration controls only came into being after WWI when a wider international system capable of administering the rapidly nationalizing politics of mobility came into existence. In this regard, actions taken by certain states during WWI (28 July 1914 to 11 November 1918) were crucial. The dissolution of the Russian (1917), Austro-Hungarian (1918), German (1918), and Ottoman Empires (1922) resulted in their former territories either being incorporated into other imperial states or claimed as new national homelands. The making of new nation-states depended on the formation of new nations, of course, the making of which was always a violent process.

As it was in the Americas, nation-state formation across Europe and Asia Minor relied on imperial discourses of autochthony. New National-Natives claimed to have an eternal and essential relationship with a particular, imagined national community and timeless sovereignty over a particular territory. The realization of national political communities required that various biopolitical groupings of people be forcibly moved. People who were not part of the People were moved *out* of national homelands, while other people claimed by the nation were moved *in*. Both processes were imagined as "homecomings," as people in both groups were imagined to be moving to where their nations existed. Both groups were used to embody the nation on whose behalf nation-states claimed to rule. The normalization of such enormous violence rested on the idea that those outside of the nation were also from outside nation-state territories and were, therefore, "people out of place." It was in these interwar years that new state categories, including National Minorities, Refugees, and Stateless were institutionalized, categories announcing the ascendancy of the national form of state power. I discuss actions taken by the 1923 emergence of the nation-state of Turkey as being emblematic of this world historic shift in how the relationship between political communities and human mobility was understood.

The very structure of nation-states meant that they portrayed themselves as ever precarious. From their formation, threats to the nation were said to be everywhere. The best-known example of this was Germany after the National Socialist German Workers' Party (Nazis) took control of the state in February 1933. The Nazi Party, formed in the years following the dissolution of the German Empire, adhered to racist, sexist, able-ist, anticommunist, and populist politics. They promoted the most limited view of German nationhood on offer and became central to normalizing fascism. In the Nazis' 1935 Reich Citizenship Law, German citizenship was further limited to people racialized as "German," loyal to the Nazi regime, and meeting fascist standards for physical and mental normativity. As a result, Jewish people, and later, people categorized as "Gypsies, Negroes, and their bastards," as well as people said to have "mental and/or genetic deformities" (Friedländer 2009) were made stateless and thus deportable. The Nazis' planned expulsion of stateless people failed, however, largely due to Allied states' refusal to dismantle the vast "paper walls" they had erected against Migrants. Refused admittance by other states, large numbers of the Nazis' victims were forced to remain in (expanding) German state territory. The first death camps were established after it became clear that Nazi plans for their expulsion were not feasible.

In the interwar years, states intensified their immigration controls. Even imperial states imposed new controls on entry into their metropoles (and sometimes into their colonies). However, except for the White Dominions, *imperial subjects* were not generally subject to such controls and retained their relatively unrestricted right to move across imperial territory.[8] Once WWII started, immigration controls were expanded greatly. As the Nazis' victims (and others) discovered, nation-states across the New World had walled themselves off, while imperial territories in Asia and Africa were officially closed to the entry of nonsubjects.[9] At war's end and with the start of the Postcolonial New World Order, controls that had largely been portrayed as temporary and exceptional were accepted as necessary and permanent features of now-national state sovereignty. As it was at the end of WWI, the expansion of immigration controls after WWII was enacted precisely when tens of millions of people across the world had been left dispossessed, displaced, and in search of new homes.

As had also occurred after WWI, in the first years following WWII, "population transfers" were used to establish the limits of national membership. In addition to the movement of people claimed by various nations throughout Europe, the partition of British India into Pakistan (East and West) and India led to the permanent movement of almost fifteen million people: the single, largest migration event known. The formation of Israel as a Jewish nation-state resulted in the forced movement of over 700,000 Palestinian people out of the new state. Roughly that same number of Jewish people moved into the new state of Israel, many fearful of continued persecution in Europe or by their recent demonization in Northern African and Middle Eastern states. With the formation of each new nation-state, new immigration controls were enacted.

In the emergent Postcolonial New World Order, immigration regulations and restrictions became a key mechanism through which inequality on a *global* scale was reorganized. Immigration policies constructed a "global apartheid" of highly differentiated rights, entitlements, and life outcomes, so that one's nationality came to comprise an international barrier to mobility and to accessing life's resources (Richmond 1994). With the hegemony of the national form of state power, the practice of human mobility from place to place—occurring since time immemorial—was pushed out of the political imagination. It was replaced with the glorification of stasis. Yet in each and every national homeland were people who were not *the People*. Nationalism thus ushered in the dual—and intimately connected—crises of emplacement and displacement. All sorts of violence, symbolic and life ending, was unleashed as a result.

In chapter 5, "The Postcolonial New World Order and the Containment of Decolonization," I discuss the creation of the post-WWII world of nation-state rule. This postcolonial world was created jointly by the victors of numerous national liberation movements in the former colonies and the nationalization of the sovereignty of the former metropoles of empires (which I discuss further in chapter 7). The transformation of a world ruled by imperial states to one in which nationness became (and remains) "the most universally legitimate value in the political life of our time" (Benedict Anderson 1991, 3) was actively championed by the United States and its insistence that imperial monopolies on trade and capital investment be dismantled in favor of national home rule.

This Postcolonial New World Order did not represent a *challenge* to the social relations of imperialism but, instead, organized new modes of managing now-national populations and situating each one within globally operative—and competitive—capitalist social relations. Postcolonialism thus worked to *contain* the revolutionary and liberatory demands to abolish the practices of expropriation and exploitation most closely associated with imperialism. Indeed, the new international system provided the institutional structures (and force of coercive action) for capitalist social relations to expand. They did so through—not against—the nationalization of states, sovereignty, territory, and subjectivities. Claiming to have liberated people, postcolonialism liberated capital instead.

These outcomes were organized by the key institutions of postcolonialism—the United Nations; the Bretton Woods institutions; the national military-industrial complexes of the First, Second, and Third Worlds; and the international "development" goals for national liberation states. *Politically* important was the United Nations and its founding charter (1945), which declared that people who could make themselves into the People of a state's territory had the right to national "self-determination." *Economically*, the institutional arrangements organized by the Bretton Woods agreements positioned national sovereignty as a disciplinary mechanism for the workers of the world. *Militarily*, the Cold War normalized the enormous buildup of a military-industrial complex across the world and shored up national mechanisms of violence.

Yet even as the Postcolonial New World Order was touted as the establishment of a horizontal system of equal and sovereign nation-states, it was both global and hierarchical. Indeed, its organizational structure ensured the intensification of racialized and gendered class disparities within and across nation-states. Disparities within nation-states and across the international system were enforced by national citizenship and immigration controls that, together, produced a global apartheid even more intense than that of the imperial system it replaced. Despite this, the Postcolonial New World Order enjoyed enormous legitimacy. Discourses of national autochthony were key to ensuring this. Postcolonial forms of ruling separated people based on nationalist notions of liberty, whereby nation-state sovereignty was glorified as a form of empowerment.

In chapter 6, "Developing the Postcolonial New World Order," I discuss how the strong, international agreement on the need for "developing" the former colonies was a crucial aspect of the expansion and consolidation of the national mode of capital accumulation and state power. The paradigm of development rested on a pseudopsychological discourse of "modernization" in which the imperial impoverishment of the now-former colonies was reframed as a result of a failure to develop. The pursuit of a minimum per capita GNP (gross national product) and a high rate of annual growth by nation-states was normalized. Heavily promoted by new international institutions, developmentalism thus normalized new, national ways of doing capitalism and entrenched the Cold War machinations of the First and Second Worlds on the Third World while doing so. Third World national liberation states, however, were far from passive victims in this process, even as most people they ruled were certainly victimized. Instead, these nation-states posited development as necessary for the *reversal* of the conditions of colonialism. The linking of developmentalism to national liberation became crucial for their construction of an overarching national identity.

Developmentalism, always speaking in autochthonous terms, argued that home rule was dependent on nation-states reducing their foreign dependency and becoming reliant on the national production of industrial and consumer goods and services. This greatly strengthened the fundamental postcolonial binary of National and Foreigner, making developmentalism a significant part of the biopolitical rule of postcolonialism in the Third World. Developmentalism—including state support for the national bourgeoisie—also became a crucial part of how decolonization itself was reframed as a process of economic modernization and not the end of practices of expropriation and exploitation. Discourses of development, therefore, helped to depoliticize newly independent nation-states' emphasis on capitalist markets as well as obfuscate the process by which how nation-states delivered more and more people to capitalism. Significantly, developmentalism, as an always future-oriented aspiration, allowed national liberation states to forever delay making good on their promises of decolonization.

The postcolonial political, economic, and military structures resulted in a world where the cyclical crises of capitalism would affect the lives of more and more people. In response to the crisis begun in the mid-1960s, shortly after the metropoles of the British and French empires were also nationalized, a set of policy reforms called the Washington Consensus were undertaken to reorganize both the Bretton Woods institutions and the policies of nation-states. Named after the agreement of Washington, DC-based institutions—the IMF, the World Bank, and the GATT—these institutions became more politicized than they already were. Using their much-needed financial capacities to demand policy changes from borrowing states, condition-laden loans (particularly from the IMF) soon became a standard source of national revenue, especially for the national liberation states.

The neoliberal reforms wrought by the Washington Consensus affected nation-state policies ranging from finances to incarceration to stepped-up immigration controls. Together these secured a shift in the balance of class relations throughout the international system. Everywhere, neoliberal restructuring strengthened the power of capital and nation-states. In the First World, there was a steady erosion of post-WWII gains made in wages, including the national social wage, and levels of labor unionization. In the Second World, workers faced greater control by state bureaucrats. And in the Third World, the pace of land grabs intensified, as did the destruction of the rural economy, both leading to greater urbanization, unemployment, and poverty. Consequently, across the world, there was, simultaneously, an enormous growth in the mobility of capital and a greater effort by nation-states to simultaneously expropriate, displace, *and* immobilize workers.

Yet neoliberal reforms were most often viewed through a nationalist lens. Despite their global character—and despite the fact that class disparities intensified between people within nation-states as well as across this system—"foreigners" were defined as being the "problem." Nationals in the former colonies and the former metropoles imagined themselves as having been "colonized" by all things—and all people—deemed "foreign." Demands for nation-states to take action against foreign corporations and foreign workers were (and remain) common. It simply could not be acknowledged that each national economy existed within a *global* capitalist system, one fundamentally based on the exploitation of workers pitted against one another within as well as across the system of nation-states, and one that persistently required fixes for its crises of profitability and control.

Instead, the deep disappointments, disillusionments, and disenchantments that accompanied the growing crises facing workers across the world resulted in what Paul Gilroy (2005) calls a "postcolonial melancholia," one that led people across the world to believe that their nation-state had simply been hijacked by "foreign capital" and/or by "foreign workers" either in other nation-states or Migrants within nation-states. Refusal to acknowledge that nationalism never could live up to its promises ironically led to further nationalism. Postcolonial melancholy shifted from sadness to rage against all things not-National. The emergence of theories of neocolonialism emanated from such a belief. Part of the "structure of feeling" of postcolonialism, ideas that people had been colonized anew kept the possibility of a future national liberation alive (see Williams 1961).

In chapter 7, "Global Lockdown: Postcolonial Expansion of National Citizenship and Immigration Controls," I discuss how by the late 1960s the entire inhabitable surface of our earth was demarcated as the (often contested) territory of one or another sovereign nation. The formation of new national liberation states across Africa, Asia, the Pacific, and the Caribbean, along with the nationalization of the sovereignty of the two largest remaining imperial states—the British and the French—resulted in a world where there was no freedom of movement. Exercising its newfound national right of self-determination—each nation-state erected barriers to the entry of people into its territories. In two tables, I show the strong relationship between the obtainment of independence and the enactment of laws governing nationality and immigration in Asia (including the Middle East) and Africa. In more narrative form, I discuss the same for the Pacific and the Caribbean.

In this consolidated Postcolonial New World Order, the separation of National-Natives and Migrants was sealed. Even as social, economic, and/or political rights of noncitizens varied greatly among nation-states, in none did Migrants have rights commensurate with Nationals. Today, one's national citizenship is the single most consequential factor in predicting how well and for how long one lives. This "citizenship premium" depends upon citizenship and immigration controls (Milanovic 2015). In the Postcolonial New World Order, the global gap in prosperity and peace has shifted from being primarily a difference between imperial metropoles and colonies to an even greater one between citizens of nation-states.

Even so, nation-states cannot ensure that only National-Natives reside within their territories. Not only is this a logistical impossibility—people will attempt to move to where they believe they can live and live better—but regardless of rhetoric to the contrary, nation-states do not see the end of immigration as a desirable outcome. Across the postcolonial world, especially in the Rich World, there is a structural reliance on the *recruitment* of Migrant Workers. The categorization of workers *as* Migrants allows nation-states to use their citizenship and immigration policies to create ever greater competition between workers. Such a strategy works because of the *nationalization of the wage*. Nationals are generally granted more workplace rights and paid more than Migrants. Thus, aside from producing nationalism as a strong territorial attachment, citizenship and immigration policies also produce Migrants as the sort of flexible and precarious worker sought by employers and states. Migrants thus show us that national states do not form a closed system but are part of a *global* one. Indeed, the expansion of capitalist social relations under conditions of postcolonialism—and the consequent growth in capitalists' need for commodified labor power—is one of the main ties that bind not only individual nation-states but also workers together into a global system.

In chapter 8, "National Autochthonies and the Making of Postcolonial National-Natives," after having analyzed one of the two main technologies of postcolonial power—the globalization of national citizenship and immigration controls—I examine the second: the national discourse of autochthony. I show how postcolonial discourses of national autochthony differ in tenor, are mobilized "from above" and "from below," and, as the examples I chose show, are exercised by people across the left-right political spectrum. By looking at events in the national liberation states of India, Sudan, South Sudan, and Myanmar; the growing power of "White Natives" in both Europe and in the former White Settler colonies; the Cherokee and Mohawk Indigenous-National Natives in the United States and Canada, respectively; and Bolivia under Evo Morales, its first self-identified Indigenous president, I show that autochthonous claims clearly differ, both in scale and effect, and take on different forms within, between, across, and at times against today's existing nation-states. The people who deploy such discourses also have wildly varying abilities to institutionalize their nationalist politics of autochthony.

What each of these examples shows, however, is that the category of National-Native carries enormous legal and moral authority precisely because it is a legacy of the autochthonization of political membership first practiced by imperial states. At the same time, postcolonialism has turned the category of Native on its head. Being Native once marked someone as a *subjugated* subject of empires. Now, being Native is to make oneself the subject of "national self-determination." Today, the exemplary National subject is someone laying claim to being a Native *of* national territory. The imperial binary of European/Native has thus been flipped into the national binary of National-Native/Migrant. Surreally—and dangerously—migration is increasingly portrayed as colonialism. A growing number of National-Natives imagine themselves as being colonized by Migrants. Such claims are perhaps most often made in the former White Settler colonies where there are two claimants for the category of autochthon: White National-Natives and Indigenous National-Natives. However different their relations to the extant nation-state is, both conflate migration with colonization. Arguing in zero-sum terms, Migrant emplacement is seen to cause National-Native dispossession.

This, once again, demonstrates that in the Postcolonial New World Order, the struggle for national liberation is a never-ending one. Many of today's conflicts, and some of the most violent ones, are represented as National-Natives struggling to oust Migrant "colonizers." Such discursive practices have only hardened under neoliberalism as the material substance of national citizenship has been "hollowed out" (Jessop 1993). Thus, claims of being Native to the nation trump formal National citizenship.

In the rest of this chapter, I try to understand how it is that autochthonous discourses are plausible—and how they work—in a remarkably wide set of circumstances, ranging from far-right political parties to the movements of some of the most exploited and oppressed people on the planet. Studying how national autochthonous discourses are deployed across the world and the political spectrum allows us to see that their similarities are neither superficial nor semantic—that is, evident only in their shared use of the terms "Native" or "Indigenous." Instead, both are technologies of postcolonial governmentality. Discourses of national autochthony allow those laying claim to Nativeness to make exclusive political claims to national identity, belonging, sovereignty, and territory. As each mobilization of national autochthony is reliant on—and productive of—the figure of the Migrant, the violence of national exclusions and even national inclusions is laid bare.

I conclude this book with chapter 9, "Postseparation: Struggles for a Decolonized Commons," in which I argue that the failure to achieve decolonization is a failure of the national form in which liberation has been imagined. National self-determination, the leitmotif of the Postcolonial New World Order, is a form of power that contains and ultimately extinguishes the goals of—and the desire for—a decolonization worthy of its name. I argue that the very real problems we face in realizing decolonization are greater than the existence of asymmetry within the global system of sovereign nation-states. The inability of nation-states to counteract the limits to equality set by global capitalism lies not in the mechanism of uneven development, as the neocolonialism thesis argues, but in the banal, everyday work done by nation-states to ensure that the lands they territorialize and the people made into National-Natives are readily available to capital. A key delivery vehicle is nation-state restrictions against free mobility. Citizenship and immigration controls serve up Migrants to capital looking for ever cheaper and more vulnerable workers, and to National-Natives debilitated by postcolonial melancholia. Looking to national sovereignty as the means to decolonization—and to the National-Native as the only subject needing or capable of realizing decolonization—only guarantees that people will be consigned to postcolonial power.

We need to take into account what was lost by the victory of national self-determination, so that we can do better in our next round of struggles. I believe that a collective and a cooperative project for decolonization is possible, one that can unite Natives and Migrants through a shared refusal to identify with these state-categories. I say this not in some flight of utopian fancy or because of some deep-seated denial of the very real harm done to people categorized as Natives or as Migrants, but with the knowledge that only by coming together can we defeat those who lord their power over us.

Such knowledge has long been put into action by many people. People who had been colonized, enslaved, and/or indentured together built maroon societies; people fighting against slavery asked, "Am I not a man and a brother?"; pirates freeing themselves from the sovereign power of ships' captains sang, "All for one and one for all"; Diggers addressed each other as "fellow creatures"; women accused of speaking out of turn declared that "God was no respecter of faces"; and many direct producers organized against capitalism under the banner of "Workers of the world, unite!" Each of these struggles to break the chains of servitude to states and capital was built on the mobile politics of solidarity. People's shared experience of the terror of expropriation, exploitation, and oppression led to people's shared resistance—and to shared subjectivities.

Tragically, their struggles were lost. The victors cemented their power by institutionalizing private property, expanding the capitalist mode of production, enhancing states' power, and weaving an interlocking web of ranked hierarchies normalized by ideas of race, gender/sex, and nationhood. Their greatest victory was the fact that many people experiencing expropriation, exploitation, and oppression saw themselves through these ruling identifications instead of with other direct producers. The acceptance and intensification of the contemporary separation between National-Natives and Migrants is the latest manifestation of such relations of "define and rule" (Mamdani 2012).

In rejecting the Postcolonial New World Order with its separated political categories of Natives and Migrants, I embrace a collective struggle for our common, borderless world. The contemporary struggle for our commons, one that I believe must be both worldly and global, is the latest effort to decolonize our world and our imaginations, another effort to make our heaven on earth, despite the jealousies and violence of those who want to be sovereign lords.

2

THE IMPERIAL
GOVERNMENT OF
MOBILITY AND STASIS

Imperialism is the export of identity.

—*Edward Said, 1993*

The postcolonial separation of Natives and Migrants is part of the legacy of imperialism. Imperial states had, of course, long separated imperial subjects through the negative duality of European/Native, even as European empires expropriated, exploited, and negatively racialized working people in Europe. Natives were the colonized subjects of imperial colonies. Europeans were the colonizers. Empires had also long established racist classification schemes, each with different sets of rights determined by degrees of distance from "European blood" and "European culture." With these still firmly in place, from the mid-nineteenth century a further separation was made *between* colonized Natives. Imperial states began categorizing colonized Natives as either "Indigenous-Natives" or "Migrant-Natives." This binary was part of efforts to maintain imperial rule in the face of heated resistance from the collectivity of Natives. The British Empire was the first to institute such distinctions, but other major European empires soon followed suit. In this chapter, I discuss how this bifurcation of colonized Natives was part of a broader shift in imperial rule from "direct rule" to "indirect rule" colonialism.

Indirect-rule colonialism was comprised of three major institutions: the Native Authority made up of appointed Native rulers as well as colonial officials and administrative staff; the Native treasury, which collected revenue to fund local staff and services; and Native courts said to administer Native "law and custom," supposedly dating from precolonial times. Each of these structures was nominally independent but rigorously policed by imperial agents and civil servants. Through such tactics, Native and imperial elites became deeply bound to one another and to the maintenance of imperial rule (D. Cheesman 2013, 10–11). Colonialism, of course, had long operated through Natives. Imperial states often superimposed their power over social and political structures in the colonies by bringing the extant ruling class into the service of empire or by producing "Native leaders" out of whole cloth—as when imperially appointed chiefs, kings, and so forth were empowered to act autocratically against other Natives.

European empires had also long engaged in biopolitical technologies of rule. The early seventeenth-century categorization of colonized people as Natives, long associated with "a person born in bondage; a person born to servants, tenants, etc., and inheriting their status," not only normalized their exploitation, but the 1604 designation of Native as one born in a particular place also grounded Natives as a part of the "resources" of specific imperial colonies (OED, "native [n.]"). By the end of the seventeenth century, nonhuman animals as well as plants began to be emplaced and defined as Native (or not). By the early eighteenth century, this intensified as places were identified by that which was said to be Native there. The imperial category of Native thus signified both the classed relations of subordination and servitude and the territorialized and racialized relations of "natural" belonging. By the nineteenth century, these related meanings combined to constitute Natives as the colonized people *of* a given colonial territory. Thus, even when Europeans were themselves born in imperial colonies, they remained European, just as Natives remained Natives of any particular colony regardless of where they actually lived. In these ways, the categories of European and Native came to be rooted in racialized geographies.

However, in the mid-nineteenth century, the process of emplacing and, relatedly, displacing imperial subjects went further. With serious tumult erupting in British colonies, the empire attempted to dissipate the (potential) collective strength of unruly Natives. Instead of continuing to rely upon Native elites to secure rule over other Natives, the British imperial state employed enhanced technologies of biopower. Imperial attention was now paid to how each and every Native was defined and positioned within the colonies. Some Natives were fixed in place as Indigenous-Natives and became the only ones regarded in imperial law as being *of* the colony. Other Natives were redefined as Migrant-Natives and, as such, out of place. Their bifurcation was not only an extension of the classic imperial policy of *divide et impera* but was part of a new policy that Mahmood Mamdani (2012) calls "define and rule." Together the new biopolitical categories of Indigenous-Natives and Migrant-Natives further territorialized imperial identity, ushering in a new imperial governmentality in the process. By naturalizing the link between rights, territory, and identity, indirect-rule colonialism became part of the genealogy of ideas about nationalized sovereignty.

INDIRECT-RULE COLONIALISM AND THE IMPERIAL DISTINCTION BETWEEN NATIVES AND MIGRANTS

Indirect-rule colonialism was a dramatic shift ushered in by a dramatic event: the 1857 Indian Rebellion in British India. In May 1857, soldiers of the Bengal army shot their British officers and marched on Delhi. Their mutiny spurred rebellion by civilians across the northern and central parts of the subcontinent. Considered the greatest challenge made to any European power in the nineteenth century and lasting well over a year, the rebellion generated fear that colonized Natives not only in British India but in other parts of the empire would overthrow imperial rule (Mamdani 2012). This was neither an exaggerated nor a fleeting worry, and its effects were felt beyond the British Empire. In the United States, for example, the "British Mutiny" played into "an anxiety toward slave revolts in the late 1850s and into the Civil War" (Bilwakesh 2011).

After putting down the Indian Rebellion, Britain passed the 1858 Government of India Act and took control from the East India Company. Ironically, direct British imperial-state control was accompanied by an "indirect" style of rule. The East India Company had expanded British control over much of the Asian subcontinent by relying on existing elites to extract wealth from Native workers and to brutally suppress their dissent. Otherwise, it ignored the day-to-day organization of their lives. The company did, however, apply a strategy of "civilizing" the Native ruling class and Native members of its military by trying to get them to adopt British laws, technology, and even Christianity. This was done in an effort to assimilate them to bourgeois European ways of life.

The British imperial state believed that the revolt had been sparked by Native resentment at such intrusions. After its suppression, British rule came to be informed by the belief that Native unruliness could be quelled by recognizing—and codifying—how the Natives were "different," not only from the British but also from each other. "The ambition of indirect rule," Mamdani argues, "was to remake the subjectivities of entire populations" such that "cultural difference was reinforced, exaggerated, and built up" (2012, 45, 48). "Protection" became the governmentality of indirect-rule colonialism. People categorized as Indigenous-Natives were temporally enclosed within "custom" and spatially identified with particular places. Migrant-Natives, declared as more "modern," were defined through their (supposed) migration and lack of territorial claims.

The construction of an increasingly separated and divided colonial population was facilitated by the labyrinth of censuses and tax rolls initiated in the colonies during the mid to late nineteenth century. Previous imperial practices of counting landholdings and household heads or collating raw numbers of human (and often plant and other animal) inhabitants gave way to the goal of making each and every colonized Native legible to empire. In British India from 1867 to 1872, British census personnel collected data on the caste, religion, profession, and age of each Native to define the content of the "character" of each group (Cohn 1987). With such methods of population data collection, the British Empire categorized Natives into separate, supposedly incommensurable, biopolitical groups. Ideas of the "sameness" of one group of Natives materialized "differences" between them so that, in true racist fashion, each was constructed as comprising a distinct *type* of Native. Under indirect-rule colonialism, then, the strategy of separating Europeans from Natives was extended to the separation of Natives.

Over time, biopolitical technologies, initially used to define juridical categories, established long-lasting social and political boundaries between separated Native groups. An example from British India helps us see how this was done. In 1862, the idea that Hindus and Muslims were wholly different types of people was shored up by identifying each as having discrete customs, culture, history, and traditions (Gottschalk 2013). The British Raj institutionalized such ideas by empowering the supposed guardians of tradition—princes, priests, and landholders—and by consolidating authoritarian British rule. The passing of separate "personal codes" or "personal laws" was part of this (Cohn 1996). The "civil" (or "personal") matters of Hindus and Muslims would be dealt with by separate Native authorities established by the British but portrayed as emanating from the "traditions" of the named group. In the subsequent decade (1862–1872), further legal and administrative reforms were enacted to "preserve" and "protect" these now-differentiated groups of Natives. The British thus actively constructed new identities—communal and individual—by institutionalizing the significance of religion in social and political life in unprecedented ways.

The construction of separate legal systems and political constituencies that produced differences between the colonized Natives also fueled antagonism between them. This was not beside the point. By 1888, just three decades after the Indian Rebellion, a member of the Council of the Secretary of State for India, Sir John Strachey, could say that "the existence side by side of the hostile creeds is one of the strongest points in our political position in India" (N. Stewart 1951, 49). As the anticolonial movement grew, in 1905 the British partitioned the province of Bengal into a "Hindu" western region (Bengal) and a "Muslim" eastern region (East Bengal and Assam).[1] The 1909 Indian Councils Act (or Morley-Minto reforms) created separate electorates for Muslims. As Hindus vied for the "Hindu vote" and Muslims for the "Muslim vote," the need to make appeals to voters across now-communal lines was nullified and the separation of Hindus and Muslims was entrenched in formal politics. Indeed, the belief that only Hindus could represent Hindus and only Muslims represent Muslims institutionalized communalism into electoral politics and led to increased demands for further partitions (Mamdani 2012, 28, 30).

With "community" membership becoming key to the making of political claims, these communities were regarded by many to be self-chosen and self-enacted. John Morley, secretary of state for India, encouraged such a view by speaking about the separate "nations who inhabit India" as a timeless feature of Native life (Madden 1979). The "invention of tradition" was, thus, accompanied by the invention of genealogies and histories (see Hobsbawm and Ranger 1983). From here it was not a huge leap for each to demand self-determination. Indeed, in 1947, the British Raj was partitioned into the separate nation-states of India—which many, including numerous leaders of the All India Congress Party, had already come to see as a Hindu place—and Pakistan, which became a separate place for Muslims. The territorialization of identity—and the demand for home rule that such identities generated—was thus a key legacy of indirect-rule colonialism.

Late-imperial territorialities not only emplaced Indigenous-Natives, but they also displaced those categorized as Migrant-Natives. They were portrayed as people Native to someplace else. The differences between the two biopolitical groups of colonized Natives hinged upon the idea of autochthony. Indigenous-Natives were defined by imperial states as autochthons, while their opposite, Migrant-Natives, became allochthons. Derived from the Greek *autos* (self) and *khthon* (earth), an autochthon was one (originally in the plural) who had literally "sprung from the earth"; the term referred to "an original or indigenous inhabitant of a place" (OED, "autochthony [*n.*]"). The term *indigenous* is also from classical Greece. To be indigenous was to be "born inside, with the class connotation of being born 'inside the house'" (Ceuppens and Geschiere 2005, 385). Like *autochthon, indigenous* denoted someone (or something) "born or produced naturally in a land or region; native or belonging naturally to (the soil, region, etc.)" (OED, "indigenous [*adj.*]").

The counterpart to autochthonous or indigenous people was the alloch-thons. Predicated on the Greek *allo*, referring to that which is other or differ-ent, and the Indo-European *allo*, referring to someone (or something) "else," and first used as a geological reference, *allochthonous* referred to something from someplace other than where it is currently found (OED, "allochthonous [*adj.*]"). It was not until the period of indirect-rule colonialism that things (and later people) were defined as allochthons (OED, "allochthon [*n.*]").

Already by the mid-seventeenth century, European imperial states had em-ployed a discourse of autochthony to sow divisions. For example, in 1646, Thomas Browne stated, "Although . . . there bee . . . swarmes of Negroes serv-ing under the Spaniard, yet were they all transported from Africa . . . and are not indigenous or proper natives of America" (OED, "indigenous [*adj.*]"). Two centuries later, they employed it to make even further separations. By the late nineteenth century, indirect-rule colonialism took these ideas further to cat-egorize those Natives who were "not indigenous" as Migrant-Natives, or the "people out of place." This made Indigenous-Natives the more authentic Na-tives of any colony.

The distinction between Indigenous-Migrants and Native-Migrants piv-oted on ideas of stasis and mobility. Saying that Indigenous-Natives were from a place was to metaphysically locate them as being *of* that place. Autochthons were defined not only as "springing forth from the land" but also as immobile subjects. In being so closely associated with a place, Indigenous-Natives were natured. Imperialists, deploying what Gilles Deleuze and Félix Guattari (1988, 15) call "tree logic," imagined Indigenous-Natives as literally "rooted" to the land. Together, the idea of their supposed stasis along with the idea that they were a natural part of a given environment informed imperialists' view that Indigenous-Natives were people with timeless and unchanging "traditions"— in short, a people without history. Ideas of indigeneity as a manifestation of racialized temporalities intensified already racialized geographies. Defining any individual as an Indigenous-Native was based not on where the person was born, but upon the birthplace of their "race." Indirect-rule colonialism thus manifested racialized ideas of essentialist origins in territorialized form.

Under indirect-rule colonialism, an ontological misrepresentation met a racialized geography. Empires established Native authorities and granted the power to allocate (or refuse) land and to recognize (or refuse) rights, a power that was well guarded. In contrast, Migrant-Natives were denied access to territory and to political representation on Indigenous-Native territories. This had the effect of further territorializing Indigenous-Natives while ren-dering Migrant-Natives placeless. In the process, Migrant-Natives became dependent on the market to possess land. Moreover, because imperial states defined Migrant-Natives as less Native than Indigenous-Natives and, thus, less governed by "tradition," they were seen as having a greater ability to at least partially engage in capitalist markets (e.g., as market gardeners or merchants) in ways that Indigenous-Natives could not. The formation of these two sets of property rules helped to materialize the supposedly natural characteristics between the two, separated groups of Natives. This too played no small part in materializing "Indigenous" and "Migrant" as political identities—which had, we will later see, profound consequences for how decolonization was fought for.

Under indirect-rule colonialism, remaining precolonial institutions and relationships were affected. The opposition constructed between Indigenous-Natives and Migrant-Natives came to dominate local patterns of organization, producing what Nicholas Dirks (2001) calls an "ethnographic state." How one saw and practiced one's religion, related to landlords and/or political rulers, saw one's self in the world, and viewed one's proximate neighbors were all informed by discourses of autochthony. In this regard, it is important to remember that the political identities of Indigenous-Native and Migrant-Native were imperial constructions designed to keep empires in power. Whichever way Natives were defined, all Natives were ultimately colonial subjects. Despite the prestige and power held by nominal leaders of Native authorities, European imperial "advisers" remained in charge. Despite whatever wealth some small number of Migrant-Natives could amass from their market activities, they were not allowed to offer real competition to metropolitan investors. It was the imperial state that enjoyed most of the benefits of taxation and set the terms of engagement with capitalist markets.

It is also important to keep in mind that imperial ideas of stasis and mobility, around which the separation of colonized Natives revolved, was not reflective of some existing reality but productive of it. Those categorized as Indigenous-Natives were no more or no less fixed in place than Migrant-Natives. Indeed, some who became Indigenous-Migrants had previously fled state power, while some defined as Migrant-Natives had been sedentarized by states. James Scott (2009) provides some examples of this in his study of "Zomia."[2] There, those who became Indigenous-Natives were often the ones whom precolonial states regarded as barbaric because they had, literally, run for the hills to avoid state rule. These later "hill people" were seen as more "primitive" than people in the valleys, who had been "civilized" by being subjugated to state rule in order to exploit their labor. Over time, Scott (2009, ix) argues, these "hill people" were "seen from the valley kingdoms as 'our living ancestors,' 'what we were like before we discovered wet-rice cultivation, Buddhism, and civilization'." Thus, because "self-barbarianization"—or a relatively stateless life—was (and remains) unthinkable, "hill people" were said to be embodiments of the past or "original" condition of humanity (Scott 2009, 173).

By the late nineteenth century, European imperial states borrowed from these prior imperial discourses for their own purposes. They too relied on notions of stasis, but this time geographical as well as temporal. Thus, even though "hill people" were in no way static, either temporally or geographically, but were instead "best understood as runaway, fugitive, maroon communities who have, over the course of two millennia, been fleeing the oppressions of state-making projects in the valleys—slavery, conscription, taxes, corvée labor, epidemics, and warfare" (Scott 2009, ix), and even though valley dwellers were less mobile than hill people were by virtue of having been captured by the state *and* had been in the area alongside those who became the Indigenous-Natives since time immemorial, they were defined as "belonging" somewhere else. Furthermore, Indigenous-Natives and Migrant-Natives were represented as having wholly unconnected histories, even though the two had a symbiotic relationship. Such practices were not limited to Asia but crisscrossed empires.

In the British imperial territory of Darfur (in western Sudan), a distinction between "Black Natives" and "Arab Natives" was first made in the 1920s British imperial census. Black Natives were defined as the "original" and, thus, Indigenous-Natives, while Arab Natives, said to "originate" elsewhere, became Migrant-Natives. This imperial distinction failed to account for the political importance of claiming an "Arab" identity for people in the area, however (Mamdani 2009, 15, 80). Before British rule, being "Arab" was a way to align oneself with the powerful. Indeed, "Arabs" had been in Darfur for at least as long as those the British designated as Black (Mamdani 2009). Yet the British Empire (and subsequently many others) racialized the political strategy of claiming Arab-ness and made the now-territorialized separation of Black-Indigenous and Arab-Migrant a part of the historiography of "Africa" (Mamdani 2009). The precolonial history of Africa came to be told as a running conflict between Black Indigenous-Natives and their "foreign" (now Migrant) Arab rulers. As a result of indirect-rule colonialism's attachment of racialized traits to demographic groupings, racialized ideas of distinct and discrete "bloodlines" permeated the making of political claims. Consequently, racialized and spatialized separation became central to imperial-state rule.

Pioneered by the British, indirect-rule colonialism became a model of colonial administration for other imperial states. Indeed, today's international reach of autochthonous discourses emerged from a shared global history of empire(s). The French imperial state, starting in piecemeal fashion in 1865, had by 1881 consolidated indirect-rule colonial principles into its Code de l'indigénat, which was in force until 1946 (although Bronwen Manby [2010, 29] argues that "its practical application lasted far longer"). First established in French Algeria, it shaped French imperial practices more broadly shortly thereafter. By 1889 it was the main juridical vehicle of French imperialism in sub-Saharan Africa and Asia. The code separated people throughout the French Empire into one of two hierarchically arranged, racialized categories of people, each with its own distinct set of political rights (or lack thereof). Those categorized as "Europeans" were placed in the higher-ranked category of French citizens (*citoyens français*), while the colonized Natives (*indigènes*) of non-European French imperial territories were placed in the lesser category of French subjects (*sujets français*).[5]

However, in addition to the distinction between (European) French citizens and (colonized) French subjects within the empire, the French imperial state made distinctions between the Natives. Baz Lecocq (in Geschiere 2012, 5) notes that the French Empire first formally employed the notion of *autochtone* in an attempt to separate "Berbers" from "Arabs" in Algeria in 1874 (Bengio and Gabriel 1999). Shortly thereafter, the French imperial state was using the distinction between autochthons and allochthons in Sudan, recently incorporated into its empire (Ceuppens and Geschiere 2005, 387). Here the French formed racialized cantons of "real *autochtones*," each administered by "traditional" power holders. These cantons formed the basis for *le commandement indigene* (Abbink 2012). Indeed, Abbink argues that *autochtonie* became "a basic principle for *la politique des races*, elaborated by the well-known Governor-General of French West Africa, William Ponty, around 1900" (2012, 22).

Such practices heralded a shift in French imperial practices from assimilation (into "French civilization") to indirect-rule colonialism's governmentality of "protection" and "tradition." From the late nineteenth century onward this led to the French system of "association." New, appointed Native rulers were organized by the French at three different levels and grades, *chef de province* (provincial chief), *chef de canton* (district chiefs) and *chef de village* (village chief). These "traditional chiefs," each of them "real *autochtones*," were empowered by the empire to collect taxes and commandeer forced labor, particularly for the production of crops.

Other imperial states also employed indirect-rule strategies to retain as well as expand their empires. In the Dutch East Indies, a system of legal pluralism established different legal codes not only for Europeans and Natives but also for Natives and "foreign Orientals" (Mamdani 2012, 40). Similarly, while the Portuguese imperial state's 1899 Indigenato Code distinguished between the racialized categories of the *não-indígena* (or, broadly, Europeans) and the *indígena*, it further differentiated between the *indígena*, now ruled by customary law, and the *assimilado*, racialized as "Asian," "Afro-Portuguese," or "Africans" (Manby 2014). Similar rules applied in Spanish, Belgian, German, and Italian colonies.

Indirect-rule colonialism, thus, changed how people in state-spaces came to know and relate to one another through racialized temporalities and geographies of stasis and mobility. Regimes of land tenure, political rights, and the minutia of daily life in the colonies were drastically changed, as were ideas of history, belonging, subjectivities, and the imagined space of "society" itself. The governmentality of protection, with its preservation of the "traditions" of emplaced Indigenous-Natives—and the displaced Migrant-Natives—produced a racialized territorialization of politics.

Not only were colonial practices altered, so too were understandings of colonialism itself. Imperial states often, but not always, put Migrant-Natives in positions of authority over Indigenous-Natives all the while retaining authority over both. They insisted that imperial acts of colonialism were no different than the actions of Migrant-Natives. Within such ideas was the view that practices of expropriation and exploitation were defined by one's relationship to place, as "outsiders" were said to have always taken that which belonged to "insiders." This informed the distinctions empires made between colonized people, but it also went no small way toward the recasting of Migrants as "colonizers" today. Indeed, the legacy of indirect-rule colonialism has reached into our present. From the last decades of the nineteenth century to now, the distinction between Indigenous-Natives and Migrant-Natives provides the basis of nationalist strategies of home rule. While not all national liberation states came to be ruled by those the imperialists categorized as Indigenous-Natives, in each, the political struggle over who would become sovereign over what territory—and over whom—increasingly centered on claims to autochthonous status. In this, they were not dissimilar to those former colonies—and now nation-states—conceptualized as White Settler colonies.

WHITE SETTLER COLONIES

The British "White Settler" colonies of the "New World"—now the nation-states of the United States, Canada, Australia, and New Zealand—are assumed to be distinct from European colonies in Africa and Asia, because people racialized as European or White eventually came to imagine these places not just as colonial possessions but also homelands.[4] Of course, in these White Settler colonies, there were colonized people whom imperial states categorized as Natives. In addition, particularly in the United States, enslaved people from Africa were forcibly brought in, and, in each of these colonies, there was a later movement of indentured, contract labor recruited as "coolies" from Asia. As a result of racist practices that separated and ranked White and non-White people, both the United States, which declared independence from the British Empire in 1776, and the British White Dominions of Canada, Australia, New Zealand, and Newfoundland, which remained in the empire until well into the twentieth century, were defined as places of—and for—a cross-class group of Whites. These distinctions between White Settler colonies and other colonies in Asia, Africa, and the rest of the New World, however, have led to a negation of the many similarities between them. In the next two sections, I outline how the practices of indirect-rule colonialism evident in Asia and Africa were also implemented in the White Settler colonies and in the same period. At the same time, I show that indirect-rule colonialism in these places continued to operate alongside continued adherence to civilizational and assimilationist discourses based on racist ideas of White supremacy.

Indirect-Rule Colonialism in the White Settler Colonies: The United States

From the mid-nineteenth century onward, some of the key practices of indirect-rule colonialism—definition, segregation, protection, and immobilization—were evident in the New World's White Settler colonies. As elites in these territories began to stake their claims to independence from British imperial rule—and even more so, when these former colonies nationalized their sovereignties, beginning with the United States in the late nineteenth century—new efforts were made to contain, count, and control the colonized Natives (also classified as "Indians" and "Aborigines"). Foremost among these strategies was the creation of "reserved" parcels of land to which Natives were economically, politically, and geographically tied. As occurred in Asian and African colonies governed through indirect-rule colonialism, the reservation systems in the United States, Canada, Australia, and New Zealand were initially organized in the name of protecting Natives. Similarly, each "tribe," "band," or, later, "nation" of Natives was nominally ruled by Native leaders appointed by the ruling state.

Notably, such a shift took place earliest in the United States, which, in 1776, achieved its independence from the British Empire, more than a century earlier than the other White Settler colonies. However, although the emergent United States had already entered into informal treaties with Natives starting in 1775, its key aim then was to maintain trade relations with them (largely in fur and skins) while attempting to "civilize" Natives into a norma-tive European bourgeois ethos. Toward these ends, an Office of Indian Trade was formed in 1806 and maintained until 1822. It was with the end of the trade (or "factory") system, when the Bureau of Indian Affairs (BIA) was established in 1824. Maintaining the "civilizing mission" of previous offices, it attempted to move Indians into European-style agriculture. The 1830 Indian Removal Act further facilitated this mission.

A shift toward indirect-rule colonialism in the United States became evi-dent in the mid-nineteenth century. In 1851, the U.S. Indian Appropriations Act authorized the forcible removal of Indians from lands already taken by the military and claimed by Whites. Displaced Indians were moved onto reserved lands located in U.S. territory mostly west of the Mississippi River. New res-ervations created after this time were comprised of territories that had been either named by treaty or already expropriated by the state. In 1868, President Grant expanded the practice of containing and segregating Indians by send-ing the U.S. Army to restrict Indians' movement off reservations. U.S. control over Indians was further intensified by the 1871 Indian Appropriations Act, which ended the treaty-making process and facilitated the further expansion of U.S. territory. The U.S. state responded to Native resistance to such prac-tices with some of its most violent and bloodiest wars waged against them.

The making of reservations and the related enumeration of Natives, I argue, are forms of indirect rule colonialism. The U.S. federal government formed "Indian tribes" whose allotted "reservations" were nominally managed by "tribal governments" led by appointed chiefs and tribal councils. Of course, each recognized Native political structure was under the authority of the BIA, which held both plenary and financial power over it. Even so, the U.S. state por-trayed the establishment of reservations, with the oft-accompanying forced relocation of "Indians" onto them, as a form of protecting them and their "traditions." As indirect colonial practices did in Asia and Africa, these led to the further destruction of prior land-tenure systems and livelihoods and significant disruptions of previous social relationships, including a massive reduction in the status of women. Philip Deloria (2004, 27) characterizes res-ervations as a "colonial dream" wherein "fixity, control, visibility, productivity, and, most importantly, docility," were the state's main objectives.

The governmentality of protection shaped the 1886 U.S. Supreme Court ruling that made all Indians wards of the U.S. government (*United States v. Kagama*). Declaring that Congress held plenary power over all "Native Ameri-can tribes," the decision stated that "the power of the general government over these remnants of a race once powerful . . . is necessary to their protection as well as to the safety of those among whom they dwell." The creation of Indian reservations was also part of the state's project of racialized classification and geographical and political segregation. In this, the 1887 Dawes Allotment Act was a critical technology defining individuals as Indians through a racialized system of "blood quantum." Together, the Dawes Act worked to expand U.S. territories and U.S. control over Indians.

Lists known as the "Dawes Rolls" were compiled by Indian agents noting each person's name and estimated percentage of "Indian blood." Access to land (divided into smaller, individual plots), revenue, as well as political power on Indian reservations were made dependent on having one's name (or the name of a close family member) on the Dawes Rolls. In enumerating and defining Indians, the United States also used the Dawes Rolls to limit the number of officially recognized Indians in order to limit its distribution of "protections." The process by which the Dawes Rolls were compiled was notorious. Indian agents hired by the U.S. government often just listed people's blood quantum as whatever they wanted, or they used the ideas of "scientific racism" to qualify—or more likely disqualify—people as Indians based on the shape of their feet, hair type, and so forth. It was through these racialized schemes of state identification that "Indianness" was materialized. As Indian tribes were made responsible for determining the proof of a person's Indian blood quantum, individuals as well as entire tribes became invested in who was—and was not—officially a member. Unsurprisingly, the state category of "Indian" became a critical aspect of people's self-identification.

The bifurcation introduced through such methods of indirect-rule colonialism in the United States, thus, was the production of two groups—one autochthonous group recognized as Indian and another that was no longer so recognized. As Ojibway writer David Treuer (2011) notes, "'As long as grass grows or water runs'—a phrase that was often used in treaties with American Indians—is a relatively permanent term for a contract. 'As long as the blood flows' seemed measurably shorter." Such practices were enshrined in the later 1934 Indian Reorganization Act, which made blood quantum "a legal marker of Indian identity in the United States at the federal level" (A. Simpson 2014, 137).

Together the federal government's creation of Indian reservations, refusal to negotiate treaties, enforcement of state-mandated racialized blood quantum criteria for Indian status, and the tying of this status to economic and political rights, entrenched legislated differences between those legally recognized as Indians and those who were not. It also organized legislated differences between Indians and other racialized, biopolitical groups. Earlier antimiscegenation laws designed to maintain the legal and affective separation of those racialized as either White or Black were extended to prohibit marriage between those defined as Indians and Blacks—for example, in Oklahoma in 1908 and in Louisiana in 1920 (Moran 2003, 1663). As we shall see in chapter 8, the legacy of those practices shape social relations between these differentiated groups to this day.

However, in the United States, practices of indirect-rule colonialism did not hold decisive sway, as they did in the Asian and African colonies. By the 1920s, U.S. policy once again emphasized assimilation. In 1924 an Indian Citizenship Act was passed, making all Indians U.S. citizens. Approximately 125,000 Indians were recategorized as U.S. citizens shortly after its passing. Previously, Indians who were "not taxed" were not guaranteed citizenship as stipulated by the Fourteenth Amendment (1868), which granted citizenship to all those born in the United States. In fact, until 1924, Indians were treated as subjects of "foreign governments," as the infamous 1856 Dred Scott decision defined them.[5] Instead, prior to 1924 only those Indians who enlisted in the military, had received individual allotments, had been granted U.S. citizenship through special treaties or statutes, or as an Indian women had married a White man, could become U.S. citizens.

With the 1924 Indian Citizenship Act, the incorporation of Indians as U.S. citizens was no longer viewed by the state as a threat but as an advantage. It was part of a broader and often contradictory reordering of the relationship of racism and nationalism in the United States. Significantly, the same year that Indians were redefined as U.S. citizens, the blood quantum rules deployed against Indians were extended to other negatively racialized groups, but in the opposite direction. While people had to reach—and prove—a high threshold of Indian "blood" to be defined as such, Virginia passed its notorious "one-drop" rule with its 1924 Racial Integrity Act. It defined as "Negro," with all of the legalized and social subordination imposed by this identification, anyone with even one (alleged or actual) ancestor from sub-Saharan Africa. The United States thus used blood quantum rules in whichever way would take away the most—and grant the least—amount of rights to various non-White people. At the same time, a de facto legal segregation of Black people was put into place in the North just when there was a significant northern movement of Black people from the South.

The Indian Citizenship Act was also passed in the same year as the 1924 Immigration Act (Johnson-Reed Act), which included both the National Origins Act and the Asian Exclusion Act. The Indian Citizenship Act and the Immigration Act worked in an opposite manner. The former expanded the number of U.S. citizens to gain greater control over Indians, while the latter severely

limited lawful entry into the United States to various groups of negatively racialized noncitizens, including, for the first time, people moving from Europe
(see chapter 3). The two processes intersected, as the Indian Citizenship Act
affected the cross-border movement of Indians whose precolonial territories
traversed the newer territorial border between the United States and Canada.
Having U.S. citizenship became necessary for Indians' unhindered movement
into the United States. Those born on the Canadian side of the border became "aliens" in the United States (and vice versa) (A. Simpson 2014, 134).

Thus in the 1920s, the United States embarked on projects that forced
political assimilation of Indians (while also maintaining that this was for
their protection), limited the rights of Black people, and enforced limits to
immigration. Together, through Indian blood quantum rules, the one-drop
rule, and the accelerated use of immigration controls designed to curtail the
entry of negatively racialized people, the idea of "bloodlines" appeared to be
"immutable and transhistorical, passed down through generations without
change" (Ngai 1999, 79). Each profoundly shaped the categories of Nationals
and Migrants and what it meant to be in either of them.

Indirect-Rule Colonialism in Other White Settler Colonies

Similar processes were under way in the other historic White Settler colonies. These are worth examining, for, in contrast to the United States, the
others—Canada, Australia, and New Zealand—remained part of the British
Empire, albeit with the additional power attached to being White Dominions, until the early to mid-twentieth century. Here practices of indirect-rule
colonialism were manifested in policy from the late nineteenth century. In
Canada, the 1876 Indian Act was passed using the powers bestowed by the
1867 British North America Act classifying Canada as a "self-governing" Dominion.[6] Canada's Indian Act defined who was—and was not—an Indian and
defined the content of what being an Indian meant (Tobias 1976). The Indian Act also established separate reservations (*réserve autochtone* in French)
for Indians, with the British Crown (not Canada) vested with legal title over
them. Separate "band councils," which Canada retained power over, were
created to govern Indians. The Indian Act also defined the rules for political
membership in "Indian bands," including participation in band council elections. Significantly, the right to reside on a reservation was governed by these
band councils, with the oversight of Canadian state officials.

The Indian Act and the practices of the band councils charged with enforcing it were significant aspects of racializing and gendering Indian membership
as well as political status in Canada (Maracle 1988; Bourgeault 1989; Ng 1993;

Iacovetta and Valverde 1992; Backhouse 1999; Mawani 2010). Indian Act rules institutionalized patriarchal social relations, as only children whose mother was married to someone Canada recognized as an Indian would be considered Indian herself. A woman's status prior to marriage was irrelevant, as Indian women marrying men defined as non-Indian lost their status, as did their children. Children born to unmarried Indian women were also denied Indian status. This had serious and long-lasting material, political, and affective outcomes for all concerned, and it profoundly shaped the subjectivities of both those identified by Canada as Indians and those who were not.

In keeping with indirect-rule colonial practices of "protection" in Asia and Africa, Indians in the radically altered political, social, and economic climate of late-nineteenth century Canada were expected to carry on with "traditional" ways of life. Yet, as did Indigenous-Natives of other colonies, Indians in Canada were prevented from fully engaging in economic activities that would have allowed them to survive in the capitalist market economy introduced and enforced by the British Empire. For example, Indians needed a permit from a government Indian agent to sell, trade, or barter (Opekokew 1980; Sluman and Goodwill 1982). Obtaining a university degree or voting in a Canadian election was declared to be "un-Indian" and, if practiced, would, until 1960, result in the loss of "Indian" status.

In Australia, where colonized Natives were called "Aborigines," similar processes were undertaken. Prior control over Aborigines held by the London Colonial Office was delegated to State (as compared to federal) Aboriginal Protection Boards (APBs), which held almost complete power over their lives. In 1839, South Australia created an office of the "Protector of Aborigines." In 1869, an Aborigines Protection Act was passed by the Aboriginal Protection Board of Victoria. Other Australian states followed suit: New South Wales established an Aboriginal Protection Board in 1883 and passed its Aborigines Protection Act in 1909, Western Australia's Aborigines Protection Board passed a number of statutes between 1886 and 1898, and Queensland passed an Aboriginals Protection and Restriction of the Sale of Opium Act in 1897, both to restrict the spatial movement of "Aborigines" and to separate them from Chinese people.

The stated aims of the various Australian APBs was, again, "protection," but, like the reservation systems in the United States and Canada, the APBs existed within the broader project of racialized and geographical segregation. Thus, the APBs created "Aboriginal stations" or "managed reserves" onto which Aborigines were forcibly moved (and removed from if their presence conflicted with other state projects). The power to determine the membership of and residence on these reserves was under the directorship of station managers. The APB era represented an intensification of control over Aborigine people in select areas of Australia. Where Aborigines could live and work, whom they could marry, their family formations, and most other aspects of their lives were governed by the APBs.

The Australian state defined who was—and was not—an Aborigine, which in turn affected one's access to reserved lands, residence at the Aboriginal stations, and continued family relations. Again, racialized ideas of blood were at play. John McCorquodale (1986, 11) notes, "The proliferation of children having 'white' blood in their veins, and the decline of the 'full-blood' population, prompted a legislative response to redeem the former and protect the latter." Legislation concerning "half-castes" was passed in numerous Australian states from 1839 (New South Wales) to 1913 (Tasmania), including the 1886 Victorian Half-Caste Act, whose intent was to physically separate Aborigines from other Aborigines designated as also having "White blood." This and other such acts led to the horror of forced removal of children from Aborigine homes, as "half-caste" children were taken from their Aborigine families and placed in industrial schools or reformatories, where they were expected to assimilate into White normative practices (Australian Human Rights Commission 2009). Formally defining Aboriginality by "blood" remained the standard until the late 1950s.

In the White Dominion of New Zealand, a similar process began in 1856 when its Native Reserves Act was passed just two years after the formation of a separate New Zealand Parliament. This act formalized a process in place since the 1840s of creating and managing "Native Reserves." Administered by the colony's Native Department, the act was said to both protect and assimilate Natives (who were also referred to as "Aboriginal" or "Maori"). Thus, Attorney General Henry Sewell argued that reserves for Natives were "the most and indeed only way of preventing their extinction" while also stating that the Native Reserves Act was "the first step to lift them [Natives] out of their present merely animal state of communism, into the position of civilized communities" (in Boulton 2004, 163).

Official enumerations of Maori people were undertaken in 1857 and 1858. Rather than listing individuals as members of families, they were listed as members of the "tribe" in which they resided in order to monitor their movements (Kukutai 2013, 36). Racialized ideas of blood were used to determine who was—and was not—Maori. Not only were Maori enumerated separately from others in New Zealand, but there was also a state obsession with the category of "full bloods" and "half-castes." By 1926, "a dazzling array of racial designations" was employed to describe Maori individuals, from "full blood Maori" to "three-quarter caste" to "half-caste" (Kukutai 2013, 37). Such identifications profoundly changed precolonial forms of self-understanding.

Actions undertaken by the White Settler colonies of the United States, Canada, Australia, and New Zealand informed and were informed by those undertaken by European empires across the world, particularly the British Empire, of which the latter three were still formally a part of until the early to mid-twentieth century. Not only were the colonial practices of "indirect rule" evident in the importance given to the discourse of "protection," but these White Settler colonies also defined the criteria for who was categorized as Native, defined which Native group (i.e., which "tribe" or "band") one was a member of, defined the place where that group was geographically bound, and defined what it meant to be a member of such a group. Just as importantly, these practices also defined who was not Native. All of these state acts affected the lives of those so defined in very real material and existential terms.

THE DISTINCTIVENESS OF THE WHITE SETTLER COLONIES

Other key aspects of the governmentality of indirect-rule colonialism as practiced in Asia and Africa after the mid-nineteenth century, however, did not take hold in the White Settler colonies. The pressure to deed more and more territory as private property to those defined as White settlers, combined with the steady political pressure to nationalize White Settler colonies from the latter half of the nineteenth century, prevented a policy of indirect rule from being fully implemented there. Instead, what was put into place was an amalgamation of direct- and indirect-rule colonialism. In contrast to Asian and African colonies where the governmentality of protection overtook previous discourses of "civilization" and "assimilation," even as the Natives there continued to be negatively racialized, in the United States, Canada, Australia, and New Zealand, discourses of "protection" worked alongside those of civilization and assimilation.

Indeed, the imperialist discourse that the colonized Natives had "timeless cultures" which ought to be preserved never fully took hold in the White Settler colonies. This, I argue, was related to the fact that White Settler colonies were able to nationalize their sovereignty earlier than most of the rest of the empire. Their ongoing efforts to forcibly assimilate Natives—most horrifyingly through segregated and violent Native "residential schools," which were established in the mid-nineteenth century in the United States and New Zealand, the late nineteenth century in Canada, and at the turn of the twentieth century in Australia (Buti 2002), were part of their ongoing efforts to become independent nation-states. In the rest of the British Empire, neither the London Office nor the local imperial administration had any such goals. Instead, their efforts to preserve the (invented) traditions of Natives were with the aim of preserving the empire.

Indeed, it was not until the mid to late twentieth century—a full century after it was deployed in Asian and African colonies—that a discourse of preservation was undertaken. Tellingly, it was often called for by Natives themselves. For example, in the United States, a series of acts emphasized the preservation and protection of Native cultures: the National Historic Preservation Act of 1966, American Indian Religious Freedom Act of 1978, Archaeological Resources Preservation Act of 1979, Native American Graves Protection and Repatriation Act of 1991, and the National Park Service's Tribal Preservation Program (Phelan 2009). Even so, such acts did not fundamentally alter the revamped civilization discourses now articulated through ideas of "development." Instead, these acts are perhaps best understood as contributing to the making of Native claims for an independent national sovereignty. As they did in Africa and Asia, the imperial "define and rule" practices of "protection" and "preservation" of "tradition" that linked one's Indigenous-Native identity to one's place and one's rights also shaped national liberation movements in the former White Settler colonies.

Another key difference in the White Settler colonies was the lack of distinction made between Indigenous-Natives and Migrant-Natives. First, in keeping with classic autochthonous discourses of Natives being the original inhabitants of a place, all colonized Natives in the New World were regarded as Indigenous-Natives. Second, the key act of defining Indigenous-Nativeness in the White Settler colonies was the state deciding to recognize a person as Native or not. Under indirect-rule colonialism, states manipulated the number of Natives they recorded by simply reclassifying many people as non-Native. Third, as select British colonies in the New World came to be defined as White Settler colonies, both the racialization of those defined as Native as well as the redefinition of others as non-Native was part of further "Whitening" of these places.

The Whiteness of these colonies was also defined against non-White people transported to these colonies for the value of their exploited labor. The meaning of Whiteness was related both to the colonization of Indigenous-Natives and to the violent suppression of enslaved people from Africa and coolie laborers as well as other workers from Asia. Of course, this was true throughout imperial space. People from Europe moved not only to the White Settler colonies but to colonies in Africa and Asia as well. Colonial administrators, military commanders, rank-and-file soldiers, teachers, nannies, and others moved from the imperial metropoles in Europe to the colonies. Moreover, colonized Natives of Africa and Asia—and to a much lesser degree, Natives of the Americas and the Pacific—were also moved throughout imperial space.

The key thing differentiating colonies in Africa or Asia from the White Settler colonies was that the labor power of European workers was crucial for the viability of these latter colonies as sites of profitable investment. This became especially important in the United States after its outlawing of the Atlantic slave trade in 1808. However, it was also important due to the fact that in the first hundred years after their initial encounter with Europeans, a massive population decline of Natives took place. Patrick Wolfe (2006) argues that alongside the large-scale recruitment of people from Europe, this massive loss of Native life made—and continues to make—"settler colonialism" unique. Wolfe contends that the project of settler colonialism—one he strips of its relationship to Whiteness—has a different elementary logic than other colonial projects do—what he terms a "logic of elimination" versus a "logic of labor exploitation."

Yet there is something in Wolfe's logic that evokes a colonial trope. It was a common feature of imperialist (and later, nationalist) discourse in the White Settler colonies that Natives were not workers. An 1886 editorial in the *New York Times* exemplified this: "Work is something [the Indian] has never done; his idleness and improvidence are his birthright." Other scholars of Native history, however, show that the exploitation of Native labor in the White Settler colonies was just as crucial to the colonial project there as it was anywhere else. Indeed, the enslavement of Natives started with the very first landing of Christopher Columbus in the Caribbean. This was followed by Native enslavement in much of what is now the United States, Canada, Australia, and New Zealand (Reséndez 2016; Rushforth 2003; Behrendt 2016; Tate and Foy 1965). Indeed, in the Americas, the exploitation of Indian slaves—estimated to number anywhere from 2.5 to 5 million people—was not, Andrés Reséndez (2016, 5, 96) argues, "a residue of colonial wars or a transitional phase until African slaves arrived in the New World in sufficient numbers, but was an established network with staying power in which a host of individuals, from imperial bureaucrats down to miners, governors, frontier captains, and Indian allies, had a stake." Indeed, Indian slavery lasted well into the late nineteenth century.

Thus, in contrast to Wolfe and others (Veracini 2011; Morgensen 2011a), who contend that the main imperial goal for the White Settler colonies was largely unfettered territorial gain through the elimination of Natives, Reséndez (2016) argues that the massive population decline in the New World was largely due to the harsh conditions of forced labor endured by the enslaved, which fatally weakened their immune systems and made them susceptible to the new diseases, which killed large numbers of Natives (Reséndez 2016, 14). To corroborate his argument, Reséndez (2016, 16) points out that "one year before Europeans began reporting smallpox [in 1509], Española's Indian population had dwindled to five percent or less of what it had been in 1492." In addition, their enslavement was accompanied by massacres to terrorize—and discipline—Native rebels. The enormous loss of life was the outcome of numerous factors, none of which was predetermined according to a "logic of elimination."

Contrary to Wolfe's formulation that living, working Natives were peripheral to the imperial project in the New World, Christopher Columbus himself recognized that "the Indians of Española were and are the greatest wealth of the island, because they are the ones who dig, and harvest, and collect the bread and other supplies, and gather the gold from the mines, and do all the work of men and beasts alike" (quoted in Reséndez 2016, 28). Thus, far from being a preplanned and unique "structure" of settler colonialism, the violent deaths of many millions of Natives was the result of the imperial project to take territory *and* exploit the labor of Natives (Wolfe 1997, 94).

Indeed, foregrounding imperial practices, rather than elementary logics, or radical and incommensurable difference, Russell Thornton (1980) notes that the massive loss of life of Natives during the process of European colonization stands in stark contrast to the results of earlier arrivals of people from Asia and, later, from Scandinavia, to what became White Settler colonies in the Americas. These prior movements, Thornton argues, did not have any significant demographic effects in the Western Hemisphere, because the practices inherent in all colonizing efforts—the expropriation of the wealth of people produced by their laboring bodies on expropriated territories—were absent. This, he argues, made all the difference in the results of encounters resulting from people's movements.

Thus, what makes White Settler colonies distinctive is not that, from the start, imperial states wanted to extinguish Native life in order to gain territory to populate with Europeans. Instead, what is unique about them is that the Whitening of one portion of the working class sowed deep and long-lasting divisions between workers recruited—usually through great force—from across the New World, Africa, Asia, and Europe to labor in these colonies. In the British colonies in North America, the Whitening of workers from Europe began in the mid to late seventeenth century. They were juridically separated from other workers in order to strategically thwart the evident, serious, and sustained resistance by a "motley crew" of workers whose collective actions had threatened to overthrow imperialist projects from the start (Linebaugh and Rediker 2000). Indeed, the Whitening of some workers did little to change the long-held beliefs of the European bourgeoisie concerning the inherent inferiority of all workers, including those identified as European.

It is thus useful to remember that by the early seventeenth century, as the British Empire established colonies in the New World, the process of enclosing common lands in England was also under way (Mingay 2014). Starting in 1604 and continuing to 1914, over 5,200 enclosure bills were enacted by Parliament. Some 6.8 million acres—over a fifth of the total area of England—was enclosed (Turner 1980, 179, 181; U.K. Parliament n.d.). In addition to mass land confiscations in Ireland, a further 1.17 million acres was enclosed in Wales (Chapman 1987, 28). The Scottish Clearances enclosed millions more acres (Richards 1985). These enclosures and confiscations were a critical part of the capitalist process of "primitive accumulation" and "improvement" that began in the English countryside and spread over the entire face of the earth.

The consequence of such massive dispossession and the "great transformation" of land into imperial territory and private property was the commodification of the labor power of the expropriated (Polanyi 1944; Wood 2002). As a result, millions of people were on the move in search of new livelihoods. Many workers in England were pressed into service, transported as felons, or kept in unfree employment relations as indentured servants under the control of their masters in British colonies in the New World. Here they joined other members of the largely unfree labor force, which included people defined by the imperial state as Natives or Negroes. The idea that workers from Europe were White would have been nonsensical at this time. Indeed, as Peter Linebaugh and Markus Rediker (2000, 208) note, all workers, including those from Europe, understood that "the 'white people' were, in code or cant, the rich, the people with money, not simply the ones with a particular phenotype of skin color."

Yet, while brutally subjugated, by the late seventeenth century, workers from Europe were elevated above all other workers through laws that invented the White race (Allen 1975). In particular, the possession of masculinized Whiteness became a necessary requirement for freedom as imperial states equated slavery with Blackness in the seventeenth century. White men were not only granted their freedom long before other workers, but they also had access to the best-paid jobs in capitalist labor markets within the empire (Hyslop 1999, 405; Federici 2004). In the process of making Whiteness a "possessive investment" (Lipsitz 1995), Whiteness became a crucial aspect of containing labor solidarity (Allen 1975, 19n63). Making the White Settler colonies White was a *product* of this process. The power of states—and of capital—grew in direct proportion to the consolidation of a "fictive community based on whiteness" (Linebaugh and Rediker 2000, 209). Arguably, the success of strategies used to Whiten workers was an initial moment in the imperial turn to biopower and informed all subsequent "define and rule" strategies of indirect-rule colonialism across the empire.

It is thus important to historicize the Whiteness of the White Settler colonies. Far from being there from the start, they became White Settler colonies as workers from Europe were made into White settlers over centuries of imperial rule. The strategic essentialism of racism as a technology of separation formed the basis for turning those colonies with large numbers of workers from Europe into White Settler colonies. The process of Whitening accelerated in the nineteenth century—the era of indirect-rule colonialism. As Whiteness was imagined—and accepted—as a cross-class project, Whitened workers became stalwart supporters of the ongoing imperial (and increasingly national) expropriation of land and the continued unfreedom of workers categorized as the Natives of the United States and the White Dominions, as well as the Natives of Africa, and later, of Asia.

The success of these imperial and national strategies of separation rested on the fact that Whiteness became a key claims-making device. Whiteness became a necessary attribute for gaining access to private property (especially in land) and to free-wage employment (Roediger 1999). Thus, what distinguished the White Settler colonies was the formation of a separate, and relatively privileged, "White working class." Sharing with the ruling classes an identity of Whiteness allowed White workers to imagine that the wealth of colonial territories was theirs too. Thus, what was also unique about the White Settler colonies was that Whites also came to see themselves as autochthons.

Indeed, after the Britain and the United States abolished the Atlantic slave trade in the early nineteenth century and the "Great Migration" from Europe began,[7] a key part of the strategy for attaining and consolidating the power not only of the White bourgeoisie but also Whitened workers was to lay claim to a specific Native belonging. The claim of Nativeness allowed them to solidify their claims to territory, to private property, and to the best (of often very bad) working conditions and wages. Indeed, the earlier discourse of *terra nullius* had already encouraged the making of such an association. The imperial representation of what became White Settler colonies as sovereignless allowed imperial elites and, later, Whitened workers to claim these places as their own. Thus did the imperial discourse of autochthony produce multiple—and always separated—groups of Natives. In the White Settler colonies, there were the colonized Natives of these colonies, Natives of Africa and Asia, and Europeans from the metropoles of empires who came to claim, quite uncannily, the status of Native for themselves.

With such claims, Whites in the White Settler colonies bridged the contradiction between discourses of autochthony and discourses of migration. In their claims to be White Natives, there was no effort to hide their movement from Europe. Indeed, by the mid-twentieth century in the United States, historians as well as heads of states promoted a discursive shift that redefined colonizers as Migrants (Handlin 1951; Kennedy 1964; Mills 1997). In an effort to erase the colonial part of White Settler colonies, everyone—except the Natives of the United States—were recast as Migrants. Colonizers, slaves, coolie laborers, and workers from Europe largely entering prior to the imposition of any immigration controls, all became Migrants. Made hegemonic in the early 1960s, just when the Postcolonial New World Order was being consolidated, this discourse was part of an effort to disavow the imperial genealogy of nation-states.

With its roots in the nineteenth century discourse by which Whites born in the United States reconstituted themselves as American "Natives" to distinguish themselves from those newly arrived from Europe, by the 1960s, the trope of the United States as an "immigrant nation" allowed Whites to define themselves as "old immigrants" in comparison to the "new immigrants" from Asia, Africa, and the rest of the Americas (Behdad 2005). This allowed them to retain their belief in their White National-Native status. Pointing to their own successful Americanization, the "We are all immigrants" narrative was deployed to demand the assimilation of non-White immigrants and to contain the civil rights insurgency of "national minorities" of Black, Native, and Asian people in the United States. The other former White Settler colonies adopted similar discourses.

The European metropoles of various empires, however—especially the two largest, the British and the French—had also nationalized their sovereignties in the early to mid-1960s (see chapter 7). Some people there also began to define themselves as Natives. In the process, the former Natives of Asia and Africa who, by the 1960s, had largely become citizens of various "national liberation states," were moved from being the imperial subjects of various European states to becoming potential or actual Migrants. By the late twentieth century, those who would have been classified as colonized Natives until the mid-twentieth century were redefined as *colonizers* of the now Native-Europeans. Each of these categorical shifts in how people were understood—and treated—is part and parcel of the emergence and consolidation of the Postcolonial New World Order of national autochthony.

CONCLUSION

While human history can be said to be a history of movement, the reasons why people moved and how their movements were understood, by themselves and by others, have certainly changed. The single biggest shift in this came with the formation of "civilizations" that were an effect of state power. Starting about five thousand years ago, the first states were formed in the Mesopotamian alluvium (Scott 2017, 3). All states since then have attempted to control the movement of people subjected to their rule, be it by facilitating their movements (e.g., transporting them as slaves) or in trying to prevent their flight. All states have also engaged in discursive practices to represent people's movements—and purported stasis—in such a way as to normalize the state's seizure of the "monopoly over legitimate movements" (Torpey 1998). However, not all forms of state power have implemented the same kind of controls or exercised the same kind of discursive practices.

The subject of this chapter—the shift in European imperial-state methods of rule from direct- to indirect-rule colonialism in the mid to late nineteenth century—and how this affected both juridical and representational practices concerning Natives as well as Europeans/Whites across empires—tracks how this shift affected state controls on people's mobility. Autochthonous discourses created a distance in imperial states between those categorized as "people of a place" and those categorized as "people out of place." This distance materialized the separation between Natives and Migrants and made such categorical identities a meaningful way for people to understand themselves and others.

The formation of new racialized geographies of autochthonous belonging was driven by efforts from imperial states to maintain their rule. After a massive, mid-nineteenth century rebellion of Natives in British India, one imperial state after another created and separated colonized natives into the two categories of Indigenous-Natives and Migrant-Natives. In the same period, in what became the White Settler colonies of the New World, the British imperial state, as well as the independent but not quite yet nation-state of the United States (see chapter 3) created a system of racialized segregation by establishing separate territorial reservations for Natives and using racialized ideas of blood quantum to limit the number of people eligible to make a life on them. Such practices, while intent on controlling Natives, were also about controlling the relationships between imperial subjects—and ensuring the separation of people who otherwise coexisted in imperial (and soon, national) space.

Indirect-rule colonialism succeeded in planting the seeds of "natural belonging," which would lead to demands for home rule and the nationalization of imperial sovereignty. Nationalism drew upon and intensified the biopolitical demographics organized by practices of indirect-rule colonialism by institutionalizing the association between a People (the "nation") and a place (territory) within the state form itself. The flattening of the world into a set of discrete "nations" begun in the late nineteenth century in the Americas marked the successful institutionalization of such ideas. Nation-states, by selectively constructing an exclusive—and exclusionary—national People from all the actual people who lived in any territory, simultaneously concretized and abstracted the ground upon which claims to autochthony would be made, claims that all nations and nation-states would rely upon in one way or another.

The first nation-states in the Americas laid the basis for the centrality of autochthony to the nationalization of sovereignties, territories, and subjectivities. Nation-states in the New World, with their deep and centuries-long histories of colonialism, slavery, exploitation, exclusion, and segregation of many sorts, also laid the basis for the uncanny politics of autochthony. Led by elites who profoundly associated with the European metropoles of the imperial states, nation-states in the New World renarrated colonialism as part of their own national origin story, one that simultaneously romanticized, competed with, and suppressed the autochthonous claims made later by those whom imperial states categorized as the Natives of the colonies. As I show in the following chapter, in this competition for autochthony were the Migrants who, structurally, could not lay claim to either story.

3

THE NATIONAL GOVERNMENT OF MOBILITY AND STASIS

On a roof in the Old City
Laundry hanging in the late afternoon sunlight:
The white sheet of a woman who is my enemy,
The towel of a man who is my enemy,
To wipe off the sweat of his brow.
In the sky of the Old City
A kite.
At the other end of the string,
A child
I can't see
Because of the wall.
We have put up many flags,
They have put up many flags.
To make us think that they're happy.
To make them think that we're happy.

—Yehuda Amichai, 1971

Indirect-rule colonialism bifurcated the colonized Natives into two separate groups—Indigenous-Natives and Migrant-Natives. But why *Migrant*-Natives? In this chapter, I show that by 1857—the year of the Indian Rebellion in British India, which precipitated its shift to indirect-rule colonial strategies—some colonized *Natives* of British India had already been categorized as *Migrants*. The parliamentary victories of the slavery abolition movement in the earlier part of the nineteenth century, and especially the 1833 British Slavery Abolition Act (UK, 3 & 4 Will. IV c. 73), led to a desperate search for new ways to produce and discipline a capitalist workforce, something essential to the continued profitability of colonial ventures. The figure of the Migrant subjected to state controls on entry was one solution. For this reason, it was at the beginning of the end of slavery in the British Empire when Migrants first appeared on the world stage.

The British Empire's categorization of some Natives as Migrants in the 1830s proved to have world-historic ramifications. The first controls placed on the movement of Native "coolies" from British India in 1835 were highly influential for future immigration controls. The first immigration law of the United States four decades later (1875), for instance, also named "coolies" as a prohibited group. By the end of the coolie trade in the early twentieth century, categorizing people as Migrants would be a well-established method of both labor control and nation-state formation across the world.

It may thus come as a surprise that the first regulations and restrictions against the free movement of British subjects across the empire in the 1830s were initially regarded as a largely illegitimate shift in prior imperial-state practice. What ensured their implementation was not only planters' demands for new sources of highly disciplined labor, but also, ironically, the demands for mobility controls made by slavery abolitionists. The latter argued that both emigration and immigration controls on the movement of coolies from British India were necessary to ensure that the movement of coolies was "voluntary" and their indentured labor "freely" undertaken. The early immigration controls in British India and British Mauritius, thus, also marked an early instance of the *governmentality of protection*—something that defined indirect-rule colonialism a few decades later.

In this chapter, I show that the initial trickle of mobility controls begun in the early nineteenth century became a torrent by the end of World War I (WWI). By war's end in late 1918, several empires had collapsed, and large parts of their territories came to be ruled by newly founded nation-states. In the brief period between the two world wars, further immigration controls were enacted, both by a now-shrunken number of imperial states and by the growing number of nation-states. Nationalist imaginaries were strengthened through the enactment of these immigration controls. These presaged the Postcolonial New World Order of nation-states established at the end of World War II (WWII). Already by the late nineteenth century it had become clear that nationalism was going to fundamentally change how states controlled human mobility. Indeed, as I show in this chapter, the enactment of immigration laws closely tracked the nationalization of state sovereignty—and people's sense of themselves as Nationals.

From the start, autochthony laid the foundation for the birth of nation-states in the mid to late nineteenth century. Discourses of autochthony gave "nations" the historical heft nationalists sought. The idea that Nationals were *native* to their national "homeland" solidified nationalist claims to being a "people of a place" and gave rise to National-Natives. Grounding their claims to national territory on autochthonous grounds provided nation-states with the rationale for enacting immigration controls that drew upon imperial policies of indirect-rule colonialism that categorized each biopolitical group of people as being of a particular place. Racist and sexist immigration laws were portrayed as a form of protection from "foreigners" who did not "belong" in national territory and, if let in, threatened the security of the nation. Such politics positioned Migrants as *allochthons* in relation to National-Native *autochthons*.

National autochthonies thus relied heavily on state and class ideas of "racial purity." The relationship between ideas of nation and race—indeed, between "national places" and "national races"—was, according to Étienne Balibar (1991c, 50), "neither a matter of perversion (for there is no 'pure' essence of nationalism) nor a question of formal similarity, but a question of historical articulation." This was true for those nations that Hans Kohn (1961) defined as "ethnic nations" *and* those defined as "political nations." Living outside of one's "national homeland" was rendered by all nationalisms as resulting from crisis and as crisis-producing (Sutcliffe 2001). In the process, human mobility across national boundaries was pathologized as a vector of contamination.

In the making of nations, the expulsion of Migrants, while not always physical (although this was indeed a well-used policy), was always juridical and social. No nation—and certainly no nation-state—existed without the presence of non-Nationals. While many non-Nationals remained (or were reclassified as) juridical Migrants, some did eventually become citizens. However, people seen as being *in* the nation but not *of* the nation were regarded (and classified) as "national minorities." Tolerated, they inhabited a highly precarious status in the nation-state, one heavy with the ever-present threat of outright expulsion or even extermination. Whether one would have the "right to have rights," as Hannah Arendt ([1951] 1973) famously said, or to paraphrase Giorgio Agamben (1998), whether one would have a right to life itself, depended on one's *nationality*, itself an amalgam between law and "national society."

In the following, I outline the historical processes leading to the institutionalization of immigration controls, first in territories claimed by imperial states and, later, by nation-states. I begin with a discussion of the 1835 Mauritius Ordinances, which mark the first time that certain, specified British subjects were regulated and restricted in their movement within the empire. I then compare the first immigration controls of Canada and the United States to show the difference that the *form* of state sovereignty—imperial or national—was to their implementation.

With the emergence—and ascendency—of the nation form of state sovereignty, I show how additional discourses of "protection" emerged. Immigration controls, first portrayed as protecting the Migrant by British antislavery campaigners in the early nineteenth century, came to be seen by nation-states (and nationalists) as protecting the National-Native. National controls on citizenship became a further crucial mechanism for the allocation and distribution of rights and resources. In the process, the entire, eons-long practice of human movement into new places was pushed out of our imagination—or, perhaps more accurately, was reimagined as a national security threat. In the process, *stasis* was glorified as the normative way of being human. All sorts of violence, both symbolic and life annihilating, flowed from this, as in each territory imagined as a national and native homeland there were people who were not part of *the People*. Nationalism thus ushered in the dual—and intimately imbricated—crises of emplacement and displacement and gave life to the negative duality of now *National*-Natives and always-already foreign Migrants.

MAKING MIGRANTS: FROM (IMPERIAL) EXIT CONTROLS TO (NATIONAL) ENTRY CONTROLS

All states control and limit human mobility (Scott 2009). However, *how* various forms of state power—monarchical, imperial, or national—do so has differed greatly with regard to whose mobility they tried to constrain. Generally, while monarchical or imperial states tried to stop the entry of suspected enemy agents, both regarded general immigration (or entry) restrictions as a *weakening* of state rule. This is because monarchical or imperial states ruled by gaining territorial control over as much of the earth and as many people as possible so as to subject them to their regimes of taxation, forced labor, and military conscription. Such states subjected people to their power by either expanding the state's territorial reach or by moving people *into* state territories. Monarchical or imperial states were also intent on stopping their subjects from falling under the control of another state or escaping into nonstate spaces. Thus it was exit controls, not entrance controls, that monarchical or imperial states viewed as key to the success of their civilizational projects ("civilization," as James Scott [2009] notes, is always an effect of state power). Indeed, the first documents we would recognize as passports were instituted against the free movement of impoverished English subjects *within* England during the reign of Henry VIII (1509–1547), himself the first king of the English Empire (Bridget Anderson 2013, 20).[1]

Imperial states, with their ever-enlarging scope of operation, not only permitted people's entrance into their territories, but they operated under what Radhika Mongia (2018) calls a "logic of facilitation" regarding such movements. People's mobility was often organized by the state and exploited by investors in the emergent plantation economies in Ireland, the Caribbean, the Americas, Asia, Africa, and the Pacific. Indeed, from the earliest European imperial venture—the 1492 voyage of Christopher Columbus to the islands of the Caribbean—people were moved into and across imperial realms for the glory of empire and for profit. Such movements became increasingly important after the emergence of capitalism in the English countryside in the sixteenth century (Wood 2002).

The introduction of capitalist social relations of production into the ruling practices of imperial states definitively changed how they operated by making them increasingly reliant on procuring and moving exploitable bodies to sites of investment. Indeed, the movement of people across the world grew exponentially as capitalism expanded through profits made at new sites of "primitive accumulation." The growth of the imperial system was thus accompanied by both the economic and extra-economic (i.e., state) displacement of people. With land either privatized or taken as public (state) property, growing numbers of people moved in search of new livelihoods. People were also moved through the institution of slavery. Historian Andrés Reséndez (2016, 3–4) notes that "Columbus's very first business venture in the New World consisted of sending four caravels loaded to capacity with 550 Natives back to Europe, to be auctioned off" in Spain where slavery was already well established and widely practiced.

With the introduction of capitalist social relations, both slavery and the character of colonial projects changed dramatically. Capitalism led to the wide-scale displacement—and movement—of peasants from the English countryside starting in the sixteenth century. The establishment of rent as a method of aristocratic enrichment, the eviction of peasants from land most could not afford to rent, and their subsequent proletarianization allowed for the greater empowerment of both capitalist investors and the British imperial state (Wood 2002).

The result was large-scale loss of life and a mass movement of people across the Atlantic. In Ireland alone, William Petty estimated that in a single decade between 1641 and 1652, about 504,000 people died (in Linebaugh and Rediker 2000, 62). The overlapping displacements and entrapment in servitude often led to coerced movements of people out of England, Ireland, Wales, and Scotland. From the 1590s, legislation dictating banishment was "aimed at the Irish, the Gypsies, and Africans"; in 1598, penal transport of British convicts began; and in the mid-seventeenth century, the Atlantic slave trade in people captured in Africa intensified (Linebaugh and Rediker 2000, 57). All this led to a transatlantic system of producing, amassing—and moving—a *global* capitalist workforce. With the enslavement and displacement of colonized Natives in the New World, Asia, and later Africa, and the high death rates of people transported to work as prisoners, slaves, indentured servants and, later, even as "free" laborers, workers' mobility became an indispensable—and ongoing—part of the conjoined project of securing territory and extracting profit from people's labor.

FROM SLAVE TO COOLIE TO MIGRANT

A key system that empires used to facilitate the movement of much-needed labor—one whose abolition led circuitously but certainly not inevitably to today's national system of immigration controls—was the cross-Atlantic slave trade. Marcus Rediker (2007, 5) notes that "over the almost four hundred years of the slave trade, from the late fifteenth to the late nineteenth century, 12.4 million souls were loaded onto slave ships and carried through a 'Middle Passage' across the Atlantic to hundreds of delivery points stretched over thousands of miles." Another five million people or so died from one stage of the slave trade to another—from capture in Africa to the Middle Passage and their first year of exploitation in the Americas (Rediker 2007, 5).

The global market for enslaved people captured and forcibly moved from Africa to (mostly) the New World (but also across Africa and to Asia) fundamentally altered social relations within and between Africa, Europe, and the New World and ushered in long-lasting modes of social organization based on racist and sexist separations (see Irwin 1977). Each side of the triangular trade—the movement of ships and their crews from Europe to Africa; the movement of enslaved people from Africa; and the movement of the commodities produced by slave labor to Europe—was enormously profitable for investors. The operation of the Atlantic slave trade also further consolidated imperial-state power. States used their military might to protect the investments of shippers, slavers, and plantation owners by ensuring the safe passage of slave ships and enforcing the labor relations of slavery.

In the process of moving people into a shared place of exploitation in the empire, the institution of slavery was further racialized. Practiced since the advent of state power (Scott 2009), slaves had long been negatively racialized—seen to be wholly different and inferior "types" of people whose domination was very much normalized. However, in the mid-seventeenth century, and in its thirteen colonies, the British imperial state ruled that workers positively racialized as White would no longer be used as slaves, while people negatively racialized as "Negroes" and "Indians" would remain enslaveable. With the legal codification of slavery by the colony of Virginia in 1661, Kunal Parker (2015, 39) explains, "Slavery soon became the dominant status of blacks in every colony. In rapid succession, enslaved blacks lost a number of public and private rights. They were excluded from the political process; barred from testifying in courts; prohibited from engaging in commercial activity; and unable to form legally recognized families." Concomitantly, White male servants were legally granted additional protections and benefits as their labor was considered to be their own property (Steinfeld 1991).

The negative racialization of slavery thus accompanied the "invention of the White race" (Allen 1994) as well as the "invention of free labor" (Steinfeld 1991). Through these processes, a chasm was created between working people racialized as White, Native, Black, and, later, Asian (Fredrickson 1988). At the same time, the gulf that capitalism created between working men and women also grew (Federici 2004). All of this had enormous political significance. Roxanne Doty (1996, 185) notes that the practices of now-freed White, male workers to differentiate themselves from their numerous Others was "a kind of statecraft from below," which allowed White men to "engage in governmental practices that reproduce[d] territorially bounded identities as natural and given."

Perhaps nowhere were these territorially bounded identities more evident than in those colonies that as a result of these racialized divisions became White Settler colonies. In the British thirteen colonies, enslaved people were usually categorized as "aliens" instead of as imperial subjects (Parker 2015, 24). Their political status as aliens placed them outside of the English common laws that allowed imperial subjects to make claims on the imperial state. This continued once the White Settler colonies gained their independence. Under the United States Naturalization Act of 1790, attainment of U.S. citizenship was restricted to "any alien, being a free white person" who had been in the United States for two years—thus excluding all non-White people, unfree workers, and most women (whom the law did not yet regard as "persons").

Hence, efforts to maintain the institution of slavery in what became the White Settler colonies (which the United States was the most dependent upon) produced both a racialized division of labor and a racialized division of political membership. The property and labor relations of slavery were primarily imposed upon those categorized as nonsubjects and racialized as being *natives of Africa* even if most enslaved people throughout the history of slavery's almost two-and-a-half centuries of operation in the United States had neither been born nor set foot there. Likewise, slavery continued for the *natives of the United States* who were also mostly categorized as aliens until 1924.

The political exclusion of enslaveable people becomes even more significant in hindsight, as the abolition of slavery in the British Empire in the 1830s and 1840s began the process by which one's national citizenship became key to one's life. The end of the Atlantic slave trade, indeed the world-historical shift that came with the delegitimization of slavery, was undoubtedly the result of the centuries-long and countless acts of opposition to it by enslaved people. Their demands were further strengthened by others joining the enslaved across the empire and against its lines of race (Hochschild 2006). As a direct result of their collective efforts, the British imperial state—the largest slave state at the time—passed its Abolition of the Slave Trade Act on 25 March 1807. The British maintained the *labor relation* of slavery for decades afterward, however, even several years after the passing of the Slavery Abolition Act of 1833.[2] In the intervening years between the end of the slave trade and the end of slavery, a desperate search was under way for a system of labor recruitment to replace it.

The British Empire's perceived need for other workers became acute during the period of slave "apprenticeship" between 1834 to 1843 when there was a precipitous decline in the productivity of plantations. Former slaves did what they could to enter paid labor markets or establish small-scale farms, while plantation owners sought to restore the control over workers that slavery allowed. Nothing that the planters tried—apprenticeship, debt bondage, indenture, tenant farming, sharecropping, vagrancy laws, regressive taxation, or coercive labor contracts—was sufficient to bring back slavery-era levels of capitalist profits. It was the coolie system of labor recruitment that turned out to be the British Empire's solution to the "problem" of the end of slavery. From approximately 1830 to the 1920s, coolieism replaced slavery to become the dominant system of obtaining workers for imperial ventures (L. Potts 1990, 69).

People categorized as coolies were moved by the millions across the empire, often on the same ships that had previously carried enslaved Africans (Lowe 2006). They became a key labor force on plantations as well as in the building of the capitalist infrastructure of roads, canals, and railroads. Under coolieism, negatively racialized people—mostly men and mostly from British-controlled China and British India—were moved across the empire (and beyond) to work under conditions of contracted, indentured servitude. While there is no definitive number on the scale of coolieism—some estimate a low of twelve million, while Lydia Potts (1990, 71) argues that even "an estimate of 37 million or more would not be entirely without foundation"—the scale and significance of the coolie system was, even at the lower estimates, comparable to the slave trade. Indeed, the coolie system surpassed African slavery in its intensity, as millions of coolies were moved within the span of less than a hundred years (73).

The start of the coolie system took place during a period of intensive colonization in Asia and Africa.[5] Between 1815 and 1914, a period referred to as Britain's "imperial century," approximately 10,000,000 square miles (26,000,000 km^2) of territory and roughly four hundred million people were added to the British Empire. Throughout the nineteenth century and into the first few decades of the twentieth, as capitalist market imperatives of competition, productivity, profit maximization, and accumulation spread, even to places not formally colonized, workers were desperately in need of new livelihoods. The ability to move workers from Asia as coolies was further shaped by shifts in the organization of the British Empire. Not only did the 1843 abolition of slavery in British India result in a greater number of workers available for transportation as coolies, but in 1858 the British Crown took authority over it from the British East India Company, which had ruled it from 1757. Consequently, across Asia, the British Empire facilitated large-scale labor migration as part of an "empire-wide sourcing of labor" (Kaur 2004, 205).

Significantly, newly implemented immigration controls were crucial to the success of the coolie labor system. By the end of coolieism in the early twentieth century, making people Migrants became a well-established mechanism of labor and social control across the world. Looking back, we can see such controls as the first bricks in the "paper walls" constructed by nation-states (Wyman 1968). Thus does Radhika Mongia (2007, 43) argue that contemporary immigration controls have a "crucial colonial genealogy."[4]

In 1835 on the British colony of Mauritius, an island in the Indian Ocean about 1,200 miles (or 2,000 kilometers) off the southeast coast of the African continent, a monumental shift in state practices on human mobility began (Mongia 2007). Mauritius was first claimed as a colony by the Dutch (1638–1710), then by the French (1710–1810), and finally by the British (1810–1968). The movement and exploitation of slave labor made it an important site for investment in a booming sugar industry. Thus it was that the impending abolition of slave labor relations on Mauritius on 1 February 1835 caused local British colonial officials grave concern over how best to maintain the productivity of the plantations and the profits of the planters. The planters' intention to recruit coolie workers from British India also worried Mauritian officials, who feared that in the absence of slave labor relations, these new workers might destabilize the colony itself. Coolie workers might turn out to be too unruly or set a dangerous example for recently freed but "apprenticed" workers. Before the forced "apprenticeship" of manumitted slaves was to end in 1839, Prosper D'Epinay, the recently appointed protector general of Mauritius, asked, "Who can say what influence this medley of individuals, with their manners, their usages, and their vices will have on our indigenous population, especially when it shall become wholly free?" (in Mongia 2007, 401).[5] Local officials addressed the issues of labor productivity and discipline through two related responses: immigration controls and contracts of indenture.

In 1835—the start of the "apprentice" system—the local British Council of Mauritius passed two ordinances regulating the entry of laborers from British India (Mongia 2007, 394). Workers recruited as coolies needed to demonstrate that they had permission to move from British India to British Mauritius, and they would only be granted such permission if they produced a contract of indenture tying them to work for a specified amount of time. These ordinances thus introduced new limits on the hitherto free mobility of imperial subjects within the British Empire. Indeed, they marked a dramatic shift from imperial concerns about the *exit* of British subjects to new concerns about their *entry* into other parts of the empire.

Indeed, the Mauritius Ordinances diverted from the imperial principle that no subject would be denied entry into any other part of the empire. Indeed, the formal, juridical equality of all British subjects was not an insignificant part of how the empire quelled dissent in its colonies. Hence, a great deal of justification was mustered when implementing immigration controls against coolie workers from British India moving to British Mauritius. Thus, even as D'Epinay began his defense of these new mobility controls by affirming that British Indian subjects had the same rights as "those who reside in any possession, territory, or dependency of Great Britain," he went on to ask whether "the term British subject, and the privileges attached to it, are not according to places and circumstances, susceptible of important division and modification." In particular, he stated that "it is a distinction common to every metropolis that their colonies are governed by special laws, because the elements of society are not the same therein as in Europe (especially when slavery existed); [hence] the same system of legislature is not applicable" (in Mongia 2007, 401). D'Epinay thus justified these new restrictions as a *racialized* regime of mobility controls in which *only* the coolies from Britain's colonial units—not Europeans from the British metropole—would face restrictions.[6] Not only was his argument for migration controls against coolies from British India quite prescient concerning the racist underpinnings of subsequent immigration controls, but his distinction between British subjects had far-reaching consequences for later developments in the British Empire, particularly as some administrative units agitated for greater independence.

In addition to the novel immigration restrictions imposed by the Mauritius Ordinances, the colonial British Indian government (then the East India Company) also implemented new *emigration* controls against coolies and against them alone. Established when exit controls on British subjects' movement out of the *metropole* of the empire started to be lifted in 1837, recruited coolies and their emigration agents were required to provide written statements outlining the terms of their labor contracts of indenture before an official of British India.[7] For the colonial governments of both British Mauritius and British India, then, the labor contract became the emblematic aspect for controlling and disciplining coolie labor by also controlling their mobility. Contracts ideologically distanced the coolie labor trade from the institution of slavery it was designed to replace. Often written in English, these contracts, which coolies signed or, most often, marked with an X (and with their fingerprint after the introduction of fingerprinting technology in India in 1858), provided documentary proof that coolies were not slaves (Tinker 1974; Lowe 2006).

At the time, such proof was *politically* necessary. As soon as the new trade in coolie labor became known, a campaign arose in both the British metropole and British India to "protect" coolie workers from a system that was regarded by abolitionists as a new slave trade. Arguing that British India's emigration regulations were insufficient to ensure that coolie workers were moving of their own volition, a report in the *Anti-Slavery Reporter*, a main publication of the slavery abolition movement, argued, "It should be observed, that, of all the thousands who have hitherto gone to Mauritius, or other colonies, there is no proof afforded that any of them went voluntarily; but, on the contrary, decisive evidence that they were either kidnapped for that purpose, and by force put on board vessels employed in transporting them, or were obtained by the most fraudulent statements" (in British and Foreign Anti-Slavery Society [1842] 2014, 47). Antislavery campaigners successfully pressured the government to appoint a special committee to inquire into the movement of laborers from British India.

Established on 1 August 1838, the committee concerned itself with the coerced character of the migration of coolies. For both slavery abolitionists and the committee, this focus was informed by a shared assumption that coolies were "ignorant and unwary" (British and Foreign Anti-Slavery Society [1842] 2014, 50). However, such a focus also allowed both to ignore existing *colonial* conditions in India, precisely the conditions that might make moving preferable to staying for coolies. Acknowledging the "helplessness" caused by poverty, they nevertheless avoided identifying the *source* of the poverty of colonial subjects—as well as ways to end it. Instead of challenging the capitalist underpinnings of British imperialism or, more specifically, the labor relations under which coolies were exploited, abolitionists instead argued that workers in British India not be allowed to move to other colonies in the empire (British and Foreign Anti-Slavery Society [1842] 2014, 50). Embedded in emerging "relations of rescue," abolitionists thus argued that mobility controls were necessary for the coolies' own protection (Pascoe 1990). Indeed, relying on autochthonous tropes valuing stasis, abolitionists went so far as to argue that mobility itself was anathema to people in British India. The *Anti-Slavery Reporter* stated that the "population, so far from desiring to emigrate from their native land to distant and foreign parts, are utterly averse to it" (in British and Foreign Anti-Slavery Society [1842] 2014, 67). In this way, campaigns to protect coolie workers contributed to the association of migration with crisis.

Initially, antislavery campaigners were successful in their efforts. On 29 May 1839, the governors of the East India Company prohibited the emigration of workers engaged in manual labor, effectively halting the movement of workers from British India to other parts of the empire. Persons effecting their emigration were liable for a then-hefty fine of two hundred rupees or three months in jail. Unsurprisingly, the planters in Mauritius (and, by now, also in the British Caribbean) worked hard to overturn the ban. In the end, the planters prevailed, and on 2 December 1842, the governors of the East India Company reversed their earlier decision. The emigration of coolies was again permitted, resulting in the movement of millions of people throughout the British Empire. That year alone, almost 35,000 coolies were shipped from British India to British Mauritius.

To avoid further comparisons with slavery, however, newly minted agents with the title of "protector of emigrants" were appointed at each departure point. Likewise, an office of the Protector of Immigrants was established in Mauritius (and elsewhere). Operating on both ends of this labor recruitment system, emigration and immigration agents were in place to certify that the movement of coolie workers was "voluntary" and their labor "free." Thus began the now well-entrenched dichotomy between "forced" and "voluntary" migration. The decision to depict the movement of coolie workers as "voluntary" negated the structural conditions precipitating either their movement or the benefits of their movement to those who would exploit their labor power.

It should come as no surprise, therefore, that neither emigration nor immigration controls actually worked to protect coolie workers. Conditions aboard coolie ships were life threatening, and their conditions of work were brutal and often deadly (Lowe 2006). Far from being free, coolie workers signed contracts the terms of which ensured that they worked under unfree employment relations (Tinker 1974). Thus, coolieism, rather than signaling the expansion of free labor, instead organized a new Middle Passage voyage that linked practices of colonial expropriation and capitalist exploitation (Christopher, Pybus, and Rediker 2007). Indeed, we may very well be moved to ask, as Eric Williams, historian and first prime minister of Trinidad and Tobago, did, "how it was possible for any country that had abolished slavery on the ground that it was inhuman to justify Indian indenture with its 25 cents a day wage and its jails."[8] The new regime of documents—both contracts and an early form of passport issued by the protector of emigrants—normalized not only the movement of coolies but also their subsequent exploitation, thus allowing empires and investors alike to continue amassing enormous profits. Indeed, once the coolie labor trade was fully implemented, planters quickly replaced the now-freed slaves with coolie laborers. As a result, throughout the Caribbean, where coolies were used extensively, sugar and cacao exports, having been threatened with a slowdown, rose significantly.

However, it is important to note that throughout the nineteenth century, the movement of those who were *not* coolie workers remained, for the most part, very much unregulated and unrestricted. The British imperial state continued to think it unwise to so openly demonstrate that the equality of British subjects—symbolized by the equality of movement within the empire—was an empty promise. In any case, both the British imperial state and its investors were most keen on ensuring a stable supply of laborers.

Nonetheless, the regulations imposed by the British on the movement of coolie workers marked the emergence of the figure—and state category—of the Migrant. The Migrant was not simply someone who moved across space, for even at the beginning of such controls, not all people's movements were regulated or restricted. Instead, *Migrants were people whose mobility was controlled by the state*. Migrant, then, did not exist as a political category prior to the imposition of state controls on (some) people's ability to move. Even though humans have moved since time immemorial, Migrants were produced out of a new regime of labor control required by investors reeling from the victories of the slavery abolitionist movement. For this reason, Mongia (2018) argues that the coolie labor system acted as a bridge between the imperial-state logic of *facilitation* and the nation-state logic of *constraint*.

Like "Native," "Migrant" was originally an imperial-state category. Both transformed as the nation form of state power became ascendant. Indeed, the groundwork laid by the 1835 Mauritius Ordinances, particularly the idea that separate administrative units of the British Empire could and ought to be allowed to enact their own immigration controls, became, I argue, a key ideological underpinning for the nationalization of states and their sovereignty. In the next section, I demonstrate the importance of immigration controls to both the ideology of nationalism and the formation of nation-states. By comparing the first immigration policies of the United States with those of Canada, I show the important difference that the national form of the state made to the United States' implementation of immigration controls earlier than Canada.

Significantly, as occurred for the British imperial state earlier in the nineteenth century, coolie workers figured large in the first immigration controls enacted by both the United States and Canada. Here the two also diverged. The first U.S. immigration law, enacted by the 1875 Page Act, explicitly restricted the entry of "Chinese coolies" and women deemed to be "prostitutes." The British Empire's White Dominion of Canada's first effort to restrict immigration concerned the entry of Natives of British India in 1914 who were not coolies and who thus retained their right to free mobility within the empire. Canada's attempt to restrict their entry was a key point of contention between it and the London Office. For both the independent state of the United States and the still-British colony of Canada, imposing restrictions on who could and could not enter their respective territories signaled the nationalization of their sovereignty. Immigration legislation gave judicial effect to the idea of the nation as a bounded territory with limited, racialized membership. Controlling entry into nation-states was therefore of critical importance to the making of nations and for the provision of the legal basis to "protect" said nations from the threat said to reside with Migrants.

COMPARING THE FIRST IMMIGRATION CONTROLS OF CANADA AND THE UNITED STATES

In 1914 in a direct attempt to nationalize its sovereignty, the Canadian government denied entry to imperial subjects from British India arriving in the province of British Columbia aboard the passenger ship the *Komagata Maru*.[9] Knowing full well that they were not arriving as coolie workers and were, therefore, free from such controls, Canada acted in the context of a growing nationalism across the "White British Dominions," in which Whiteness was the quintessential criteria for an emergent national membership.

In 1914, Canadian officials racialized all but twenty of the 376 passengers from British India (mostly from the Punjab, a key recruitment site for the British imperial military) as "undesirable" for inclusion in the "Canadian nation."[10] The issue for the Canadian government was not the entry of people per se. A year earlier, over 400,000 people had arrived in Canada, mostly from Europe, including many non-British subjects (Kazimi 2012, 43). In contrast, the fellow British subjects arriving on the *Komagata Maru* were rejected because they were not White, a view captured in the lyrics of "the most popular beer-parlour ballad" of the summer of 1914 when the *Komagata Maru* made shore:

> To Oriental grasp and greed
>
> We'll surrender, no never.
>
> Our watchword be God Save the King
>
> White Canada Forever.
>
> (in Kazimi 2004)

Two months to the day that the *Komagata Maru* first docked in Vancouver's harbor, the Canadian government ordered troops from several regiments as well as a Royal Canadian Navy vessel to force the ship's departure and deport its passengers to Calcutta (Mawani 2018). Speaking in Canada's House of Commons in October 1914, former Prime Minister Sir Wilfrid Laurier (1896–1911), stated, "The people of Canada want to have a white country" and that "certain of *our fellow subjects* who are not of the white race want to come to Canada and be admitted to all the rights of Canadian citizenship. . . . These men have been taught by a certain school of politics [liberalism] that they are equals of [White] British subjects; unfortunately they are brought face to face with the hard facts when it's too late" (in Mongia 1999, 550; emphasis added).

In rejecting those passengers, Canada cited its 1910 Immigration Act, which had created a separate category of "Canadian domicile" to distinguish between British subjects elsewhere in the empire and those resident in Canada.[11] Knowing that any ship leaving British India had to stop to refuel, the 1910 act had further required all ships transporting passengers to Canada to maintain a "continuous journey" from their point of departure. The arrival of the *Komagata Maru* was a direct challenge to this affront to the free mobility rights of imperial subjects in British India. The passengers on board well knew that Canada was resorting to legal subterfuge to circumvent London Office strictures against curbing the entry of any British subject who was not recruited as a coolie worker—and were willing to challenge it (Mawani 2018). That Canada was able to force their departure thus marked a break in the Canadian government's previous acquiescence to British imperial concerns. In its aftermath, the 1914 British Nationality and Status of Aliens Act conceded that White Dominion legislatures and governments should not be prevented "from treating differently different classes of British subjects" (in Bridget Anderson 2013, 38). Thus, the *Komagata Maru* incident signaled the start of a distinct Canadian national sovereignty and another step toward the end of a broader definition of imperial subjecthood (Mongia 1999). Afterward, it became crucial to be considered a "desirable" member of the Canadian "nation" to enter Canada.

In 1922, Canada's prime minister, Mackenzie King, consolidated Canada's ever-bolder assertions of a separate—and national—sovereignty by informing the British imperial government that the Canadian Parliament would no longer follow its decisions in foreign affairs. A year later, Canada passed its 1923 Chinese Immigration Act, which imposed an outright ban on the entry of people from China. In contrast to its 1885 Head Tax regulation, which was a (thinly) *veiled* effort to prevent the entry of workers from China, Canada was able to pass an act *explicitly* excluding people subject to the power of the British Empire once its claims to a distinct national sovereignty were recognized by the London Office. In 1931, the British Parliament formally recognized this in its Statute of Westminster, which allowed colonial (Canadian) laws to supersede imperial statutes.

In contrast, the United States passed its first immigration law[12]—the 1875 Page Act—almost half a century earlier than Canada's 1923 Chinese Immigration Act.[13] It explicitly prohibited the entry of those categorized as "Chinese coolies," convicted felons, and women "imported for the purposes of prostitution

(US 1875, chap. 141, sec. 5).[14] With slave labor relations having been outlawed a decade earlier (1865), U.S. trade unions, much like abolitionists in British India in the 1830s, lobbied for immigration controls by representing coolies as a "relic of slavery" (Lowe 2006). However, the term "coolie" in the United States denoted *any* "unskilled" worker from China, not only those working under contracts of indenture.[15] Hence, the U.S. ban on Chinese coolies also affected workers outside of the coolie system.

Additionally, the primary effect of the bar on "prostitutes" was to restrict the entry of unmarried women from China as a response to racist fears that they would marry and raise families in the United States. Eithne Luibhéid (2002, 36) argues that "the common perception that all Chinese women were likely to be enslaved prostitutes had direct connections to scientific racism, because some scientific racists held that the status of women within various groups mirrored larger racial hierarchies." Thus, not only did the figure of the "Chinese prostitute" have the broader effect of reproducing the heteropatriarchal wife/prostitute dichotomy within U.S. immigration (and other) laws, inaugurating the now long-standing association between criminality and immigration in the process, but it also became central to the portrayal of all people from China as a "yellow peril" endangering the emergent "American nation" (Luibhéid 2002, 38).

The 1875 Page Act began the nationalization of U.S. sovereignty. Until then, the United States not only had imperial ambitions, but had acted like an imperial state. Thus, it had not imposed general restrictions on the entry of people into its territories. Quite the opposite. In 1844, for example, it signed the Treaty of Wangxia/Wang-hiya with the Chinese emperor; followed by the 1858 Treaties of Tianjin (Tientsin) and the 1868 Burlingame Treaty.[16] Indeed, the United States lobbied China to loosen its imperial exit controls so as to encourage people's movement to the United States. The Page Act reversed this and in so doing signaled a shift in the *form* of the U.S. state. With its restrictions against the entry of particular categories of people, the Page Act institutionalized a national "logic of constraint" with regard to people's entry to its territories. Through the Page Act—passed almost a full century after the writing of the U.S. Constitution—the United States announced itself as a *nation-state*, one whose nation-ness was defined by Whiteness.

The nationalization of Whiteness in the United States was further advanced by the 1882 Chinese Exclusion Act, the first to explicitly prohibit immigration on the basis of one's racialized nationality.[17] The Chinese Exclusion Act removed any reference to "coolie" or "forced" labor and simply prohibited the entry into the United States of *all* workers from China, skilled as well as unskilled, for a period of ten years. This expanded in 1884 to include any-one from China. In 1889, the U.S. Supreme Court's decision in *Chae Chan Ping v. United States*, or the "Chinese Exclusion Case," confirmed the nationaliza-tion of U.S. sovereignty in stating that "the power of exclusion of foreigners being an incident of sovereignty . . . cannot be granted away or restrained" (United States 1889). Chae Chan Ping, like approximately 20,000 others, left the United States after the 1882 Chinese Exclusion Act passed with the assur-ance that Chinese subjects previously resident in the United States had the right to return. Indeed, the federal government issued reentry certificates to these residents. The 1888 Scott Act voided these reentry certificates, how-ever, and categorized reentrants as "illegal aliens" (Motomura 2006). Thus, not only were workers from China the first to be affected by U.S. immigration laws, they were also the first to be categorized as "illegal."

The Supreme Court ruling against Chae was significant for a number of reasons. First, the decision defined immigration controls as an exclusive fed-eral jurisdiction and created the plenary power doctrine governing immigration law, thus insulating the government from constitutional challenges by nonciti-zens denied entry. Additionally, by overturning the federal government's com-mitments under the Burlingame Treaty with China, the Chinese Exclusion Case established the federal government's authority to *unilaterally* abrogate interna-tional treaties. Significantly, each of these new federal powers was defended on the grounds that regulating and restricting immigration was an integral part of U.S. sovereignty. The Supreme Court found that the right to exclude "aliens" from U.S. territories stemmed from the sovereign powers defined by the 1789 Constitution. In its 1889 ruling, the Supreme Court argued that the federal gov-ernment had the right to "preserve its independence and give security against foreign aggression and encroachment whether from the foreign nation acting in its national character or from vast hordes of its people crowding in upon us." In doing so, it read the association between sovereignty and immigration con-trols *back* to the late eighteenth century, a time when the United States was not interested in *constraining* movement into its territories, but was actively *facilitat-ing* it with its continued participation in the Atlantic slave trade.

The hundred-year gap between the ratification of the U.S. Constitution in 1789 and the *Chae Chan Ping* ruling that redefined U.S. sovereignty to include the right to restrict immigration—as well as the forty-one-year gap from when the United States passed its 1882 Chinese Exclusion Act and when Canada passed similar legislation in 1923—demonstrates the difference that the na-tionalization of state sovereignty makes with regard to the implementation of immigration controls. By racializing and gendering both the emergent figure of the Migrant, and the National Citizen to which it was opposed, these first immigration controls of both the United States and Canada also demonstrate the racist and sexist underpinnings of nation-state formation. Indeed, immigration controls were enacted in the name of protecting the "White nations" actively under construction in U.S. and Canadian territories. By the end of the nineteenth century, immigration controls were portrayed as protecting the nation from the figure of the Migrant.

Demands for further immigration controls only increased as the nation-state's territorial borders quickly became the point at which the nation protected itself from "contamination." Successive immigration acts worked to simultaneously accentuate the value of Whiteness while limiting its definition. Almost fifty years after the passing of the 1875 Page Act barring the entry of "Chinese coolies" and "Chinese prostitutes," in 1921 the United States imposed its first controls on the entry of (certain) people from Europe. Through this legislation, people in southern, central, and eastern Europe also came to be defined as undesirable.

THE MAKING OF NATIONAL SOVEREIGNTY THROUGH IMMIGRATION CONTROLS

Former White Settler colonies were far from alone in nationalizing their sovereignty and engineering a racialized nation through immigration controls. By 1915, almost all of the independent states on the American continents had nationalized their sovereignties through the same means.[18] These controls, along with restricted criteria for national citizenship, helped to construct those positively racialized as members of the new nations as *National-Natives*. The long road in their transformation from imperial-state territories to nation-states began with the end of their colonial status.

By the 1820s, the reign of the Spanish and Portuguese Empires in the New World was more or less over (only Cuba and Puerto Rica remained under Spanish rule), and that of the British and French Empires was reduced. However, like the United States, these new independent states did not nationalize their sovereignty right away. There was often a decades-long (or longer) gap from independence to nation-statehood. Across the American continents, aristocratic creoles had been powerful agitators for independence. Their aim was to create imperial powers of their own. Thus, though Benedict Anderson (1991) is correct that nation-states first formed in the New World, they did not become *nation*-states in the early nineteenth century, as he assumed. While the ideology of nationalism was indeed prevalent then, states did not nationalize their sovereignty until the late nineteenth century. Even then, as

I show in chapter 4, it was not until the start of WWI when the nation-state form prevailed in the Americas.

In 1819, the former Spanish imperial colonies of today's Colombia, Venezuela, Ecuador, Panama, northern Peru, western Guyana, and northwest Brazil, led by the creole aristocrat Simón Bolívar (known as *El Libertador*), declared independence and formed the territory of *Gran Colombia* (Great Colombia). Established as a federal republic with Bolívar as its president, *Gran Colombia* was to be built into a continental empire able to compete for domination of the Americas with the United States (also an imperial aspirant at the time). Likewise, in 1822, a year after Mexico became independent from the Spanish imperial state, a new Empire of Mexico was declared. Ruled by Agustín de Iturbide (reigning as Agustín I of Mexico), it annexed the Federal Republic of Central America, which included present-day Chiapas state, Costa Rica, El Salvador, Guatemala, Honduras, and Nicaragua. A year later, Iturbide abdicated, and the wealthy creoles of the Central American provinces declared themselves independent of Mexico and reestablished the Federal Republic of Central America. By 1831, not only had Bolívar (who had ruled as dictator from 1828 to 1830) died, but so too had ideas of a *Gran Colombia*.

With the end of European imperial rule over the Americas and the political turbulence resulting from the failures of the now "independent" states, the United States rushed to fill the political void. So too did the British Empire. In 1823, U.S. President James Monroe sent the British a warning by declaring in Congress that "the occasion has been judged proper for asserting, as a principle in which the rights and interests of the United States are involved, that the American continents, by the free and independent condition which they have assumed and maintain, are henceforth not to be considered as subjects for future colonization by any European powers . . ." (Avalon Project n.d.). Nothing was said about efforts by the United States to establish its own control (but not political incorporation) over the region. Indeed, this Monroe Doctrine formed the basis of such efforts. This would not be the last time the United States would interpret other states' independence as a means to deploy its own power (see chapter 5).

The British were not so easily deterred. Like the United States, however, the British did not, for the most part, try to annex territories in the Americas into its empire. With its 1840s free trade strategy, the British Empire established itself as both a commercial and political power in Latin America (Kaufman and Macpherson 2005, 247). This saved the British the administrative cost of territorial expansion, staved off a broader continental (or federalist) political project in the Americas, and ensured that investors and financiers reliant on the British Empire could freely operate in the region. Thus, Britain too saw benefit in formally recognizing the new states' sovereignty. Indeed, already in 1824, British Foreign Secretary George Canning had remarked that "Spanish America is free, and if we do not mismanage our affairs sadly, she is English" (in F. S. Weaver 2000, 45). British influence in the region remained strong until the end of WWI, when the United States secured its hegemonic hold across the Americas (F. S. Weaver 2000).

The ruling classes in each newly independent state struggled to get the most they could from these power plays. Capitalist investment in the region grew as new markets for commodities emerged in Britain (and to a lesser extent in the United States and France). In Argentina, for example, the wealth of the new ruling class was heavily dependent upon exports to Britain. Production for commodities required workers, and as in the Spanish colonial era, these workers had to be brought in. Embedded in a wider set of global movements of peoples at the time were those of people moving from Europe to the Americas, which grew enormously after 1870. Indeed, rates of immigration to Argentina far surpassed those to the United States and Canada during most of the late nineteenth century (Goebel 2016, 140). The production of new commodities and the new trade routes of capitalist exchange they traveled on provided fertile ground for ideas of a nationalized state sovereignty to germinate. Throughout Latin America in the late nineteenth century, liberal elites profiting from the new free trade led a "new economy of representation" centered around ideas of national identity (González-Stephan 2003; also see Guerra 2003).[19] They deployed *nativism*—the idea that the "native-born" needed protection from the threats posed by "foreigners"—in their efforts to gain wider support. Consequently, demands for immigration controls and their establishment became central to the formation of nation-states.

The nationalization of state sovereignty was declared through the regulation and restriction of mobility into state territories. Everywhere such restrictions were selectively applied to people deemed unfit for national membership. Across the Americas, immigration controls were first enacted against the entry of negatively racialized people. At the same time, the mobility of those constituted as Europeans was actively encouraged until the period between the two world wars. As they did in the British Empire and in the United States, new immigration controls throughout Latin America came on the heels of the end of African slavery and the search for new state technologies for labor discipline. Like slavery, each new set of immigration controls was racialized.

Two decades before the United States did so, Peru was the first state to nationalize its sovereignty by enacting racist immigration laws. In 1853, it barred the entry of people from China arriving on a boat where there was "illness, rebellions or killings." This was followed in 1856 with a ban on coolie workers arriving from Asia. By 1891, Peru declared that immigrant recruitment would be made up "exclusively of the white European race" (Fitzgerald and Cook-Martin 2014, 374). Costa Rica was the next state to nationalize its sovereignty in 1862 by barring the entry of Black people and people from China (358). Demonstrating the interstatal field in which immigration controls operated, its prohibition on Black people was Costa Rica's preemptive move against President Lincoln's suggestion to ship freed Black slaves from the United States to Central America (Cleven 1925).

One by one, states in the Americas announced their national sovereignties by enacting their first, always racist, immigration policies. After Costa Rica (and the United States in 1875) was Argentina. Having declared independence from the Spanish Empire in 1810, its first immigration restrictions were not enacted until 1876. Due to a significant labor shortage, it had the least restrictive immigration policy of any new nation-state in the Americas; nonetheless, Argentina stated its "preference" for people categorized (by the state's constitution no less) as "Europeans." The greatest wave of new nation-states came in the 1880s and 1890s. El Salvador, independent in 1821, nationalized its sovereignty in 1886 by barring Chinese people, whom it labeled as "pernicious foreigners." It also subjected to immigration controls anyone who had not previously been a citizen of the former Federal Republic of Central America (Fitzgerald and Cook-Martin 2014, 430n120). In quick succession, the rest of the states in Central and South America followed suit. Colombia, independent in 1810, enacted its first immigration restrictions in 1887 by banning the entry of Chinese people.[20] Ecuador, independent in 1822, passed its first immigration restrictions in 1889, which prohibited the entry of Chinese people. Bolivia, independent from Spain since 1825, decreed its first limits in 1899 by barring people from Asia. Uruguay, independent in 1828, passed its first immigration controls in 1890, which "absolutely prohibited" the entry of people racialized as Asian, African, Bohemian, and *gitanos*, or "gypsies."

Brazil declared its independence from the Portuguese Empire in 1822 and established the new Empire of Brazil. Its imperial aspirations ended in 1889 with the establishment of the Brazilian Republic. Brazil had abolished slavery a year earlier (1888). In 1890, Brazil passed its first racist immigration controls. Containing about 40 percent of all slaves transported during the Atlantic slave trade, Brazil now prohibited "Natives of Asia and Africa," while encouraging immigration from Europe (C. R. Cameron 1931, 37). In 1891, Venezuela, independent since 1811, passed its first immigration restrictions by barring people from Asia and from the English or Dutch Antilles, effectively prohibiting the entry of Black people. By 1912, Venezuela declared that "individuals not of the European race" were barred (Fitzgerald and Cook-Martin 2014, 379). Guatemala's first immigration restrictions were passed in 1896 and prohibited the entry of people from China. Nicaragua, independent since 1821, enacted its first restrictive immigration policy in 1897 by declaring that "the immigration of Chinese naturals is absolutely prohibited." That same year, Nicaragua expelled Chinese people residing on its Mosquitia coast.

At the dawn of the twentieth century, the remaining states in the Americas also declared their national sovereignty by enacting racist immigration controls. Honduras, independent since 1821, enacted its first immigration restrictions in 1902 by regulating the entry of all coolie workers employed on labor contracts as well as people racialized as Chinese or Black. Paraguay, independent since 1811, passed its first immigration law in 1903 by denying entry to people of the "yellow race," Black people, and *gitanos*. Panama, independent since 1821, enacted immigration restrictions in 1904 by prohibiting the immigration of "Chinese, Turk, and Syrian" people. Chile, independent since 1818, passed its first immigration controls in 1915, singling out people from China for extra visa fees and restrictive entrance quotas.

Mexico did not pass its first comprehensive immigration laws for almost a century after it declared independence from Spain in 1821. This is largely due to much internal strife, the numerous changes in government in its first fifty years, and wars with vying empires (Spain, France, and Britain) as well as with a United States intent on expanding its territories. In 1909, Mexico first restricted immigration by prohibiting the entry of "undesirable" people, including those with specified contagious or chronic ailments that would prevent them from working, children under sixteen years old, anarchists, mendicants, and prostitutes. In the years between WWI and WWII (see chapter 4), Mexico racialized its immigration controls by barring people from China (1921); people from British India (1923); Black people, especially Afro-Latinos (1924); "Gypsies" (1926); Palestinians, Arabs, Syrians, and Lebanese (1927); Poles and Russians (1929); Hungarians (1931); Malays and East Asians (1933, except Japanese citizens); and Soviet citizens, Lithuanians, Czechs, Slovaks, Armenians, Turks, Latvians, Bulgarians, Romanians, Persians, Yugoslavs, Greeks, Albanians, Afghans, Ethiopians, Algerians, Egyptians, Moroccans, and Jewish people (1934) (Fitzgerald and Cook-Martin 2014, 256).

Mexican rulers grounded their claim to national sovereignty on the corollary policy of *indigenismo*, which simultaneously celebrated Native-ness while believing that only people with Spanish and Portuguese "blood" could initiate a new "universal era of humanity." Thus, the declaration of the rise of *la Raza Cósmica* (the "cosmic race") of *mestizo* Mexicans—one of the contenders for National-Native status—was made possible by the forced assimilation of the Natives of Mexico *and* the exclusion of a broad range of negatively racialized groups through immigration restrictions (Knight 1990; Vargas 2000).

Prior to the start of WWI, several formal colonies in the Caribbean also gained their independence from imperial states. Like the states on the American continents, many of these early independent states did not nationalize their sovereignties or enact immigration controls until (usually much) later. In 1804, Haiti, which now claims the western territories of what was Spain's first colony in the "New World," namely, Hispaniola, became the second state in the Western Hemisphere, after the United States, to gain its independence.[21] Purposely departing from states on the continents that valorized European/ White identities, Toussaint L'Ouverture, leader of the Haitian Revolution, declared himself the leader of a sovereign *Black* state of Saint Domingue in 1801. The 1805 Constitution declared Haiti a "Black Republic" by recategorizing all Haitian citizens as "Black" and, in an effort to prevent the re-enslavement of Black people, barring most Whites from obtaining citizenship (Dupuy 2004, 9). By 1816, all "Africans, Indians [of the Americas and Caribbean], and those of their blood" who resided in the state's territories longer than a year were granted automatic citizenship. No immigration restrictions were enacted until almost a century later when, in 1903, Haiti prohibited the entry of "any individual called Syrian or thus named in the popular language" (Fitzgerald and Cook-Martin 2014, 366–367 and 432n168). Significantly, and in keeping with the times, this racialized ban was presented as necessary for the maintenance of a Black sovereignty over Haiti (Plummer 1997).

The Dominican Republic (DR), claiming the eastern part of Spanish Hispaniola, declared its independence from Spain in 1821. This was known as the "Ephemeral Independence," however, as Haiti occupied it from 1822 to 1844. That year, the DR once again declared its independence (not recognized by Haiti until 1874). It passed its first immigration regulations in 1905 by restricting the entry of people from the West Indies, effectively curtailing the entry of Black people (Fitzgerald and Cook-Martin 2014, 360). For those states becoming independent prior to WWI, Cuba was the last. It became independent from Spain in 1898 but was "administered" by the United States until it became a republic on 20 May 1902. Even then, Cuba was not formally sovereign, as the United States retained a legal basis to control Cuban governmental policies. As such, the 1882 U.S. law on Chinese exclusion was applied to Cuba

(Cervantes-Rodríguez 2010). With exceptions for periods of high labor demand, this policy was largely kept in place until 1943.

In summary, each of the world's first nation-states formed in the Americas was imagined as a racialized political community. The ruling classes, which largely initiated and led nationalist projects in the both White Settler colonies of the United States and Canada and across much of the rest of the Americas and in the Caribbean, understood themselves as the representative members of the nations they made. Each ruling group imagined itself as *National-Natives*: the rightful "people of the place" with the autochthonous right to sovereignty over it. Each new nation-state, except Haiti, valorized Europeanness, often recoded as Whiteness, as a necessary component of the national body. Haiti turned this on its head by valorizing Blackness. No nation-state—and no nationalist project—could imagine itself without immigration controls to "protect" itself from the figure of the Migrant, however.

CONCLUSION: MAKING NATIONAL AUTOCHTHONS

The compulsion, need, and desire to move grew alongside the expansion of European empires. From the start of European imperial penetration into the New World in the late fifteenth century and the emergence of capitalist social relations in England in the sixteenth century, and their global spread ever since, people across the world have been under pressure to *move*. At the same time, people were forcibly immobilized by imperial-state practices of colonialism, slavery, indentureship, and the ever-expanding capitalist market in labor power. Imperial states simultaneously *facilitated* large-scale movements of people as laboring bodies for rapidly multiplying colonial ventures while passing laws *restricting* people's mobility to create a ready and increasingly disciplined supply of exploitable bodies.

Through these twin processes, a global proletariat was made. Imperial states enslaved the people they colonized and categorized as Natives, organized a massive trade in enslaved people taken out of Africa, transported a large labor force from Europe for both military and commercial ventures across the empire (but especially in the New World), and, starting with the end of the British slave trade and later the end of slave labor relations, indentured a millions-strong labor force of coolie workers recruited largely from British-controlled Asia. Collectively, this global proletariat was made to toil for the glory of empires and their investors.

At the same time, the global proletariat also built movements of its own. Each one of the innumerable insurrections, revolts, and attempted escapes from imperialism elicited a violent response from rulers. Destroying their shared identification as the direct producers of wealth was key to weakening workers. To divide them, empires separated them through elaborate taxonomies of race, nation, and gender/sex. Colonialism created workers as either Europeans or Natives, separating them from one another through differential treatment in the law and in everyday practice. In the late seventeenth century, workers from Europe began to be enfolded into the Whiteness that earlier was the preserve of the wealthy. Given (relative) labor market freedom, Whites were shown significant amounts of "mercy" in contrast to the ongoing terror of slavery experienced by "Negroes" and colonized Natives across the world (Rediker 2007). People sexed and gendered as men were given preferential access to the capitalist wage and to women's labor, while across the world women were either denied access to wages or were highly subordinated within capitalist labor markets (Federici 2004). In either case, women were denied autonomy over their own labor and over their own bodies. The differential racialization of women positioned some as "mothers of the race" while others were vilified as "racial degenerates" (Bock 1983).

Yet none of these imperial efforts were easily enforced. There is a long—and largely untold—history of direct producers refusing to be separated and pledging their solidarity to one another (see Linebaugh and Rediker 2000). One such successful effort was the slavery abolition movement. Led by the enslaved themselves, people in the colonies and in the metropoles joined in protest against slavery and the slavers (Hochschild 2006). By the early part of the nineteenth century they had successfully forced some of the key slave trading states (especially the British Empire) to outlaw the slave trade and, later, to free people from the relationships of slavery itself. Power responded with a new form of immobilizing people: immigration controls.

First implemented by the British imperial state against workers recruited through the coolie system, the earliest immigration controls were also labor controls. Through them arose the figure of the Migrant: the person whose entry into state territory was regulated and restricted. The category of the Migrant was given further force in the mid to late nineteenth century when states began to nationalize their sovereignty. Nation-state power was produced—and normalized—with the idea that states represented the political community of the "nation." Membership in this community of rights-bearing citizens was limited from the start by ideas of race and normative gender/sex roles. By barring negatively racialized and nonnormatively gendered people from entering their territories, immigration controls announced the nationalization of states' sovereignty and were productive of a nationalist imaginary made up of Nationals and their Migrant others.

The formation of cross-class nations destroyed global lines of solidarity between workers and gave birth to national nativism(s) demanding that states protect "national interests." Mere decades after the success of the slavery abolitionist movement, separating Nationals from Migrants became a crucial aspect of the governmentality of nation-states. Migrants were the foil against which nations could be mobilized and on whose shoulders the source of very real miseries—and immiseration—of worker-citizens could be placed.

Nationalisms are a legacy of imperialism. Drawing upon imperial practices from the late nineteenth century on that created and separated Indigenous-Natives from Migrant-Natives, nation-states constructed an exclusive—and exclusionary—*People* from all the people living in their territories. Ideas of *autochthony* were central to the nationalization of sovereignties, territories, and subjectivities. Autochthony was evoked as the ground of national belonging by both colonized Natives and "Europeans." In the (former) White Settler colonies, ruling-class White men retold the history of colonialism as their own origin story, one competing with the autochthonous claims made later by colonized Natives themselves. By definition, Migrants, because they could not be narrators of nations, were made into allochthons.

Thus, in the late nineteenth century, both imperial states and the new nation-states in the New World had institutionalized the association between ideas of *people* and *place*. Both indirect-colonial rule and citizenship and immigration controls were productive of autochthons claiming to be the "people of a place" against allochthonous Migrants who were the "people out of place." The figure of the Migrant was thus a necessary corollary to the figure of the Native and the figure of the National. The National and the Native were both defined through stasis, while the Migrant was defined through movement into National-Native space. Yet because no one is always on the move or always stationary but always both, our ideas of people placed in the categories of either National-Natives or Migrants were deformed in the process, as were our ideas of human mobility. Now, human movement across the ideational borders of "nations" or the territorial borders of nation-states was made into a crisis, one to be constantly addressed by further state regulations and restrictions on people's mobility.

In the next chapter, I examine the synchronous nationalization of state sovereignty and expansion of immigration controls with the start of WWI. Between the end of WWI and the start of WWII, the spatialized logic of autochthony and the racist logic of antimiscegenation informed the birth of evermore nations and, with the dissolution of several large empires, evermore nation-states. The expulsion and/or "return" of "lost populations," the partitioning of territories, and immigration controls against Migrants were animated by assertions of the distinctiveness—and separation—of each nation. Such rationales were also given for the murder of those now constructed as the "enemies of the People."[22] In this way, the ideas of nation and race became interchangeable within a discourse of autochthony. The interwar period, and the actions taken by states during WWII, laid the groundwork for the emergence of the Postcolonial New World Order and the institutionalization of the antagonism of National-Natives against their Migrant others.

THE JEALOUSY
OF NATIONS

Globalizing National Constraints
on Human Mobility

In the nightmare of the dark
All the dogs of Europe bark,
And the living nations wait,
Each sequestered in its hate.
Intellectual disgrace
Stares from every human face,
And the seas of pity lie
Locked and frozen in each eye.

—*W. H. Auden, 1939*

By the early twentieth century, a clear association between the national-ization of state sovereignty and the enactment of immigration and citizen-ship controls was well established. By limiting entry and membership, such controls allowed each new nation-state to institutionalize the relationship between a nationalized People and state territory, thereby making ideas of national autochthony central to the national form of state power. In this chapter, I examine the formation of new nation-states and their new immi-gration and citizenship controls in the years from the start of World War I (WWI) in 1914, through the interwar years, and to the period during World War II (WWII, 1939–1945). During this period, there was a significant strengthening of nationalism, and with it, the formation of evermore nation-states. In the process, the negative duality between National-Natives and Migrants was consolidated, and the stage was set for the making of the Postcolonial New World Order at the end of WWII.

The ascent of nationalism and the concomitant expansion of immigration controls came with the collapse of several imperial states. In the last, bloody years of WWI, the Russian Empire (February 1917), the Austro-Hungarian Empire (October 1918), and the German Empire (November 1918) collapsed. By 1922, the Ottoman Empire, long in decline and decisively weakened by the Young Turk Revolution of 1908, had dissolved. In the interwar years, their vast imperial territories were swallowed up, mostly by other empires, especially the British, which expanded dramatically as a result.[1] However, in a small number of former imperial territories, new nation-states were established. This too was an enormously violent process. Particularly emblematic of such nation-building practices were the Greco-Turkish "population exchanges" in the 1920s. As it made evident, the national *stasis* upon which ideas of national autochthony rested depended on a great deal of forced *movement*.

No study of the murderous consequence of nation building—and the centrality of regimes of citizenship and immigration to them—would be complete without examining the normalization of the Nazi's genocide against those defined as "out of place" in the German nation. Understanding how central the stripping of German citizenship from Jewish people was to the Holocaust that followed shows how important the figure—and legal category—of the Migrant was to normalizing violence within nationalized societies. I end this chapter by discussing how, by the end of WWII, the system of imperial states—along with their political legitimacy—would itself collapse and be replaced by our present, postcolonial system of nation-states. And how, with it, the pace of immigration and citizenship controls would increase dramatically.

WORLD WAR I

As we have seen, most of the states in the New World had nationalized their sovereignties by the start of WWI. Even so, a fully developed system of immigration controls only came into being when an *international* system of states interested and capable of administering immigration controls emerged. The actions of certain states during WWI helped to bring about such a system. In examining these actions, we see in retrospect that the start of hostilities in Europe was the beginning of the end of (relatively) free movement into European territorial states (many of which were still imperial in form). Yet at this time, immigration controls were enacted in purported states of emergency

Research paper point?

and often portrayed as *exceptions* to states' usual powers. They were widely viewed as only tolerable during periods of war, thus demonstrating just how nonhegemonic immigration controls were in Europe at this time.

Nonetheless, by August 1914, there was an abrupt curtailment of free movement both out of and into the "major powers" of Europe. Possession of a passport became necessary for moving across state borders for states' subjects and nonsubjects alike. Subjects required passports to leave the metropolitan territories of empires, while "aliens" were required to show passports when entering to appointed immigration officers recording and monitoring their movements. Additionally, some states required that aliens have preissued visas stamped in their passports, thus extending states' reach beyond their own territories and enabling what Aristide Zolberg (1997, 308–309) has called the "remote control" of the border. Each measure relied upon interstate agreement and cooperation.

Although exit controls had long been part of the repertoire of imperial mobility controls, the imposition of *entry* controls into imperial territories in Europe during WWI was new. Such restrictions had important ramifications, for as John Torpey (2000, 111) argues, they "led to the consolidation of views about foreigners and methods for restricting their movements that would prove to be an enduring part of our world." By requiring that "aliens" possess identification papers marking themselves as such, these documents solidified the idea that states were distinct, enclosed "societies," which "must be defended" from Migrants (Foucault 2003).

Britain enacted its first restrictions on the entry of aliens into its imperial metropole a few years before WWI. Its 1905 Aliens Act now required non-British subjects, or aliens, to possess valid passports and be registered upon arrival by officials of a new immigration bureaucracy. As was similar legislation in the Americas, Britain's 1905 Aliens Act was racist, designed primarily to stem the entry of Jewish people trying to escape pogroms in the Russian Empire. This act not only produced the figure of the "undesirable immigrant" in British law (Bashford and McAdam 2014), it also "implemented a system of class discrimination in the procedures of immigration control" by excluding those who could not afford a cabin on the ships bringing them to Britain (R. Miles 1993, 147).

The advent of WWI led to the intensification of British immigration controls. Not only was a recognizably modern British passport, complete with photograph and other biometric information, introduced, but also the British Nationality and Status of Aliens Act of 1914 required "foreign-born" persons to carry an alien registration card. This empowered the British state to monitor the mobility of aliens within the United Kingdom. Moreover, after 1914, women marrying a foreign-born man would lose their British status. Finally, as discussed in chapter 3, this same legislation allowed British White Dominions such as Canada to impose racist immigration controls on British subjects who were deemed undesirable. The 1914 act, thus, enhanced the gendered and racialized idea of Britishness by enhancing controls against Migrants (Baldwin 2001). Importantly, however, and reflecting the imperial form of British state power, this Britishness was not yet *national*. Instead, the key legal separation between people remained the duality of subject and alien (R. Miles 1993, 153). Indeed, the act also stipulated that naturalization by *any* British possession had the same effect as naturalization granted in England.

The start of WWI was also the start of immigration controls into the French imperial metropole. Indeed, "the greatest country of immigration in Europe went so far as to permit immigration only within the limits of quotas" established during the war (Plender 1988, 76). Primarily intended to regulate the entry of a large and much-needed labor force, new state categories of workers were differentiated by their status in the empire. There was the "national civilian" workforce of the metropole, the "colonial" workforce of Natives of French colonies, and the "foreign" workforce. Through such categories, the idea of a national labor market, as well as the category of Immigrant Worker, began to emerge (see Ng 1988; Torpey 2000, 112). In 1917, France also made passports and foreign identification cards mandatory for non-French citizens and subjects over the age of fifteen in the metropole (Noiriel 1996, 61).

In 1914, the German imperial state also implemented passport restrictions. By 1917, it required all foreigners to possess a state-authorized identification document, including a certified picture of the bearer. In 1915, Italy reversed its prewar policy and not only imposed passport requirements for foreigners but also required visas issued by Italian authorities abroad. Foreigners were further required to report to public security officials within twenty-four hours of arrival (Torpey 2000, 114). Again, however, across the imperial metropoles in Europe a distinction remained between imperial subjects and foreigners, with the former largely continuing to have unrestricted entry.

U.S. immigration restrictions also intensified during WWI, even though the United States entered the war late (6 April 1917). As discussed in chapter 3, the United States had implemented racist immigration controls since 1875. In 1915, however, it implemented its own passport requirements, and in February 1917 Congress passed a sweeping new Immigration Act (overriding the veto of President Woodrow Wilson) imposing literacy tests, creating new categories of inadmissible persons, and barring immigration from the "Asia-Pacific

Zone." Tellingly, not everyone moving from this zone of exclusion was barred. People racialized as Europeans moving from sites in the Asia-Pacific zone— who often held the same political status as colonized Natives (e.g., British subject)—retained their ability to enter the United States. Indeed, the act had two primary purposes: preventing the entry onto the U.S. mainland of Natives of Japan working as indentured plantation laborers in Hawai'i (which the United States had annexed in 1898) and barring the entry of Natives of British India. This differential treatment of people according to where they were "Native" to in U.S. immigration law further consolidated the racialized territorialization of people and place.

Though Europeans from the barred zone were not excluded, the 1917 act did mark the first time that significant numbers of people from Europe came under immigration controls, with some denied entry to the United States. All new entrants were screened at a U.S. port of entry. Anyone over sixteen years old had to pass a literacy test. Those with dangerous politics (e.g., "anarchists") or who were unable to meet normative standards of good mental or physical health (e.g., "idiots," epileptics," and "insane persons"), good character (e.g., people convicted of a felony or crimes of "moral turpitude"), or good family life (e.g., polygamists) were deemed inadmissible (see Ngai 1999). Including normative rules within the emergent regime of immigration controls enhanced immigration and border agents' discretionary powers. Moreover, the construction of the "good Migrant" in U.S. immigration law also affected what it meant to be the normative "good citizen." Indeed, as Bridget Anderson (2013) notes, not only Migrants but the hierarchy of "good," "tolerated," and "failed citizen" were all produced though such immigration controls.

In addition, during WWI, states that had partially lifted restrictions on people exiting their territories in the nineteenth century reinstated them. In wartime, preventing subjects or citizens from leaving state territory provided young, male bodies to prosecute the states' wars and female bodies to repopulate the decimated population. Thus, throughout WWI, subjects within European metropoles were required to bear a passport for all border crossings, including when leaving state territories. For the first time, the U.S. 1918 Wartime Measures Act also required its Nationals to do the same while also regulating the entry and exit of aliens.

Although policies undertaken during WWI helped to create the avalanche of travel documents so familiar to us now, many states were unable to fully enforce their new passport or visa requirements (Torpey 2000, 113). European mobility controls during WWI, employed as they were by imperial states, mostly did not impose controls on the entry of their imperial subjects into their European metropoles. Thus, even though imperial states were increasingly challenged by the nationalisms within their colonies *and* their metropoles, they did not generally restrict the cross-empire movement of their subjects. For instance, under its 1914 immigration controls, all British imperial subjects—approximately 412 million people—retained their right to freely move to the British metropole (Maddison 2001). Again, maintaining the mobility of imperial subjects was part of how an imperial authority was normalized. Hence, the category of "alien" applied mostly to *nonsubjects* of empire.

It is also important to note that large-scale movements of people were precipitated by WWI. In August 1914, the German Empire's occupation of Belgium, northern France, Poland, and Lithuania; the Austro-Hungarian Empire's invasion of Serbia; the Russian Empire's occupation of Germany's territories in East Prussia; and the German and the Austro-Hungarian Empires' invasion of the Russian Empire led to the flight of millions of people. In the Ottoman Empire during WWI, Turks in its metropole, clear that the empire had been fatally weakened, came to see Armenians as a threat to their nationalist aspirations and organized for their expulsion, a forced exodus leading to a massacre known as the world's first genocide (Raphael Lemkin 1946). Although not usually counted in most discussions of migration, over sixty-five million soldiers were also mobilized during WWI across vast territories of empires, many from military garrisons in the colonies. In addition, millions of civilians were conscripted, especially in imperial colonies. In British East Africa, for instance, approximately one million people were conscripted as carriers (Paice 2010).

INTERWAR YEARS

The supposedly temporary and exceptional restrictions enacted during WWI were made permanent during the fragile (and brief) peace between the two world wars. In those states remaining imperial in form—Britain and France being the two largest—immigration restrictions, as well as the monitoring of aliens within state territory, became a part of everyday state practice. In Britain, the 1919 Aliens Restriction Act (further amended by the Aliens Order of 1920) extended the wartime act of 1914 indefinitely. The discourse of "race" was again deployed in this act. By April of that year, approximately 19,000 Nationals of Germany were forcibly repatriated to "cleanse" Britain of "German blood" (Cesarani 1987, 6). Additionally, under threat of deportation, all aliens were required to register with the police when looking for paid work or housing. Such restrictions against alien residents made a sharp separation in the law—and were productive of the category of Migrant Workers. Aliens were excluded from the right to engage in job actions, thereby weakening their ability to

challenge employers' demands and affecting the strength of the entire working class. In France, the law requiring all aliens to possess identity cards during wartime was also made permanent. A 29 July 1922 decree demanded that
all aliens be screened upon entry to meet specified "health prescriptions"
and show they were economically "necessary." Only aliens meeting these two
entry criteria would be given an identity card, the contemporary equivalent
of a temporary resident permit (see Rygiel n.d.).

Those states that had already nationalized their sovereignties also made
their wartime controls permanent and added new categories of "inadmissible
aliens." These were in no small part due to racist paranoia about the entry of
people displaced by WWI and deemed undesirable. In 1919, the U.S. Congress
made permanent its 1918 "exceptional" legislation targeting dissidents. In 1921,
it passed another immigration act that, for the first time, imposed broad limits to immigration from Europe. Premised on the "undesirability" of receiving
people from Southern and Eastern Europe and the "desirability" of receiving
people from Northern Europe, the act stipulated annual quotas limiting lawful entry to no more than 3 percent of the total number of immigrants from
any specific state already residing in the United States as recorded in its 1910
census (Higham [1955] 2002). The result was that, while the numbers of people
entering the United States from Northern European states remained the same,
the numbers of people entering from Southern and Eastern European states
dramatically declined. Prior to its passage, approximately 685,000 people
per year had entered the United States. The 1921 act mandated that no more
than 175,000 people would be admitted from Southern and Eastern Europe
(Higham [1955] 2002).

Racism thus intensified in U.S. immigration law in the interwar period. In
addition to the ban on people from the Asia-Pacific zone (which remained
in place) and new limits to immigration from Southern and Eastern Europe, a 1924 act effectively barred the entry of almost all Jewish people. It
also expanded the system of "remote control," as U.S. consuls abroad were
tasked with issuing "national origin" immigration visas and conducting police
checks, medical inspections, financial responsibility determinations, and political interviews of potential immigrants prior to their arrival at a U.S. port
of entry (Torpey 2000, 120). The U.S. Border Patrol was created in 1924 to
enforce this growing number of immigration regulations and restrictions.

By the 1930s, the process of nationalization had proceeded so far in the
United States that acceptance of the Philippines' independence became more
politically plausible than continuing to allow Filipinx relatively unrestricted
entry to the United States. Because it would remove Filipinx from the cate-

gory of U.S. Nationals, the independence of the Philippines (a U.S. colony since 1898) would subject Filipinx to immigration controls. It was thus portrayed as a "safeguard to the United States" (Madison Grant, quoted in Tyner 1999, 68). Indeed, Philippines' independence and restricting Filipinx immigration were inextricably linked. Senator Millard Tydings, coauthor of the 1934 Philippine Independence Act, stated, "It is absolutely illogical to have an immigration policy to exclude Japanese and Chinese and permit Filipinos *en masse* to come into the country. . . . If they continue to settle in certain areas they will come in conflict with white labor . . . and increase the opportunity for more racial prejudice and bad feelings of all kinds" (in Takaki 1998, 3). Although a ten-year process for achieving the independence of the Philippines was started with the passing of this act, immigration to the United States from the Philippines effectively ended.[2] It was only with the 1965 Immigration and Nationality Act that general immigration from the Philippines was once again permitted.

Across the rest of the Americas, nation-state after nation-state intensified its already racialized immigration restrictions. As discussed in chapter 3, from the early 1920s onward, Mexico barred various biopolitical groups said to be a threat to Mexican society, including Jewish people in 1934. In Honduras, a 1929 decree added a special entry fee on "coolies" as well as on Black, Arab, Turkish, Syrian, and Armenian people. By 1934, all these people as well as those categorized as *gitanos*, Palestinians, Lebanese, Poles, and Czechs were barred from entry (see Fitzgerald and Cook-Martin 2014, 367–368). In 1930, Nicaragua barred people categorized as Turk, Arab, Syrian, Armenian, and Black, as well as *gitanos* and coolies.

The growing importance of nationalist discourses was central to the story of intensified immigration controls in the interwar years. Across the world, ideas of "nation-ness" were on the ascent. The belief that state territories were exclusive homelands to particular nations took hold and (so far) has not let go. Yet because nationalist rhetoric never matched the reality on the ground, a variety of further state practices of "culling" people to make *a People* were consequently undertaken (Fitzgerald and Cook-Martin 2014). Immigration of negatively racialized people was restricted, if not wholly barred. Expulsions of negatively racialized people deemed unfit for national membership were organized. Most catastrophically, there were planned and purposeful exterminations of people portrayed as a national threat.

Tragically, the lists of people barred from entering one state's territories often corresponded with another state's lists of people targeted for expulsion or murder. Indeed, in many cases the lists overlapped. "Enemies of the people" in one state were another state's "inadmissible aliens." As Aristide

Zolberg (1981, 22) notes, "The reorganization of the world as a whole according to the principles of state nationalities . . . gave rulers a warrant to achieve ethnic homogeneity—or at least to reduce ethnic pluralism." Each of these violent acts shared the same underlying premise: national rights were the rights of *autochthony*. Ideas of essential national homelands worked to territorialize political membership, societal belonging, and, crucially, state-granted rights along highly racialized lines.

NATIONAL POPULATION EXCHANGES, EXPULSIONS, AND EXTERMINATIONS

What flowed from nationalist ideas of home rule was the sorting of "populations."[5] The idea that nation-states ought to be comprised *of* and *for* those whose nationality matched that of the state began its rapid ascent. With the dissolution of many empires party to WWI, some significant parts of their territories were redefined as national homelands by those hoping to govern new, nationally sovereign states. As nationalists everywhere viewed nations as having an "eternal" and essential sovereignty over certain territories, autochthony was given a new, *national* lease on life.

As Nationals autochthonized themselves into National-Natives, those defined as outsiders to the nation were made allochthons. In each new nation were people redefined as "foreign" bodies, people racialized as originating from a place that those "of their type" were from. As foreigners were portrayed as existing within national territories only because they had moved there from someplace else, nationalist origin stories not only narrated the timeless and territorial nation but also narrated a *migration story* for the others. For this reason, each partition and forced population transfer was portrayed as a return, a *sending home* of Migrants to "their own" eternal and essential national territory.

Thus, the formation of national communities, each imagined as static, unleashed large-scale migrations. With the collapse of the Russian Empire in 1917, approximately 1.5 million people regarded by the new states as foreigners were forced to leave, including an estimated 350,000 people constituted as Assyrians, Greeks, and Turks, who "returned" to places the vast majority had never stepped foot in. After the war, over one million people constituted as German were forcibly removed from territories annexed by victorious states (Dowty 1989, 87). The partitioning of the Austro-Hungarian (1918) and Ottoman (1922) imperial territories also resulted in a tremendous culling of now-national populations. About 570,000 people constituted as Polish were forced to move and sought refuge in the now-national Poland. Moreover, about 250,000 people constituted as Bulgarians were forced to leave Greece,

Serbia, and Romania; 50,000 Greeks were forced out of Bulgaria; 200,000 Hungarians were forced out of Romania; and 20,000 Serbs were forced out of Hungary (Dowty 1989, 86–87).

The formal defeat and dissolution of the Ottoman Empire in 1922 and the creation of the new nation-state of Turkey in 1923 is perhaps emblematic of the world-historic shift in how human mobility was understood—and how nation-states would treat it. For people living in Ottoman imperial territories, WWI did not end until the signing of the 24 July 1923 Lausanne Treaty. This is when the Allied Powers[4] recognized the *national* sovereignty of Turkey over the territories regarded as the former seat (or metropole) of the Ottoman Empire. In exchange, the new nation-state of Turkey renounced its claims to the rest of Ottoman territories (which were mostly incorporated into the British Empire).

Already before the outbreak of WWI, the nationalist Young Turk government had seized power through a 1913 coup and quickly embarked on a process of "Turkification." They were spurred on, in part, by events in the Balkans, where new nation-states had been carved out of the still-extant Austro-Hungarian and Ottoman Empires through two regional wars regarded as a "prelude" to WWI (R. Hall 2000). Bulgaria, Greece, Montenegro, and Serbia imagined themselves as "nations." The existence of people meeting their criteria of nation-ness but who lived elsewhere became grounds for much nationalist agitation to "reunify" the "nation" and, initially, the expansion of their newfound national territories. While awaiting their "homecoming," new Balkan nation-states went about sorting the existing people into Nationals and Migrants. Muslim Albanians, Bosnians, Pomaks, and Tatars were defined as "people out of place" and were forced to move to Turkey, where most had never been but where they were said to "belong" (Şeker 2013, 728).

Meanwhile, those in control of the new state of Turkey launched murderous attacks against Armenians, formally Ottoman subjects but now constituted as foreign to the emergent Turkish nation. In 1915, the Young Turk government passed the Temporary Law of Deportation authorizing the state to expel anyone constituted as a threat to a rapidly nationalizing security. From 1915 to 1917, anywhere from 600,000 to 1.5 million Armenians and Assyrians died during their forced expulsion from Turkey (Dadrian 1986, 342). By 1921, Turkey and the Soviet Union had partitioned what had been Ottoman Armenia between them through the Treaty of Kars.

All of these enormously violent events informed the negotiations of the January 1923 Lausanne Convention, a settlement of the Greco-Turkish War of 1919–1922 (which preceded the Lausanne Treaty). Signed by the Greek and Turkish governments, the Convention Concerning the Exchange of Greek and Turkish Populations was the first internationally ratified compulsory population exchange agreement. It mandated the movement of the "Muslim inhabitants of Greece" to Turkey and the "Christian Orthodox inhabitants of Turkey" to Greece. Not only were these events "a humanitarian disaster of world-historical proportions" (Watenpaugh 2010, 1316), but they came to be regarded as a model for future nationalizing efforts and future partitions, including the 1947 partition of British India into Pakistan and India (and the subsequent partition of Bengal into its Indian and Pakistani components) as well as the 1948 partition of Palestine and Israel. As such, I believe this initial population exchange is worth discussing at some length.[5]

see print
in p42.

Members of the "Greek population" residing in Turkey or the "Turkish population" residing in Greece were said to *originate* in the nation whose territory lay elsewhere and, as such, to be National-Natives *of* the places they did not live in. This was in contrast to the practices of the Ottoman Empire, which separated and categorized its subjects into religiously affiliated groups (e.g., Muslim, Christian, or Jewish *millets*) but considered them as part of one political community (Kazamias 2009). As such, a member of any millet was able to live throughout the empire. The basis of the 1920s population transfer of "Christian Greeks" and "Muslim Turks," on the other hand, was the nationalist insistence that territorial state sovereignty be embodied by a newfound nationalized identity.

The nation-state of Turkey was said by its founders to be *of* and *for* "Muslim Turks," while the nation-state of Greece was *of* and *for* "Christian Greeks." Consequently, "Muslim Turks" had no rightful claim to land or life in Greece, and "Christian Greeks" had no such rights in Turkey. Such nationalist sentiments were enshrined in Article 7 of the Convention Concerning the Exchange of Greek and Turkish Populations, which identified expelled persons as holding the nationality of the nation-state they were moved to. To ensure this outcome, the two nation-states agreed to a process of compulsory "denaturalization" of the expelled. Those forced out were thus juridically reconstituted as *deported* Migrants. In total, about 2 million people were forcibly expelled from the places where they had made their lives: 1.5 million people were moved from Turkey to Greece, and 500,000 people from Greece to Turkey.[6] They were forced to align their religious identities (often established through conversion) with the new national identities of the territories they were relocated to.

This first internationally mandated population transfer was grounded in autochthonous claims, and it cemented the racialized criteria for national belonging. It was said that differentiated groups of National-Natives were incapable of living as part of the same political community—even though members of various religious groups had done so for centuries. Nationalists insisted that it was "natural" for each People to have its own territory *and* to be sovereigns of it. In this, population transfers were seen by nationalists on all sides as a great—and necessary—"unmixing." National formations became gigantic antimiscegenation programs, ones that profoundly reshaped the practice of racism. Importantly, by framing and normalizing their expulsion across the Aegean Sea as a "sending home," Greece and Turkey muted the violence of their expulsion.

What was also muted was the racist character of deportations (as well as other immigration controls). In the new Republic of Turkey, the engineering of the national population did not end with the Armenian genocide or the population exchange between Greece and Turkey. Alongside continuous expulsions of people defined as "out of place," Turkey passed its first immigration law on 14 June 1934. Tellingly titled the Resettlement Law (no. 2510), it restricted entry to only those with "Turkish descent and culture." This was defined by the state according to criteria of "language, culture, and blood."

MAKING "NATIONAL MINORITIES," "REFUGEES," AND THE "STATELESS"

With the carving up of former imperial territory into separate nation-states, and the resultant dispossession, displacement, and death of tens of millions of persons, a new state category of people emerged—Minorities.[7] Comprised of those either unable to constitute themselves as a nation or, having done so, being so far unable to secure their own sovereign state, Minorities are those people outside of the mainstream of nationhood. The state category of Minorities is what allows nation-states to reckon with the fact that the world is not naturally organized along the Wilsonian idea (and ideal) of *national* self-rule.

After WWI, emergent nation-states were thought of as unwilling or incapable of protecting Minorities; thus, they were seen to be in need of *extrastate* protection. The League of Nations, formed in 1919, was the body mandated to protect Minorities through negotiation and enforcement of Minority Treaties.[8] It was the signing of these treaties that led Hannah Arendt ([1951] 1973, 274–275) to famously remark that "the nation had conquered the state." She argued that entrusting the League of Nations to enforce the rights of those residing in nation-states amounted to a recognition of their *communitarian* basis. Minorities existed in the context of National Majorities *for whom* states purportedly ruled. Writing in the aftermath of WWII, Arendt recognized that

National Minorities were easily susceptible to being denied—or stripped—of their citizenship, thus ceasing to have the "right to have rights" within the nation-state (Arendt [1951] 1973, 293, 297).

As such, the League's Minority Treaties were far less important for the protections they offered Minorities—which were quite minimal, since the League rarely acted upon complaints about their ill-treatment[9]—than they were for organizing the governmentality of an emergent international order. This new order increasingly centered the nation form of state power and favored stability of this system over the needs and desires of those who had been minoritized. Indeed, by the late 1930s, Minority Treaties were ignored altogether by member governments as it became evident that another world war was looming. However, the idea that nation-states had their Majorities (i.e., the "nation") and their National Minorities stuck. After WWII, key legal principles of the League's Minority Treaties were incorporated into the founding 1949 Charter of the United Nations (UN) and its declaration—and significant expansion—of the right to "national self-determination," as well as the UN's subsequent international treaties and human rights commissions.

However, in the interwar years, when it became increasingly difficult to imagine a world without nations, Minorities were increasingly represented as "people out of place"—that is, as Migrants. At the same time, some National Minorities became increasingly convinced that their best interests lay in making themselves into a National Majority. Attesting to the ascendancy of nationalism, a growing number of people represented themselves as part of nations deserving their own nationally sovereign state. Indeed, a long-term effect of the League's Minority Treaties was the emergence of a new, national style of geopolitics wherein protection of National Minorities of one state said to be part of National Majorities in other states became a tactical rationale for state efforts to expand their territory. Bellicose claims of either *irredentism* (the political claim that some members of the nation were outside of the nation-state's territories and needed to be brought in) or *revanchism* (the claim that part of one's national homeland was controlled by another state and needed to be reclaimed) led to the promotion of war to ensure demands for the return of either the People or their territory.

In the ensuing violence and unease, another new state category of people was constructed: Refugees—people persecuted by states and national populations, often because they were portrayed as threats to the security of new national societies. The state category of Refugee reflected and regulated their flight from certain forms of national violence. They too were part of the collat-

Ppl. have a right to live, but need a state to live in.
(current system)

eral damage of a world increasingly being comprised of separate and distinct nation-states. Indeed, at the end of WWI, people spoke not only of Refugees but of a "refugee problem" said to challenge new interstate relations (J. H. Simpson 1938).

As it was for National Minorities, the League of Nations was empowered to act as the extrastate agency "protecting" Refugees. Its refugee system was an open acknowledgment that not only WWI but also the emerging international order of nation-states was leading to the displacement of millions of people. From the start, defining who was—and was not—a bona fide Refugee became central to both geopolitics and national politics (McAdam 2013). Yet even people whose persecution was acknowledged encountered problems not only in leaving dangerous state spaces, but also in gaining permission to enter states due to the erection of significant controls on immigration. Thus, in 1921, as it became evident that nation-states were unwilling to act on behalf of Refugees, the League created the Office of the High Commissioner for Refugees. Initially imagined as filling a temporary need, its first brief was to address the needs of the approximately two million people displaced as a result of upheavals from the 1917 Russian Revolution. The office of the High Commissioner for Refugees soon found itself addressing a growing number of displacements, including the more than one million Armenians who continued to be forced out of Turkish Asia Minor, as well as the 1923 forced population transfer between Turkey and Greece. Ironically, it was the League's first High Commissioner for Refugees, Fridtjof Nansen, who led and oversaw the expulsions organized by Turkey and Greece.

As part of his work with Refugees, Nansen took part in the negotiations addressing another new state category: the Stateless. At the 1922 Intergovernmental Conference on Identity Certificates for Russian Refugees, the issuance of "stateless persons passports" was agreed to. These were necessary because many people were now left without any recognized legal right to live in *any* state's territory. As such, they had none of the state identity documents now required to move across borders. Popularly referred to as Nansen passports, these extrastate documents provided people with an avenue to lawfully enter states. First used to move the approximately 800,000 Russian expatriates whose Russian citizenship had been revoked for having fled Russia after the revolution and the ensuing civil war, it was extended to include those from Turkey rejected from that state's criteria for National-Nativeness, especially the approximate 300,000 to 400,000 Armenians and Assyrians remaining there until 1923. Holders of Nansen passports were lawfully permitted to cross into state territories whose subject or citizen status they did not possess. Although states were not supposed to deport them, these passports had to be renewed each year and were not infinitely renewable.

Nansen passports for the Stateless, while certainly live-saving and life-enhancing for many of their holders, were also a technology through which states' immigration controls, each now requiring identity documents, were further normalized as a regular and necessary part of statecraft. Indeed, historian Peter Gatrell (2017) argues that "innovative though it was, the Nansen passport was as much about assisting host states as it was about giving refugees a degree of legal status, since it enabled the state to keep track of refugees who came and went." Indeed, by making Nansen passports primarily available to Stateless Russians and Armenians but not to millions of others whom states refused to recognize as bona fide Refugees (e.g., those displaced by nationalist violence in the Balkans), the power of states to sort people into different migration categories in order to halt some of their movements was further enhanced. Indeed, *most* Stateless people were not described as victims in need of protection (the discourse of the League) but as people of an "abnormal status," "homeless," "undesirables" and, tellingly, "a new class of international people" (in Rürup 2011, 116). Out of the approximately four million Stateless people in Europe and the Near East during the interwar years, Nansen passports were only issued to less than half a million (Thompson 1938).

By the late 1930s, it was increasingly accepted that one's identity emanated from one's state-issued—or in the case of the Nansen passports, extrastate-issued—identity documents. However, more to the point, if identity documents granted someone their identity, then as Miriam Rürup (2011, 113) has pointed out, "the reverse was also true: The lack of valid papers expressed one's lost link to human society." This is oddly reflected in Dorothy Thompson's 1938 comment that, "there is no doubt that by and large, the Nansen certificate is the greatest thing that has happened for the individual refugee [for] it returned his [sic] lost identity" (in Giaimo 2017). While Nansen passports certainly did not ensure their holders would be granted the political status of the states they entered—the only official identity of Nansen passport holders was Refugee—Thompson's remark shows the growing importance of states' monopolization of the "legitimate means of movement" (Torpey 1998).

Indeed, the reality of people made (and kept) Stateless was to be subject to the authority of *any and every* state they encountered while lacking the "right to have rights" in each. With tongue firmly in cheek, Bertolt Brecht (1940, in Rürup 2011, 113), reflecting on his own recent experience of fleeing Nazi Germany, wrote, "The passport is the most noble part of the human

Nationalism

being. It also does not come into existence in such a simple fashion as a human being does. A human being can come into the world anywhere, in the most careless way and for no good reason, but a passport never can. When it is good, the passport is also recognized for this quality, whereas a human being, no matter how good, can go unrecognized." People made Stateless by states thus offered a clear negative counterpart to the growing ranks of National-Native citizens. Indeed, the creation of Minorities, Refugees, and Stateless people reflected the violence of ordering the world along the lines demanded by nations and nation-states.

However, in the early interwar years, even as immigration controls were rapidly being implemented, the national "logic of constraint" had not completely eclipsed the imperial "logic of facilitation" (Mongia 2007). Thus, at the 1920 League conference in Paris, some of the delegates made recommendations to *reduce* peacetime restrictions on movement. Later, at the 1921 Inter-Parliamentary Union conference in Stockholm, passports and other limits to people's mobility were condemned as unacceptable breaches of liberty by not a few participants (Torpey 2000, 127). Such criticisms of the growing system of border controls were largely ignored, however. Instead, new interwar immigration controls were represented as a new regime of protection.

In the interwar years, immigration controls as well as tariff walls on the import of commodities were portrayed as necessary to "protect society." Great Britain, Germany, Austria, Italy, the Netherlands, Belgium, and France each raised its import tariffs after 1928 (Hynes, Jacks, and O'Rourke 2012). In addition to producing the figure of the Migrant worker, the interwar period, Eric Hobsbawm (1990, 132) notes, was also when the idea of a national economy emerged in Europe. Karl Polanyi (1944) saw the nationalization of economies and cultures as crucial to the consolidation of the "great transformation" toward a "market society." Polanyi (1944, 202) argued that at this time, "Protectionism everywhere was producing the hard shell of the emerging unit of social life. . . . The new crustacean type of nation expressed its identity through national token currencies safeguarded by a type of sovereignty more jealous and absolute than anything known before."

During the interwar period, the "jealousy" of nationalized sovereignties was keenly felt *within* nation-states. Nazi Germany was one of the deadliest examples of this. The roots of the ascendance of the National Socialist German Workers' Party in February 1933 lay in the dissolution of the German and Austro-Hungarian Empires and the nationalist political climate of the interwar years. From the Italian *fascio*, or "bundle," fascists saw no difference between a racialized nation and the political community, thus making all "non-Nationals" enemies of the People. Indeed, the Nazis' long-standing adherence to racist, sexist, able-ist, anticommunist, and populist views promoted the most limited view of German nationhood on offer. The Nazis' 7 April 1933 Law for the Restoration of the Professional Civil Service claimed to "re-establish" a "professional" *and "national"* civil service by dismissing all teachers, professors, judges, and other government workers who were of "non-Aryan descent" or who were political opponents of the Nazis. On 14 July 1933, the Law for the Prevention of Hereditarily Diseased Offspring mandated compulsory sterilization for people classified with a range of hereditary, physical, or mental "abnormalities."

The passing of what came to be known as the Nuremberg Racial Laws on 15 September 1935 depended on discourses of national autochthony to make "German-ness." State attention to ideas of the German race was grounded in ideas of German place, or *völkische Staat.* The Nazis' claim to a mythical "Aryan" identity helped to *autochthonize* German-ness by creating a specifically German historiography, one that located "German-ness" back into the mists of a "national" prehistory and allowed for the narration of "Germans" as the people with eternal claims to "German lands." The Nazis thus represented their political project as a national reawakening of a slumbering and complacent German nation that had allowed its historical homeland to be polluted by the entry and infiltration of foreign-Others (Holton 2005). This is evident in the preamble to the Nazis' Law for the Protection of German Blood and German Honor, where the state declared that, "entirely convinced that the purity of German blood is essential to the further existence of the German people, and inspired by the uncompromising determination to safeguard the future of the German nation, the Reichstag has unanimously resolved" to outlaw "marriages between Jews and citizens of German or related blood" (Article 1), ban "sexual relations outside marriage between Jews and nationals of German or related blood" (Article 2), bar Jewish people from employing "female citizens of German or kindred blood as domestic servants" (Article 3) and forbid Jewish people from displaying "the Reich and national flag or the national colors" (Article 4).

Ideas of national autochthony also underwrote the 15 September 1935 Reich Citizenship Law, which revoked the German citizenship of Jewish people. The juridical basis of this revocation was Article 2, which limited membership in the German nation-state to those having "German or related blood." Defining Jewish people as outside of the racialized German *Herrenvolk* (or "master race") allowed them to be defined as non-members of the German nation. The assumed association between "German blood" and loyalty to "the German people and Reich"—also served to define Jewish people as outside of the German nation. On 26 November 1935, a supplementary decree also stripped German citizenship from people categorized as "Gypsies, Negroes, and their bastards" as well as people deemed to have "mental and/or genetic deformities" (in Friedländer 2009).[10]

All those whose citizenship had been stripped were now legally deportable. Indeed, a July 1938 order authorized the state to expel all those whose German citizenship had been revoked (Torpey 2000, 135). In his 24 January 1939 edict, Hitler further ordered Hermann Göring to establish the Reich Central Office for Jewish Emigration in Berlin for the purposes of "solving the Jewish question by means of emigration or evacuation" (Browning with Matthaus 2004, 195–196). Thus, the initial Nazi technology of ensuring a "national reawakening" was through a population transfer, a national practice that, it is worth noting, was accepted as legitimate by signatories to the Lausanne Convention just fifteen years earlier (in 1923).

By the late 1930s, it was clear that fascist governments across Europe were attempting to displace—and endanger the lives of—large numbers of people through laws attacking people imagined as outside of the national race, as well as the mob violence such acts encouraged. Again the League stepped in. In the years preceding WWII, two League of Nations treaties were signed: the July 1936 Provisional Arrangement concerning the Status of Refugees Coming from Germany[11] and the February 1938 Convention concerning the Status of Refugees Coming from Germany (which was extended in September 1939 to include people fleeing Austria).[12] In a 1938 speech, Hitler responded to these treaties: "I can only hope and expect that the other world, which has such deep sympathy for these criminals, will at least be generous enough to convert this sympathy into practical aid. We, on our part, are ready to put all these criminals at the disposal of these countries, for all I care, even on luxury ships." Neither the signatories of these treaties nor other states were "generous," however—quite the contrary. The Allied states refused to diminish—never mind abolish—their vast immigration controls. Consequently, most people rendered Stateless since 1935 were unable to leave Nazi Germany, not initially because the Nazis would not permit their exit, but because other states would not permit their entry.

The outcome of a 1938 meeting of the League-established Intergovernmental Committee on Refugees (ICR) held in Évian-les-Bains, France, made it clear that as it had failed to protect most Minorities, Refugees, and other Stateless people, the League would also fail to protect the victims of fascism. The main concern of the parties at the Évian conference was to maintain the emergent interstatal system of immigration controls—*not* to protect those in need of safe passage and new places to live. Indeed, in its 1938 report, it presented *people's movement*—and not the actions precipitating it—as the crisis. The report prefaced its recommendations by noting "that the involuntary emigration of people in large numbers has become so great that it renders racial and religious problems more acute, increases international unrest, and may hinder seriously the processes of appeasement in international relations" (in Gutman and Margaliot 1999, 96).

Indeed, except for the Dominican Republic, all states, imperial or national in form, refused to offer asylum to those targeted by Nazi rule.[15] One by one, the signatory states offered various arguments for their unwillingness to offer real assistance to the Nazis' victims (Wyman 1968, 197). Their biggest concern, which they presented as perfectly normal, was the need to defend their highly racialized version of society. As noted by Ervin Birnbaum (2009), France insisted it was "saturated." Britain was willing to accept some Jewish children (almost 10,000 eventually arrived), but not their parents, because, it stated, "a sudden rush of Jewish refugees might arouse anti-Semitic feelings" (in Birnbaum 2009). Britain also refused to allow Jewish people to immigrate to anywhere else in the British Empire (including the territories of its Mandate for Palestine). "Switzerland," its government declared, "has as little use for these Jews as Germany has, [and] will herself take measures to protect Switzerland from being swamped by the Jews" (in Birnbaum 2009).

In the Americas, with their long-standing racist entry controls, the sentiment was similar. The Central American states released a joint statement with thinly veiled anti-Jewish racism that declared their unwillingness to offer asylum to "traders and intellectuals" (in Birnbaum 2009). Brazil stated that all visa applicants required a certificate of Christian baptism. Peru, referring to the U.S. refusal to increase its immigration quota of 25,957 for Germans and active restriction of Stateless Jewish people, caustically stated that the United States provided the rest of the world an example of "caution and wisdom" (in Birnbaum 2009).

Indeed, prior to the start of WWII, U.S. immigration quotas for Germany and Austria were left unfilled. The year 1939 was the first time the United States filled its combined German-Austrian quota (now including annexed Czechoslovakia), but even this meant that it accepted only 27,000 people out of the approximately 309,000 Jewish applicants from Germany, Austria, and Czechoslovakia that year. From 1933 to 1945, the United States took in only 132,000 Jewish refugees, with the vast majority entering before the outbreak of war (see Wyman 1968). From December 1941 to the end of WWII in September 1945, "only 21,000 refugees were allowed to enter the United States," or about "10 percent of the number who could have been legally admitted under the immigration quotas during that period" (Wyman 1992, 217). Knowing full well that Nazi Germany had stripped Jewish people of their citizenship and labeled them as "criminals," the United States demanded that Jewish refugees produce certificates of good conduct from the German police.

Fuck off.

In denying entry to victims of the Nazis, Australia declared, "As we have no real racial problem, we are not desirous of importing one" (in Birnbaum 2009). Canada, in another barely disguised anti-Jewish policy, stated that it would only accept people experienced in working in agriculture.[14] The year of the Évian Conference, Canada's director of the Immigration Branch, Frederick Blair, stated, "Pressure by Jewish people to get into Canada has never been greater than it is now, and I am glad to be able to add that after thirty-five years of experience here, that it has never been so carefully controlled" (in Abella and Troper 1998). Between 1933 and 1939, Canada admitted fewer than five thousand Jewish people, one of the lowest numbers in the world.

Most states, thus, not only upheld their existing immigration controls against the victims of the fascist states, but intensified them. In 1938, the year before WWII began, only about 36,000 Jewish people were able to leave Germany and Austria (Holocaust Encyclopedia n.d.). For this reason, Birnbaum (2009) termed the Évian Conference "The Most Fateful Conference of All Times in Jewish History." In addition to refusing people asylum, those in attendance sent the message that states, especially the major powers, would not make Nazi treatment of its victims a political issue. Notably, the large-scale brutal assaults on people targeted by the Nazis, including their mass transportation to concentration camps, took place *after* Évian. Indeed, the *Kristallnacht* ("Night of Broken Glass") pogrom across Germany took place just months afterward, in November 1938. Thus, it is safe to conclude that the full horror of the "jealousy" of nation-states was realized—the state directed extermination of approximately 11 million people in Europe—when an operative *interstatal* system of immigration controls was in place to prevent the flight of those seeking a safe haven.

While the Holocaust cannot wholly be laid at the feet of these immigration controls, it is not an unimportant fact that only after the deportation of "undesirables" from Nazi-controlled territories across Western and Eastern Europe became impossible did the Nazis begin their systematic, mass exterminations of those deemed "enemies" of the racialized German nation. It was in late 1941 when the Nazis first erected extermination camps.[15] Indeed, in October 1941 the Nazis outlawed the emigration of Jewish and Romani or Sinti people from greater Reich territories, including occupied Europe (Reich

Main Security Office 1941). The order was sent to German embassies in Nazi satellite states. German naval patrols began to police the waters to halt those fleeing. While this decision—coming almost a decade after the Nazis initially took power in Germany—was no doubt prompted by the Nazis' failure to quickly seize Russian territories (where they had wanted to deport people to), the refusal of other states to allow for the entry of the Nazis' victims was critical (Browning 1986, 498).

The Chelmno camp in occupied Poland, the Nazi's "first killing center," opened after the October 1941 order ending emigration. In 1942, newly constructed extermination camps were opened—Belzec, Sobibor, and Treblinka—in the interior of Poland. A few months later, the first gas chambers were installed. That same year, trains crammed beyond capacity began to transport Nazi prisoners, including about 250,000 to 300,000 people deported between July and September 1942 from the Warsaw Ghetto (erected in 1940). In these camps, the Nazis carried out a mass and systematic execution of Jewish people and other "enemies" from across Europe, three million of whom were Polish Jews.

WORLD WAR II AND ITS AFTERMATH

Immigration controls preventing the entry of victims of Nazism were part of a broader intensification of mobility restrictions within states as well as across state borders during WWII. Nation-states across the New World walled themselves off to a growing number of people, while nonimperial subjects were denied entry to imperial territories in Asia and Africa. Both the United States and Canada, for example, enhanced their immigration controls. Even before it officially entered WWII in December 1941, the United States passed the 1940 Alien Registration Act expanding the grounds for deporting aliens and required all aliens over the age of fourteen to register, be fingerprinted, and report to state authorities every three months (Daniels 2006, 107). Once the United States became party to the war, it declared all citizens of Japan, Germany, and Italy over the age of fourteen and resident in the United States to be "alien enemies" who were "liable to be apprehended, restrained, secured, and removed" (in Daniels 2006, 114n8). In mid-January 1942, the more than one million people affected were ordered to reregister and were given new identification certificates that they were required to carry at all times. President Roosevelt's 19 February 1942 Executive Order 9066 authorized the incarceration of subjects or nationals of Japan, Germany, and Italy—but also many U.S. citizens racialized as Japanese, German, and Italian—in War Relocation Authority camps (Executive Order 9066 1942). Japanese-Americans (as well as resident Japanese subjects who at this time were ineligible for naturalization into U.S. citizenship) bore the brunt of this order. Approximately 120,000 "Japanese" were interned. Reflecting the racialized imagination of the United States as a "White nation," 62 percent of these "Japanese" people were U.S. citizens (Harth 2003).

Canada also tightened its criteria for immigration with the start of WWII. For example, the minimum amount of money required for admittance was tripled from $5,000 to $15,000, and any new immigrants were made to work as farmers. Like the United States, Canada also constructed prison camps for those categorized as "enemy aliens," most of them British subjects. Since Canada did not yet offer separate citizenship (or passports), "enemy aliens" were defined by a 1940 Order in Council as "all persons of German or Italian racial origin who have become naturalized British subjects since September 1, 1922." By late-1941, both subjects of Japan and British subjects racialized as "Japanese" were added to the list and became its main victims. Approximately 22,000 "Japanese" people were interned, 14,000 of whom were British subjects domiciled in Canada. That year, in a gross understatement of its historical record, Frederick Blair, director of the Immigration Branch, noted to Parliament that "Canada, in accordance with generally accepted practice, places greater emphasis on race than upon citizenship" (in Abella and Troper 1982, 230).

Amid the turmoil of WWII, autochthonous discourses of which racialized group belonged in which state's territories normalized deportations, population transfers, and mass exterminations across Europe. The Japanese imperial state committed grave atrocities against those deemed inferior. In both German- and Soviet-occupied territories of Poland, there were forced expulsions of people. In the initial period of Nazi-occupied Poland, up to two million people were deported to territories further east. By war's end they had been "replaced" by upwards of half a million "Germans," people who themselves had often been deported from the USSR, the Baltic region, Romania, and Bessarabia (many of whom were, once again, forced to move after Germany's defeat). From 1940 to 1941, anywhere from 300,000 to 1.5 million people were expelled from Soviet-occupied Poland (see Siemaszko 1991).

After the Nazis invaded the USSR in June 1941, the Soviet government deported the "Volga Germans" to Kazakhstan, Altai Krai, and Siberia, where many were interned in labor camps and worked to death. From 1943 to 1944, Crimean Tatars, Kalmyks, Chechens, Ingush, Balkars, Karachays, and Meskhetian Turks were deported by the Soviet Union to other Soviet-controlled parts in Central Asia or Siberia. The 1940 Soviet occupation of the Baltic States (Estonia, Latvia, and Lithuania) also led to forced deportations—60,000 people from Estonia alone (Buttar 2013). Further, with Finland's cessation of Finnish Karelia to the Soviet Union in 1940, approximately 410,000 persons known as "Finnish Karelians" were "transferred" into remaining Finnish territory. In turn, with the Finnish occupation of East Karelia from 1941 to 1944, the Finnish state deported people deemed to be "Russian" while moving tens of thousands of persons deemed to be "Finnish" in. When Finland ceded this territory back to the USSR in 1944, the "Finnish" population was once again moved, this time in the name of "evacuation."

In the Axis-occupied Balkans, the Nazi puppet state of Croatia was carved out of occupied Yugoslavia. It enacted Nazi-style race laws declaring Jewish, Roma, and Sinti people its "enemies." Serbian people were also systematically targeted for expulsion and murder. By war's end, approximately 330,000 to 500,000 Serbs, 32,000 Jews, 26,000 Roma, and between 5,000 and 12,000 Croatian political opponents of the regime had been killed (Gutman 1990). Another 500,000 Serbs were either expelled or forced to convert to Catholicism. In Bulgarian-occupied Macedonia, approximately 30,000 Serbs were expelled. In mainland Greece, about 20,000 Cham Albanians were expelled. In late 1944, after the Soviets and Yugoslav Partisans retook northern Yugoslavia, more than 200,000 "Danube Swabian" people were expelled, including about 30,000 people who were deported to the USSR to work as slave laborers.

All these movements of people, each actively organized by states, most of which had nationalized their sovereignties by the start of WWII, demonstrates that while nation-states certainly did operate under what Mongia (2007) terms a "logic of constraint," they also *facilitated* much mobility as well. The key difference between their facilitation of movement and the "logic of facilitation" which informed the practices of the imperial states preceding them, was that nation-states, in addition to engaging in "population transfers," which, in part, moved people *into* state territories, engaged in many acts that moved people *out* of nationalized territories through deportation regimes targeting those denied (or stripped of their) national citizenship. Moreover, as the raging jealousies of nationalism, inflamed by war, ushered in unprecedented limits to global human mobility, they also gave greater impetus *for migration*. At the end of WWII, tens of millions of people were left dispossessed and displaced. In Europe alone, an estimated thirty million people were in search of new lives and livelihoods. As Gunther Beijer (1969, 42–43) notes, in the first ten years after WWII, the number of people expelled from one European state to another was similar to the number of people leaving Europe during its Age of Migration from the early nineteenth century to the first decade of the twentieth century.

Untever the global equivalent of
2, nation B ...

The greatest movement of people in the immediate post-WWII period was of those constituted as "Germans" living outside of Germany. The Potsdam Agreement, signed by the United States, the United Kingdom, and the Soviet Union, organized the expulsion of about fourteen million people deemed to be "German" from several Eastern European states (mainly Poland, Hungary, and Czechoslovakia). In an employment of autochthonous logic, many were "returned" to their "racial" and "national homeland" of Germany (soon to be divided into East and West Germany) where, like previous (and subsequent) victims of population transfers, most had never set foot (Torpey 2000, 143). One of the signatories to this agreement, Winston Churchill, was quite sanguine about this massive displacement: "I am not alarmed by the prospect of the disentanglement of populations," he said, "not even by these large transferences, which are more possible in modern conditions than they were ever before" (in Walters 2010).

In this immediate post-WWII period, it was not only in Europe where people experienced massive levels of displacement. There was an equally massive dislocation of people throughout Asia and what was now being called the "Middle East," each also organized along autochthonous lines. The end of the British Raj was violently ushered in with the partition of British India in 1947 and the subsequent creation of the nation-states of Pakistan and India. Marking their national sovereignty, Pakistan and India instituted a forced population transfer involving anywhere from ten million to fourteen million people. Taking place over the space of a few months, it was the single largest forced migration of people thus far in human history. At least one million people were killed and tens of thousands of women raped, usually by men on the other side of the religious and national divisions unleashed in no small part by the machinations of the British Empire during the period of indirect-rule colonialism (Butalia 2000). They were not alone. With the formation of the new, explicitly Jewish nation-state of Israel, over 700,000 Palestinians were forced, by one means or another, to flee (Israel 1952; UN 1951). In turn, roughly that number of Jewish people moved into the new state of Israel, many fearful of continued persecution in Europe as well as their recent demonization in Northern Africa and other states in the Middle East.

CONCLUSION

From WWI onward, the nationalization of state sovereignty was accelerated by a multipronged process. Emergent as well as established nation-states expelled many regarded as allochthonous (outsiders) to the nation, encouraged the movement of members of the "nation" into their territories, used their military force to expand their territories to encompass missing pieces of their "national homelands," and placed new and ever intensifying immigration restrictions on those deemed to be "undesirable" or even "enemies of the people." Together these processes created a massive reordering of people's relation to place, to states, and to one another. The process of nation building in Europe alone led to over *100 million people* crossing newly created borders from the start of the Balkan Wars (1912–1913) to 1968 (Beijer 1969, 42–43). As "nations" were "reawakened," various people were forcibly "returned" to places they were now said to be National-Natives of. Deportations were represented as "home-sendings" while the transference of people in were portrayed as "homecomings." For the victims of forced population transfers, the cruel irony of being told that one's dispossession and displacement was a "return" to a national homeland was not lost on anyone affected, even as it was roundly celebrated by nationalists.

In addition to those millions caught up in forced movements, millions of others were also on the move. With new national economies integrated into globally expanding capitalist markets for land and labor, many were moving because they needed new livelihoods. Those people who were *not* a People (at least not in the places they lived and needed to work) encountered a world in global lockdown. From the start of WWI, throughout the interwar years, and during WWII, immigration controls became more and more intense. By the end of WWII they were accepted as a permanent, necessary, and even "timeless" feature of state sovereignty. Thus did nation-state practices of regulating and restricting people's movements produce some as "people of a place" and others as "people out of place."

Both National-Natives and the Migrants they were distinguished from came to be fixed in time and space. Ideas of a shared world and a shared social condition were largely eclipsed by nationalisms declaring their own, distinct place in the world. In addition to immigration controls, limits to "nation-ness" were set through ideas of a shared history and a shared future. Both were deeply informed by ideas of "race"—or its correlatives "blood," "ancestors," and "genealogy"—to buttress claims for their "eternal" existence. Together, spatial and temporal limits to the "nation" helped define *where* the national society belonged, *who* belonged in any given national homeland, and who they ought to be *with* when they were there. For each "nation," separation became both a necessity and a virtue.

Immigration controls thus contributed greatly to the territorialization of people's consciousness. Each time national border controls were enacted and their reach made greater, a national form of life was granted to Nationals and disallowed for Migrants (Foucault 1978, 138). For the growing number of states nationalizing their sovereignties, national citizenship became key to determining whether or not one had "the right to rights," whether or not one could lawfully work in rapidly nationalizing labor markets, whether or not one had access to the national social wage of state welfare provisions, and whether or not one could be deported by the nation-state. It was not only Nationals-Natives who lived in nation-states, of course, but also those classified as "foreign bodies." To manage this, alongside the category of National, the number of Migrant categories proliferated during the period under study. People were classified as refugees, permanent residents, guestworkers (or temporary foreign workers), illegals, and stateless, each arrayed hierarchically against the normative nationalist subjectivity of the National-Native. Immigration and citizenship policies, thus, created another sort of partition, or perhaps, more accurately, an *apartheid*, between Nationals and non-Nationals not only across the span of the globe, as Anthony Richmond (1994) pointed to, but also *within* any nation-state's territory (Sharma 2006). Indeed, controls on immigration rapidly became a key mechanism through which inequality on a *global* scale was reorganized after WWII in the emergent Postcolonial New World Order of nation-states.

In this regard, and to bring it back to the beginning of the end of (relatively) unrestricted movement into state territories, it is important to note that the coolie labor system largely collapsed with the start of WWI. The growing nationalism—and immigration controls—in the Americas, as well as the growing resistance to this system by coolie workers themselves, made their recruitment increasingly difficult.[16] Just as coolieism replaced slavery as a key system for both labor recruitment and labor discipline, the category of "Migrant worker" replaced that of coolie worker. National immigration controls (across the Americas and in the former imperial territories of the Russian, German, Austro-Hungarian, and Ottoman Empires), alongside the enactment of entry controls to the metropoles of the remaining European imperial states, each led, in their own way, to immigration restrictions and regulations shaping the supply, price, and individual as well as collective strength of those recruited now as Migrant workers.

In the following chapter, I examine the post-WWII emergence of what I call the Postcolonial New World Order, the system and the condition for possibilities we find ourselves in today (H. A. Baker et al. 1995). In it, I show how postcolonialism, far from ushering in a period of decolonization, marked instead the hegemony of nation-states. From the outset, postcolonialism was shaped by the convergence of nationalist demands from the colonies with the demands of the most powerful nation-state (the United States) and the most powerful capitalists (largely based in the United States). Through newly formed international institutions, capital became more mobile, while human beings faced increasing restrictions on their ability to move. Indeed, the actions taken by states after the end of WWII solidified the link between the sovereignty of states, the nationalization of society and membership in it, and the regulation and restriction of human mobility. Access to entering old and new nation-states mapped firmly onto the global distribution of wealth, creating a new global apartheid of a "Rich World" and a "Poor World."

From the start of the Postcolonial New World Order, the sovereignties of nation-states, and therefore the nationalities people were hailed into, were far from equal. Whether people would face more or less restrictions on their movement became dependent on which nationality they possessed and which passport they held. So too did the obtainment of paid employment, living-wage levels, adequate housing and education, social welfare programs, and much more. Indeed, the organization of the *nationalization of the capitalist wage and the nationalization of the social wage* created and solidified ideas of National-Nativeness. Thus, in the next chapter, I argue that the gross inequalities that lasted—indeed intensified—after the end of imperial-state rule are best understood not as neocolonialism or neoimperialism but as *postcolonialism.* The Postcolonial New World Order is one in which nation-states with their national "societies" organize and normalize discrimination based on the always-already autochthonous, racist distinction between National-Natives and Migrants.

5

THE POSTCOLONIAL
NEW WORLD ORDER
AND THE CONTAINMENT
OF DECOLONIZATION

When the ax came into the woods, many of the trees said,
"At least the handle is one of us."

—Proverb

NATIONAL SELF-DETERMINATION

Shortly after the end of World War II (WWII), the rapid normalization of
the national form of state ushered in what I call a Postcolonial New World
Order. With it, nation-states came to be widely regarded as the only legitimate form political communities could take. By the 1960s imperial states effectively ceased to exist. They were replaced by an international system of
nation-states whose governing idiom was home rule, a system wherein state
control over territory and people was deployed in the name of the "nation."
With the success of postcolonialism, ideas of decolonization were reduced
to, and I argue, contained by nationalism.

"National self-determination" became a fundamental principle of the
contemporary international legal regime. As stated in the founding Charter
of the aptly named United Nations (UN), the organization's very purpose was
"to develop friendly relations among nations based on respect for the principle of equal rights and self-determination of peoples, and to take other ap-
propriate measures to strengthen universal peace" (Chap. 1, Article 1, part 2).
Its declaration stood in marked contrast to the formation of the League of

Nations in the aftermath of World War I (WWI). While the *prima facie* rationale for the existence of the League was U.S. President Woodrow Wilson's expressed doctrine of "self-rule," "self-governance," and even the "consent of the governed," it was not—nor was it meant to be—applied generally to the *colonies* of imperial states (Manela 2007, 22).

In his famous Fourteen Points speech in 1918, Wilson outlined the League's basic structure by declaring, "An evident principle runs through the whole program I have outlined. It is the principle of justice to all peoples and nationalities, and their right to live on equal terms of liberty and safety with one another, whether they be strong or weak." Yet at this time, when the most powerful states were still largely imperial in form, the League did not consider all people to be *Peoples*—that is, "nations." Instead, the League argued that the colonies of empires had not yet "reached a stage of development where their existence as independent nations can be provisionally recognized."[1] Consequently, the League asserted, they must remain under colonial "tutelage." Ironically, nationality was then a mark of *imperial distinction*. In the interwar years, many people in the world remained colonized *subjects* of one or another imperial state.

Applying the principle of national self-determination to people in the colonies emerged not from the League of Nations, but as part of the machinations of the United States trying to become a global hegemon during WWII. In August 1941, President Franklin Roosevelt convinced British Prime Minister Winston Churchill to sign an "Atlantic Charter." Not a formal treaty, the Atlantic Charter instead reflected the vision of the United States of a Postcolonial New World Order. Significantly, it was the first agreement between powerful states that did not disqualify colonized people from self-governance. Article 3 declared that Britain and the United States would "respect the right of all peoples to choose the form of Government under which they will live; and they wish to see sovereign rights and self-government restored to those who have been forcibly deprived of them." The United States succeeded not only in getting Churchill's concession to eschew territorial gains at the conclusion of WWII (in stark contrast to the expansion of the British Empire after WWI) but also to agree to respect "the freely expressed wishes of the peoples concerned" (Atlantic Charter 1941). Both signing parties knew that fulfilling the terms of the Atlantic Charter would sound the death knell of the British Empire.

Yet Churchill signed the charter, not because Britain acknowledged the horrors of imperialism and wanted them to end, but because it was in desperate need of continued U.S. financial aid to fight in WWII. In addition to the June 1940 German occupation of France, the September 1940 start of the German "blitz" of the United Kingdom, and the May 1941 German defeat of British, Greek, and Yugoslav forces in the Balkans, there was a very real and immediate threat that Germany could soon cut off access to British India through the Suez Canal. There was the additional possibility that the Japanese Empire's occupation of British colonies across Asia would fatally weaken its hold in this part of the world. The United States parlayed these British weaknesses into support for its postwar goals and laid the groundwork for its ascendency to global hegemon (see Cull 1996, 4–5). Once the United States officially entered the war (on 8 December 1941), it became the main supplier of military and nonmilitary supplies to the Allies and was a critical force in defeating Germany in North Africa and Western Europe and in defeating Japan in the Pacific.

Ever hopeful that the empire could be retained at war's end, Churchill tried to refashion his agreement with the United States as one concerned "primarily, [with] the restoration of sovereignty, self-government and national life of the States and nations *of Europe* now under the Nazi yoke" (Winston S. Churchill 1942, emphasis added). On 1 January 1942, three weeks after the United States formally entered WWII, the "United Nations," a term coined by President Roosevelt, was launched. Established to prevent any Allied state from making a separate peace with Germany, Italy, or Japan, the UN had signatories to its formative declaration subscribe to "a common program of purposes and principles embodied in the Joint Declaration of the President of the United States of America and the Prime Minister of the United Kingdom of Great Britain and Northern Ireland dated August 14, 1941, known as the Atlantic Charter." A month later, Roosevelt publicly refuted Churchill's interpretation of the charter and stated, "We of the United Nations are agreed on certain broad principles in the kind of peace we seek. *The Atlantic Charter applies not only to the parts of the world that border the Atlantic but the whole world*" (in Nwaubani 2003, 507; emphasis added). Later that year, U.S. Undersecretary of State Sumner Welles, "a proponent of supporting anticolonial nationalism," was even more blunt. With the signing of the Atlantic Charter, he baldly stated, "The age of imperialism is ended" (in Nwaubani 2003, 509).

Roosevelt's anticolonialism was far from principled, however. It was strategic. As Ebere Nwaubani (2003, 512) argues, "Roosevelt left little doubt that his prescription meant no more than the substitution of United States economic penetration for European imperialism." Indeed, for the United States, "national self-determination" was a way to break up imperial monopolies over the wealth of their colonies. U.S. support to end empires was to replace imperial markets with its much-vaunted "Open Door" policy, thus ensuring entry for the United States into new markets for natural resources, labor, and consumers. As a U.S. State Department statement put it in 1944, "Overseas trade will be more important than ever before. . . . Our country will not be able to maintain our heretofore standard of living or even to approximate it unless we can produce more, export more, and help by our overseas trade *to all lands* to raise the standard of living of backward peoples so that they may absorb more and more of the products of American agriculture and industry" (in Nwaubani 2003, 514; emphasis added).

The United States expected that the new postcolonial order of sovereign nation-states would be an enormous boon for its position in the world and for the capitalists whose bottom line it championed. It is important, therefore, to read the Atlantic Charter's principle of self-government for *all* people (or, more accurately, all *Peoples*) not as its endorsement of anticolonialism, but as a means of achieving U.S. hegemony over a post-WWII world. The charter was thus a significant step toward the principle of "national self-determination" that was later to be enshrined in the UN, a key institution of postcolonialism. Indeed, the UN itself regards the Atlantic Charter as "a milestone" to its creation and "the first real step towards a world organization" (Brazier 2015).

U.S. support for the principle of self-government was thus central to the making of a Postcolonial New World Order. By January 1942, twenty-six of the Allied states (some of them, like "British India," British imperial colonies) had signed the "Declaration by United Nations" upholding the idea of self-governance for all "people." By war's end, twenty-one more states (some of them in exile) acceded to the declaration. This declaration formed the basis for the 1945 United Nations Conference on International Organization (UNCIO), a convention of delegates from fifty Allied states (including British imperial colonies) held in San Francisco, where the UN's charter was drafted and signed. Its ratification in 24 October 1945 enshrined the *national* right of "self-determination" into the post-WWII international regime (and its emergent laws) and signaled the beginning of the end of the hegemony of imperial states. It also signaled the start of a new world order of postcolonialism, with its global system of nation-states.

One particular nation-state—the United States—was firmly in control. The United States had little to fear—and much to gain—by demanding that the markets controlled by imperial states be opened up. During WWII, the productive capacity of firms (private and those built by state funds) in the United States grew by 50 percent, largely by producing military supplies. At the same time, powerful capitalist firms in Europe and Japan were significantly diminished by the war (Luard 1983). At war's end, U.S. government investments in industry, including foreign aid, troop deployments, military procurement policies, and the state's provision of relatively cheap oil worked to ensure the profitability of what President Dwight Eisenhower would come to call the "military-industrial complex." Ideas of "free trade," "free enterprise," and the "free world" captured the postcolonial zeitgeist and the preeminent place of the United States in it.

The financial clout of the United States in the global capitalist economy ensured its domination. In addition to $17 billion in Marshall Plan funds channeled to various European states, the United States extended other substantial loans to Western European states, particularly Britain, as well as to those in the Far East. From 1945 to 1962, the formative period of the Postcolonial New World Order, the United States expended $103 billion in both economic and military aid. Of this, $71.5 billion was on economic aid ($40 billion in grants, $23 billion in long-term loans, and $8.5 billion in food) and $31.5 on military aid.

A key requirement for recipient states was to make their currency convertible. This was particularly important with regard to Britain. Indeed, a key condition of the 1946 $3.5 billion Anglo-American loan was the full convertibility of sterling pounds, allowing states with sterling balances to convert these to U.S. dollars. Convertibility led to the withdrawal of almost $1 billion from British reserves and, by 1949, to a more than 25 percent devaluation of sterling pounds. Another key condition attached to U.S. loans was trade liberalization between European states—*including their colonies*, thus guaranteeing U.S. entry into markets previously closed to them, especially the integrated market of the British Empire. This, along with the replacement of the British Sterling Bloc with the U.S. Dollar Bloc ensured that U.S.-supported capital could trade with (still) British dominions such as India, Egypt, Iraq, and Palestine. While Britain used large portions of its Anglo-American loan to support its overseas spending, mostly in the Near East (Egypt, Iraq, and Palestine) and in British India in an effort to maintain its imperial power, the devaluation of their currency forced the British to make dramatic cuts in both domestic and overseas expenditures, making British retention of its colonies extremely difficult.

It became increasingly clear after WWII that maintaining imperial territorial domination was not necessary for practices of expropriation and exploitation. By the early 1960s, even the most powerful imperial states entering WWII—Britain and France—had nationalized their sovereignty (see chapter 7 and Cooper 2005). However, this does not mean that processes of territorialization were no longer important. The end of empires and the strong territorial attachment that nationalism produced to nationalize both state sovereignty and people's subjectivities created a Postcolonial New World Order of nominally independent nation-states tied firmly together through the coercive power of those states that had more financial capital to distribute. The United States used this postcolonial system to gain concessions from individual nation-states.

The numerous movements for national liberation waged within the colonies were a crucial part of assuring the ascendancy of postcolonialism. Fierce battles for home rule were fought, and mostly won, by anticolonial activists deploying nationalism.[2] They were able to unite many of the direct producers with the old (aristocratic) as well as new (capitalist) ruling classes in successful struggles for national self-determination. After the end of WWII, and with astonishing speed, the near-global space of imperialism was nationalized. Between 1945 and 1960, three dozen new nation-states in Asia and Africa were formed. Postcolonialism was thus marked from the outset by the convergence of nationalist demands from the colonies with the demands of the most powerful state (the United States) and the demands by capitalists seeking new markets (the largest of which were headquartered in the United States).

In this new postcolonial world, practices of controlling and extracting wealth from older and newer nation-states did not fundamentally diverge from the patterns of expropriation and exploitation emblematic of the old imperial world order. Indeed, under postcolonialism, capitalist social relations *expanded*. Across the planet, as much of the stuff of life was enclosed within capitalist markets—land and food being perhaps the most crucial— more and more people joined the ranks of the proletariat. The dramatic spread of capitalist social relations mirrored the expansion of nation-state power. Whether in the form of the post-WWII welfare state, the warfare state, or the "developing" state, both the nation-state and capital made unprecedented penetrations into people's lives. Indeed, as James Scott (2009, 324) notes, in the post-WWII period, people's ability to escape their expropriation and exploitation was severely weakened, if not rendered impossible.

In this chapter, I discuss how a new postcolonial world of nation-states, far from challenging the social relations of imperialism, only implemented new, nationalist forms of regulating capitalism, managing "populations" and, crucially, *containing* the revolutionary and liberatory demands of people across the globe. The nationalization of states, sovereignty, territory, and subjectivities placed severe constraints on continuing efforts at decolonization. Indeed, the twofold processes of globalizing capitalist social relations while nationalizing states and subjectivities was the *governmentality* of postcolonial power. National-autochthony was crucial to create and sustain the idea—and the affect—of national self-determination so central to new modes of capital accumulation and state power. In the process, both states and capital were seen as nothing more than rightful possessions of the "nation" of autochthons. The post-WWII period is rife with exhortations from the state, from capital *and* from large segments of the working class itself, to support one's "national capital" against that of "foreigners." Not surprisingly, the virtues of national capital were extolled precisely when new markets were forcibly created and existing ones expanded.

To discuss the governmentality of postcolonialism, I bring together several lines of analysis of the post-WWII period. Assembled by the former colonizers, the formerly colonized who are now "independent," and those currently seeking a national sovereignty of "their own," the nationalist link between identity, territory, and sovereignty fundamentally reorganized the political basis of making claims. Under postcolonialism, being part of the people who were the "people of the place" became absolutely essential. Hence, the National was always already the Native. Non-National others were, by definition, *allochthons* or "people out of place." This distinction was institutionalized through further controls on obtaining national citizenship and on immigration. Indeed, actions taken by states after WWII solidified the link between nation-state sovereignty and citizenship and immigration restrictions. It became unimaginable that states would not—and should not—control the entry of people into their territories or determine who could become their citizens.

I examine a variety of institutional responses that organized postcolonial social relations in order to maintain practices of expropriation and exploitation, while containing demands for decolonization through nationalist demands for sovereignty. *Politically* important was the United Nations and its founding charter declaring that all people who are a People have the right to national self-determination. *Economically*, the institutional arrangements organized by the Bretton Woods agreements positioned national sovereignty as a mechanism of disciplining the workers of the world. *Militarily*, the Cold War normalized the enormous buildup of a military-industrial complex across the emergent Three Worlds through discourses of national security. An examination of the *juridical* territorialization of rights and subjectivities through an ever expanding system of national immigration laws will be examined in chapter 7.

THE UNITED NATIONS

Enshrined in the UN's 26 June 1945 founding charter, national self-determination was institutionalized as the form that liberation from colonialism would be recognized as in the law. Across the world, and across the political spectrum, the power of (mostly new) nation-states was normalized. By 1960, the hegemony of the national form of state power was firmly in place. That year, and in a textbook example of the cart chasing the horse, the UN unanimously approved Resolution 1514, the Declaration on the Granting of Independence to Colonial Countries and Peoples (or the Declaration on Decolonization). In Article 1, the UN declared, "The subjection of peoples to *alien* subjugation, domination and exploitation constitutes a denial of fundamental human rights, is contrary to the Charter of the United Nations and is an impediment to the promotion of world peace and co-operation" (emphasis added). The UN was "convinced that all *peoples* have an inalienable right to complete freedom, the exercise of their sovereignty and the integrity of their national territory" (UN General Assembly 1960; emphasis added). This declaration signaled that as far as the world of nationally sovereign states was concerned, national independence resolved the relations of colonialism.

By making *home rule* the accepted vehicle for decolonization, the problem of colonization was presented, first and foremost, as a problem of foreign rule. Consequently, people's ongoing struggle against "subjugation, domination and exploitation" became separated from the struggle against colonialism. As I discuss later, such practices were only associated with the *continuation* of colonial practices if the rulers and profiteers were not "one's own." On the other hand, the power of nation-states and/or those seen as "national capitalists" to expropriate the wealth of labor and planetary resources contained within national territories was normalized as a sort of nonpower, or perhaps more aptly, as part of the *"Peoples'* power." This too was the work that nationalism did. U Nu, a leading nationalist in the Burmese movement for independence from the British in 1948 and the first prime minister of the new nation-state of Burma (now Myanmar), knew this well. Harking back to its original 1942 purpose, he remarked in 1955 that the UN Charter "is in effect one great mutual security pact" (in Prashad 2007, 48).

Nevertheless, and despite the protestations of nation-states who had shed their colonial status and become possessors of national sovereignty, it was evident from the start that like the UN structure itself, the global system of nation-states would be organized in a profoundly undemocratic and hierarchical manner. Within the UN, the balance of power lay firmly with the five major Allied powers—the United States, the United Kingdom, the Soviet Union, France, and China—who established themselves as permanent, *veto-wielding* members of the UN's new Security Council. Charged with the "maintenance of international peace and security," the Security Council was the only UN body authorized to take action on behalf of *all* of its members and the only body able to enforce its resolutions. Formally the General Assembly was the UN's highest decision-making body, yet it was given no direct powers to formulate international law or even take decisions (except on the internal operation of the UN—for example, its budget). The Security Council alone could make binding decisions on UN member states, including imposing trade sanctions and authorizing military intervention.

None of this prevented the UN (or its individual member nation-states) from issuing a continuous stream of platitudes about equal rights and the equality of all people. The one with perhaps the greatest gulf between rhetoric and reality was the UN's 1948 Universal Declaration of Human Rights, which declared, "Everyone has the right to work, to just and favourable conditions of work and to protection for himself [sic] and his family [and] an existence worthy of human dignity. . . . Everyone has the right to a standard of living adequate for the health and well-being of himself and his family, including food, clothing, housing and medical care." The obvious and wholesale neglect of these "universal human rights" lay in the *power* that nation-states had to recognize and act on them—or not. Their failure to secure these rights was not always simply negligence. As I discuss below, even if they wanted to, individual nation-states were *structurally* incapable of acting to secure such rights within a world where capitalist social relations were evermore global. However, while the "human rights" of many National Citizens were not recognized, respecting such rights for foreigners was *always* out of the question. Nowhere was the inherent contradiction of postcolonialism—the global expansion of the material basis for capitalism and its normalization through nationalism—more clearly organized than in the Bretton Woods institutions implemented under the auspices of the UN.

BRETTON WOODS

The Allied states formulated the economic scaffolding for the Postcolonial New World Order prior to the end of WWII at the UN's Monetary and Financial Conference held between 1 and 22 July 1944 in Bretton Woods, New Hampshire. The U.S. nation-state and the soon-to-be decimated British Empire dominated negotiations. Indeed, the Bretton Woods conference was the culmination of over two years of U.S.-British discussions regarding the postwar reorganization of power. At Bretton Woods, the United States extracted from the British all that Prime Minister Churchill had not fully conceded in the 1941 Atlantic Charter. Tellingly, Britain ratified the Bretton Woods Agreement after war's end in December 1945 as the United States agreed to its Anglo-American loan.

By making the U.S. dollar the central global currency, the Bretton Woods institutions ensured the clear transference of global dominance from the British Empire to the United States. Noting the impending shift in global power from imperial to international, Roosevelt stated at the opening of the Bretton Woods conference that "the economic health of every country is a proper matter of concern to all its neighbors, near and far." Such concern was institutionalized in the two main institutions established in 1944: the International Monetary Fund (IMF) and what came to be known as the World Bank (formed by the International Bank for Reconstruction and Development and the International Development Association). The third main institution, the General Agreement on Tariffs and Trade (GATT), was formed in 1947. Together this troika established a framework of rules and regulations for the central banks of member-states, thus setting the global rules and procedures for international financial and commercial relations. The U.S. goal of opening up new capitalist markets and making participation in these markets an imperative was ensured by making access to international finance and markets dependent on participation in these institutions. Reflecting U.S. domination of this system, member states fixed their exchange rates by tying their currency to the U.S. dollar (which was backed by gold until 1971).

The Bretton Woods institutions were institutionally structured to ensure that they would monitor—and exert influence over—the policies of nominally sovereign states. Although all UN member states were voting members of the Bretton Woods institutions and administered and helped to fund them, power to effect their decisions was highly uneven. The number of voting rights granted to a nation-state was determined by its number of shares in the institution. These shares, in turn, were proportionate to the size of that state's economy. This guaranteed that the most powerful and wealthy states would dominate. The states in what soon came to be known as the "First World" held 80 percent of all votes in the IMF and the World Bank, of which the United States initially held 30 percent.

The World Bank, headquartered in Washington, D.C., provided capital to states in the form of long-term loans or grants for reconstruction and/or development. Its funds were directed primarily at constructing the infrastructure needed for "national development" and establishing an international trading regime between member states. Across the world, hydroelectric dams, mills, smelters, plants, even sports stadiums, were built with World Bank funds. So too were bridges, highways, and air and water ports to transport commodities, militaries, and people. Each World Bank loan or grant was *conditionally* made and was highly skewed to favor the priorities of dominant states seeking greater "free market" measures (B. Baker 2011, 67).

The World Bank required all its member states to first join the IMF, also headquartered in Washington, D.C. The IMF was designed to oversee international monetary and financial systems, monitor international exchange rates, provide conditional, short-term loans of reserve currencies to states facing an international trade deficit, and ensure that each member state's policies provided an attractive return on capital investment. Charged with ensuring that member states' trade deficits would not be so great as to produce a devaluation of currency and a resulting decline in imports, the IMF not only helped ensure a system of international trade but also sheltered private banks in the First World states from drops in the fiscal viability of debtor states. It enforced its mandate through its "country reports," in which member states were evaluated on a number of competitive indexes. Those performing poorly were penalized as high-risk debtors and charged higher interest rates on loans. In these ways, the IMF used its finances to tether debtor-states to a globally operative capitalism.

The purpose of the GATT, headquartered in Geneva, Switzerland, was the promotion and facilitation of "free international trade." Considered the first worldwide multilateral free trade agreement, it rejected the protectionism practiced by numerous states in the interwar years. Instead, its mandate was to "expand the production and exchange of goods," produce a "substantial reduction of tariffs," and secure the "elimination of discriminatory treatment in international commerce" (Iriye and Saunier 2016, 441). The GATT's most important provision was its requirement that each member state confer "most favored nation status" to every other member. This had the effect of excluding (as "discriminatory treatment") the type of tariffs and customs policies followed by empires in the age of imperialism.

The GATT's pressure on states to reduce tariffs, however, was never equally applied. A number of key economic arenas were, for all intents and purposes, omitted or barely affected. This worked to advantage dominant states, particularly in their agricultural markets. Tariffs against agricultural commodities coming from the new national liberation states, which were disproportionately reliant on them, were not lifted. Concomitantly, farmers in dominant states, especially in the United States, where the industrialization of agriculture was most advanced, were massively subsidized. Thus, even the GATT's ineffectualness (i.e., its *retention* of tariffs and state subsidies) worked to benefit dominant states and capital investors in them. Indeed, far from fostering free competition in global trade, the greater purpose of the GATT was to eliminate the special arrangements that imperial states, especially the British, had used to organize the imperial world order. Imperial economies— including in the now mostly *former* colonies—were "freed" so that capital investment and commodities from around the world, especially the United States, could enter. Not unlike the imperial world order it replaced, then, the Bretton Woods institutions organized a world heavily reliant on the expropriation and exploitation of the wealth of resources and labor from what would soon be termed the "Third World." The major difference was that in the Postcolonial New World Order, most of the people there were no longer colonized but were citizens of nationally sovereign states who were also members of Bretton Woods institutions.

PAX AMERICANA

As we have seen, the ascendency of the United States was secured further through its enormous capacity to grant or loan billions of dollars, primarily to Western European states but also to a number of states in the Far East. Like its support for "national self-determination," the grants and loans offered by the United States came with the demand that recipient states lower trade barriers and reduce regulations in order to open markets to U.S. commodities. Additionally, in Europe, where there was strong state support for key industrial sectors such as steel, automotives, and heavy machinery, Marshall Plan grants and other loans were used as capital. The state virtually took up a monopoly position in these industries and provided the main force for economic growth. This was also true in Japan, where the policies enacted through the Ministry of International Trade and Industry (MITI) provided the necessary state support for the resurgence of privately held Japanese companies. Japan received some $2.4 billion in U.S. grants and credits, the largest grants made outside the Marshall Plan. Other nation-states in Asia also received U.S. funds: Taiwan ($1 billion), South Korea ($894 million), the Philippines ($803 million), India ($255 million), Indonesia ($215 million), and Pakistan ($98 million). An additional $282 million went to Israel and $196 million to other states in the Middle East. Together, U.S. power in the Bretton Woods institutions and its financial clout vis-à-vis the Marshall Plan and other large monetary loans inaugurated the *Pax Americana*.

Despite borrowing the terminology of past empires, the Pax Americana was not a new imperial system. It was the U.S. nation-state's dominance of the postcolonial world system of nation-states. As such, U.S. power plays after WWII circulated *through* individual national sovereigns. The formation of

European subsidiaries of U.S. companies is one example of this. In the 1950s and 1960s, subsidiaries were created to comply with rules of the European Economic Community (EEC), formed in 1957. Its member states organized a common, tariff-free market for all companies operating within its jurisdiction while imposing tariffs on imports from non-EEC states. Initially, U.S. firms with European subsidiaries were the main beneficiaries. Journalist Jean-Jacques Servan-Schreiber (1971, 35), noted, "Already, in the ninth year of the Common Market, this European market is basically American in organization." With their worldwide supply chains and transportation facilities, imports of manufactured components from the United States, greater financial resources, growing reach in international markets, and deposits of profits and dividends to mostly U.S.-based shareholders, U.S. firms in Europe enhanced the global power of capital headquartered in the United States and the U.S. nation-state supporting them.

In a world of nation-states, the United States did not have to "colonize" Europe to enhance its global power and reach. Unlike imperial states, the United States did not territorially incorporate European territories into itself, claim sovereignty over them, or incorporate people there as its subjects. In contrast to imperial assertions of sovereign control over territories and people, after WWII, Europe was left as a collection of separate and sovereign states. Indeed, this was preferable. The United States thus ruled *through* European states, not *over* them. Thus, while some view Pax Americana as a new imperial formation, the power wielded by the United States was firmly based on the *globalization of national sovereignty*.

At the same time, no nationally sovereign state was "independent" of the others. Entering the global system established by Bretton Woods required states to observe its conditions. Failure to do so was likely to result in losing access to international finance and government aid, as well as possible trade and other sanctions that could stop short any efforts at "independence." John Maynard Keynes, a main architect of the Bretton Woods regime, understood this well. In discussing his plans for a Clearing Union (CU) with European Allies in February 1943, he noted that member states' "readiness to accept super-national arrangements" was an essential feature of the new system (Keynes 1971, 25:89). However, far from forming a sort of proto–world government, as its critics bombastically called it, such arrangements would very much operate *through* member states.

The Bretton Woods institutions, along with the billions in U.S. international grants and loans, increased the flow of capital from the United States to the rest of the world, leading to the amassing of enormous profits by capital headquartered in the United States. International trade doubled during the 1950s and then more than doubled again in the 1960s. By 1960, there was approximately $66 billion worth of "foreign direct investment" (FDI),[5] most of it concentrated in raw materials extraction and resource-based manufacturing. By the early 1970s, when some Bretton Woods arrangements were being restructured to address challenges in postwar regimes of regulation (Aglietta 1979), the global amount of FDI had grown to $213 billion. Whereas from 1870 to 1914, most FDI flowed from the United Kingdom and went to both British imperial colonies or to the United States, between 1945 and 1960, the United States became the main source—about 85 percent—of all new FDI, with most of it going to member states of the Organization for European Economic Co-operation (OEEC, itself a creation of the Marshall Plan). In the 1950s, only 20 percent of total U.S. FDI went to the nation-states formed from the former colonies, and this was overwhelmingly invested in resource extraction. A gradual increase in FDI channeled to manufacturing in these states occurred during the 1960s, the very early period of the neoliberal turn in state policy.

Within the United States, the Pax Americana marked the emergence of the so-called American Dream. After WWII, the consumptive capacity of some parts of the working class in the United States grew enormously. For them, the postwar tripartite compromise between state, capital, and labor unions ushered in a sense of great and never-ending prosperity, predominantly for those seeing themselves as White National-Natives. Trade union membership in the United States peaked in the 1950s, and labor unions won long-term and relatively lucrative contracts for their members (who remained largely White and male). The GDP of the United States more than doubled in the twenty years after WWII, and the number of large shopping centers, each containing numerous stores, grew exponentially: from eight at the end of WWII to 3,840 by 1960.

The legitimacy of the national form of state power grew alongside the power of the United States over the rest of the planet. In some senses, the power that the United States wielded in the Postcolonial New World Order was seen as *resulting* from its nationalized sovereignty. The hegemony of the nation-state is reflected in the commonplace assertion that the relative lack of power of other nation-states, especially, but not only, in the former colonies, was due to their not having *enough* national sovereignty. Yet the power of the United States was simultaneously portrayed as a new form of imperialism. This was a sentiment continuously expressed by the leaders of the USSR.

Notably, while the Soviet Union participated in the initial planning of the Bretton Woods institutions, it withdrew in 1947. The USSR thus rejected

Marshall Plan aid and prevented its allied states in Eastern Europe from accepting those funds. The Soviets well understood that the conditions attached to U.S. grants or loans, as well as the financial credit offered by the IMF or World Bank, would be conditional upon the USSR extending its "economic cooperation" with the United States and Western European states. Lenders would also have the power to scrutinize the USSR's financial situation and influence its policies. The Soviets realized that acceptance of either would lead to the exercise of U.S. control over the policies of the USSR and over the newly nationalized states in the Eastern Bloc, its own orbit of influence.

Instead, the USSR established a financial system and avenues for international trade that it dominated. By 1947 the Soviet Union had constructed its Molotov Plan. What Bretton Woods and the Marshall Plan did for U.S. hegemony, the Molotov Plan did to secure Soviet control over new nation-states in the Eastern Bloc. In one example, the USSR gave Poland the equivalent of $450 million in aid, large supplies of industrial equipment, assistance in establishing industrial production facilities, and 200,000 tons of grain after it refused Marshall Plan grants. The USSR and Poland also entered into a five-year trade agreement. Other states in the emergent Eastern Bloc quickly followed the Polish example. Credit, aid, trade, and political influence circulated between the USSR and these states. By 1949 they formed the USSR-dominated Council for Mutual Economic Assistance (or COMECON). Yugoslavia under Josip Tito was the sole exception in rejecting the Soviet "alternative." However, Yugoslavia showed that no state could remain independent from one or the other main international creditor: in 1949, it requested and received U.S. aid.

The Soviet Union's refusal to join the Bretton Woods institutions or receive Marshall Plan funds was a crucial element in the precipitation of the Cold War between the United States and the USSR. In his 1947 speech to the UN, the Soviet deputy foreign minister, Andrei Vyshinsky, accused the United States of imposing its will on "independent" states through promises of financial and other economic resources. In an escalating rhetoric of stark binaries, the United States labeled the Soviet Union a "totalitarian" state and itself the leader of the "Free World" ("free" being the moniker attached to the expanding international trade and capitalist markets the U.S. championed), while the USSR labeled the United States a "fascizing" power and positioned itself as the champion of the colonized and the proletariat.

The psychologized duality of a "neurotic" USSR and a United States overcome by "war psychosis" concealed the ways in which the Cold War expanded both states' control across the world as well as within their own territories. While the U.S.-led Western Bloc faced tense internal dynamics among its allies (most notably a bristling Great Britain undergoing the process of losing its empire and becoming a nation-state), the tensions within the Eastern Bloc were no less significant. This was aptly demonstrated by the 1948 expulsion of Tito's Yugoslavia from Cominform (the Information Bureau of the Communist and Workers' Parties) and the USSR's involvement in a coup d'état in Czechoslovakia in 1948. The United States, meanwhile, intervened to severely weaken communist or socialist parties across the world.

THE COLD WAR ESTABLISHMENT

With its bifurcated poles of influence centered in Washington and Moscow, the Cold War was the dominant *military* framework for normalizing the political and economic contours of the Postcolonial New World Order. Intimations of the Cold War were in place even before the end of WWII. At the end of the February 1945 Yalta Conference, Churchill declared, "The Soviet Union has become a danger to the free world." By the July 1945 Potsdam Conference, the Allies openly disagreed about a number of issues: the division of Germany, the size of its postwar reparations, and Soviet policy in Eastern Europe. At the same time, the U.S. delegation, intent on making the UN the key postwar international institution, tried to convince the Soviets to join it. Joseph Stalin agreed once it was clear that as a permanent member of the UN Security Council, the USSR would receive veto power over all UN actions.

With the end of WWII, the victorious Allied states separated into two blocs, each incorporating some of the former Axis states' territories. The Western Bloc was comprised of the United States, the other member states of the North Atlantic Treaty Organization (NATO, established in 1949),[4] and Japan, which the United States occupied from 1945 until 1952. The Eastern Bloc emerged by 1955 as the Warsaw Pact and was comprised of the USSR and Central and Eastern European states.[5] In classic Manichean manner, and playing to the fears fostered during WWII, each side portrayed the other as a threat to world peace and order.

The first discursive shots in the Cold War came in the form of two telegrams that established the tenor of the conflict for decades afterward. The first was sent by George Kennan, the U.S. chargé d'affaires in Moscow (and, later, ambassador to the Soviet Union), to James Byrnes, U.S. secretary of state, on 22 February 1946. The second was sent by Nikolai Novikov, the Soviet ambassador to the United States, to the leadership of the USSR on 27 September 1946. Kennan's "long telegram" was precipitated by the Soviet's refusal to join the Bretton Woods institutions. In it, he expressed the necessity of preventing the expansion of the USSR's area of influence by military, economic, and ideological means.

Kennan asserted that the USSR was *incapable* of envisioning a "permanent peaceful coexistence" with the Western Bloc (Kennan [1946] 1993, 17). Employing a racialized, pseudopsychological discourse, Kennan characterized leaders of the USSR as having an outlook that, "at bottom" was a "neurotic view of world affairs" that, in turn, contributed to an "atmosphere of oriental secretiveness and conspiracy" and represented a "traditional and instinctive Russian sense of insecurity" (20, 22). The result, Kennan argued, was that "they have learned to seek security only in patient but deadly struggle for total destruction of rival power, never in compacts and compromises with it" (22). The United States, he argued, had "here a political force committed fanatically to the belief that with us there can be no permanent *modus vivendi*, that it is desirable and necessary that the internal harmony of our society be disrupted, our traditional way of life be destroyed, the international authority of our state be broken, if Soviet power is to be secure" (28). Stating that the USSR was "impervious to logic of reason," Kennan insisted that it was, nonetheless, "highly sensitive to logic of force." However, U.S. "resistance" to USSR fanaticism, he argued, could, "if situations are properly handled," be handled with "no prestige-engaging showdowns" (29).

Kennan's telegram provided the subsequent basis for the Truman Doctrine of "containment." Kennan argued that it was necessary for the United States to act as the "world's policeman"; to fatally weaken communist parties as well as "labor, youth and women's organizations" around the world, but especially the "international labor movement"; to destabilize any state whose policies would strengthen the Soviet position; and to support "anticommunist" regimes regardless of their actions (Kennan [1946] 1993, 28, 25–26). Kennan was particularly concerned about the Soviets' "internationalism," even as it was clear that the USSR had abandoned such a position in the 1920s in favor of Stalin's nationalist, "socialism in one country" approach. Regardless, Kennan (22) argued that the Soviet Union's greatest strength was its "new guise" of "international Marxism, with its honeyed promises to a desperate and war torn outside world," particularly "colonial areas and backward or dependent peoples." In this struggle, Kennan (27) argued, "no holds will be barred" by the Soviets: "Mistakes and weaknesses of western colonial administration will be mercilessly exposed and exploited. Liberal opinion in Western countries will be mobilized to weaken colonial policies. Resentment among dependent peoples will be stimulated," and they will be "encouraged to seek independence of Western Powers." For these reasons, in the international arena, Kennan argued that the United States not concede ground to the Soviets but come out forcefully as the *champion of national self-determination.*

At the same time, Kennan insisted that the United States also needed to seek and expose "communist sympathizers" *within* the Western Bloc, since the USSR wanted to destroy the United States (and "the West" in general), by setting "poor . . . against rich, black against white, young against old, newcomers against established residents, etc." Any effort within the United States "to disrupt national self-confidence, to hamstring measures of national defense, to increase social and industrial unrest, to stimulate all forms of disunity," including "grievances, whether economic or racial," Kennan argued, weakened the United States (Kennan [1946] 1993, 27). To fight communism, he argued, was to protect U.S. "national security." For the United States, the USSR and communism were synonymous. This went no small way in shoring up the idea that the USSR was actually communist.

Nikolai Novikov articulated the Soviet side of the growing Manichean divide. In his telegram, he summarized the reorganization of post-WWII power by stating, "The political foundations of the British Empire . . . [are] appreciably shaken" as "crises [arise], for example, in India, Palestine, and Egypt," and the "economic devastation" of "all of the countries of Europe and Asia . . . [provides] American monopolistic capital with prospects for enormous shipments of goods and the importation of capital into these countries—a circumstance that would permit it to infiltrate their national economies" (Novikov [1946] 1991, 528). Novikov correctly concluded, "Such a development would mean a serious strengthening of the economic position of the United States in the whole world and would be [a] stage on the road to world domination by the United States. . . . This is the real meaning of the many statements by President Truman and other representatives of American ruling circles: that the United States has the right to lead the world" (529).

Noting the tension between the United States and Great Britain in the "Near East and the Mediterranean Sea," Novikov ([1946] 1991, 536) maintained that "the United States . . . is not interested in providing assistance and support to the British Empire in this vulnerable point, but rather in its own more thorough penetration of [these areas], to which the United States is attracted by the area's natural resources, primarily oil." In particular, he pointed out that "the American interest in Palestine, outwardly expressed as sympathy for the Zionist cause" such as its "demand that 100,000 Jews from Europe be permitted to enter Palestine, actually only signifies American capital wishes to interfere in Palestinian affairs and thus penetrate the economy" (531).

In response, Novikov positioned the USSR as saving the world from "U.S. imperialism." Presciently predicting that the emerging U.S. policy of "containing communism" would result in the violent overthrow of elected governments around the world, he framed U.S. efforts as "limiting or dislodging the influence of the Soviet Union from neighboring countries" in order to put into place "new governments that would obediently carry out a policy dictated from the United States" (Novikov [1946] 1991, 536). In contrast, he portrayed the USSR's *own* territorial and geopolitical expansion as a "democratic reconstruction" and tried to present the USSR as an alternative beacon of democracy and anticapitalism (532).

Both the United States and the USSR thus portrayed themselves as reluctant but willing warriors for liberty, equality, democracy, and international peace. Shortly after war's end, the United States shifted from holding diplomatic relations with the Soviet Union to maintaining a Cold War footing. In the summer of 1947, key administrative vehicles for the execution of the Cold War were created by the U.S. National Security Act: a unified Department of Defense, the Central Intelligence Agency (CIA, the first peacetime intelligence agency in the United States), and the National Security Council.

In 1947, Stalin's USSR established the Information Bureau of the Communist and Workers' Parties (or the Communist Information Bureau, Cominform). The first official forum of the international communist movement since the 1943 dissolution of the Comintern, Cominform coordinated policies and actions between the various Soviet-controlled communist parties to address the changed circumstances brought about by the creation of the Eastern Bloc. Funds channeled through the Council for Mutual Economic Assistance (COMECON), bound the Soviet Socialist Republics as well as Eastern Bloc states to the USSR's planned "state capitalist" economy (Goldman 1935; Avrich 1973).[6] A series of bilateral trade agreements between COMECON states reoriented trade patterns to benefit those who ruled the USSR. From 1946 to 1947, the USSR directly annexed several Eastern European states as nominally sovereign Soviet Socialist republics, including eastern Poland, eastern Finland, eastern Romania, and Latvia, Estonia, and Lithuania (which had been brought into the Soviet sphere of influence under the 1939 Molotov-Ribbentrop Pact between the USSR and Nazi Germany). Others, such as East Germany, Bulgaria, Hungary, Czechoslovakia, and Albania, became satellite states firmly in the orbit of the USSR.

However, as the United States brutally crushed communists and their supporters around the world (or assisted allied regimes in doing so), the USSR steadfastly crushed those considered to be "anticommunist." Not unlike the

U.S. label of "un-American," "anticommunist" was a political label used to discredit anyone who disagreed with the policies or direction of the Soviet state. From torturous gulags within USSR territory, the execution of rivals for leadership of the state or party, or the forced removal of governments that fell out of favor, the leadership of the Soviet Union also violently maintained its own power. The United States and the USSR thus contained not only each other but also any revolutionary forces within their states or across the world offering alternatives to the Postcolonial New World Order. Both did so in the name of "national security."

This was evident in the first deadly conflagration of the Cold War, which took place in response to the Greek Civil War (1946–1949). In a speech to Congress on 12 March 1947, Truman argued that "the foreign policy and the national security of this country" was dependent on events unfolding in Greece. He argued that the United States was "threatened by the terrorist activities of several thousand armed men, led by communists" in Greece. The U.S. decision to intervene on the side of the right-wing, anticommunist Greek government violently marked the end of the WWII alliance between the United States and the USSR.

U.S. support for the Greek government also signaled the decline of the power and influence of the British Empire. While the British had stopped the National Liberation Front (effectively, the Greek Communist Party) from taking Athens in 1944, by late 1946 the British could neither ensure the same outcome nor continue to prop up the right-wing Greek government. The British openly turned to the United States, thus explicitly acknowledging U.S. global hegemony for the first time. The United States, with bipartisan approval in Congress, committed $400 million to support the right-wing Greek government in the civil war. Although Yugoslavia (a WWII ally of Greece against Nazi occupation), Bulgaria, and Albania supported the Greek Communist Party, Stalin's USSR did not, thus precipitating the political fallout between Yugoslavia's Tito and Stalin. Unsurprisingly, given the greatly uneven financial and material support given by the United States to the anticommunists—and denied by the Eastern Bloc—the right wing in Greece won. The Cold War lurched from one crisis to another.

In September 1949, as the Communist People's Liberation Army (Red Army) gained control over mainland China and the USSR exploded its first atomic bomb, the Cold War heated up considerably. In 1950, war broke out on the Korean peninsula. The peninsula, which had been part of the Chinese Empire until the late nineteenth century and a formal Japanese colony from 1910 until the empire's collapse in 1945, was partitioned into a North Korea (controlled by the Soviets) and a South Korea (controlled by the United States) at the end of WWII. This arrangement fell apart when North Korea, supported by the USSR and the People's Republic of China (PRC), attempted to take over South Korean territory. The UN Security Council—which the Soviet Union was then boycotting and which did not recognize the PRC until 1971—formed and dispatched a UN military force, 88 percent of which were U.S. troops. The loss of life in the three-year war was extensive: approximately 1.2 million people were killed on all sides (Lacina and Gleditsch 2005).

Hardly any part of the world was spared the violence of the Cold War. A few notable examples include the opening in Panama of the U.S. Army School of the Americas in 1946, which signaled that the United States considered Latin America a part of its "sphere of influence"[7]; CIA involvement in the defeat of popular communist parties in the Italian and French elections of 1947; the 1954 U.S.-backed coup d'état in Guatemala that forcibly removed President Jacobo Arbenz and installed Carlos Castillo Armas; the 1954 CIA overthrow of the elected Iranian government of Premier Mohammed Mosaddeq and his replacement with Shah Mohammad Reza Pahlavi; the U.S. war in Vietnam, which began in the 1950s as the United States began to fund French troops in an effort to restrict the expansion of communist forces in the region; the Soviet invasion of Hungary in late 1956; the construction of the Berlin Wall in 1961; the Cuban Missile Crisis in 1962; the U.S.-supported 1964 armed overthrow of Brazil's President João Goulart and the establishment of a military dictatorship, which lasted until 1985; the Soviet occupation of Czechoslovakia in 1968; the 1973 Arab-Israeli war; and USSR-U.S. interventions in Afghanistan from the 1970s. All of these and many more violent conflicts were undertaken as proxy wars between the United States and the Soviet Union. A dominant characteristic of the Cold War was the constant and real threat of nuclear annihilation, as each side amassed and justified an enormous nuclear arsenal through the doctrine of mutually assured destruction (MAD).

Despite all of these interventions (military, financial, cultural, and otherwise) across large parts of the world and affecting billions of people, *neither* the Western nor the Eastern Bloc was imperial in form or character. These blocs were instead made up of a growing number of "independent" nation-states. While many of the new nation-states only had nominal independence, nonetheless, their existence *as nation-states* was important for the exercise of postcolonial power. Even the Soviet socialist republics depended upon their nominal and national sovereignty to normalize their subordination to Moscow.[8] Postcolonialism, thus, *deployed* the power of nation-states to maintain the global dominance of both the United States and the USSR.

The national character of the Postcolonial New World Order was further demonstrated by the establishment of a third bloc comprised of what Vijay Prashad (2007) calls the "national liberation states." Those involved in the creation of the Non-Aligned Movement (NAM) attempted to intervene in international politics by stating their unwillingness to be buffeted by the Cold War bipolarity. Led by former imperial colonies transformed into independent nation-states, the NAM sought a "third way." It was French demographer and public intellectual Alfred Sauvy who first used the term *Third World* in reference to the NAM nation-states (in Keyfitz 1990). Tellingly, his 1952 usage referenced the Third Estate, a term coined by the Abbé Emmanuel Joseph Sieyès, an early French bourgeois nationalist, who, in challenging the First Estate of the clergy or the Second Estate of aristocratic nobles in the late eighteenth century, defined the true "French nation" as comprised of its Third Estate, or "common people" (see Foucault 2003). Sauvy, paraphrasing Sieyès, wrote, "This third world, ignored, exploited, despised like the third estate, also wants to be something" (in Keyfitz 1990). The attachment of the class politics evident in ideas of a Third Estate to ideas of "Third World liberation" confused—and conflated—demands for national sovereignty with the working-class demand for the end of exploitation. Referring to "national liberation" as an abolition of slavery of sorts, replete with discourses of "casting off of the shackles," represented all colonized Natives as equivalent to a *class* of exploited people. The presentation of "liberated nations" as the emancipated subject of history, therefore, was the particular Third World style of producing the "national community" as a *cross-class* one. With their Third World project, the NAM states further solidified the link that nationalist parties had made between anticolonialism and nationalism.

Third World nation-states, however, also wanted to be powerful players on an international stage. They understood that to do so, they must join together in what Prashad (2007) calls a "Third World project." The Third World's first significant meeting was in Bandung, Indonesia, in 1955. For participating heads of nation-states, Bandung was a meeting of national sovereigns wishing to exercise their newfound independence by refusing to be drawn into either the Western or Eastern Bloc. Instead, they wanted to assess the advantages that either—or neither—side might provide them. India's first prime minister, Jawaharlal Nehru; Indonesia's first president, Sukarno; Egypt's second president, Gamal Abdel Nasser; Ghana's first president, Kwame Nkrumah; and Yugoslavia's first president, Josip Broz Tito, were the unofficial leaders of the NAM. Hosted in Bandung by Sukarno, the NAM accepted the Five Principles formulated by Nehru as its political basis. These called for mutual respect for each other's territorial integrity and sovereignty; mutual nonaggression; mutual noninterference in domestic affairs; equality and mutual benefit; and peaceful coexistence. Central to all of these principles of national sovereignty was the commitment to remain neutral in the Cold War.

Despite its "third way," the members of the NAM were not, however, in fundamental disagreement with the Postcolonial New World Order. Instead, their protest focused on the obviously subordinate position of most national liberation states in the new international arrangement of power. Their policy formulations, thus, were largely efforts to even the postcolonial playing field by reorganizing various elements of the dominant Bretton Woods system. While the NAM was an international body, their key policy formulations were distinctively national. A key plank of their project was support for "their" national capitalists against "foreign" ones. Their main concern was that national liberation be profitable to (a select few of the) National capitalists (Chatterjee 2004).

The NAM states' idea of economic justice was threefold. First, they rejected the U.S. demand for reduced trade barriers for its exports to the Third World. Instead, they wanted a reduction of barriers to the entry of commodities from the Third World to the First World and tariffs on products imported from the First World. These were part of the effort to erect a system designed to strengthen the Third World "national bourgeoisie" and allow it to be both nationally and globally competitive. Second, the NAM states demanded greater access to the postcolonial finance system. They wanted access to Marshall Plan–like grants and the ability to repay bank loans in their new national currencies, instead of the "hard currency" of the U.S. dollar. Finally, the NAM states wanted to develop an institutional framework for international trade, such as cartels of primary commodities that they hoped would create a "new international economic order" more attune to their demands.[9]

These measures, supposedly taken to "raise the standard of living of the masses," were the NAM's particular version of the cross-class trickle-down theory of wealth redistribution (see Prebisch 1962, 1). Policies benefiting "national capitalists" would supposedly enrich "national workers" (the very people without whom anticolonial struggles would not have been won). The NAM states failed, of course, and did so for very predictable reasons. Not only did the Postcolonial New World Order rather easily absorb capitalists in the Third World while weakening the power of workers there, but long before Bandung—indeed, long before "independence"—many national liberation leaders, while fighting imperialists, also fought communists who held a view of liberation that called for the abolition of class rule. Once in control of newly sovereign nation-states, these leaders, including the ones who initiated the Bandung meetings, did not support a transformation of the social relations of capital. Instead, they tended to support the rural, landed gentry; merchants; and nascent bourgeoisie in their territories—*always at the expense of the direct producers* (Prashad 2007).

Moreover, by the time of Bandung, six of the nation-states meeting there had already joined various international bodies with the former imperial powers: Pakistan, the Philippines, and Thailand joined the 1954 South East Asian Treaty Organization with the United States, the United Kingdom, France, Australia, and New Zealand, while Turkey, Iran, Iraq, and Pakistan joined the 1954 Central Treaty Organization with the United States and the United Kingdom. Moreover, like the United States and the USSR, most Third World nation-states used government funds (often borrowed at exorbitant interest rates) to support national military-industrial complexes to protect their national security. Some of this had to do with defending their territories from attacks by other nation-states. However, most national liberation states primarily used their costly militaries within their own borders and against those they considered "internal" threats to national security, most notably communists. For these reasons—and more that I discuss in chapter 6—the Third World project did not offer people living in the national liberation states a way out of either the Cold War or the social relations established by the Postcolonial New World Order. NAM states were therefore crucial to the normalization of postcolonial power. Indeed, by accepting the very basis of postcoloniality, even while lobbying for a redistribution of the world's wealth into the pockets of the "national bourgeoisie," "national liberation" seemed little, if anything, like the anticolonialism that so many had worked so hard to realize.

CONCLUSION

After WWII, the Postcolonial New World Order of nation-states and their international bodies provided the institutional structures (and force of coercive action) for how global capitalism would operate after the end of empires. The UN channeled anticolonialism into postcolonialism by normalizing the organization of political communities as nationally sovereign states. The Bretton Woods institutions worked through nation-states' power to foster the conditions for capitalist profits, especially evident in the idea of the "national bourgeoisie." Thus, while the Postcolonial New World Order was based on the establishment of putatively sovereign nation-states, it remained both a global and a deeply hierarchical system. Indeed, it was organized in such a way as to ensure the *further* globalization of capitalist social relations. Each nation-state offered (private or state) capital the best conditions for profitability while erecting the postcolonial architecture of global competition. Each nation-state (or set of nation-states in the case of cartels or customs unions) competed against one another in capitalist markets. Indeed, what Susanne Soederberg (2005) has called the "competition state" was there from the start of postcolonialism.

Across all political stripes and across the First, Second, and Third Worlds, postcoloniality was fundamentally structured by the Cold War's consolidation of the discourse of national security. Importantly, the Cold War was organized not as competing *empires* maneuvering for expanded territories (and the wealth of the people on them), but as *three international alliances,* each claiming to respect and safeguard the sovereignty of nation-states. In the overblown rhetoric of the First, Second, and Third Worlds, respectively, President Truman famously described the Western Bloc as the protectors of the "free world" and promoters of "national self-determination"; the leaders of the USSR, always in a disadvantageous position over the United States, described themselves as the anti-imperialist protectors of "national Peoples"; and Third World leaders cloaked themselves in the mantle of "national liberation." Each would act on the words of Truman (1947) that the nation-state would protect itself from either "armed minorities" within or from "outside pressures." At the heart of the Postcolonial New World Order and its Cold War was the battle for trade, profit, and the aggrandizement of nation-state power. Such relationships only intensified once the Postcolonial New World Order was fully consolidated by the 1960s.

This is evident in postcolonial schemes of "development" in the Third World, the response to the "crisis of capitalism" in the mid to late 1960s, and the crisis of the legitimacy of nation-states that followed in the 1970s. In the absence of political discourses that could compete with the enormous power of nationalism, citizenship and immigration controls *hardened* with the political maturation of the neoliberal turn in state policies in the early 1980s. Thus, in the Postcolonial New World Order of nation-states, it was a *neocolonialism* and a *neoimperialism* that were pointed to as the cause of much misery and greater immiseration. Each of these processes shored up the autochthonous return to the Native as the main claimant of National place and the Migrant not only as a threat to national security but also, now, as a *colonizer.* I discuss each of these in turn in chapter 6.

6

DEVELOPING
THE POSTCOLONIAL
NEW WORLD ORDER

You can cuss out colonialism, imperialism, and all other kinds of ism,
but it's hard for you to cuss that dollarism.
When they drop those dollars on you, your soul goes.

—Malcolm X, 1965

The expansion of both state power and capitalism with the rise of the Post-colonial New World Order showed that "national self-determination" did not lead to decolonization—not if decolonization meant ending practices of ex-propriation and exploitation for all dispossessed and displaced people. With the end of empires and the nationalization of state sovereignty came new land grabs, new methods for mobilizing and disciplining labor in the service of capital, and new means of separating people. With nation-state rule, national borders were made and marked, citizenship and immigration controls were enacted and enforced, and people's subjectivities were further territorialized.

In this chapter, I discuss the postcolonial agreement on the need for "development"—defined both by individual nation-states and international governing bodies as a high rate of growth and the obtainment of minimum per capita GNP (gross national product). By the mid-1950s, the discourse of "fighting underdevelopment" through financial assistance, global commodi-ties trade, export of advanced technologies, transportation infrastructures, and more became a central part of how postcolonial rule was normalized in and across the First, Second, and Third Worlds. The United States saw de-velopment as the importation of U.S. manufactured goods and services and the further opening up of the world to capital investors it supported. The USSR saw it as a key mechanism to advance its own industrialization. The Non-Aligned Movement (NAM), on the other hand, pursued import substitution programs and tried to diversify exports away from low value-added raw resources to encourage industrial production within its member states. Each saw development as crucial for its "national security."

Developmentalism, with its pseudopsychological and racist discourse of "modernization," articulated with the technologies of postcolonial rule and shaped the political character of the postcolonial world of nation-states (see Shils 1955; Bell 1960). Indeed, developmentalism was a significant part of how the Cold War was fought. In 1951, U.S. Undersecretary of State James Webb sent a memo entitled "U.S. Policies and Programs in the Economic Field Which May Affect the War Potential of the Soviet Bloc" in which he stated that *ensuring* development was a key plank of the United States' "defense" of the "free world" (see Webb 1951). In it, he made it clear that the United States could also deploy its power to *prevent* development by blockading the movement of commodities and technologies to its enemies—as it did to the Eastern Bloc, Communist China, Manchuria, and North Korea. The USSR, meanwhile, pursued many of the same techniques. Both within the Eastern Bloc as well as outside of it, the Soviets used promises of development assistance—or its abrupt end—to influence policies in other nation-states.

As development was the rubric under which a significant amount of international financial capital moved, nation-states worked to maneuver its flow to their advantage. For example, the final communiqué of the Bandung conference, in perfect awareness of how development—and its denial—was a weapon of the strong, opened with a pledge of "economic cooperation" and the pursuit of "economic development," including "the investment of foreign capital." However, the communiqué was necessarily sensitive to how anticolonialism had become equated with "national liberation" by participating nation-states, and its authors wanted to avoid equating "foreign capital" with "foreign rule." Thus, the communiqué added that such investments would be "on the basis of mutual interest and respect for national sovereignty" (Asian-African Conference 1955, 94).

POSTCOLONIAL SCHEMES FOR DEVELOPMENT

The Third World was the main target for development, both for the obvious reasons and for the less obvious ones. Comprised mostly of the former colonies of imperial states, it had, in some cases for centuries, been incorporated into global capitalism as a producer of wealth and power for imperial rulers and capitalist investors in the metropoles. Yet, in British India, for example, just as the British Empire was placing land, food, and shelter (and much else) into capitalist markets, it argued that limiting most colonized Natives' access to credit or, increasingly, the capitalist wage was tantamount to "protecting" villagers and agricultural workers (Catanach 1970). Indeed, through the governmentality of indirect-rule colonialism from the mid-nineteenth century on, imperialism held the colonized in a position of subordinated *stasis* while concealing the very active *disruptions* that imperialism organized. It was not accidental that such practices had the effect of limiting competition from Natives and ensuring the dominance of European capitalists. Moreover, by defining modernity as the culture of the colonizers and tradition as the culture of Indigenous-Natives, indirect-rule colonialism laid the groundwork for the postcolonial discourse of "modernization."

With their "independence" from imperial states, most heads of national liberation states *demanded* development to gain some advantage from global capitalist markets. However, it is safe to say that most people who fought colonization did not fight for new and better terms for incorporation into global capitalism. Upon independence, the vast majority of new Nationals in the Third World relied directly on the land for their livelihoods (farmed land, forests, mountain pastures, swamps, rivers, oceans, and more). Most engaged in anticolonial movements for guaranteed access to land, an end to hunger and disease, and a life of dignity and peace. In other words, they fought for liberation from expropriation and exploitation. A smaller number of people incorporated into the waged proletariat fought for fairer wages and working conditions, often demanding that these be on par with wages in the metropoles of the same empire (see Cooper 1996). A much smaller number fought for capitalist development. But it was this last group that dominated national liberation states. For them, developing "national capitalists" was central to this strategy.

Though the discourse on development was part of an earlier imperial discourse, its particular *postcolonial* character was twofold. First, development was now said to be necessary for the *reversal* of the conditions of colonialism. Development thus became seen as an essential part of *home rule*. Second, and relatedly, developmentalism promised to turn capital into a tool for national self-determination. Developmentalism allowed the national liberation states to argue that their primary goal was to sustain effective economic demand for industrial expansion and ensure investors' profits. Indeed, Vijay Prashad (2007, 86) argues that national liberation states relied on the development of capitalist markets (especially in food, land, energy, and labor) for their construction of an overarching national identity.

Such an identity was, of course, a binary one. The promotion of national development in the Third World was predicated on the national autochthonous assumption that the very raison d'être of nation-states was to end foreign dependency and become reliant on national capitalists and national workers' production of industrial manufacturing and consumer goods, all to cohere the nation. Consequently, developmentalism strengthened the fundamental postcolonial binary of National and Foreigner. Expropriation and exploitation were now equated with imperialism and foreign rulers, while the same practices undertaken by nation-states and national rulers were normalized as nothing more than "developing" the nation. The discursive practice of development thus reframed decolonization itself as nothing less than a process of *economic autochthonization* of both capital and the proletariat. The idea that what was good for national capital was good for all Nationals helped to *depoliticize* newly independent nation-states' emphasis on—and naturalization of—capitalist markets.

The majority who remained impoverished were portrayed as being poor *because* they were "traditional" (Bell 1960). Those who remained unconvinced by developmentalism were chastised for trying to keep the nation in the "Stone Age." In one example, one of the shining lights of NAM, India's Prime Minister Nehru, rejected a 1948 resolution to adopt a socialist economy proposed by a parliamentary opposition member, Kazi Syed Karimuddin. Responding to Karimuddin's challenge, Nehru stated that it was not socialism but science and technology that would provide the "basis of all future growth" in India (in D'Souza 2003, 104). That same year, Nehru put science and technology into action by laying the first slab of concrete for the Hirakud Dam, whose production of hydroelectric power for nearby factories would flood the farm lands that over 100,000 villagers relied upon and lead to their dispossession and displacement. Speaking to some of the affected villagers just one year after "independence," Nehru blithely told them, "If you are to suffer, you should suffer in the interest of the country" (in Marino 2012).

Developmentalism made it possible to destroy many people's nonmarket and nonindustrial uses of land and water, while declaring that it was all for the national good. As Edward Said (1993, 290) notes, armed with a "truly amazing conceptual arsenal—theories of economic phases, social types, traditional societies, systems transfers, pacification, social mobilization, and so on," developmentalism enabled states to mobilize other ideas such as "productivity" and "economic growth" in their efforts to attenuate social conflict. In the Post-colonial New World Order, it was the nation-state that would improve people by *intensifying* the flooding, damming, mining, polluting, monocropping, or razing of land for the development of public and/or private enterprises. Such acts of developmentalism so came to define the Third World project that, as Rodric Braithwaite (2012, 33) notes, "the term 'Third World' quickly lost its political meaning for most observers" and simply became synonymous with that part of the world defined as "underdeveloped."

While developmentalism had attained hegemonic status, across the First, Second, and Third Worlds, there were serious disagreements on how development should proceed. In 1955, the NAM called on the United Nations (UN) to implement a Special UN Fund for Economic Development (SUNFED) and an International Finance Corporation, both designed as a sort of Marshall Plan for developing the Third World. Both were roundly rejected, largely because the United States refused to agree to the funding. This is not to say that the United States discouraged development—far from it. The United States argued that development should take place primarily through private capital investment or through loans made on standard banking terms by either the International Bank for Reconstruction and Development (IBRD) or the American Export-Import Bank. Not coincidentally, both were designed to finance sales of U.S. exports. The U.S. view largely dominated. Developmentalism became the main "aid" to the Third World. The terms were always set by those with capital, including states in each of the Three Worlds, but especially the First and Second Worlds, as well as international bodies.

Yet though there were significant differences in how to achieve development, each based on which states and which capitalists would benefit, the flow of investment (state and/or private) was central to the postcolonial relationship between *all* nation-states and capital. This is evident in the UN's First Development Decade, begun in 1960. The decade began with the independence of seventeen former colonies in Africa, resulting in a hundred UN member states (from fifty-one in 1945). President John F. Kennedy, then keen to control UN activities, proposed and launched the Development Decade at the UN in September 1961. There he asserted that development would work to "lessen the gap between developed and underdeveloped countries, to speed up the processes of modernization, and to release the majority of mankind from poverty" (in Jolly 2004, 86). UN Secretary General U Thant agreed. Drawing from the first paragraph of the UN Charter, which states that a major aspect of "national self-determination" is to "employ international machinery for the promotion of the economic and social advancement of all peoples,"

U Thant defined development as "economic growth plus social change." Yet, the UN General Assembly made it clear that development equaled capitalist growth when it established the Development Decade's goal as ensuring a minimum annual growth rate of 5 percent in aggregate national income for the "underdeveloped" countries by 1970.

It was also made clear that achieving development was primarily the responsibility of those underdeveloped nation-states. President Kennedy had signaled this approach in his 1961 inaugural address by declaring, "To those peoples in the huts and villages of half the globe struggling to break the bonds of mass misery, *we pledge our best efforts to help them help themselves*" (Kennedy 1963; emphasis added). Likewise, UNICEF (United Nations Children's Emergency Fund) would state that "the countries of the 'third world,' having cast off their colonial status, now also needed to cast off their poverty." To do so, both the United States and the UN argued, "they needed aid in the form of funds and know-how from their richer neighbours" (UNICEF n.d.). Development thus became a national problem, while the wealthier, more powerful nation-states became global benefactors, a role that they gladly took up.

Throughout the Third World in the 1950s and 1960s there was indeed widespread industrialization and capitalist economic growth, but not the annual growth of 5 percent the UN had called for. On average, throughout the 1960s the estimated yearly increase in per capita output in the developing world was about 2 percent, which, when averaged out, amounted to about three dollars per person. This less-than-expected result came not only from how developing states were managed, but also from the decisions of globally operative capital investors (state and private). National development freed up capital, and investors in developed and developing nation-states alike put it where they could get the best returns on their investments. Investment was especially strong "in the extractive industries, particularly oil," the President's Council of Economic Advisers 1967 annual report found, something that resulted in capital investment being "unevenly distributed among countries" (CEA, U.S., 1967). Thus, as Denis Goulet (1992, 550) notes, "No basic changes . . . occurred in class relationships and the distribution of wealth and power; the larger social system remain[ed] structurally exploitative." Acknowledging this, Amartya Sen (1983, 757), writing at the start of the UN's Third Development Decade, stated, "There is no . . . relief for the third of the Indian rural population who go to bed hungry every night and who lead a life ravaged by regular deprivation. . . . The quiet presence of nonacute, endemic hunger leads to no newspaper turmoil, no political agitation, no riots in Indian parliament. The system takes it in its stride."

What broke the system's stride were the structured, patterned, and cyclical crises of capitalism. Promoted as a cure for hundreds of years of imperialism, developmentalism could not prevent the crisis that became evident in the midst of the first UN Development Decade. This first major capitalist crisis of postcolonialism was marked by a noticeable drop in the rate of profit, a steady concentration of capital in various sectors, a weakening of consumer markets, and periodic collapses in the markets for credit. As they did with each crisis, capital and states responded by restructuring state policy.

In the first two decades after WWII, the Bretton Woods institutions and their counterparts in the Second World were formulated to address the capitalist crisis of the interwar years—a crisis shaped by the closed markets of empires—by opening up newly nationalized states to greater penetration by capital and/or commodities. By the mid-1960s, it became evident that these same institutions were no longer adequate in their present form. In the early 1970s, with the "Nixon shock" of ending the dollar's convertibility into gold, the devaluation of the U.S. dollar, and the growing U.S. trade deficit, the cry that Bretton Woods had failed was increasingly heard. Stagflation (high inflation and unemployment combined with stagnant demand) roared across the world. A consensus emerged among nation-state leaders and capital investors that something had to change—and it had to change both dramatically and quickly.

Across the world, the post-WWII "compromise" between state, capital, and labor was restructured. Capital, nation-states, and international bodies worked together to formulate a new policy paradigm, known now as neoliberalism. Everywhere, neoliberal policies reshaped the rights and services obtained through national citizenship. In the First World, post-WWII, nationally organized welfare state benefits, along with rates of labor unionization, steadily eroded. In the Second World, growing corruption (including false data reporting to central planners) and the rise of the informal economy led to greater insecurity. In the Third World, the pace of land grabs intensified, and livelihoods in the rural economy declined precipitously. Across the world, neoliberal policies led to large-scale movements both of people from the countryside into huge urban slums across the Third World and of more and more people across national borders (see chapter 7).

First World welfare capitalism, which had provided a social wage largely to National Citizen–workers, thus enhancing their bargaining power in nationalized labor markets, was increasingly represented as a harmful state intervention with powerful moral hazards (Murray 1984). The subsequent "rolling back [of] the state" was very much an exercise in further shifting the balance of power to capital over workers (Scharpf 2000). Workers reliant on welfare benefits faced increasing stigmatization and, as Bridget Anderson (2013) argues, were reduced to "failed citizens" unable to meet neoliberal, normative standards of "good citizens" fully engaged in the labor market.

The neoliberal approach to welfare for workers stood in stark contrast to the continued support nation-states offered to capital investors. By the late 1980s, when neoliberalism reached its *political* maturation and was pursued by nation-states regardless of the political party of their leaders, any alternatives to it were rejected out of hand—at least once electoral power was gained. Reductions in state funds for education, health care, and infrastructure; the implementation of more regressive tax codes; and the expansion of private property rights were all systematically pursued. The further liberalization of international trade, the sell-off of previously nationalized industries, and the deregulation of protections for workers and the environment became the defining features of neoliberalism.

While such reforms were made possible by substantial nation-state support for capital, neoliberalism was also coordinated at an international level. It is not for nothing that neoliberalism was known as the "Washington Consensus." The Washington, DC–based institutions of the IMF and the World Bank, after all, actively promoted neoliberal policies of deregulation, privatization, and trade liberalization. The financial capacities of these institutions, especially the IMF, were used to demand policy changes from borrowing nation-states. In the context of the broader crisis of global capitalism, loans from the IMF made conditional on implementing neoliberal reforms became a standard source of revenue, especially (but not only) for the national liberation states. By the 1980s, neoliberalism so defined nation-state policies that international commercial banks were able to take over much of the IMF's basic monetary functions.

The result was massive indebtedness of nation-states, especially in the Third World. Skyrocketing interest rates in the First World led to a dramatic increase in the cost of servicing the debts of Third World states. Consequently, by the late 1970s, the Third World became a net *exporter* of capital (Potter 1988, 9). From 1978 to 1982, the World Bank estimated that while approximately $80 billion in loans and investments flowed *into* the seventeen most indebted developing states, $130 billion flowed *out* in the form of service charges (Marchak 1991, 211). This situation hardly changed by the end of the 1980s, when the amount of money leaving developing states to service international debts was about $40 billion a year more than what came in as development loans and aid.

The international "debt trap" was set. No longer able to afford the terms of private loans, Third World states turned back to the IMF. Indeed, commercial banks and the IMF often worked hand in hand. Many major commercial banks flatly refused to make further loans until condition-laden IMF agreements were signed. Despite the fact that, as Ankie Hoogvelt (1990, 120) describes, "nobody, not even the IMF/World Bank and the global private financiers, den[ied] that the debt burden . . . [was] being carried by the masses who [bore] neither a moral nor a material responsibility for incurring the debts in the first place," a standard package of "structural adjustment programs" was demanded by the IMF and the World Bank that further harmed direct producers disproportionately. These "adjustments" generally included reductions in real wages, rising interest rates limiting the availability of credit, cuts in subsidies to agricultural sectors resulting in huge price hikes for basic subsistence goods (e.g., grains and cooking oils), reversals of any previous land reforms, approval of resource extraction and megadevelopment projects (with the blessing and funding of the World Bank), removal of export duties and import tariffs, and further mobilization of capital as massive outward transfers of profits by corporate subsidiaries were permitted (see Hoogvelt 1990).

In the 133 nation-states that the World Bank labeled as "developing," the debt rose from $18 billion in 1973 to $612 billion by 1982 (Duménil and Lévy 2005, 9–19). By the end of the 1990s, their total debt was approximately $2.2 trillion. By 2012, it was $4.8 trillion. At the same time, private capital held in the Third World fled to safer and more lucrative profits in the First World, thereby ignoring their much-vaunted role in the development stories of national liberation states. In the period from 1979 to 1984, the movement of capital held by Nationals of various Latin American nation-states alone totaled at least $130 billion (Marchak 1991, 210). In addition, the noted kleptocracies in national liberation states depleted much of the capital held by those states (Hoogvelt 1990, 121). The massive build-up of Third World militaries—again, used primarily within each state's territorial borders—depleted much of the remaining funds. Indeed, as people across the Third World protested austerity, the national liberation states increased their use of repression, leading to the phenomenon known as the "IMF riot" (see Stiglitz 2006).

The repressive use of nation-state power was not limited to the Third World, of course. The United States, operating under the Cold War "Reagan

Doctrine," provided direct aid to anticommunists across the world. These funds enabled both state militaries (often trained by the United States) and private mercenaries to move against social movements and state governments offering even tepid challenges to neoliberal policy reforms. Murderous forces, including the Nicaraguan contras, the Afghani mujahedeen, and the National Union for the Total Independence of Angola (UNITA), were beneficiaries of billions of U.S. dollars (Prashad 2007, 210). The Reagan Doctrine evoked the postcolonial discourse of protecting the United States' national security to normalize the violence it exercised often thousands of miles from U.S. territory.

POLITICALLY MATURE NEOLIBERALISM

Neoliberalism signaled a shift in the balance of class relations both within nation-states and across the international system. Capitalists benefited from increasingly regressive tax policies, laws that further secured private property rights, and regulations that gave them greater access to new sources of profits. This was nowhere more true than throughout the Third World. There, as markets were increasingly unregulated and investment procedures liberalized, capital investment grew, particularly in markets for land and labor as new laws severely weakened workers' unions. In a 1979 speech to the UN General Assembly, Sinnathamby Rajaratnam, deputy prime minister of Singapore (and founder of the People's Action Party along with Lee Kuan Yew), declared, "The policies that work best are those based on free market competition" (in Prashad 2007, 211). Officially speaking on behalf of the "nation," Rajaratnam represented those with major capital investments in Singapore. One of the "Four Tigers," and a part of the "East Asian miracle," Singapore, despite being a NAM member, was long allied with the U.S.-led Western Bloc.

From 1960 until the 1997 financial crisis, the economies of the export-driven Tigers (Singapore, South Korea, Taiwan, and Hong Kong) grew at a rapid rate. While most of this growth benefited the top of the class hierarchy, and while large number of workers, many of them women, newly arrived from the various peripheries within and beyond the nation-state were recruited for "3D" work (dirty, dangerous, and demeaning), poverty rates in the Tiger states were lowered, people's incomes generally grew, and income distribution improved. The Tigers' export-oriented approach was more successful than the import-substitution approach followed by other nation-states in the Third World in meeting UN development goals. Indeed, according to historian Chalmers Johnson (1999), the Tigers were exemplary "developmental states." By the late 1970s, the World Bank intoned that "these market-oriented aspects of East Asia's experience can be recommended with few exceptions" (in Prashad 2007, 248). Thus, the rest of the Third World was encouraged—and coerced through conditional loans—to follow suit.

Exhortations to other Third World nation-states to model themselves on the Tigers, however, failed to acknowledge the specific combination of circumstances that led to their "success." Their political alignment with the United States led to the Tigers receiving substantial U.S. financial aid—$13 billion to Taiwan and $5.6 billion to South Korea between 1945 and 1978, for example—but each of the Tigers was also a secondary recipient of the enormous funds expended on the U.S. military-industrial complex (Schaeffer 2003, 134). Moreover, the concentration of capital in the Tigers, especially South Korea, depended on a system of corporatism or "state entrepreneurialism." Much state revenue was allocated to build and finance the expansion of capitalist investments. Moreover, in each of the Tigers, a dictatorial state was in place at one point or another in the post-WWII period. Singapore has been a de facto single-party state since it became a "self-governing" part of the British Empire in 1959, and it has continued to be one after its "independence" in 1965. South Korea (1960–1988) and Taiwan (1949–1996) were both ruled by dictatorships and Hong Kong was a British colony until 1997, after which it became a "special" part of the People's Republic of China (PRC).

Increasingly, capital investment in the Tigers was concentrated in their growing number of export-processing zones, where laws protecting workers and the environment were nonexistent. Moreover, across the Tigers a super-exploited workforce of Migrants was created. Finally, with the help of the Tiger states, capital moved farther afield, to production sites set up in other nation-states with much lower wages. Many of these strategies overlapped. For example, capital based in South Korea won lucrative construction bids in the oil-producing states of the Middle East and brought with them a workforce from South Korea who labored as Migrant workers (Gardezi 1995).

While Third World critics of the Tigers' approach (and that of the PRC by the 1980s) saw their practices as a renunciation of the national liberation project (Bullard, Bello, and Mallhotra 1998), they were, in fact, in keeping with it. Indeed, capitalists benefited not only from strategies taken by the Tigers but also from those taken by the non-Tiger Third World nation-states. State-led "import substitution" policies, the nationalization of banks and select industries, and high national tariff barriers for competitors had allowed the "national bourgeoisie" in particular to amass capital. However, by the 1980s, these capitalists wanted to liberate their capital and thus they also became champions of neoliberalism. While their wealth was created by "developmental" policies, they now viewed such policies as a hindrance to the *further* growth of their capital (Prashad 2007, 216). Instead of seeing the adoption of neoliberal policies as "effectively leas[ing] its economic sovereignty to the wiles of foreign capital," as Vijay Prashad (2007, 225) does with regard to 1970s neoliberal reforms in Jamaica, then, it is more useful to recognize that *no* nation-state escaped neoliberalism. This is not because they had "sold out" national liberation, but because each nation-state was an integral part of a global capitalist system, one that persistently required "fixes" for its crises of profitability and control. *Indeed, national liberation was one such capitalist crisis-fixing strategy in the immediate post-WWII era.*

Neoliberalism was not a reversal of national liberation or a break from the Bretton Woods institutions, but a response by nation-states to the capitalist crisis begun in the 1960s. As the first iteration of the Bretton Woods institutions did from the mid-1940s to the mid-1960s, the Washington Consensus on neoliberalism worked for some time—at least for capital and for those controlling nation-states. From the mid-1980s to mid-1990s, the first decade in which neoliberalism had been normalized, there was a fifteenfold increase in cross-border trade and a greater than 500 percent increase in foreign direct investment (Ruggiero 1996, 2). By the late 1990s, the international trade in goods and services had a combined value of approximately $6 trillion, with transnational corporations controlling over 70 percent of it (Shiva 1997, 113). A growing proportion of the world's labor force produced for globally dispersed markets.

The adoption of neoliberal reforms looked different in various nation-states, but the result was the same: greater control and concentration of capital by either state or private owners of capital, and a working class that was unable to effectively resist it, in no small part because the discourse of nationalism and the organizational structure of nation-states had eliminated the common language of anticapitalism and the political community of workers. Predictably, then, alongside the growth in trade and profits grew disparities in the distribution of wealth, power, and peace, both within nation-states and across the international system. Between 1960 and the late 1990s, a significant widening of world income distribution took place. Indeed, the extent of the disparities surpassed those during the Age of Empires (ILO 1997, 3–4). Instead of calling the Postcolonial New World Order into question, this reorganization of wealth and power only further consolidated it.

A particular "structure of feeling" came to be associated with the deep disappointments, disillusionments, and disenchantments accompanying the growing expropriation and exploitation practiced by postcolonial nation-states. Paul Gilroy (2005) has given a name to the affective response to these processes: "postcolonial melancholia." Not long after the initial and deeply felt euphoria that many experienced with the end of imperial rule, soon enough a postcolonial malaise settled in and hardened nationalism in the postcolonies. For some it took days and for others months, even years, after formal independence to realize that national liberation did not live up to their dreams of decolonization. Yet, instead of seeing postcolonial schemes of development, nation-state support for capital, and the resultant immiseration of so many as reasons to stop supporting the *national form* of liberation struggle and seek other, more effective routes to decolonization, the mounting failures of national liberation states were deflected onto all things—and people—regarded as foreign.

Many came to believe that the national liberation project failed them not because of any structural limitations inherent to it, but because it was "hijacked" by "foreign capital," "(neo)imperialist states," or government leaders and bureaucrats who had been corrupted. While perfectly able to identify the postcolonial condition of "hunger, misery, illiteracy; inequality of every kind, sexual discrimination, economic exploitation; corruption, commercialisation, fanaticism; spreading slums, [and] looting of the environment" (P. Anderson 2012, 34), melancholic responses could not acknowledge that nation-states and global capital were wholly incapable of—and uninterested in—addressing these to achieve *liberation*. To acknowledge this would lead to the death of nationalisms and the governmentality of postcolonialism. Instead, like other forms of melancholia, the effect of its postcolonial variant was to *keep* the possibility of a future "national liberation" alive. This allowed National-Natives to continue to narrate themselves into the nation and imagine themselves as sovereigns.

No concept was as important in upholding the appeal of nationalism as the concept of "neocolonialism" and its variant, "neoimperialism." Those employing these concepts held that the well-documented failures of the national liberation states resulted from the continued expropriation and exploitation of the Third World by foreign capital and foreign states that were recolonizing them through new, international political and economic institutions. In the framework of neocolonialism, the national liberation project itself was not challenged. One slight exception to this was the critique that national liberation was easily hijacked by the national bourgeoisie, whose class interests turned it away from the rest of the nation (see Fanon 1965). However, even this insight left room for a national liberation project that could somehow achieve what it promised its supporters.

The conceptual framework of neocolonialism, although clearly astute about how the institutions of the Postcolonial New World Order pillaged the resources and labor of working people in the Third World through international terms of trade and finance, also provided *a refuge* for national liberation states. It ignored the fact that national liberation states were not outsiders to the Postcolonial New World Order of nation-states but had helped to create and maintain it. More importantly, the discourse of neocolonialism ignored how national liberation states exercised considerable power over the lives of their national populations even as they were in no way dominant within the international system.

Most importantly, theories of neocolonialism failed to account for the ways that the national liberation states did not offer a fundamentally different view of the Postcolonial New World Order than did the dominant states (or capital). Both wanted development, which they understood as an expansion of industrialized, capitalist social relations (privately or state driven). Both wanted to accelerate the process of proletarianization in the name of modernization. Both wanted global commodity trade and the generation of market demand for their national products. And so on. The key difference between the two was that the Third World (and neocolonial theorists) wanted an end to unequal or uneven development, unequal exchange, and the free trade policy agenda of First World states, corporations, and banks that favored the Rich World nation-states (see Arghiri 1972; Amin 1977). This was an important difference, of course, but it rested on two false assumptions: first, that the Postcolonial New World Order of nation-states *could* somehow be made equal or even at an international level and, second, that the continued existence of class relations prevailing in each and every nation-state was compatible with calls for equality. By seeing the postcolonial system of nation-states as *capable* of realizing liberation for all, discourses of neocolonialism disavowed the fact that postcolonial ruling relations were predicated on cutthroat competition between capital, between workers, and between states, along with the assured destruction of the planet's ecology.

Far from illuminating the workings of the new system, then, the concept of neocolonialism profoundly misrepresented it. And in so doing, it bought time for national liberation states. Mistaking postcolonialism for imperialism and mistaking powerful nation-states, such as the United States, for imperial states kept the idea of the nation and its liberation alive. It also kept alive the idea that people were still colonized. It thus allowed for the reproduction of a "nation" forever *awaiting* liberation from its "colonizers." As it had during earlier anticolonial struggles, the identification of the problem as one of (neo)colonialism or (neo)imperialism offered *more nationalism* as the solution.

Analyses of neocolonialism, then, simultaneously revealed *and* concealed the hollowness of national sovereignty. They showed that far from being discrete and separate, each nation-state was positioned against others in a hierarchically organized system wherein some nationally sovereign states were far more powerful than others. Those mistaking postcolonialism for neocolonialism thus argued that through coordinated efforts such as the NAM or by forming cartels, national liberation would be achieved. Yet at the same time, the discourse of neocolonialism shored up the nationalist fantasy that a low place in the international hierarchy was the result of an insufficient level of national sovereignty. Because concepts of neocolonialism accepted the postcolonial myth that national sovereignty could override class and state power, they were a fundamental misreading of ruling relations.

It is useful to reexamine the emergence of the concept of neocolonialism to see the work it did to mask the realities of the Postcolonial New World Order. The term "neocolonialism" was coined by Ghana's first postcolonial leader, Kwame Nkrumah, a key leader of the NAM as well as of the Pan-Africanist movement. Neocolonialism appears in the 1963 preamble to the Charter of the Organization of African States (OAS) that Nkrumah helped to create and, of course, in the title of his 1965 book, *Neo-colonialism: The Last Stage of Imperialism*. Recognizing that, at least in much of the Third World, identifying a process as "colonialism" would grant legitimacy to those who opposed it, Nkrumah used the concept of neocolonialism to argue that "national self-determination" was not being achieved because of the actions of forces *external* to the national liberation state. Nkrumah's (1965, x) assertion that "a state in the grip of neo-colonialism is not master of its own destiny" helped to position national liberation states as *victims* of foreign forces that were thwarting their national aspirations. He argued, "The essence of neocolonialism is that the State which is subject to it is, in theory, independent and has all the outward trappings of international sovereignty. In reality its economic system and thus its political policy is directed from outside" (ix).

Thus, central to the thesis of neocolonialism was the existence of a "new colonizer" who, like the old one, could only ever be "foreign." Employing the autochthonous character of nationalism, neocolonial theorists portrayed

National-Natives as once again colonized because of their lack of sovereignty over their territorial homelands. Yet because under neocolonialism "independence" *had* been achieved and leaders like Nkrumah *did* rule the nation-state, the character of "foreignness" was reframed. Once again, development was at issue. The national liberation state, Nkrumah argued, "can only become developed through a struggle against the external forces which have a vested interest in keeping it undeveloped" (xx). Such a framing helped to portray national liberation states as the continued agents of a forestalled decolonization.

The discourse of "national development" allowed Nkrumah—and other Third World leaders—to conceal the national liberation states' support for the extension of capital and the nation-state into more and more areas of people's lives (and livelihoods). We can see this in Nkrumah's argument that "the struggle against neo-colonialism is not aimed at excluding the capital of the developed world from operating in less developed countries. It is aimed at preventing the financial power of the developed countries being used in such a way as to impoverish the less developed" (x). The concept of neocolonialism thus whitewashed the incredibly violent process of nation building undertaken in the name of national liberation, especially the expropriative and exploitative practices of the national liberation state itself. Thus, although it is most certainly true that the Third World project's inability to rearrange the international system to its benefit failed in part because of First and Second World nation-states' refusal to go along, any analysis of this process must take into account how national liberation states actively participated in expropriating the wealth of their territories and the people living there. Yet, because they did not fundamentally question the basis of postcolonial power, theories of neocolonialism helped to reproduce it.

This is evident in the reign of Nkrumah himself. In 1958, only one year after national independence, Nkrumah outlawed labor strikes, passed the Preventive Detention Act that gave the state enormous powers to arrest and detain people for up to five years without charge, and established the powerful and brutal National Security Service. Nkrumah eliminated even the pretense of (liberal) democracy by declaring that his party, the Convention People's Party, alone could stand for election, thus transforming the newly liberated Ghanaian nation-state into a de facto dictatorship. He did all of this in the name of "national unity" and "national development," even as it was obvious that those in Nkrumah's entourage stood to be personally enriched.

As India's Prime Minister Nehru did in 1948, Nkrumah made major infrastructural development projects, such as the Volta River Dam (now called the Akosombo Dam), key to the "development" of Ghana. Indeed, as Andrzej Krassowski ([1974] 2011, 52) notes, "For its most ardent supporters, this project . . . had become both vehicle and symbol of a total transformation of the Ghanaian economy." Its construction, funded in part by the World Bank, flooded an enormous area where approximately 80,000 people lived, most of them subsistence farmers. The flooding was contained within Lake Volta, the largest human-made lake in the world, one covering almost 4 percent of the land area of Ghana. Approximately 700 villages were destroyed, and the tens of thousands of people displaced and dispossessed by the dam were moved by the nation-state to fifty-two "resettlement villages" it had quickly erected. The long-term effects have been devastating to both people and the environment. The people most affected by the dam have been found to have both increased economic risks and higher rates of poverty (Obeng 1977).

Most of the electricity first generated by the Akosombo Dam went to the aluminum industry. The building of an initial aluminum smelter to process imported alumina was directed by Kaiser Aluminum, a U.S.-based corporation. Once Nkrumah's government assured the financiers that the company running the smelter would be exempt from taxes on trade and receive discounted electricity from the dam, its funding was supported by the Export-Import Bank of Washington, DC. However, that the World Bank and a U.S. corporation were involved in this prestige project was seen by some in Nkrumah's ruling party as a "sell out." In response, Nkrumah began parallel negotiations with the USSR. These were suspended, however, when Nkrumah lost interest. However, after a visit to the Soviet Union in late 1961, Nkrumah ordered state control over much of the private sector. Nkrumah's new Seven Year Plan (modeled on that of the USSR) for state investment could not be met because of insufficient state funds, the lack of demand in domestic markets, and limited bureaucratic capacities. As a result, there were major cuts in government expenditures. Funds were reduced the most for housing and social services, as well as general government services (Krassowski [1974] 2011, 63). Both for the (largely) subsistence farmers displaced by dam construction and for others whose means of social reproduction were greatly reduced, the ring of national liberation began to sound hollow. It was in this context that Nkrumah penned his theory of neocolonialism the same year that the Akosombo Dam opened.

Some of the earliest postindependence literary works in the Third World were about the hollowness and hypocrisy of the national liberation state and its rhetoric of national unity. Author after author began to capture people's discontent with the results of their transformation from colonized Natives to "independent" Nationals. Novels, music, and films tried to capture how this postcolonial "rot," as novelist Ayi Kwei Armah called it, had been in the national liberation project all along. Armah's 1968 novel, *The Beautyful Ones Are Not Yet Born*, written toward the end of the UN's First Development Decade, was an early example of the postcolonial novel. The novel's main character, called "the man," was faceless and nameless. Marking a stark contrast to the First World counterculture's all-powerful figure of "the Man,"[1] "the man" of postcolonial Ghana was a lonely railway worker defeated over and over again by the dictatorial rule that marked Ghana's first postcolonial government of Nkrumah. In Armah's novel, the postcolonial nation-state seeks to abort the birth of "the beautyful ones" who could create the urge to positive social change. Armah's novel spoke directly to the carrying out of such terminations during Nkrumah's regime.

Following the arts, postcolonial theorists also began to show the continuities between the actions of imperial states and those who led national liberation states. The research agenda began to include questions of how new nation-states failed the vast majority of the people who resided in them while enriching and empowering National rulers (private and public). Postcolonial theory thus questioned the work done by both the nationalist and the statist aspects of the national liberation project. Trying to undo the hyphen that normalized nation-state power, a discernible postcolonial vocabulary was employed. Antonio Gramsci was particularly helpful for understanding how "subalterns"—those whom he described as having "no part in the state"—experienced the Postcolonial New World Order (in Spivak 2014, 12).

For postcolonial theorists, it was precisely the power of the national liberation states and how they were being deployed *against* people that needed to be addressed. Indeed, in contrast to those deploying the concept of neocolonialism, postcolonial theorists in the Third World were crucial in acknowledging that the current basis, as well as current governmentality, of power *involved* the national liberation states. Postcolonial social theory was used somewhat later to understand the First World nation-states, but no less powerfully as a result. An exemplary study was *Policing the Crisis* (S. Hall et al. [1978] 2013), in which a particular British version of postcolonial melancholia was analyzed (although it was not called this). The authors captured the growing sense of a "crime crisis," an all-pervasive sense of "risk" in neoliberalized Britain, and the consequent desire for greater "national security." They showed how responsibility for the crisis was laid firmly at the feet of negatively racialized young people imagined as outsiders to the British nation. Crucial to their analysis was how the "loss of a fantasy of omnipotence," inextricably tied up with the transformation of the imperial metropole into a nation-state from the 1960s onward, felt to many like a diminishment of their own power (S. Hall et al. [1978] 2013, 108). As it was across the world, the response in Britain was more nationalism and more violence against Migrants.

Postcolonial theory thus made us aware of how the legacies of imperialism shaped life not only in the former colonies but also in the former metropoles. We could see how the practices of imperialism were being sanitized as both imperial states and their colonies nationalized their sovereignties, and, relatedly, how the empire was increasingly becoming a source of nostalgia. Thus, as both the spectacular and mundane atrocities of imperialism were brought into the scholarship about the former metropoles as well as the former colonies, the continuities between imperialism and contemporary nation-state practices of racism, police brutality, torture, genocide, and policies that left more and more people impoverished were exposed. Together, critical investigations of First and Third World projects showed that people's displeasure with the current state of affairs stemmed not only from the deep sense of disillusionment felt by many who had pinned their hopes on the nation but also from people's actual experience of the national *form* of state power.

However, because the idea that nation-states work for "the People" remains largely unchallenged, people's actual experiences of its very real failures have not been—and cannot be—acknowledged. Consequently, the loss of the dream of national liberation—indeed, its ongoing nightmare—has not been rechanneled toward a more liberatory project. Instead, our feelings about "our nation" and "our" nation-state remain deeply melancholic. As melancholic responses often do, postcolonial melancholia has produced a great deal of violent conflict, much of it centered on nationalist claims over land, jobs, education, and state services, all of which are imagined as belonging exclusively to those who belong to the nation. Across the world, the nation for whom a state supposedly rules has shrunk even further. The criterion for national belonging is increasingly defined as possessing autochthonous claims to the nation and its sovereign territory. Such criteria hinge on being the people *of* a place and, thus, having a right to be on national territory and to what is available there. Recourse to the ideas of autochthony—the elevation of Nativeness or indigeneity to a first principle—depend on the idea that national self-determination can save the day. Consequently, just when more and more people have been left with little to no access to land, and little to nothing but their labor power to try and sell in ever more competitive labor markets, the autochthonous-nationalist discourse of land and place dominates.

CONCLUSION

In the years during and immediately following the end of WWII, postcolonial technologies of domination and postcolonial technologies of the self managed the end of the legitimacy of imperial states and constructed the hegemony of the Postcolonial New World Order of nation-states. The deployment of nationalism during the imperial era helped to shift anticolonial struggles away from efforts to end practices of land theft, forced labor, and immiseration, and toward the achievement of "national self-determination." Those who would, in actuality, *determine* what happened to people within each nation-state were those who held the reins of nation-state power and those with capital to invest in their territories.

Thus, not long after "national liberation" had been institutionalized in national liberation states, it quickly became clear to at least some that while the "national" was everywhere, the liberation associated with it was absent. This was structural: while the Postcolonial New World Order was based on the establishment of putatively sovereign nation-states, it remained very much a hierarchical and global system. Indeed, it was organized *in order to* ensure the further globalization of capitalist social relations. Each nation-state offered capital the best conditions for profitability. Moreover, each state (or set of states in the instance of cartels or customs unions) competed against one another. All this aptly demonstrated that the national sovereign no more worked on behalf of people than did the imperial sovereign.

The failure to achieve national liberation, however, did not diminish the power of nationalism. Instead, nationalist conceptual frameworks such as neocolonialism were employed to understand not only the continuity but the growth and deepening of the inequalities that had been sown in the imperialist era. This concept helped to organize the deep-set melancholia that had settled over people who were offered national sovereignty as a way to end colonialism. A signal response was defense of the nation against all non-National Others. As a result, nationalism was—and firmly remains—*the* governmentality of postcolonialism.

Right across the world, the nation-state is the model for political community. At the time of this writing, there are 193 nation-states. The process of nation-state making is far from complete, as numerous battles rage in efforts to dismantle existing nation-states and establish new nationalized sovereignties in their place (the longed-for "nations" of Scotland, Quebec, Palestine, Kurdistan, Punjab, Kashmir, Hawai'i, and many more). Much of social life continues to be contained within nationalized spaces (e.g., labor markets, educational systems, welfare provisions). Each of these forms of regulation contributes to the organization of society as national. And certainly, most people's subjectivity is wholly informed by whichever national community we imagine ourselves to be part of. People across the political spectrum argue for more state intervention on behalf of the nation. Fewer or more taxes; less or more policing; less or more regulation; fewer or more groups able to marry; fewer or more Migrants—the demands made to the nation-state by people imagining themselves as powerful because they are National-Natives are endless. In these ways, the nation-state represents an expansion of the penetration of power into our lives.

In the Postcolonial New World Order, nation-states provide the institutional structures (and force of coercive action) for the way that a globally operative capitalism has been organized (and reorganized). In the process, as I discuss in chapters 7 and 8, new biopolitical subjects—Migrants and National-Natives—have been produced. Indeed, the practices that organize globally operative capital, nationally regulated capitalist economies, and the construction of National-Natives and Migrants are deeply interconnected.

7

GLOBAL LOCKDOWN

Postcolonial Expansion of National Citizenship and Immigration Controls

The newly triumphant politicians seemed to require borders and passports first of all. What had once been the imaginative liberation of a people—Aimé Césaire's "inventions of new souls"—and the audacious metaphoric charting of spiritual territory usurped by colonial masters were quickly translated into and accommodated by a world system of barriers, maps, frontiers, police forces, customs and exchange controls.

—*Edward Said, 1993*

What the peoples think upon this subject is shown by their incessant emigration across these lines on the map.

—*Basil Davidson, 1986*

In the Postcolonial New World Order, as empires were rapidly dismantled and their former colonies—and later, their European metropoles—were re-placed by nation-states, capital from outside of the empires was able to more freely penetrate previously closed imperial economies. At the same time, *people* faced increasing barriers to their movement. As almost all people became *a People* of one or another nation-state, identifying people by their nationality—and requiring them to bear state-issued papers attesting to this when crossing national borders—became universal. Whether one was categorized as a National Citizen or a Migrant within nation-states thus also became more consequential.

In this chapter, I discuss the deep association between the nationalization of state sovereignty and the enactment of new citizenship and immigration controls. Examining this relationship across new national liberation states in Africa, Asia, the Pacific, and the Caribbean, and situating the significance of such controls in the transformation of British and French imperial metropoles into nation-states, allows us to see that the emergence of a truly international and interstatal system of mobility controls led to a system of global apartheid in which nationality became a major vector of inequality, injustice, and indifference.

Most do not see this global system of nation-states as unjust, however. Quite the opposite: national sovereignty is seen as the rightful exercise of power by the nation over its territory. Immigration controls are regarded as crucial for the realization of such home rule. Taken for granted are the ideas that only those at home in the nation are its members, that only members have the inherent right to a life in national territory while everyone else is a non-National who, at the very least, should seek permission to enter the nation's homeland. Such views are enshrined in the UN's definition of national sovereignty as the "right of each country to determine the number and categories of international migrants to be admitted into its territory" (UN 2013b, 38). Consequently, analytic distinctions have been made between human mobility within nation-states and international migration. National stasis is normalized, while moving outside one's national borders is seen as deviant.

Embedded in this national discourse of migration is one borrowed from an older, imperial one: the discourse of autochthony. Informed by the imperial discursive production of Indigenous-Natives who were both *natured* and *emplaced*, nationalisms are grounded in a fantasy of familiarity on the part of those seen to share *origins*. National historiographies of shared ancestors ("blood") and shared territory ("soil") emerge from this belief (Kristeva 1993, 3). Origins, in the autochthonous politics of nationalism, are both racialized and geographical: one's race defines one's nation and, thus, one's place (or, more accurately, one's national territory). It is an axiom of postcolonialism that nation-states belong to members of the nation. No feathers would be ruffled were one to say that India belongs to "Indians," Jamaica belongs to "Jamaicans," or, increasingly, Britain belongs to the "British."

However, because one's obtainment of formal national citizenship is not automatically translated into membership in the nation, nationalism is not perfectly expressed through state citizenship laws. Not every citizen *in* the Indian, Jamaican, or British nation-state is regarded as a Native *of* those nations. Indeed, a constant shuffling of who does and does not belong is part of how conflict is managed within and across the system of nation-states. Citizenship and immigration policies are constantly revamped to address new political and economic realities. However, one thing is clear. Around the world, and with each passing decade, citizenship has become more difficult to obtain while the global grid of immigration restrictions has been tightened. What has also grown, however, is the number of people moving. In addition to the mass expulsions often organized in the process of nation building (or nation maintenance), the postcolonial expansion of capitalist social relations has led many to move within and, increasingly, across national borders. In chapter 8, I show that as postcolonialism has matured, a further hardening of the autochthonous basis of nationalism has taken place.

In this chapter, I examine the formation of a new postcolonial global hierarchy based on one's nationality. This works in two ways. At an international level, people are juridically separated by their different nationalities. Within nation-states, people are further separated by different citizenship and immigration categories, each corresponding to very different sets of rights—and, for a growing number, a wholesale absence of rights (e.g., from "citizen," to "permanent resident," to "refugee," to "temporary foreign worker," to "illegal").[1] While the social, economic, and/or political rights of Migrants vary among nation-states, no nation-state provides Migrants with rights commensurate to those held by National Citizens. This has resulted in a world in which one's national citizenship has become the *single most consequential factor* in determining how and for how long one will live (Milanovic 2002).

Differences in geographical location, as well as whether one is placed in the nation (or not), are behind most global inequality today. Nationals in Rich World nation-states are provided with a "citizenship premium" (Milanovic 2012, 25). Moreover, mobility within the world of nation-states is also firmly mapped onto nationality. People with nationalities of Rich World nation-states experience the least restrictions on mobility, while most people with Poor World nationalities face a form of coerced "emplacement" (Malkki 1995). This can be termed a *mobility premium*. It is precisely because of these citizenship and mobility premiums that citizenship and immigration controls are key mechanisms through which global inequality is organized along national lines. The global gap in prosperity (and peace) has thus shifted from one between the metropoles and colonies of imperial states to one between people holding different nationalities.

At the same time, there is a continued—and in many cases, an increased—reliance on workers recruited from a world market for labor power. In many nation-states, both state and private capitalist ventures rely on the immigration of people simply to ensure an adequate supply of exploitable labor. However, because the *governmentality* of nation-states depends on privileging Nationals over Migrants, the *nationalization of the wage* ensures that National-Native workers are generally paid more and have more workplace rights than do Migrant workers. Moreover, jobs (at least the better-paying ones) are seen to belong to those who, likewise, belong in the nation-state.

The balance between nationalist governmentality privileging National-Native workers and the demand for an exploitable workforce explains why citizenship and immigration controls—no matter how brutal—do not keep everyone out. Instead of reducing the number of people entering nation-states to work, there is a steady reduction in the rights of people classified as Migrants within nation-states. For example, until the 1970s, when most formal labor immigration was almost completely curtailed, post-WWII labor migration into Western Europe was mainly reliant on a rotation of Migrant Workers who were not granted permanent residence rights or the rights associated with it (see Castles, Booth, and Wallace 1984). In Canada, where labor immigration is still permitted, permanent residency status became more difficult to obtain after the 1970s. Since then, most people admitted by Canada have been categorized as "temporary foreign workers" (Sharma 2006). After the 1980s, a similar process occurred in the United States (Sharma 2008). Such a shift toward evermore subordinated immigration statuses is not an isolated phenomenon but is evident globally. In this way, national citizenship and immigration controls turn Migrants into a specific *labor market category* available to capital within nation-states, one that is increasingly subject to superexploitation (Ng 1988).

The growing subordination of Migrant Workers is reflective of the power imbalance between "sending" and "receiving" nation-states. This too is part of the global legacy of imperialism. Postcolonial patterns of migration often involve the movement of people from former colonies of empires into their former metropoles (Sassen 1988). Indeed, a unique feature of postcolonial migration is that a large part of the movement of persons worldwide is now from less developed nation-states to developed ones—a major shift from previous migration patterns in which people from richer places tended to move to less rich places (Kritz and Keely 1981, xv; see Henning and Hovy 2011 for figures). "Receiving" states clearly control the process; they dictate the numbers, terms, and qualifications of lawfully admitted Migrants as well as the status they will be given upon arrival. "Sending" states carry very little, if any, weight in these decisions. This relationship, like all postcolonial relations, is one in which national liberation states participate. Indeed, since the 1950s, their use of *emigration* as a means to exteriorize both unemployment and political and social challenges, and their growing reliance on the billions of dollars sent by Migrants as remittances ($466 billion in 2017), have led them to encourage emigration (see World Bank 2018). Indeed, Migrants' remittances are now built into many "sending" nation-states' development plans (Stahl 2003, 40). "Sending" nation-states thus compete with one another to be the supply of Migrant Workers by trying to ensure that their Migrants comply with the terms set by "receiving" states.

As a result, the nationalist politics of anti-immigration are a significant aspect of how capitalism is organized in the postcolonial world. Given the continued hegemony of nationalist self-identification, the normalization of the legally elevated status of Nationals and the legally substandard status of Migrants not only intensifies the "race to the bottom" that many National workers erroneously believe they stop by their anti-immigrant politics, but it also stems the possibility of solidarity across—and *against*—the Postcolonial New World Order of nation-states. Both politically and economically, then, citizenship and immigration controls are part of what Barry Hindess (2000, 1495) calls the "international management of population" and what William Walters (2010, 90) terms the "global police of population."

THE POSTCOLONIAL WORLD OF NATIONAL CITIZENSHIP AND IMMIGRATION CONTROLS

In the decades after WWII, the restriction of people's mobility *into* state territories that had begun in the nineteenth century was largely completed. In this section, I examine the relationship between declarations of independence and the implementation of citizenship and immigration controls in the national liberation states in Asia, Africa, the Caribbean, and the Pacific. In table format, I condense information on the year when national independence was declared and the year when citizenship and immigration controls were first enacted. From there, I examine the implementation of immigration controls in the metropoles of the British and French Empires in the 1960s—largely aimed at limiting the entry of their former colonial Natives—and the consequent nationalization of their state sovereignty. I end with an examination of the intensification of immigration controls across the world, with a special focus on the Rich World, a growing destination for many of the world's people on the move.

Across the space we now call "Asia," the movement of people, ideas, and goods (primarily luxury products until the advent of capitalism) has taken place for millennia.[2] With the formation of the world's first states in Near East Asia approximately five thousand years ago, the main restrictions on free human mobility concerned *emigration* (often portrayed as desertion). With the formation of new European empires starting in the late-fifteenth century and their subsequent territorial expansion, millions of people were moving (and being moved) across and out of Asia to work. So important was this movement that the British Empire—the most extensive empire on the continent—categorized its various Asian colonies as either being "labor-scarce" or having a "labor-surplus" (Ullah 2012, 84; see also Kaur 2004).

By the start of WWII, most of the land mass of the Asian continent was formally incorporated as a colony of a European empire. A few colonies (and imperial metropoles) in the Near East declared their independence in the 1920s and 1930s, but most contemporary nation-states in Asia were formed after WWII. Across Asia, immigration controls were generally not passed—and certainly not rigorously enforced—until the dawn of the Postcolonial New World Order after WWII, even in those states that had nationalized their sovereignty in the interwar era (Turkey in 1923, Iran in 1925, and Saudi Arabia and Iraq in 1932) or even during WWII (Lebanon in 1943). In contrast to nation-states formed in the interwar years, those formed after WWII tended to enact citizenship and immigration laws much more quickly after their independence.

As table 7.1 shows, the Asian continent is very large and incredibly diverse in terms of its postcolonial history. What is clear, however, is that Asia today is a continent of nation-states. People's freedom to move into and throughout Asia is highly regulated and restricted. Most people in Asia must have national passports and visas to lawfully enter states whose nationality they do not possess. For those seeking new livelihoods and new homes, and especially for those who are officially Stateless, like many Palestinian and Rohingya people, the Postcolonial New World Order can be deadly.

One cannot generalize about any continent, and Asia is no exception, particularly as it is where more than half of the world's people currently reside. It contains nation-states with a very high GDP (China, Japan, and South Korea) and some with among the lowest GDPs on earth (e.g., Mongolia, Laos, Afghanistan, Cambodia). China has the world's second-largest national economy, while India has the largest number of impoverished people on the

TABLE 7.1

ASIA (INCLUDING THE MIDDLE EAST):
FIRST CITIZENSHIP AND IMMIGRATION LAWS

Nation-State	Year of Independence	Year of First Citizenship or Nationality Law (NL)	Year of First Immigration Control
Turkey (republic)	1923	1924	1950
Cyprus	1960	1960	1960
Saudi Arabia	1932	1954	1952
Kuwait	1961	1959	1959 (under British control)
Bahrain	1971	1963	1965
Qatar	1971	1961	1963
Oman	1970	1972	1973
United Arab Emirates	1971	1972	1973
Iraq	1932	1924 (British Mandate)	1978
Jordan	1946	1928 (British Mandate); 1949	1927 (British Mandate); 1973
Lebanon	1943	1946	1962
Israel	1948	1952	1950
Syria	1945	1951	1960
Yemen	1990 (unification of North and South Yemen)	1990	1991
Iran	1925 (Pahlavi dynasty installed)	1928	1931
Afghanistan	1919	1936	1935
India	1947	1950	1950
Pakistan	1947	1951	1952

(continued)

TABLE 7.1 (CONTINUED)

Nation-State	Year of Independence	Year of First Citizenship or Nationality Law (NL)	Year of First Immigration Control
Bangladesh	1971	1971	1952 (from Pakistan)
Sri Lanka	1947	1948	1948
Bhutan	1949	1958	1958
Nepal	1768 (kingdom)	1948	1958
Maldives	1965	1967	1965
Myanmar	1948	1948	1947
Thailand	1932 (constitutional monarchy)	1913	1928
Indonesia	1945 (declaration); 1950 (republic)	1945 (constitution) 1958 (NL)	1956
Vietnam	1976 (socialist republic)	1988	1990
Philippines	1934 (declared) 1945 (enacted)	1935	1940
China (PRC)	1949	1980	1979
Taiwan	1947	1947	1952
Hong Kong	1997 (from British)	1949 (HK residents)	1951 (area closed along China border)
Cambodia (kingdom)	1953	1996	1994
Laos	1953	1990	1998
Malaysia	1957 (Malaya) 1963 (Malaysia)	1947 (under British rule)	1959 (Malaya) 1963 (Malaysia)
Singapore	1959 1963 (union with Malaysia until 1965)		1959 (Singapore) 1966 (post–withdrawal from Malaysia)

TABLE 7.1 (CONTINUED)

East Timor	2002 (from Indonesia)	2002	2003
Brunei	1959 (internal administration) 1984 (independence)	1962	1958
Japan	1947 (occupied by United States, 1947–1952)	1950 (NL)	1951
North Korea	1948	1963	1950
South Korea	1948	1948	1949
Mongolia	1990	1995	2001

planet. Of course, in contrast to nationalist rhetoric, no nation-state is homogenous. China not only has the second-largest economy, but it is also second only to India for its number of impoverished people (World Bank 2014).

Reflecting the enormity and diversity of Asia, the picture for migration also varies dramatically. Having said that, Cornelius and others (2004) show that there is a convergence in the various Asian nation-states' immigration policies. In general, nation-states in Asia produce Migrant Workers through a system of work permits, quotas, and levies. Regulations that produce Migrant Workers—and produce their legal right to work within nation-states as a temporary one—include tying Migrant Workers to their employers, denying visas to their family members, outlawing the marriage of Migrants to National Citizens, and restricting their mobility while denying them rights and entitlements in the nation-states they work in (Hugo 2005, 114–115). This is most evident in the member-states of the Cooperation Council for the Arab States of the Gulf (or Gulf Cooperation Council, GCC), which I discuss separately below. Additionally, while Singapore and Hong Kong have created special policies to permit and even encourage the permanent residency and citizenship of a select group of Migrants (Ullah and Rahman 2012, 9), most Migrants across Asia are generally prevented from naturalizing their citizenship. Immigration policies across Asia, as elsewhere, are premised on the idea that Migrants despoil national culture (see Castles 1995).

There is indeed an undisguised racist current within the national immigration policies of many Asian states. Some, such as Japan, South Korea, Taiwan, and Hong Kong SAR, have established special preference policies for those racialized or ethnicized as being "like" the normative national subject. Even these people are typically admitted on a temporary basis. However, unlike their negatively racialized counterparts, they are given ready avenues to permanent residency and citizenship (Rahman and Fee 2012, 22). Other states use their immigration policies to direct Migrant workers to particular sectors of the economy according to their country of nationality. In Malaysia, Nationals of India are only permitted to work in the service, construction, and plantation sectors, while Nationals of Indonesia, Thailand, Cambodia, Nepal, Myanmar, Laos, Vietnam, and the Philippines are permitted to work in manufacturing, service, plantation, and construction sectors, and Nationals of Turkmenistan, Uzbekistan, and Kazakhstan are permitted to work in the manufacturing, service, and construction sectors (Rahman and Fee 2012, 31).

The racism embedded within immigration policies has not stopped international migration, but it has normalized the subordination of Migrants. Thus, Asia has nation-states with some of the highest rates of *immigration* in the world (to the GCC member states) and some of the highest rates of *emigration* (Hugo 2005, 94). Almost 38.5 million people moved out of the top five Migrant-sending nation-states in Asia (India, 11.4 million; China, 8.3 million; Bangladesh, 5.4 million; Pakistan, 4.7 million; and the Philippines, 4.3 million). Most emigrants from nation-states in Asia move to other parts of the world. However, approximately 43 percent of all Migrants in Asia move to other Asian nation-states.

Where people move to within Asia varies. Since the early 1980s, there has been a sustained growth of Migrant Workers employed in the relatively prosperous countries of the GCC and of East and Southeast Asia, particularly Singapore, Malaysia, South Korea, and Japan. The GCC nation-states are so heavily reliant on Migrant guest workers that, together, they have the highest ratio of Migrants to Nationals in the world. From 2010 to 2015, Migrants comprised 48 percent of the total number of people in the GCC: 33 percent in Saudi Arabia, 44 percent in Oman, 52 percent in Bahrain, 69 percent in Kuwait, 86 percent in Qatar, and 89 percent in the United Arab Emirates (Gulf Research Center 2016). By the early 2000s, the GCC states had an estimated 22.5 million Migrants residing in their national territories, most of them from other parts of Asia (Fargues and Shah 2012). In Singapore and Hong Kong, 40 percent and 39 percent of people, respectively, are classified as foreign born. As in the GCC, most Migrant Workers in these nation-states have few rights and are denied access to national citizenship (Rahman and Fee 2012, 251).

While there is a relatively small number of wealthy Migrants within Asia, mostly employees of large transnational corporations operating on the continent, the general trend in Asia is for Nationals of the more impoverished nation-states to move to richer ones. Thus, more and more Migrants are Nationals of India, Bangladesh, Pakistan, the Philippines, Indonesia, Nepal, Myanmar (formerly Burma), Laos, Vietnam, Cambodia, and Sri Lanka (Rahman and Fee 2012, 19). Unsurprisingly, these nation-states also top the list of states heavily reliant on Migrants' remittances (Ullah 2012, 85).

At the same time, explains Graeme Hugo (2005, 115), in 2001 a quarter of the nation-states in Asia "had policies to try and lower current levels of immigration. This represents a trebling of the number of such countries since 1983 and is indicative of a hardening of destination country attitudes towards immigrants." Once again, this has not led to less immigration. Instead, it has led to a shift in people's immigration status so that more and more people are forced to live and work as "illegal" Migrants. Indeed, the International Organization for Migration (IOM 2013) notes that Asia "hosts the largest undocumented flows of migrants in the world." Asia is also the site of a very high number of Stateless people. People identified as members of "minority ethnic groups" have either not been recognized as National Citizens of the states they reside in or have had their citizenship nullified as a result of autochthonous nation-state policies (see the discussion of Rohingya in Myanmar in chapter 8). Their de jure Migrant status amplifies the violence directed against them and, ironically, creates the impetus for them to move out of the persecuting nation-state for their very survival.

The nationality laws of most Asia states are primarily of the *jus sanguinis*—or the "right of blood"—variety and, as a result, are racialized and often gendered. Indeed, in Asia, only Pakistan has unrestricted *jus soli*—or the "right of the soil"—laws. Usually, criteria for obtaining *jus sanguinis* citizenship pivot on whether one is regarded as an autochthon or Native of the nation. For example, South Korea's first 1951 Nationality Law limited nationality to people whose father was a national of the Republic of Korea when the person was born. This was a legal (and practical) difficulty, however, since in 1951, one's father would have been born before the republic even existed (1948). The provisional rules establishing South Korean nationality thus stated that a person was a Korean national if the father was a "Korean," or *joseonin*. With such a definition, Koreanness was racialized to include only those persons who could claim undisputed membership to a presumed community of Koreans. This criterion was based on having undisputed ancestral ties to previous Korean imperial states, particularly the Joseonin Dynasty, which began in

1392 and lasted until the Japanese imperial state colonized Korea in 1910 (Lee 2003, 127). Until today, very few non-*joseonin* have been able to gain permanent residency in South Korea, and even fewer have been able to gain South Korean nationality.

Gulf Cooperation Council (GCC) Nation-States

The GCC was formed in 1981 as an economic and, to some extent, defense alliance. Its member states are Bahrain, Kuwait, Oman, Qatar, Saudi Arabia, and the United Arab Emirates. Fixed territorial state borders and passports were only introduced across the Persian Gulf region with the collapse of the Ottoman Empire and the incorporation of its territories into either the British Empire or new nation-states. As Jane Kinninmont (2013, 51) notes, "Prior to that, borders were more fluid, and merchants, traders and tribes in the Gulf's port cities enjoyed a mobility that gave them some leverage over their rulers." Today, however, they are ubiquitous and regarded by the National Citizens of GCC member-states as absolutely essential to the preservation of their national culture and society. These nation-states each have a modified system of *jus sanguinis*. Citizenship is conferred through one (usually the father) or both parents, who must be Nationals of the state.

Beginning with massive infrastructure projects in the Gulf from the 1950s and then rapidly growing after the 1973 oil boom, the exploitation—indeed *superexploitation*—of people *as* Migrant guest workers is a major effect of GCC nation-states' citizenship and immigration laws (Winckler 1997). From the oil industry to the personal services sector, tens of millions of workers have been recruited and rotated out. Since the 1970s, Migrant guest workers have been recruited, first from the surrounding Arab states, then from other parts of Asia, and then increasingly from Africa (Kapiszewski 2001). In all GCC nation-states, various international labor brokerage systems are in place, accompanied by the *kafala* (or sponsorship) system, which legally binds guest workers to their employers (*kafil*) and immobilizes them in unfree employment relationships. Like the agreements made by "coolie" laborers before them, the contracts signed between employer/sponsor and guest worker cover over the structural inequalities between the two. Indeed, an enormous disjuncture exists in the *kafala* system between the wages, working hours, and type of employment promised to workers and what employers actually provide (Gardner 2012).

The vast majority of Migrants are denied any possibility of national citizenship. Migrant guest workers' lack of citizenship also makes them deportable. This serves employers well: the state grants them the right to expel Migrant Workers on short notice while requiring guest workers to give employers three months' notice of leaving their jobs or risk losing their wages (Hertog 2014, 13). Indeed, most Migrant guest workers cannot change employers or leave the state's territory without the sponsoring employer agreeing. Migrant guest workers who do so are subject to imprisonment (Bajracharya and Sijapati 2012). Through the surveillance and punitive powers of the GCC member states, Migrant guest workers are made wholly dependent on their employer.[5]

At the same time, the *kafala* system ensures that National Citizens of GCC nation-states are effectively guaranteed employment, mostly in the public sector, from which most guest workers are barred by law (Hertog 2014, 4). Along with the other protections of national citizenship—for example, those regarding minimum wage,[4] working conditions, dismissal procedures, and entitlements such as pensions and health care—there is an enormous differential in the wages between National Citizen workers and Migrant guest workers. Steffen Hertog (2014, 7) writes that in Abu Dhabi, "the 'bonus' for being a National can amount to 600 per cent of the equivalent foreigner's salary." Such a highly material difference between National Citizens and Migrant guest workers presents Nationals with a strong contrast that only strengthens their nationalist consciousness of themselves.

As GCC nation-states try to quell unrest and uprisings of National Citizens, the situation has deteriorated. Since the 2000s, many GCC member states have embarked on (or further intensified) their policies privileging National Citizens (Hertog 2014, 14). Saudi Arabia, with the largest number of National Citizen workers in the GCC, created 300,000 new public-sector jobs for them, subsidized their employment in parts of the private sector, levied new fees on employers of guest workers, and starting in 2012, targeted "illegal migrants" for deportation. From November 2013 to April 2014, Saudi Interior Ministry officials deported approximately 427,000 illegal migrants (Human Rights Watch 2015). By late 2014, over one million guest workers had been deported. Similarly, after 2011, Bahrain created 20,000 new public-sector jobs for National Citizens. In 2013, the UAE announced a hike in the wage subsidies paid to National Citizen workers.

Like postcolonialism itself, the *kafala* system is an international one. It would not operate without the assistance of nation-states whose nationality the guest workers hold. Indeed, "sending" states stabilize this system by organizing the recruitment, training, financing, placement, and disciplining of their citizen workers. Increasingly, these states also organize nominal protections and support for these workers or their families through efforts financed, in part, by the remittances received from guest workers' wages. In 2012, workers' remittances from the GCC, which are usually sent through—and taxed by—state-controlled channels, added up to approximately $61 billion.

Africa

By the start of WWI, almost the entire African continent had been incorporated into the territories of seven European imperial states: Britain, France, Germany, Belgium, Spain, Portugal, and Italy. With multiple and competing European imperial states vying for exclusive claims to particular territories, both of extant state territories and of large lands where people lived in non-state spaces, each empire established imperial administrative colonies to organize commercial routes for the development of capitalist markets. After WWII, as elsewhere, these colonial administrative units were largely reorganized as new, national liberation states. Almost all contemporary nation-states on the African continent are national liberation states formed during the 1950s and 1960s. A few other colonies, mostly of the Portuguese Empire, gained their independence in the 1970s. Several newer nation-states have been created in Africa as a result of secondary national liberation struggles (e.g., Eritrea, Namibia, and South Sudan).

In each nation-state in Africa, Aderanti Adepoju (1984, 427) notes, "the achievement of independence transformed the erstwhile free movement of persons across African countries." He adds, "The emergent nation-states enacted immigration laws and regulations governing conditions for entry, residence and employment of non-nationals." According to the Economic Commission of Africa, "The elaborate development of visa and passport regulations, or customs and controls, of the need for foreign workers to obtain work permits, or restrictions on the repatriation of savings" fundamentally changed both how and where people moved (cited in Adepoju 1984, 428).

While a minority of nation-states did not immediately pass immigration laws upon independence, instead governing lawful residency with a mix of colonial-era laws on the movement of subjects and "aliens," they nonetheless had extensive categories of "prohibited" or "undesirable" Migrants, as well as a long list of offenses for which Migrants could be deported, often without trial. Moreover, each new nation-state used nationality laws to control entry, residence, and the rights of people to work in its territory. These laws, sometimes embedded within states' constitutions, often barred certain groups from accessing naturalization provisions and, thus, worked in tandem with immigration laws to maintain people as Migrants. In the words of Angola's first immigration law (1978), each state saw such controls as an "essential measure to ensure the security of the state."

As in Asia, the post-WWII period of postcolonialism changed the ways that states which had gained formal independence earlier, such as Liberia (1847), Egypt (1922), and Ethiopia (1930), controlled immigration. Having passed laws governing nationality immediately upon independence, they did not enact immigration laws until after WWII. Examining events in Liberia, South Africa, and Zimbabwe (formerly Rhodesia) will, I believe, help us better understand the significance of nationalism to the making of citizenship and immigration controls.

Liberia, named for the Latin for "land of the free," was Africa's first republic and was "founded" by the American Colonization Society (ACS). Freed slaves were moved from the United States and the Caribbean to the West African coast (present-day Liberia and Sierra Leone) beginning in 1822. An independent Republic of Liberia was unilaterally declared in 1847 by Americo-Liberians (with the United States recognizing its sovereignty in 1862). Before then, the ACS wrote a Constitution of the Commonwealth of Liberia in 1839 that established a governor and a colonial secretary who oversaw the day-to-day operations of the colony. In it, freed slaves were legally distinguished from the several "African tribes" living along the coast. The distinction—and hierarchy—between "Americo-Liberians" and "African tribes" was maintained in the Republic of Liberia's 1847 constitution, which defined "the people of the Republic of Liberia" as "originally the inhabitants of the United States of North America." Until 1904, only Americo-Liberians were granted birthright citizenship.

Like the United States, which did not enact an immigration law for almost a hundred years after its independence, Liberia passed its Aliens and Nationality Law in 1956, which enforced new immigration controls, during the era of postcolonialism. Today, Liberia has the most restrictive of all nationality laws in Africa. Article 27 of its 1986 constitution states that "in order to preserve, foster and maintain the positive Liberian culture, values and character, only persons who are Negroes or of Negro descent shall qualify by birth or by naturalization to be citizens of Liberia" (Liberia 1986).

South Africa, a territory colonized at different times by the Dutch and British imperial states, changed its approach to governing people's mobility and political membership as it transitioned from an imperial colony to a sovereign nation-state. In 1897, the British colony of Natal (which was granted "responsible government" in 1893) passed an Immigration Restriction Act to limit the entry of British subjects from British India who were *not* "coolies." However, as

Natal was still bound to the empire's policy of formal equality among British subjects (except coolies; see chapter 3), this restriction had to operate surreptitiously through unevenly applied and discretionary language tests.

After the 1910 formation of the Union of South Africa (including Natal), an act *explicitly* targeting Natives of British India was passed. Significantly, the 1913 Indian Immigration and the Immigrants Regulation Act not only further limited the entry of the Natives of British India, it also limited the mobility of the Natives of the Union of South Africa (racialized as Black people). Black people in South Africa were defined as aliens and, as such, subject to this act. Their entry into the Orange Free State was prohibited, along with their movement between provinces. In 1930, the Union passed its Jewish Immigration and the Immigration Quota Act. Upon gaining self-governance status in the British Empire (1931), it passed the 1937 Aliens Act.

In 1949, a South African Citizenship Act was passed in which "South Africa renounced common citizenship arrangements existing among members of the Commonwealth" and established a lesser type of citizenship for "Asians" (Riley 1991, 17). A decade later, in 1959, South Africa passed a Bantu Self-Government Act, declaring that all Natives of South Africa were now Nationals of "Bantustans," or "Black homelands" that it had created. The existence of these Bantustans, first established by the British in the period of indirect-rule colonialism when the Natives of South Africa were placed in "reserved" lands, became the legal basis for South Africa to treat Black people as Migrants, thus legitimizing their subordination within South Africa. The 1970 Black Homelands Citizenship Act further entrenched this distinction.

During the apartheid era (in which period the republic was formed in 1961), the government encouraged the immigration of people positively racialized as White, including those fleeing the new national liberation states in the rest of Africa, and offered them travel subsidies and other assistance. At the same time, the 1962 Commonwealth Relations Act and the 1964 Residence in the Republic Regulation Act created a temporary foreign worker scheme for non-White people who were Nationals of other states. South Africa's 1991 Aliens Control Act, which intensified immigration restrictions, was considered "apartheid's final act" (Crush and McDonald 2001, 1).

The post-apartheid Republic of South Africa rewrote its Nationality Law in 1994, eliminating separate "Bantustan" citizenship for Black people as well as lesser levels of citizenship rights for "Asian" and "coloured" "national minorities." South Africa's new 1997 constitution enshrined these rules. There were high expectations that immigration policy would also be dramatically altered, and three important shifts did occur. First, the obvious racist immigration criteria were eliminated, but they were replaced with a dramatic decrease in the number of people admitted as permanent residents (something that changed only after 2001, after many South Africans had left and new immigrants were needed to replace professional workers; see Crush and McDonald 2001). Second, between 1996 and 2002, three amnesties for undocumented Migrants were implemented. This granted permanent residency status to some minors, Nationals of Southern African Development Community member states, and people fleeing turmoil in Mozambique. Third, in 1995, postapartheid South Africa became a signatory to both the UN and the Organization of African Unity refugee conventions and passed a new Refugee Act in 1998.

However, the apartheid-era Aliens Control Act remained largely in place. In fact, South Africa's postapartheid minister of home affairs declared that the state had hitherto been too lenient in its treatment of Migrants and, under its 1995 Aliens Control Amendment Act, authorized new powers to police entry into South Africa and increase deportations. Deportations increased that year by 75 percent (Crush and McDonald 2001, 6). Such practices, Klaaren and Ramji (2001) argue, are "dramatically similar" to those of the apartheid era. Perhaps the most dramatic continuity with apartheid-era policies is the recruitment of contract, temporary Migrant Workers. Not only has their proportion in the mining sector increased from 40 percent at the start of the 1990s to 55 percent by its end, but Migrant Worker schemes for the agricultural sectors have expanded to include women workers.

Since the early 1990s, there has also been a steep rise in the violent nativist politics of anti-immigration. Not all Migrants are targeted, however. Instead, anti-immigrant politics largely target the entry of Black people from other African nation-states, thus continuing the apartheid-era representation of the northern border as a source of danger. The danger is no longer defined as Black but as *Migrant*. Apartheid-era stereotypes and images of Black people have been superimposed on people labeled as *kwerekewere*, or "foreigners," who are portrayed as a fundamental threat to the newly minted "Rainbow Nation" of South African National Citizens. Thus, what has been represented as xenophobia in South Africa is a predictable part of the technologies of nation building (B. Harris 2002, 169).

Indeed, the political subjectivities of postapartheid South Africa rest on the deployment of a nationalist discourse of autochthony. Michael Neocosmos (2008, 587) argues that "a politics of nationalism founded on stressing indigeneity [lies] at the root of post-colonial xenophobia." He further argues, "This politics of fear has at least three major components: a state discourse of xenophobia, a discourse of South African exceptionalism and a conception of citizenship founded exclusively on indigeneity" (587). Notably, South Africa passed new, comprehensive immigration legislation in 2002. Portrayed as an effort to end xenophobia (but with no acknowledgment of the state's role in fomenting it), it offered a "skills-based" approach to selecting new immigrants. In effect, this approach further shut down people's access to both permanent residency and to citizenship (Segatti 2006, 57). That same year, South Africa intensified the number of deportations it carried out, expelling 250,000 people (Southern African Migration Project 2008, 18). In additional to the tightening of South Africa's visa regime, the result was an increase in the number of people classified as illegal Migrants.

The situation in Zimbabwe is not entirely different. First established as a territorial state in 1890 by the British South Africa Company headed by Cecil Rhodes, by 1923, "Southern Rhodesia" was classified as a self-governing (White) Dominion of the British Empire. By the early 1950s, however, and facing strong opposition to ongoing racist discrimination in favor of Whites, Britain created the short-lived (1953–1963) Central African Federation (CAF), an association dominated by Southern Rhodesia. In 1963 Southern Rhodesia declared its independence from the CAF and became the new independent nation-state of Rhodesia. Present-day Zimbabwe emerged from negotiations between White power brokers, the British government, and the heads of the main political (and military) opposition. Independence was granted by the British in 1980. Tellingly, in the lead up to its declaration, an Immigration Act was passed in June 1979 (by Zimbabwe Rhodesia, an unrecognized state briefly existing from 1 June 1979 to 12 December 1979).

Throughout the colonial era, Southern Rhodesia selectively encouraged the entry of White people from Europe and other British colonies. It offered them assisted passage and land upon arrival. At the same time, the entry of non-White people into Southern Rhodesia was actively discouraged from the late nineteenth century. Borrowing from Natal's 1897 discriminatory legislation surreptitiously barring Natives of British India, a 1903 Southern Rhodesia Immigration Restriction Ordinance likewise barred anyone unable "by reason of deficient education to write out and sign, in the character of any European language, an application" (in Emigrants Information Office 1908, 84–85). An Immigrants Regulation Ordinance in 1914 reaffirmed this stipulation. As in South Africa, Southern Rhodesia recruited workers from other African colonies as Migrant Workers for the mining and agricultural sectors at the same time. Within Southern Rhodesia, racist laws directed Black and other non-White people to the poorest paid and most dangerous jobs. Non-Whites in Southern Rhodesia were also "subject to a vast array of institutionalized controls and constraints on their freedom of movement and settlement in urban areas" (Crush and Tevera, 2010, 23).

In the first decade after the formation of Zimbabwe in 1980, large numbers of White Rhodesians permanently emigrated. At the same time, a major shift in immigration policy took place. Zimbabwe moved away from an "active encouragement of permanent residence to the granting of time-limited residence and employment permits to [high-skilled] immigrants" (Zinyama 2002). Predictably, this led to large growth in the entry of people as illegal Migrants. After 1990, the movement of people immigrating virtually halted, as related economic and political crises resulted in the out-migration of as many as 25 percent of people living in Zimbabwe. The number of people emigrating grew in the late 1990s and throughout the 2000s as Robert Mugabe's regime began to seize White-owned commercial farms and engaged in urban "cleansing," which included the criminalization of informal housing and employment (D. Potts 2010). Most who fled were unable to secure either permanent residency status or a new nationality and have, instead, been forced to live as temporary migrants, sometimes illegally, in the places they have moved to. Many have endured violent attacks. For example, Jonathan Crush and Daniel Tevera (2010, 21) report that in South Africa in 2008, "scores of Zimbabweans, along with migrants from other African countries, were hounded out of their homes and communities by rampaging mobs."

Liberia, South Africa, and Zimbabwe share a long history of racialized political membership—and discrimination against those defined as lacking the criteria for full belonging in the state. Restrictions in citizenship and immigration have changed along with the form of state power. While state-enforced exclusions have been continuous, one change that was world-transforming took place when exclusions previously understood to be racist were reproduced in the name of the nations many believed had *ended* injustice. By shifting the formal basis of discrimination from racialization to nationalization, exclusions enacted against Migrants were normalized and largely rendered unpolitical.

Most other nation-states in Africa, each established after WWII, usually enacted citizenship and immigration acts upon gaining independence (see table 7.2). A number of nation-states in Africa governed people's movements into state territory through their nationality or citizenship laws (often embedded in their constitutions) and/or late-colonial-era laws. In each, however, the legal distinction between National Citizens and Migrants was a central component of their nationalized sovereignty. As elsewhere, the interplay of citizenship and immigration laws in the African national liberation states was informed by economic nationalism. State development schemes were

TABLE 7.2

AFRICA: FIRST CITIZENSHIP AND IMMIGRATION LAWS

Nation-State	Year of Independence	Year of First Nationality Law	Year of First Immigration Control
Liberia	1847	1847	1956
Egypt	1922 (declaration) 1956 (British occupation ends)	1926	1960
South Africa	1931 ("self-governance" as a White Dominion of Britain) 1961 (republic)	1949	1913 (White Dominion) 1962 (republic)
Ethiopia	1930 1944 (Anglo-Ethiopian Agreement)	1930	1969
Libya	1951	1954	1989
Morocco	1956	1958	1934 and 1949 (French laws)
Tunisia	1956	1956	1968
Sudan	1956 2011 (republic)	1957	1960
Ghana	1957	1957	1957
Guinea	1958	1958	1987
Madagascar	1960	1960	1958 (upon becoming an "autonomous state" within the French Empire)
Nigeria	1960	1963	1963
Burkina Faso (Upper Volta)	1960	1961	1960
Ivory Coast	1960	1961	1960

TABLE 7.2 (CONTINUED)

Republic of the Congo	1960	1961	1972
Democratic Republic of the Congo	1960	1965	1970
Senegal	1960	1961	1963
Gabon	1960	1962	1968
Central African Republic	1960	1961	1970
Togo	1960	1961	1987
Mali	1960	1962	1998
Benin	1960	1965	1986
Mauritania	1960	1961	1974
Chad	1960	1959/1960	1967
Niger	1960	1960	1982
Somalia	1960	1962	1984
Tanzania	1961	1961	1961
Sierra Leone	1961	1961	1963
Cameroon	1960 (French) 1961 (British)	1968	1997
Algeria	1962	1963	1963
Rwanda	1962	1963	1963
Uganda	1962	1962	1969
Kenya	1963	1963	1967
Malawi	1964	1964	1964
Zambia	1964	1964	1967
Gambia	1965	1965	2008

(continued)

TABLE 7.2 (CONTINUED)

Nation-State	Year of Independence	Year of First Nationality Law	Year of First Immigration Control
Lesotho	1966	1967	1983
Botswana	1966	1966	1968
Swaziland	1968	1968	1964 (under British rule)
Mauritius	1968	1968	1968
Equatorial Guinea	1968	1968	1968
Guinea-Bissau	1974	1973	1975
Cape Verde	1975	1980	1979
São Tomé and Príncipe	1975	1975	n/a
Mozambique	1975	1975	1989
Angola	1975	1975	1978
Comoros	1975	1979	1988
Seychelles	1976	1979	1979
Djibouti	1977	1977	1977
Zimbabwe	1980	1980	1979
Eritrea	1993	1992	1992
Namibia	1990	1990	1993
South Sudan	2011	2011	2011

characterized by a drive to increase or gain *national* control over capitalist enterprises on their territories, "especially alien owned enterprises" (Adeoye Akinsanya in Olaniyi 2008, 5). Making possession of the state's nationality a criterion for gaining rights of property ownership or employment in key sectors of the economy, especially the state sector, was one way to achieve this goal. Immigration controls, particularly the powers of deportation, were another. Examples of such linkages include Ghana's Nationality and Citizenship

Act and the Deportation Act, both passed in 1957; Botswana's 1966 Immigration Act and its 1968 Employment of Visitors Act; Nigeria's 1963 Immigration Act; Sierra Leone's 1963 Immigration and Quota System; and Sudan's 1960 Passport and Immigration Act and its 1974 Manpower Act.

A nation-state's Nationals were often defined in autochthonous terms. After independence, this became especially evident in East and Central African states, such as Kenya, Uganda, Tanzania, Congo, and Rwanda, but it also shaped national politics across the continent. Whether the allochthons, or the "people out of place," were defined as Asian Migrants or as Migrants from elsewhere in Africa, national territory was increasingly claimed for the exclusive benefit of the National-Native "people of the place." Who was recognized as a National-Native became evermore limited in the decades after independence, as autochthony came to be defined not only at the national level but increasingly at the local, substate level. The ensuing conflicts have led to expulsions of allochthons (e.g., Uganda in 1972), the formation of some of the world's newest states (e.g., South Sudan in 2011), and genocides (e.g., Rwanda in 1994). They have also heightened nativist violence against those moving across nation-state borders, again, most notably in South Africa (Neocosmos 2008).

BRITAIN AND FRANCE: FROM METROPOLE TO NATION-STATES

It was not only the former imperial colonies that nationalized their sovereignties after WWII. So too did the imperial metropoles. In this section, I focus on the British and French imperial metropoles in Europe, latecomers to the postcolonial party of nation-states. I do so because they were the two largest European empires entering WWII. By the mid-1960s, both their European metropoles became nation-states. The enactment of new immigration controls against their former subjects marked this shift. The loss of the vast majority of their former colonies precipitated this transformation, but so too did nationalism within the former metropoles. New immigration restrictions targeting the former Natives of the colonies, ironically, were central to producing "British" and "French" as *National-Native* identities.

The nationalization of British and French metropoles in the 1960s pointed to the maturation of the Postcolonial New World Order. By looking at when—and under what political conditions—Britain and France became nation-states, we see more clearly the significance of border controls to the nationalization of state sovereignty. We also see the importance of the mobilization of a national subjectivity to the postcolonial politics of autochthony. Thus, postcolonial migrations into Britain and France are significant not because they are the first large-scale movements of people from Africa, Asia, or the New World into these two states—they are not—but because restricting the entry of former colonized Natives was crucial to the implementation of a Europe-wide system of national border controls.[5]

As discussed in chapter 2, until the outbreak of World War I (WWI), human movement into European state territories was mostly unrestricted.[6] Neither passports nor work permits were needed at the start of this war (Marrus 1985, 91–93). As discussed in chapter 3, wartime regulations were concerned largely about potential spies and political agitators. However, there was a discernible shift to controls over the entry of *workers* at this time as well. Ostensibly temporary, laws targeting workers during WWI were made permanent in the 1920s and 1930s (and were never revoked thereafter). By the start of WWII, such measures prevented people from receiving asylum from the murderous policies of fascist regimes.

Following WWII, there were large-scale migrations within and to Europe. The greatest movement of people consisted of the organized population transfer of "Germans" outside of Germany by the Allied states. Most European states also actively organized large-scale entries of people as workers. However, in keeping with autochthonous nation-building projects, this movement was regulated as a movement of "guest workers." Coming mostly from Southern Europe (especially Italy) to more-northerly states, along with people recruited either from former colonies (e.g., Algeria) or nearby non-European states (e.g., Turkey), people categorized as guest workers were wanted for their labor power but not as members of the newly formed national political community. Switzerland and France had already implemented a patchwork of guest worker programs in 1945, followed by West Germany in the mid-1950s.

At the same time, greater numbers of people resident in the former or soon-to-be former colonies began moving to the metropoles of former empires, particularly to the United Kingdom (especially England), France, the Netherlands, and Portugal. From the colonies (many now independent) came both the colonized Natives as well as a significant number of people categorized as "European." These movements into the British metropole had already begun during WWII, as workers from Africa, Asia, and the West Indies were recruited to work in its defense industries. However, after the creation of new, national liberation states, so-called New Commonwealth Migrants steadily increased.[7]

The metropoles responded with new immigration controls, which had the effect of nationalizing imperial sovereignty. I turn now to examine the transformation of the British and French states from imperial to national formations through the implementation of laws that for the first time restricted and regulated the entry of those from the former colonies. In doing so, they too became postcolonial states. As a result, by the end of the 1960s, the nation form of state sovereignty was near universal. This served to further intensify antagonism toward Migrants—and cross-border mobility writ large—and led to the further autochthonization of politics.

Immigration Controls and the Making of the British Nation-State

For most of the history of the British imperial state there were numerous controls on the mobility of its subjects from both within and outside its metropole (the United Kingdom); however, entry into it remained largely unrestricted. Exceptions to this mostly concerned issues of state security, as those suspected of being spies of competing states were formally barred from entry. By the nineteenth century, most exit controls had been lifted, and entry into the United Kingdom remained relatively free. British subjects as well as aliens could cross the border in both directions (R. Miles and Solomos 1987, 76–79). At this time, Britain even began to proudly claim its respect for the principle of asylum (Porter 1979).

This changed with the United Kingdom's 1905 Aliens Act, the first to restrict the entry of "aliens," that is, anyone who was not a British imperial subject (see chapter 3). In an atmosphere of rising nationalism within both the metropole and the colonies of the British Empire, this act defined and produced the figure of the undesirable Migrant and laid the groundwork for post-WWII immigration controls. Thus, while the Aliens Act was limited in scope—it did not regulate the entry of all aliens, but those defined as undesirable[8]—it was nevertheless, a crucial step in the decades-long process of nationalizing British identity. This process was consolidated and institutionalized in 1962, when Britain passed its first comprehensive immigration policy.

That it was the 1962 Commonwealth Immigrants Act that announced the nationalization of British state sovereignty is evident in an examination of British immigration controls from the end of WWII. At that time, about 700 million people lived under British rule across the world. Each was a *British subject*—not an "alien." As one former colony after another gained its independence during the 1940s and 1950s, Britain was mostly concerned with *losing* British subjects, not with keeping them out of the United Kingdom. Thus, even as a British Nationality Act (BNA) was passed in 1948 that substituted citizenship for subjecthood both in the United Kingdom as well as in its remaining and former colonies, it was largely an attempt to hang on to the *imperial* character of the British state. Indeed, the impetus for passing the BNA was Canada's 1946 Citizenship Act, which declared that Canadian citizenship now stood above (but did not dissolve) British subjecthood. The BNA was, thus, a *defensive* piece of legislation, one that allowed for each of the members of the new Commonwealth (including the national liberation states) to offer a distinct national citizenship while allowing Britain to retain them as British citizens. The BNA thus created two groups of "British citizens": "citizens of the United Kingdom and its colonies" and "citizens of the Commonwealth." Citizens in both categories had the status of British citizen and were to be known as either British citizens or Commonwealth citizens with *identical* rights (R. Miles 1993, 153). Thus, large numbers of people possessing the nationality of an independent nation-state were not considered aliens in the United Kingdom (Layton-Henry 2003, 65) and, as such, retained the right to enter and reside in the United Kingdom.

Indeed, at this time, maintaining the imperial "logic of facilitation" regarding the movement of Commonwealth citizens into the United Kingdom was seen as crucial to the retention of what was left of British imperial power. "There ought to be an open door," Sir Maxell Fyfe stated in the 1948 House of Commons debates over the BNA, adding that "we must maintain our great metropolitan tradition of hospitality to everyone from every part of our Empire" (in R. Miles 1993, 162). This was used as leverage in the rapidly emerging postcolonial world of nation-states: shared British citizenship allowed the British state to represent the United Kingdom, its remaining colonies, *and* the new independent national liberation states as a single, still-powerful entity.

In any case, in the immediate post-WWII period, there were not enough workers within the United Kingdom to rebuild the war-ravaged metropole. It was initially assumed that much-needed workers would come either from Europe (e.g., from displaced persons camps in West Germany and Austria or recruited through the European Voluntary Worker [EVW] Scheme) or from the White Dominions (renamed the "Old Commonwealth" in the 1960s) and Ireland (from where the largest number of people moved to the United Kingdom in the prewar years). Most state officials believed that any movement of people from the "New Commonwealth" would be either insignificant or temporary. Initially, this was indeed the case.

About 25,000 former prisoners of war (POWs) held in the United Kingdom (primarily Ukrainian, German, and Italian nationals) continued to work as farmworkers after war's end (R. Miles 1993, 157). By 1949, about 127,900 Polish citizens were resident in the United Kingdom (156). They were joined by about 81,000 aliens recruited as EVWs. Another 16,000 people entered the United Kingdom through a number of smaller schemes. Most significantly, by 1951 about 533,000 National Citizens of the Irish Republic (who enjoyed unrestricted entry) had moved to the United Kingdom. At the same time (1946–

1951), about 319,800 British subjects entered the United Kingdom, mostly from the White Dominions. About 88,000 people entered the United Kingdom from the New Commonwealth, most of whom were racialized as White, had been born in the United Kingdom, and were employees of the British Empire (R. Miles 1993, 154–155). The number of non-White British citizens from the New Commonwealth arriving in the United Kingdom between 1948 and 1951 numbered approximately 5,000 people, many of them students (Hansen 1999, 90).

Of the over one million people arriving in the United Kingdom in the immediate post-WWII period, it was the entry of these 5,000 non-White British citizens that was widely portrayed as a problem for the United Kingdom. Indeed, even before the 22 June 1948 disembarkation of the first group of approximately five hundred people sailing on the *Empire Windrush* from the British colony of Jamaica, members of the Cabinet questioned their right to land. An 18 June 1948 Cabinet Memorandum stated that their entry into the United Kingdom "was certainly not organized or encouraged by the Colonial Office or the [British] Jamaican Government. On the contrary, every possible step has been taken by the Colonial Office and by the Jamaican Government to discourage these influxes" (in Hansen 2000, 57). However, as Colonial Secretary Arthur Creech Jones pointed out, "The government of Jamaica has no legal power to prevent their departure from Jamaica and the Government of the United Kingdom has no legal power to prevent their landing" (in Hansen 2000, 57). The minister of labor added that he hoped that "no encouragement will be given to others to follow their example" (in Pilkington 1988, 19). At that time, discouragement, including, from September 1949, the withholding of British passports from people without funds or deemed to be "unsuitable" for regular employment, was the only action the Labor Cabinet could take.

A year later, *and for the first time*, the British Cabinet began to discuss limiting the "time-honoured principle" that all British citizens had the right to enter and reside in the United Kingdom (in Hansen 1999, 91). In May 1950, the new colonial secretary, James Griffiths, was asked to submit a Cabinet memorandum on the "problems" associated with the entry of "coloured people" intending to reside permanently in the United Kingdom (in Hansen 1999, 91). His memorandum led to the formation of a special Cabinet Committee of Ministers to ascertain *how* "coloured immigration" into the United Kingdom could be restricted (in Hansen 1999, 91). However, even before this memorandum or special committee report was issued, the Labor government sent instructions to colonial governments to use further informal methods to discourage British citizens from exercising their right to enter the United Kingdom. On 18 May 1950, the Home Office instructed immigration officers in the United

Kingdom to refuse permission to land to anyone without documented evidence of British citizen or British Protected Person status (in Hansen 1999, 92).

Even in this highly charged background, on 12 January 1951, Labor Home Secretary James Chuter Ede, speaking for the special committee, recommended *against* formal controls. His reasons were twofold. First, it was understood that if Britain were to keep its remaining colonies and if the former colonies were to remain in the British sphere of global influence, British citizenship needed to be meaningful. Chuter Ede stated, "The United Kingdom has a special status as the mother country, and freedom to enter and remain in the United Kingdom at will is one of the main practical benefits enjoyed by British subjects" (in Hansen 1999, 92). Second, the committee could find no uncontroversial way to control the entry of largely non-White New Commonwealth citizens without doing the same for the largely White citizens of the Old Commonwealth. Prominent Conservative politician Viscount Swinton spoke of "a continuous stream of persons from the old Dominions to the United Kingdom who come here, with no clear plans, to try their luck; and it would be a great pity to interfere with this freedom of movement" (in Hansen 1999, 89n108). The entry of New Commonwealth citizens into the United Kingdom was therefore tolerated for the time being, both to maintain the imperial structure of the British state, with its supposed equality among citizens, and to maintain the freedom of entry for White citizens.

Such toleration ended on 1 July 1962 with the passing of the Commonwealth Immigrants Act. Citizens of Commonwealth states lost their status and were reclassified as foreign Nationals, which meant that they were now subject to immigration controls. Their previous right to enter Britain as well as their "right of abode" were both nullified (Bridget Anderson 2013, 39). The act legislated that only "Citizens of the UK and Colonies" retained the freedom to enter, reside, or work in the United Kingdom.[9] By 1962, Jordan (1946), Pakistan (1947), India (1947), Ceylon (now Sri Lanka, 1948), Israel (previously the Palestine Mandate, 1948), Burma (now Myanmar, 1948), most parts of China (1949), Sudan (1956), Malaysia (1957), Ghana (1957), Cyprus (1960), Nigeria (1960), Tanzania (1961), Kuwait (1961), Sierra Leone (1961), Uganda (1962), Jamaica (1962), and Trinidad and Tobago (1962) had all become nation-states. After 1962, the citizens of national liberation states were no longer able to move freely to the "mother country" but would now be regulated by a system of labor vouchers. Criteria for obtaining these vouchers were not formally racialized, but their use resulted in severely limiting the entry of non-White citizens of the New Commonwealth. For this reason, Hugh Gaitskell, leader of the Labor opposition in Parliament, called the Commonwealth Immigrants Act a "cruel and brutal anti-colour legislation" (in Panton 2015, 547).

Three things are worth noting here. First, parliamentary debates in 1947 had already racialized all movements of people into Britain by talking about the "racial" implications of immigration. For example, Member of Parliament (MP) David Renton, speaking on the proposed British Nationality Act (passed in 1948), claimed that some migrants "are British in the *full sense*. Mostly British born, they are *racially* British and are recognizable as such" and could be distinguished from those who were *legally* British but who "have little or no *British blood* in them" and, as such, "have *no real right* to our protection" (in R. Miles 1993, 160, emphasis added). Second, significant and violent agitations targeting people from the New Commonwealth *preceded* the passing of the 1962 act. In 1958, days-long riots took place in England against the entry of non-White people—whether they were British citizens or not. A key demand of the rioters was to "keep Britain White." Notably, immigration was not the issue per se. As Robert Miles (1993, 133–134) observes, throughout the 1950s and 1960s, "the total number of aliens resident in Britain (415,700) was larger than the number of British subjects originating from the Caribbean and the Indian subcontinent." However, David Cesarani (1987, 64) notes that the riots demonstrated that "non-white people who were British subjects [*sic*] with a perfect right to enter Britain were constructed differently to white people who were technically alien, but whose Otherness was less threatening." Third, Nationals of the nation-state of Ireland (who were no longer British citizens after 1949 when Ireland left the Commonwealth) were made *exempt* from these immigration controls, even though they were the largest group of people to come to Britain after WWII (R. Miles 1993, 133). Indeed, in 1961, approximately 645,000 people with Irish national citizenship lived in Britain. To avoid accusations of racism, the 1962 act granted formal powers to the government to control immigration from Ireland, but with the understanding, made clear in Parliament, that it had no intention in doing so (Hampshire 2005, 29).

The transformation of subjects of former colonies—and later, British citizens of the Commonwealth—into Migrants marked the ending of the United Kingdom's status as an imperial metropole. The 1962 Commonwealth Immigrants Act thus announced the *nationalization* of the British state and its sovereignty. Now, one was a U.K. National or a Migrant. The 1962 act was a template for immigration controls exercised on an ever broader scale thereafter. With each new mobility control, the autochthonization of Britishness was further entrenched in British politics. As the figure of the Migrant was negatively racialized, being British in the "full sense" increasingly required being a White National-Native.

The 1968 Commonwealth Immigrants Act that followed introduced the principle of *patriality* as a criterion of entering the United Kingdom or naturalizing into U.K. national citizenship. Only those born in the United Kingdom or who had at least one male parent or grandparent born there would continue to hold the right of entry and guaranteed citizenship. This had the predictable effect of restricting the entry and rights of non-White British citizens from the New Commonwealth—very few of whose parents or grandparents had been born in the United Kingdom—while maintaining this right for Old Commonwealth citizens, many of whom could meet this criterion (Blake 1982). It is no wonder, then, that like the 1962 act, the 1968 act was also referred to by its critics as a "camouflaged colour bar" (in BBC 1971).

The 1968 act was also enacted amid racist violence targeting "Asians" (who were in fact British citizens) fleeing the autochthonous "Africanization" policies of East African national liberation states such as Kenya, Tanzania, and Uganda. Having already been portrayed by the leaders of these new nation-sates as a barrier to the success of "Africans," a category they racialized as Black, many Asians had elected not to accept a new nationality but, instead, retained their British passports (as they were permitted to do under existing law). They used these British passports when trying to enter the United Kingdom (Hepple 1968).[10] Under the 1962 act, Asians in East Africa who were citizens of the United Kingdom had every right to enter. The 1968 act removed this right. Introducing legislation deemed to be "both urgent and essential," Labor Party Home Secretary James Callaghan claimed, "Immigration control should be extended to citizens of the United Kingdom and colonies who did not belong to this country in the sense of having any direct family connection with it or having been adopted here" (in Hampshire 2005, 35). By further presenting the need for new immigration controls as a response to the record numbers of Asians entering Britain in 1968 (approximately 7,000), Callaghan left little doubt *whose* mobility the new proposed legislation intended to restrict.

On this, Labor was in agreement with Conservative MP Enoch Powell, who in his infamous 20 April 1968 "Rivers of Blood" speech stated that "by stopping, or virtually stopping, further inflow" and "by promoting the maximum outflow," the government could eliminate the threat of the White British becoming a "persecuted minority" in "their own country" by a gaggle of "charming, wide-grinning piccaninnies" (Powell 1968). Acting quickly the Labor government introduced emergency legislation—the Commonwealth Immigrants Act 1968—that included new immigration restrictions. As Lord

Lester of Herne Hill, Queen's Council, depicted it in the European Court of Human Rights in 1973, Parliament "drove it through all its parliamentary stages in three tumultuous days and nights.... [A]s members of all political parties, the press and the general public recognised at the time, the real purpose of this provision was to deprive the British Asians of their right of entry on racial grounds."

In the process of shoring up patriarchal claims to family ties to Britain, the 1968 act furthered an autochthonous view of Britishness. In arguing that British citizens racialized as Asians did not belong in Britain because of their lack of genealogical ties to it, the autochthonous politics of "Africanization" in East African national liberation states was met with the autochthonous politics of White British nationalism. Again, Powell made the autochthonous character of these new, racist immigration controls most evident when, just a year later, he stated, "The West Indian or Asian does not, by being born in England, become an Englishman. In law he becomes a United Kingdom citizen by birth; in fact he is a West Indian or an Asian still" (Powell 1969, 237).

Such politics only intensified. A former empire that had colonized much of the world and exploited as many as a quarter of its people was now worried that its national sovereignty was threatened by a purported invasion of Migrants. In 1971, Powell, speaking in favor of the Conservative government's 1971 Immigration Act eliminating the "right of abode" for all "Citizens of the Commonwealth," stated, "It is . . . truly when he looks into the eyes of Asia that the Englishman comes face to face with those who would dispute with him the possession of his native land" (in Gilroy 1987, 45). In short, Commonwealth Citizens were made Migrants who required official permission and legal documents to enter, live, and work in the United Kingdom. They also had to register with the police and reapply for permission to continue to stay every twelve months. Only those who had lawfully lived and worked in the United Kingdom for five years could naturalize into U.K. citizenship. Demonstrating once again that ideas of race and nation, not numbers, were the issue, after passing the 1971 legislation the United Kingdom joined the European Economic Community (EEC) in 1973 and, in so doing, agreed to end immigration controls over other EEC nationals entering Britain to work.

By 1981, when the Conservative government of Margaret Thatcher passed a new British Nationality Act, the United Kingdom's ties of shared citizenship with the vast majority of the inhabitants of its former colonies were effectively severed. Ironically, for a party (and government) known for its rhetorical celebration of empire, it was argued at the Conservative Party Conference in 1980 that "we have got finally to dispose of the lingering notion that Britain is somehow a haven for all those whose countries we once ruled" (Timothy Raison, in Blake 1982, 182). Arguing for this new act, the Thatcher government claimed that the 1948 BNA was no longer in line with current British immigration acts (Blake 1982, 179). The 1948 BNA had indeed maintained the British state as an *imperial* one, since both U.K. citizens and Commonwealth citizens were treated identically, while the post-1962 immigration acts established the British state as a *national* one by restricting the right to enter only to people with British citizenship. The 1981 BNA was the British state's effort to rectify this discrepancy.

The new act ushered in two significant changes. First, it modified the previous principle of citizenship obtainment through *jus soli* (i.e., citizenship by virtue of birth on national "soil"). After 1981, being born in the United Kingdom no longer guaranteed British citizenship. Only those people with a parent in possession of either British national citizenship or permanent residency rights would become National Citizens.[11] Second, although the 1981 BNA created three categories of British citizenship, only one, "British Citizenship," guaranteed freedom from immigration controls and thus the right to enter, reside, and work in the United Kingdom. To be a "British citizen," one also had to be a citizen of the United Kingdom. The other two statuses—"British Dependent Territories Citizenship"[12] and "British Overseas Citizenship"—did not come with these rights. Of the three, "British Overseas Citizenship" was the most restrictive, as it carried no right of abode anywhere other than the place of one's (non-British) nationality. Tellingly, in rejecting an amendment that would have given people holding all three categories of British citizenship the status of "British national," the Foreign Office minister, Lord Trefgarne, said that applying the term "national" to citizens of British Dependent Territories or citizens of the former colonies "would imply some sort of eventual immigration commitment" (in Blake 1982, 182). Thus, only U.K. citizens were also "British nationals." All the rest were now (potential) Migrants subject to British immigration control. Practically, this was most consequential for the five to six million citizens of Hong Kong, which remained a British colony until its transfer to China in 1997.

Together, the immigration controls introduced from 1962 to 1981 constructed a British *national* identity and, as Bridget Anderson (2013, 40) argues, merged "the Alien and the colonial subject into the Immigrant." Ever stricter controls on lawful entry, including further restrictions on the issuance of work permits, resulted in significant limits to people's ability to lawfully enter or reside in the United Kingdom and obtain its national citizenship. After these changes, the largest groups of people immigrating to the United Kingdom were White citizens of the United States, Canada, Australia, New

Zealand, and South Africa, for they were most likely to gain access to U.K. citizenship under the 1968 act's rule of patriality. The only new and significant *lawful* entry of non-White people occurred through growth in the number of people granted refugee status or those entering through family reunification programs (which the 1962 and 1971 acts did not eliminate).

When it was an empire with global reach, Britain gave people whom it had colonized the status of British subject as a means of bringing them under its sovereign control. After 1962, Britain marked its transformation from an imperial state to a nation-state by placing most people it had colonized into the category of alien, whose movement into the United Kingdom would be restricted. With the incorporation of the United Kingdom into the new post-colonial world of nation-states, the gross disparities wrought by imperialism were reconfigured into a world system of nation-states, a system whose structure of apartheid—different laws for "different" people—was regulated by citizenship and immigration controls. From the start, the idea of who constituted a U.K. (or British) National and who was a Migrant depended on a national discourse of autochthony to normalize the idea that the "White British" were National-Natives.

Immigration Controls and the Making of the French Nation-State

When WWII began, the French Empire was the second largest in the world after the British. At that time, it ruled over 110 million people, including in its metropole in Europe. As discussed in chapter 3, until the start of WWI, movement *into* the French metropole was largely unregulated and unrestricted. In the interwar period, immigration controls intensified. Although the French metropole adopted its first restrictions against the entry of "foreigners" in 1932 and its first restriction on the freedoms and rights of foreigners with its 1945 Code of Nationality, neither set of restrictions applied to France's colonial subjects.

After the end of WWII, there were large-scale movements of people, largely from North Africa and especially from Algeria, to the metropole. Much of this was encouraged by the French imperial state. In 1945, and for the first time, a French National Immigration Office (ONI) was established. On 19 March 1946, just months before the establishment of the Fourth Republic, Muslim French Algerian subjects had their status shifted to French citizens (Cooper 2011).[15] In 1947, and in keeping with the imperial "logic of facilitation," France stepped up its efforts to encourage Algerian French citizens to come and work in its metropole. Eminent demographer Alfred Sauvy (1946), the one who coined the term "Third World," argued that France needed at least five million new citizens.

This was a policy goal that political leaders of France actively supported in the immediate post-WWII years, at least rhetorically. As late as 1962, Charles de Gaulle envisioned a state of "100 million Frenchmen" in French Europe, almost the population of the entire French Empire prior to WWII (Kulski 1966).

However, the state's bureaucracy, particularly the Ministry of Labor, influenced by labor unions demanding restrictions against entry into a labor market that they imagined as *national*, opposed granting Migrants permanent residency status, a status that would enable them to become citizens. Instead, the Ministry of Labor implemented a temporary work permit system. In 1946, Minister of Labor and Communist Party member Ambroise Croizat implemented a bilateral accord with Italy. From the early 1950s to the mid-1960s, France negotiated additional "manpower" agreements with Germany (1950), a second one with Italy (1951), Greece (1954), Spain (1961), Portugal (1963), Yugoslavia (1965), and Turkey (1965).

These accords established quotas for the numbers admitted from each state and imposed an inferior set of legal rights and obligations on those now constituted as Migrant Workers. Yet, as the entry of French colonial subjects or citizens were not yet restricted by immigration controls, they were able to enter metropolitan France outside of the work permit system. Many did so. Moreover, as enshrined in France's Constitution of 1946, all French citizens (including Algerians) were formally granted access to public housing and other benefits (France 1946). Many new Nationals of former French colonies in Africa also entered metropolitan France, although the latter group did face certain restrictions.

The extension of citizenship status—and the rights and benefits that came with it, particularly the right of free movement—to colonial French citizens was a strategic effort to subdue growing agitation against imperial rule in the colonies. Doing so buttressed imperial contentions that there were benefits to remaining in the empire. The French imperial office well knew that imposing restrictions on people's entry from France's colonies into European France would become important propaganda for national liberation movements, especially in Algeria, where the Front de Libération Nationale (FLN) was increasingly active and effective. At the same time, French efforts at maintaining its empire through violence—especially the French war to keep Algeria (1954–1962) and the First Indochina War (1946–1954)—also prompted large-scale movements of people from the colonies to the relative safety of the metropole. Between 1956 and 1961, over 400,000 French citizens of the colonies had moved to the French metropole. Additionally, after 1961, when the results of the 8 January 1961 Algerian referendum on national self-determination showed overwhelming support for it, about 900,000, or 90 percent, of the *pieds-noirs*, the "European" population in Algeria, also moved to metropolitan France.

Notably, after Algeria achieved its independence in 1962, French immigration policy decisively changed. The 1962 Évian Accords ending the Algerian war guaranteed that Algerian Nationals would continue to have the right to enter the metropole freely. However, this right was eroded in 1964 when a Franco-Algerian Accord imposed immigration controls on their movement. The accord was designed to bring immigration from Algeria into France's work permit system. A bilateral "manpower" agreement was signed that year with Algeria. Similar accords were signed with Morocco, Tunisia, Senegal, Mali, and Mauritania in 1964, all of which had gained national independence before Algeria. In 1966, the Directorate of Population and Migrations was created within the Ministry of Social Affairs to put an end to the imperial "logic of facilitation" and start implementing immigration restrictions.

The main shift—one that concretized the nationalization of French sovereignty—took place on 1 July 1968 when France unilaterally placed a limit on the number of people allowed into France to work, *including* those from its former colonies. On 29 July 1968, the Ministry of Social Affairs issued a *circulaire* that led to the refusal of residence permits to those seeking work and stopped the practice of "regularizing" most undocumented workers. These measures were precipitated by two factors: France's lessening concern about whether or not its former colonial possessions disapproved of its policies, and the 1968 protests in metropolitan France. Following explosive protests that spring and summer, France undertook a series of "collective expulsions" targeting Migrants, including Nationals of its former colonies (Howley 2006–2007, 117).

Throughout the 1960s, policies of autochthony used by the French Empire to reshape its colonies from the late nineteenth century also informed the formation of the French nation-state. France's Economic and Social Council commissioned a report on "the problem of foreign workers" in 1968 (Silverman 2002, 73). The ensuing 1969 report by Corentin Calvez led the council to endorse a racist policy differentiating between European and non-European non-French citizens. The council favored the naturalization into French citizenship of Europeans while arguing, "It seems desirable, therefore, more and more to give to the influx of non-European origin, and principally to the current from the Maghreb, the character of a *temporary* immigration for work" (Calvez 1969, 315; emphasis added). Moreover, like Britain, just when France began to develop full-fledged immigration controls against the Natives of its former colonies, it lifted restrictions against the entrance of nationals of the

European Economic Community (EEC). These measures finalized the end of the French Empire and, with it, the imperial pretense that French metropolitan citizens and colonial citizens were equal. The imperial idea of *la plus grande France* ended and was replaced with a muscular French nationalism.

The end of the free movement of former colonial subjects reshaped the obvious inequalities of imperialism into a form actionable in the Postcolonial New World Order. With the end of the legitimacy of imperial states came new, postcolonial methods of disciplining and controlling people through national citizenship and immigration controls. The decisive shift toward a full-fledged system of restrictive immigration controls took place in 1974. In 1972, two *circulaires* by the government of Georges Pompidou significantly reduced the numbers of both Migrant residence and work permits. On 3 July 1974, the government of Giscard d'Estaing announced that all further immigration was to be temporarily suspended, a suspension declared to be indefinite in 1975. Between 1978 and 1980, France attempted to follow the autochthonous policy of "repatriation" and offered most lawful Migrants from North Africa financial remuneration to leave the nation-state of France, which was increasingly defining itself as White.

In both Britain and France after WWII, the discourses of racism embedded within imperial practices, which had produced separated categories of Europeans and colonialized Natives and then, later, had further separated colonized Natives into binary categories of Indigenous-Natives and Migrant-Natives, was transferred to that of citizenship and immigration controls. The post-1945 movements of people from the (former or extant) colonies into Britain and France were signified as movements of Natives widely understood as constituting distinct "races" through reference to their skin color, "blood lines," and "stock" (see R. Miles 1993, 129). In the process, it followed that "the British" or "the French" also belonged to a separate race with separate genealogies. From here, the idea that immigration *imported* the problems of the colonial situation (i.e., agitations for equality and freedom) quickly followed. The national autochthonization of the British or French nation thus provided the basis for the expression of postcolonial racism. Citizenship and immigration regulations and restrictions were key technologies of nation building. They were also central to turning formerly colonized Natives into Migrants. Together they produced the figure of the Migrant as a distinct— and separate—race, one often viewed not only as unassimilable but also as a danger from which the nation and its Nationals needed protection.

CITIZENSHIP AND IMMIGRATION CONTROLS
IN THE RICH-WORLD NATION-STATES

The actions taken by the British and French states as they nationalized their once-imperial sovereignty were similar to those taken across the First World, where, shortly after WWII, there was enormous economic growth. In Europe, this was stimulated by large capital inflows from the United States. In the United States itself, the growth in markets for its goods (both in Europe and in the rapidly nationalizing former colonies) led to a large postwar boom. International migration was a crucial component of the post-WWII global economic structure. Reconstruction or expansion could not have happened without people moving to these states as workers. From 1945 until the mid-1970s, people were actively recruited to work in all First World states. The number of people admitted to work in Western Europe nation-states alone approximated thirty million.

The demand for workers in the labor markets of the Rich World led to significant policy changes. Two different processes were under way depending on when states had nationalized their sovereignty. From the mid-1960s to the early 1970s, some states with long-standing immigration controls (e.g., the United States, Canada, Australia, New Zealand) lifted restrictions against the entry of previously prohibited groups. At the same time, there was a growing economization of immigration regulations. Canada's development of a "points system" for skilled workers in 1967 became a model for this process. For those European nation-states that had nationalized their sovereignties prior to the end of WWII, ever finer levels of citizenship and immigration controls were put into place. In all European imperial states still standing after WWII, new immigration controls were imposed aimed at limiting the entry of former imperial subjects into the metropoles. In the process, these states nationalized their sovereignty.

All Rich World states (re)introduced guest worker systems and other forms of creating and controlling unfree Migrant labor. By restricting rights available within nation-states to National Citizens (and to a somewhat lesser extent to Migrants admitted as permanent residents), nation-states in the Rich World were able to deny Migrants any number of rights (civil, economic, social) simply by categorizing them as temporary. As Stephen Castles (2006, 742) puts it, states employing guest workers were "trying to import labor but not people." Indeed, Castles adds (743), guest worker programs were predicated on the assumption of the inferiority and separation of the foreign worker. Guest workers, issued work permits whose validity was time-limited (usually for a year) and could only be renewed by approval of the state and/or the employer, were meant to constitute a rotating foreign workforce within nationalized labor markets. Their ability to bring family members with them was therefore restricted to provide a further compulsion to leave.

The United States, the dominant state in the post-WWII era, was a leader in such initiatives. Its Bracero Program was first implemented in August 1942 as part of the U.S. war effort to ensure a workforce in key sectors. From then until the end of the program in 1964, it recruited millions of people, mostly men, from Mexico as contract laborers legally tied to specific employers. Bracero workers were mainly employed in the agricultural sector or in maintaining the U.S. railroad system. The severe restrictions placed on their labor market mobility as well as outright abuses, including failure to pay wages, disciplined these Migrant Workers and kept them in work that was generally seen as undesirable by most National Citizens constitutionally guaranteed the freedom to change or refuse jobs. The U.S. deportation regime also acted as a significant disciplinary device. Its 1954 Operation Wetback deported 1,075,168 people to Mexico that year. Recruiting a temporary and unfree Migrant workforce and using deportation as a method of intimidation and expulsion came to embody the dominant form of the postcolonial regulation of human mobility across the First World.

Similar schemes were implemented in the 1940s in Great Britain, France, Belgium, and Switzerland. Throughout the 1950s and 1960s, all nation-states in Western Europe had guest worker programs—with West Germany, Switzerland, and France leading the way. In the initial post-WWII period, only Great Britain, the Netherlands, and France permitted the entry of persons as permanent residents, particularly of people from their former or extant colonies. However, they too employed some sort of temporary Migrant Worker scheme. By the 1950s and 1960s, most workers moving to Europe were admitted for contractually time-limited work. By the end of the 1960s and early 1970s, avenues for permanent residency in European nation-states were quickly closing. Such actions were part of a broader European shutdown of lawful migration for almost everyone other than EEC (and later European Union) Nationals. With the first "oil shock" of 1973–1974 and the stock market crash that followed, the lawful entry of people from Southern to Northern Europe, including Nationals of EEC-member states, as well as of guest workers from North Africa, Turkey, and Eastern Europe, was stopped. By this time, only the United States, Canada, and Australia granted permanent residency to any significant number of Migrants (Kritz and Keely 1981, xiv). By the late 1970s and early 1980s, even in these nation-states, most people filling key demands in the labor market were accorded either a "temporary" or "illegal" status (Sharma 2006 for Canada; Sharma 2008 for the United States).

Even before the global recession of 1973–1975, guest workers in Europe, along with Citizens negatively racialized as being *of* the former or extant colonies, were already problematized as disruptive and destructive of the nation. Terms such as "overforeignization" (in German: *Überfremdung*) were bandied about (Kritz and Keely 1981, xxiv). Once again demonstrating that the issue was the racialization of the nation and not numbers, the transformation of the EEC into the European Union (EU) in 1993 and its subsequent expansion occurred just as lawful entry into member states was made nearly impossible for most people from Latin America, Oceania, Asia, and Africa. It also led to one of the great seismic shifts in international migration since the end of WWII: the reduction in the movement of Europeans out of Europe and the growing movement of people across and into European nation-states as illegal migrants.[14] Indeed, despite the growing number of restrictions against lawful entry into European nation-states, people from Asia, the Middle East, Africa, and the former Soviet republics have entered the EU but have mostly been forced to live and work there without a status allowing them access to the wage levels and protections available to Nationals.

Today in nation-states across Europe, Migrants are increasingly portrayed not only as interlopers but, with the intensification of autochthonous discourses, as *colonizers*, foreigners attempting to rule over the Natives of European nation-states. As one right-wing blogger put it, "Why is colonialism bad, except when my country [Norway], which has no colonial history, gets colonized by Third World peoples?" (SAFE 2008).[15] Perhaps Karl Marx's (1963, 1) quip that history repeats itself "first as tragedy, then as farce" is apt here. The subjectification of Europeans as Natives is a case of improbable situations, an overwhelming and confusing plot, a large number of twists and random events, and the deliberate use of absurdity. I discuss this in greater detail in chapter 8.

CONCLUSION

The two most pertinent features of the Postcolonial New World Order are the existence of more and more nation-states and the expansion of capitalist social relations. Indeed, the specificity and distinctiveness of *international* migration can only be understood within the context of nationalized state sovereignties and the growing competition within global capitalist markets. The postcolonial governmentality of human mobility rests on the organization of the world into numerous territorial nation-states, each with its own racialized, autochthonized ideas of who constitutes the proper "national subject" and, relatedly, each with its own limits to national membership enforced by citizenship and immigration controls against Migrants. Citizenship and immigration controls thus not only create and define sovereign nation-states and nationalized societies, but they secure the Postcolonial New World Order. They are the technology through which juridical as well as social limits to national belonging are defined, established, and enforced. The resultant expansion of the need to document one's nationality in order to gain access to all sorts of life's necessities materializes the significance of nationality in people's lives.

With each new nation-state come further citizenship and immigration controls. The Postcolonial New World Order has thus created a world in global lockdown for the vast majority of its inhabitants. "We have established all the barriers we could think of," states François Crépeau (2003, 174). Today we see ever more stringent criteria for authorized entry; reinforced border controls at the subnational, national, and international levels, including international police cooperation and government intelligence sharing on cross-border movements; the criminalization of unauthorized movements; armed intervention to prevent border crossings; "readmission" and "safe third country" agreements that facilitate faster deportations and larger numbers of them; economic cooperation agreements that are often preceded by the "cleansing" of sites used in the clandestine journeys of people on the move; carrier sanctions on transportation companies; the empowering of carrier and airport personnel to act as border police; and "short stop operations," in which state employees are sent abroad to screen people setting off for their territories. Increasingly, across the world, we are seeing the criminalization of solidarity between those categorized as Nationals and Migrants. And, at the end of the day, "people with guns are prepared to enforce the boundaries" (Carens 1995, 2). After all, as Michel Foucault (2003) noted, "society must be defended," and society today is decidedly national. We have "border zones, detention centres, holding areas, a panoply of partitions, segregations, and striations" to shore up the territorial governance of national populations (Walters 2010, 94). Postcolonial forms of "population control" have thus been secured through the conjoined principles of global separation and national exclusion and segregation. Making national territory *the place* where Nationals belong makes the nation-state a place that *belongs to* National-Natives.

At the same time, the expansion of capitalist social relations during this time—including, crucially, the consequent growth in capitalists' need for the commodity of labor power—has bound individual nation-states together into a global system. Indeed, the international movement of workers across national borders in the post-WWII period is a constitutive part of the global system of nationally sovereign states and reflects the acute disparities between them on almost any measure (wealth, health, education, life expectancy, and more). The disparities between nation-states are reproduced within any nation-state through the differential statuses accorded to different biopolitical groups of people. There are National Citizens and Migrants, who are further divided into a hierarchy of statuses ranging from "permanent residents" to "illegals." Indeed, nation-state controls on mobility into its territories—and the "citizenship premium" that results—has intensified not only global inequalities but also the interdependency of purportedly separate national societies. First World nation-states are dependent on immigration controls to produce Migrants who are denied whatever protections from capitalist markets Nationals have secured (e.g., the social wage, the minimum wage, and workplace protections), while Poor World nation-states are especially dependent upon Migrants' remittances.

The ascendency and global institutionalization of the nationalist idea that only people who are *a People* (i.e., "nations") have the right to self-determination (sovereignty) over their territories, along with the post-WWII expansion, intensification, and racialization of immigration controls, has led eventually and through a long, circuitous but certainly not inevitable route to the postcolonial condition of increased mobility rights for capital and their commodities and increased restrictions on the ability of people to move. In this sense, national forms of state power, and the limits on citizenship and immigration that define them, have *territorialized* the power of states—and people's attachment to them—more so than any previous form of state power. The heart of this process lies in the association made between nationality and access to state-granted rights in any given territory. Immigration controls not only assume that Nationals have a right to be present upon national territory and that Migrants do not, but they also ensure that the anti-immigrant discourse of autochthony becomes the (increasingly violent) site of nationalist politics.

With the production of Nationals and their Migrant Others, previous imperial categories of Indigenous-Natives and Migrant-Natives have not disappeared, however. Instead, they have adhered to these postcolonial distinctions. While the limits that immigration controls set to national membership are always already racialized, gendered, and classed, autochthonous discourses are crucial to producing Nationals as the "people of a place" and Migrants as the "people out of place." Under the competitive conditions of postcoloniality, those claiming unqualified standing as Nationals increasingly identify themselves as National-*Natives*, while all others become Migrants. With the postcolonial delegitimization of formal, territorial colonialism, defining Migrants as colonizers is a significant part of normalizing their demonization.

Thus, it is not a coincidence that it was precisely when being a racist became anathema to most—racism's *legitimacy* dying with millions of people in Nazi gas chambers—that ideas of distinct "races" shifted to ideas of separate "nations" whose sovereignty was *defined* by the power to decide who was or was not able to enter, stay, or have rights in the nation-state. Another way of putting it, of course, as Robert Miles (1993, 35) does, is to say that it is difficult to overestimate the significance of citizenship and immigration controls for practices of racism. In chapter 8, I study how autochthonous discourses are deployed across the political spectrum. This tells us something very important about the character of power in the Postcolonial New World Order. It reveals to us that the differences posited between autochthons and allochthons—Natives and Migrants—is a *fundamental* political, as well as ontological and epistemological, challenge we must address to achieve something that can live up to our aspirations for liberty. This is because, contrary to ideals of separation, National-Natives and Migrants are cotemporal (they have a shared time), they are cospatial (they have a shared space), and they are coproductive (they have a shared history).

8

NATIONAL AUTOCHTHONIES AND THE MAKING OF POSTCOLONIAL NATIONAL-NATIVES

There is and will be rousing language to keep citizens armed and arming; slaughtered and slaughtering in the malls, courthouses, post offices, playgrounds, bedrooms and boulevards; stirring, memorializing language to mask the pity and waste of needless death. There will be more diplomatic language to countenance rape, torture, assassination. There is and will be more seductive, mutant language designed to throttle women, to pack their throats like paté-producing geese with their own unsayable, transgressive words; there will be more of the language of surveillance disguised as research; of politics and history calculated to render the suffering of millions mute; language glamorized to thrill the dissatisfied and bereft into assaulting their neighbors; arrogant pseudo-empirical language crafted to lock creative people into cages of inferiority and hopelessness.

—*Toni Morrison, Nobel lecture, 1993*

In the Postcolonial New World Order, defining oneself as a member of a nation is essential for gaining the internationally recognized right to be self-determinative. In the politics of postcolonialism, no figures are as well positioned to claim *National* status as those able to make Native claims to territory. While not all claimants to National-Nativeness realize their demands, autochthony establishes limits to who can—and cannot—claim national sovereignty. Autochthonous claims, ultimately based on some sort of ancestral or genealogical relationship to those seen as the original sovereigns over national territories, are therefore simultaneously geopolitical and biopolitical. Discourses of autochthony result in a hardening of nationalist discourses, for they are productive of both National-Natives and their Others, people who can never belong to the nation because they are not Native to its territories.

Claiming National-Nativeness therefore embeds people in certain kinds of relationships. It positions oneself in the dominant half of the negative duality in which "ancestral lands" need to be safeguarded against "strangers" who are imagined to be soiling Native patrimony (see Ceuppens and Geschiere 2005, 385–386). In the Postcolonial New World Order, no one is stranger to its system of nation-states than Migrants. Rights of national self-determination make the rejection of Migrants—or allochthons—a national right. Migrants, because they are not National-Natives where they actually live and work, are portrayed as inherently unworthy of land, livelihoods, and rights there. Further, within the politics of national autochthony, Migrants are also portrayed as the *cause* of Native displacement. Not only does this normalize national controls over access to citizenship and immigration, but, because such controls are portrayed as necessary to ensure home rule, anti-immigrant politics come to be seen as essential to the project of decolonization itself.

By creating, maintaining, and normalizing separations between National-Natives and Migrants, autochthonous politics are key to the biopolitics of the Postcolonial New World Order. For those whose autochthonous identities align with the nation-state they find themselves in, as well as those who imagine themselves as Natives but lack national sovereignty over claimed territories, autochthony is a key political identity for making claims to nationalized resources. Making claims to autochthony buttresses one's national claims, while the labeling of others as Migrants delegitimizes theirs. Hence, autochthonous vilification of Migrants—calls to "keep them out," "send them home," or demand they "stand behind" National-Natives—is a mainstay of the politics of national autochthony.

 Under imperial states, being categorized as Native was the mark of colonial subordination. In the Postcolonial New World Order, this has been turned on its head. As discussed in chapter 2, the road to claiming what I call National-Nativeness was paved by two sets of imperial practices, both aimed at ensuring the continued profitability and viability of colonial rule. The first was newly enacted regulations and restrictions on the movement of "coolie" labor within the British Empire as a way to discipline and control workers after its post-1835 abolition of slavery. The second was practices of "indirect rule" colonialism with its bifurcation of colonized Natives into two opposing groups, Indigenous (or autochthonous) Natives and Migrant (or allochthonous) Natives. In both instances, Migrants as well as Migrant-Natives were represented as dominating those said to be Native or as *more* Native.

The defining binary of the Postcolonial New World Order—National/Migrant—is grounded in these previous imperial discourses of autochthony. Not only were all those crossing new national borders categorized as Migrants, but in many of the "national liberation states," so too were those who had been previously categorized by imperial states as Migrant-Natives. From the start, possession of formal National citizenship did not immunize people imagined as allochthons against national exclusion. Sooner or later, various biopolitical groups within nation-states were *redefined* as Migrants, which worked to recast them as *oppressors* of National-Natives. Some were stripped of their citizenship. If they retained their citizenship, they were, nonetheless, *socially* positioned as "not Nationals." The struggle for national liberation, therefore, was not a one-time event, but a never-ending battle fueled by a mission to search out, identify, and exclude (by expulsion or even extermination) the Migrants within the nation.

In this chapter, I show that the postcolonial separation of National-Natives and Migrants is neither insignificant nor isolated. And *against* autochthonous discourses, I argue that it is not natural or timeless either. Each autochthonous discourse has its own historical specificity, organized through layers of imperial legacies and nationalist politics, including electoral contests over who rules the nation-state. Some of the people portrayed and targeted as Migrants are, in fact, the co-National Citizens of those claiming autochthonous status, while others are not. However, in each instance, it is the idea that the "people of a place" *should* rule that is drawn upon.

I discuss both the centrality and the variance in the deployment of autochthonous discourses in the claims made by Buddhist National-Natives in Myanmar; Hindu National-Natives in India; Hutu National-Natives in Rwanda; Black National-Natives in Sudan; White National-Natives in both Europe and the former White Settler colonies; First Nations National-Natives in Canada; Indian Tribal National-Natives in the United States; and Indigenous National-Natives in Bolivia. I do not argue that these different usages of autochthony are equivalent. They differ in tenor and tone and in scale and intensity. Autochthonous discourses are deployed "from above" and "from below" and are mobilized by people across the left-right political spectrum. Autochthonous claims take on different forms within, between, across, and, at times, against, today's existing nation-states. And variously constituted autochthons have differing relationships to the institution of national citizenship. Most importantly, the people who deploy such discourses have wildly varying abilities to institutionalize their politics of autochthony. Indeed, it is not unusual that those making autochthonous claims have few alternatives when trying to affect national politics or global markets. It is equally the case that not all contemporary discourses of autochthony advocate or mobilize physical violence against allochthons. Indeed, some people make autochthonous claims to argue for the collective care of planetary ecologies, each other, and the generations of life to come. This can especially be true when autochthonous discourses are deployed by people who seek but have not yet secured a national sovereignty of their own.

However, bringing these highly variant autochthonous discursive practices from across the world together allows us, I believe, to better understand that the similarities between them are neither superficial nor merely semantic. Their correspondence is evident not only in their shared use of the term "Native" or "Indigenous," but in how autochthonous claims elevate and amplify political claims to national sovereignty, territory, identity, and belonging. Across their various permutations, *all* autochthonous discourses rely upon—and *all* are productive of—essentialist and ahistorical ideas of nation and race, both of which are then made the fundamental basis of legitimate political claims. *All* autochthonous discourses assert that National-Natives are the original and ultimate source of law and the grantors of rights. *All* transform land into nationally sovereign territory. And, in classic postcolonial style, *all* claimants to autochthonous national sovereignty imagine themselves to be engaged in anticolonial resistance. In the process, colonialism is redefined as the usurpation of National-Natives' place as sovereigns over specific territories. This is why, as the nationalisms defining the governmentality of postcolonialism intensify, the ongoing demonization of the figure of the Migrant proceeds by representing Migrants as colonizers who "settle" on National-Native territories. Today, this is the surest way to *delegitimize* not only their presence but also their political demands.

All mobilizations of national autochthonous discourses thus view indigeneity as a *first principle* of political action. In classic Aristotelian thought, first principles are concerned with discerning a particular kind of distilled truth or essence in a given social phenomenon. They are understood to be generative, as the first basis from which something is known. As discussed in chapter 2, the spatial or temporal truth claimed in discourses of autochthony is that there exists an original link between an individual, group, and territory. Further, such a link is said to be the only rightful basis for power in and over a place—in the past, today, and into the future (Zenker 2011, 67). Since that which is elevated to a first principle is its own validation, within autochthonous discourses, having "Native rights" to national sovereignty is presented as self-evident. As Olaf Zenker (2011, 67) states, autochthony is usually represented as "'authentic,' 'primordial,' 'natural' and 'self-evident.'" As with any essentialist discourse, its empirical truthfulness is *presumed* in order to foreclose any effort at further explanation or inquiry. For this reason, autochthonous discourses are profoundly *depoliticizing*. Claims made on the basis of autochthony are rendered "unpolitical" (W. Brown 1995, 14) to immunize them from the critical practice of deconstruction. As autochthony is said to be *originary*, it becomes divorced from contingency, interpretation, or history. Consequently, and in a deeply ironic and troubling move, autochthonous discourses constitute National-Natives as being a People without history.

The special relationship autochthons claim to have to land or to place is thus a metaphysical one. Foucault (1977, 142) pointed out in regard to other metaphysical worldviews that the search for an origin (*Ursprung*), one that attempts to "capture the exact essence of things, their purest possibilities, and their carefully protected identities," allows one to be confident in the belief that "things are most precious and essential at the moment of their birth." The idea of autochthony as the originary source of political power is what undergirds autochthonous claims to land and place. *All* things, of course, have a relationship to the land (and water and air) they live on or in. Within autochthonous discourses, what only National-Natives have is a sovereign claim to territory. Unlike demands for a return of *land* (and water and air) in order to liberate people from exploitative relationships such as demands for the return of the commons (see chapter 9), demands for *territory* are political claims that define the extent of the sovereign's domain over land (and water and air) as well as the labor of the people living on it.

This is why laying a claim to autochthonous territory entails the territorialization of people. It is through this process that National-Natives become the "people of a place" while Migrants are made the "people out of place" in the places they actually live. Claiming to be the "original people" or the "original sovereigns" is not merely an historical observation (one that is often disputed) but is about laying claim to being *of* a particular place in order to lay claim *to* that place and to a particular *place* in that place. Today, claiming autochthony is about claiming the power of national sovereigns. Autochthonous claims to national sovereignty are, like most discourses of "nations," productive of ideas of race. Through a discourse of shared origins, autochthony proposes an imagined sameness of the nation's members (Kristeva 1993, 3). The basis of this sameness—ideas of ancestral genealogies, kinship, and/or blood—easily folds into ideas of race. "Origins" in autochthonous politics thus is both territorialized *and* racialized. National-Native land becomes a racialized place of sovereign power.

In this chapter, I try to understand how it is that autochthonous discourses are plausible—and how they work—in a remarkably wide set of circumstances ranging from far-right political parties to the movements of some of the most exploited and oppressed people within existing nation-states. An answer lies in the centrality and normalization of nationhood in the Postcolonial New World Order and, relatedly, in the interlocking relationship of the *racialization* of nations and the *territoriality* of power. Being a National indicates a certain status and set of rights within nation-states, and being a nation does the same in the international system of nation-states.

Claims to nationhood remain crucial for any claims of national sovereignty. Without them, one is relegated to being a "minority," someone *wholly unable* to lay claim to sovereignty over national territories. This helps to explain why National-Natives without national sovereignty resist being cast as "just another minority" within the nation-states whose sovereignty they contest (Ward Churchill and Hill 1979, 39–40; V. Deloria 1986, 3). Claims to autochthonous status may not allow people to actually gain national sovereignty, but they do make people *Nationals* whose claims for territorial sovereignty can at least be *heard* by the international system of sovereign nation-states (and by other nationalists). Within the Postcolonial New World Order, autochthons—or National-Natives—are thus the exemplary National citizens.

In what follows, I start with a discussion of the deployment of autochthonous discourses in the national liberation states. It is here where we most clearly see how discursive practices of national autochthony not only have been perverted but have *thwarted* projects for decolonization. Here, the successful claims of National-Natives to national sovereignty have led to a procession of partitions, expulsions, and even genocide, each accompanied by an ever-deeper antipathy to people constituted as Migrants. From these examples in Asia, Africa, and the archipelagos in the Pacific, I move to a discussion of select examples from the former White Settler colonies. In these nation-states, there are *two* biopolitical groupings of people representing themselves as National-Natives—Indigenous National-Natives and White Supremacist National-Natives. Both do so to bolster their own, different autochthonous claims to sovereignty over national territory.

The discourse of White Supremacist National-Natives borrows heavily from imperial discourses that connect sovereignty to capitalist discourses of "productive" or profitable exploitation of land and labor. The claims of Whites to autochthonous status rest on their being the first to turn land into both private property and state territory. On the other hand are the autochthonous claims of people formerly classified by imperial states as the Natives (or "Indians" or "Aborigines") of the colonies that existed prior to extant nation-states. Contemporary autochthonous claims made by Indigenous National-Natives, on the other hand, rest on the principles of first settlement as well as sometimes revisionist claims to first national sovereignty. While in many progressive or left-wing circles the dominant view is that the autochthonous claims of Indigenous National-Natives are wholly unproblematic, I discuss how in these too, the Migrant on Native territory is increasingly identified as a menace, a threat, and increasingly, as a settler-colonist.

Discourses of White Supremacist National-Natives are also found in Europe. It is perhaps here that it is most patently obvious that autochthonous discourses foreclose, rather than advance, the struggle for liberation and justice. As in the former White Settler colonies, Europeans—the very biopolitical groups placed in the *dominant* half of the imperial binary of European/Native—have unabashedly come to identify themselves as Natives. Across Europe, White Supremacist National-Natives have increasingly become successful in electoral politics by claiming an autochthonous identity of their own. This helps them to separate—and elevate—themselves from all those who were categorized as Natives during the imperial era. In their continued imagination of themselves as European and as White (with some National variant of such), they mobilize a discourse of autochthony in order to position themselves as oppressed victims assaulted, invaded, and even colonized by Migrants. The imperial binary of European/Native has thus been uncannily flipped into the *national* binary of Native/Migrant. An increasingly common refrain is that the autochthons of Europe are being "replaced" by Migrants (Nossiter 2017). Central to claims of postcolonial autochthony across Europe is a deep-set, anti-Migrant politics aimed either at ending immigration or "repatriating" those not Native to European nations.

Examining each of these historically specific sets of autochthonous discourses *together* demonstrates the centrality of the Native/Migrant binary to the Postcolonial New World Order. Having shown in chapter 7 how crucial citizenship and immigration controls were to the nationalization of state sovereignty, I discuss how the limits to political membership in nation-states, each resting on an autochthonous basis, have *intensified* as the promised fruits of nationalism have proven to be rotten. Nowhere is this rot more evident than in those former colonies where the colonized Natives achieved "their own" national sovereignty. Examining events there is perhaps the clearest way to discuss the work done by the postcolonial discourse of autochthony. Such an examination forcefully shows that national liberation did not result in decolonization, nor *could* it have.

THE NATIONAL-NATIVES OF NATIONAL LIBERATION STATES AND THEIR MIGRANT-OTHERS

We have seen that successful national liberation movements declared their national sovereignty by enacting citizenship and immigration controls (chapter 7). The policing of territorial borders worked in tandem with a discourse of autochthony *within* national liberation states. Autochthony established the criteria for which people belonged in new nationalized societies and, as such, the racialized basis for laying claim to national sovereignty. In this section, I show that national liberation states repackaged the practices of "define and rule" implemented by indirect-rule colonialism into postcolonial politics that determined national membership. Such politics produced the postcolonial figures of the National-Native and its Migrant Other. Not only noncitizens but also select non-Native citizens found themselves excluded from national belonging by this latter category.

I highlight select sites in the Third World where the politics of autochthony have been highly consequential. While my emphasis is often on nation-states in Africa, this is not because there is any greater prevalence of autochthonous discursive practices there or of the violence these have engendered, but because scholars of African nation-states have, so far, done the most extensive and impressive work on their growing use.[1] Despite this emphasis, it is clear that across the world, the struggle for national liberation is still being waged. Today's nationalisms often define Migrants as their colonizers, some of whom are their fellow Nationals. The outcomes of autochthonous battles have included partitions between National-Natives and Migrants, including their expulsion from national territory, as well as the dissolution of older national liberation states and the formation of new ones. While these processes are not easily disentangled, for heuristic purposes, I show the significance of each.

Postcolonial Partitions

Some national liberation states were formed through the formal partitioning of territory and a violent sorting and expulsion of people. The independence of Pakistan and India in 1947 was an exemplar of this process. In both nation-states, new national populations were produced through normative ideas of sameness, with religion a key marker. Even though India declared itself a secular state, Hindu nationalism deeply informed the discourses of national belonging as well as the practice of nation-state power (P. Anderson 2012). In contrast, Pakistan (West and East) was explicitly formed as a Muslim nation-state (Khan 1985). However, national culling and calls for further national liberations did not end with their formation, as is evident with the creation of Bangladesh in 1971 from the territories of East Pakistan and the contemporary fascist politics of Hindutva (or "Hindu-ness") in India.

A powerful political force in British India since the 1920s, Hindu nationalism informs criteria for belonging to the Indian nation perhaps now more than ever. Since the 1980s, Hindutva has become a powerful electoral movement as well as one that has fundamentally shaped ideas of national belonging. In 2014 the Bharatiya Janata ("Indian People's") Party (BJP) won a landslide parliamentary victory under Narendra Modi. With long-standing ties to the Hindu nationalist Rashtriya Swayamsevak Sangh (RSS), Chetan Bhatt (2001, jacket copy; emphasis added) argues that the BJP's "Hindu nationalism is based on the claim that it is an *indigenous* product of the primordial and authentic ethnic and religious traditions of India." The BJP separates the Indian nation-state's polity into two groups: National-Natives, comprising primarily Hindus (but also, for now, Buddhists, Jains, and Sikhs), are separated from the followers of "foreign religions," including Muslims, Christians, Jews, and Parsis (or Zoroastrians) (Bhatt 2001). For Hindutva supporters, Muslims are especially targeted as threats to the sacralized *Bharat Mata* (Mother India). This is evident in the destruction of Muslim sites of worship and in repeated attacks against Muslim citizens. It is also evident in Prime Minister Modi's growing rhetoric on "illegal" Muslim Migrants in India.

In his 2014 election campaign, Modi referred to undocumented Migrants said to be from Bangladesh as "infiltrators" and pledged to deport them en masse. This rhetoric came on the heels of growing violence against Muslims across India. In 1992, the sixteenth-century Babri Mosque in Ayodhya was destroyed by a Hindu nationalist mob of thousands spurred on since the 1980s by the BJP and the Vishva Hindu Parishad (VHP), a quasi-political group of the *Sangh Parivar* or "Joint Family" of Hindu nationalist organizations affiliated with the ruling party. In 2002, an anti-Muslim pogrom in the state of Gujarat left 790 Muslims and 254 Hindus dead, another 2,500 people severely injured, and 223 more people missing (Dhattiwala and Biggs 2012). About 20,000 homes and businesses and 360 Muslim places of worship affecting approximately 150,000 people were destroyed (Sinha and Suppes 2014). During these atrocities, Modi was Gujrat's chief minister, and he is accused of complicity in them. Mayaben Kodnani, Modi's confidante and one of his senior ministers at the time of the pogrom, was convicted in 2012 of murder, arson, and conspiracy for her involvement in the massacre of Muslims, largely women and children (G. Harris and Kumar 2012).[2] There have been continuous acts of Hindu nationalist violence against Muslim citizens of India and, increasingly, against Indian citizens who are Christian. Since May 2015, self-appointed "cow protectors," many of them associated with the ruling BJP, have enacted "a violent vigilante campaign" against the sale, purchase, consumption, and slaughter of cows (Human Rights Watch 2017).

Prabhat Patnaik (1993) has referred to Hindutva organizations (including those of the BJP) as examples of Hindu fascism for their employing of *communalist* tactics (constructing differentiated "communities" and fomenting violence between them) in order to promote a broader authoritarian program. Through a discourse of violent masculinity, Hindutva constructs an aggrieved and supposedly homogenous Hindu National-Native majority and juxtaposes them with an equally homogenous (mostly) Muslim minority who is seen to embody an emasculating presence that is foreign to India. The subservience, expulsion, or, for some, even the extermination of these allochthonous others is portrayed as necessary for the purification of the Indian nation. Patnaik (1993, 71) describes how the Hindutva organizations attempt to achieve their aims through "physical threats against opponents; the unleashing of burning, looting and killing mobs; 'action plans' directed against the so-called infiltrators (i.e. in minority-inhabited areas); and open incitement to violence."

In this era of institutionalized Hindutva rule, Modi's labeling of undocumented Muslim Migrants as infiltrators casts all Muslims, whether citizens or not, as outsiders to the Indian nation. In Narendra Modi's 2015 election campaign tour of Bengal, he promised to send all illegal migrants "back to Bangladesh"—a clear reference to Muslims—although he reassured his audience that those who would come to worship the Hindu goddess Durga would be "welcomed home as sons of Mother India" (Friese 2015). To concretize Modi's efforts, the VHP offered some fifty-seven impoverished Muslim families ration cards and jobs in return for "converting back" to Hinduism. As for Modi, so it is for the VHP—namely, conversion, or what Hindutva supporters call "reconversion," is viewed as a "homecoming" (*ghar wapsi*). Both reinforce the idea of Indian state territory as the home of an autochthonous Hindu nation.

Autochthonous Expulsions and Exclusions

In other national liberation states, the national population was defined through the process of "indigenization." Autochthonous discourses were crucial for defining those who were *of* the nation and those who were *in* the nation but not *of* it (Falola and Jennings 2002). Sometimes the process took place at a regional level. Some people in sub-Saharan Africa were defined as "its" Natives and, as such, were seen as more *authentic* and *relevant* for the process of decolonization than their Migrant-Others. Indeed, these others were defined as a barrier—or even an outright threat—to such projects. Thus, many new nation-states—most infamously Uganda—insisted that only Black "Africans" were autochthons and, thus, the only "true" Nationals. The opening of new universities and colleges during the 1960s in Africa was a crucial element in the creation of this autochthonous historiography of Africa (Brizuela-Garcia 2006, 85–86). Often done in the name of providing employment opportunities for the "true" Nationals (Peil 1974), autochthonous politics led to calls to expel the allochthons. The project of "Africanization" did not prevent new nation-states from also expelling those who were racialized as (Black) Africans but not as Nationals. Indeed, many of these expulsions were done under the guise of providing employment opportunities for those Africans also defined as the state's Nationals (Peil 1974). These dual processes were central to the production of the category of National-Native.

Immediately upon its independence in 1960, Nigeria expelled those seen as Ghanaian (Manby 2010). It did so again in 1983 when approximately three million people were expelled, of which an estimated one million were Ghanaians (Aluko 1985, 539). Likewise, throughout the 1960s Ghana, which became independent from the British in 1957, expelled hundreds of thousands of "foreigners," including those born in Ghana. In 1969, the Pan-Africanist president of Ghana, Kwame Nkrumah, relabeled Yoruba people as "aliens" from Nigeria, portrayed them as threats to the "national interest," and deported them en masse (Sudarkasa 1979). Indeed, a popular term to identify Yoruba people in Ghana was *Mubako*, meaning "You are going" (Olaniyi 2008, 10). Guinea, which gained its independence in 1958 from France, expelled fishermen who went to Ghana. Cameroon, Ivory Coast, Ghana, and Zaire each expelled traders who went to Nigeria. Ivory Coast and Niger expelled civil servants who went to Benin. Ghana and Ivory Coast expelled farmers and laborers who went to Togo. Unsurprisingly, the discourse of autochthony haunted the deportees. They faced many difficulties as a result of being referred to as "newcomers or new arrivals" upon their entry to nation-states viewed as their autochthonous homelands by those who deported them (Olaniyi 2008, 21).

Uganda, which obtained its independence from the British Empire in 1962, mobilized both a racialized discourse of Africanness as well as a nationalist discourse of Ugandanness. In 1972, people classified as Asians were expelled to further the autochthonous claims of "indigenous Africans" to

National-Native rights to land, political power, and capitalist markets (Mamdani 2001; Espeland 2011). Yet such autochthonous politics did not subside after the subsequent collapse of Uganda's economy, a disastrous attempt at invading Tanzania, and the ouster of Idi Amin in 1979. In the early 1980s, President Milton Obote, one of the leaders of Uganda's national liberation movement, expelled tens of thousands of Banyarwanda people. Included in this group were about 40,000 people who claimed Ugandan citizenship (Van Hear 1993).

In 1995, Uganda changed its constitution to restrict national citizenship from birth to those persons "one of whose parents or grandparents is or was a member of any of the indigenous communities existing and residing [as well as having been born] within the borders of Uganda as at the first day of February, 1926." That year was chosen because it was in 1926 when sugar cane plantations began operation and people from British India were brought in as indentured workers. People in groups such as the Aliba, Aringa, Banyabutumbi, Banyaruguru, Barundi, Gimara, Ngikutio, Reli, and Shana were successful in being reconstituted as one of the "indigenous people of Uganda," but because of the timeline restriction, people racialized as Asian in Uganda were not (Manby 2010, 42).

Severe discrimination against "Asians" with regard to employment and ability to engage in trade was commonplace in Kenya as well after its independence in 1963. The 1964 Africanization policy of Jomo Kenyatta required adequate knowledge of Swahili (or English, but only if one was racialized as being of "African descent") to naturalize into the new Kenyan national citizenship. Consequently, the vast majority of Asians did not take on Kenyan citizenship and kept their British citizenship (and passports) instead. As noncitizens, Asians were not permitted to work in certain occupations or lawfully engage in trade throughout much of Kenya. Kenya's 1967 Immigration Act solidified their Migrant status by requiring them to acquire work permits. Later on, expulsions of mostly Kikuyu peasants in Western Kenya and in the Kenyan Rift Valley also took place (Veit 2018). In the ever-intensifying politics of autochthony there, Kikuyu peasants had been redefined as "settlers" by those identifying as Kalenjin (Kagwanja and Southall 2013, 79). Having moved from one part of Kenya to another, they too were re-presented as Migrants who had "stolen" the land of other groups. As Peter Veit (2018) reports, "Clashes throughout the 1990s left thousands of people dead and over 350,000 displaced." Kenya was far from alone in engaging in such practices.

Other national liberation states embarked on a seemingly endless series of coup d'etats to politically expel those recategorized as Migrants and prevent them from holding state power. In postindependence Fiji, politics continued to be organized along the racialized lines first established by the British Empire. Fiji's Constitution of 1970 was largely based on the previous, British-era Constitution of 1966 and followed its "indirect rule" policies. In the voting registration, all National Citizens were classified according to their membership in differentiated colonial categories of membership, each organized through ideas of autochthony and allochthony. There was "Fijian" for the colonial-era Natives of Fiji, "Indian," for the descendants of one of the more than 60,000 people transported to Fiji from British India from 1879 to 1916 as "coolie" indentured laborers, and "General," for all those citizens not easily fitting into these two categories.

Less than a decade after Fiji's 1970 independence, an "Indian" dominated party, the National Federation Party (NFP), narrowly won the 1977 parliamentary elections over the Alliance Party and the Fijian Nationalist Party (the latter of which ran on a platform of repatriating Indians to India and garnered 25 percent of the "Fijian" vote). However, the "Fijian" governor general, Ratu (or Chief) Sir George Cakobau, bypassed the NFP and instead called on Ratu Kamisese Mara (a fellow chief and distant cousin) of the defeated Alliance Party to form an interim government while new elections were called (Tomlinson 2004, 666). Mara won the new elections. A decade later, Fiji's new Labour Party (a merger between the Labour Party and the NFP) won the April 1987 elections. One month later, the new prime minister, "Fijian" Timoci Uluivuda Bavadra was deposed in a military coup led by Lieutenant Colonel Sitiveni Rabuka, who claimed that he was seizing power to protect autochthonous Fijians from "racial discrimination" at the hands of allochthonous "Indians." After Fiji's Supreme Court ruled the coup unconstitutional and the governor general opened talks with both the Labour Party and the Alliance Party in an effort to form a new government, Rabuka staged another coup in September 1987 and declared Fiji a republic. He appointed a new government and handpicked the new president and prime minister. Subsequent and violent riots led to the burning and looting of the homes and businesses of "Indians," forcing thousands to leave Fiji. Of course, because of the "paper walls" erected worldwide, not all those wanting to leave could get out. Most Indians who left Fiji had the financial means, education, and skill sets to gain the necessary visas to emigrate, including medical professionals, teachers, engineers, and accountants.

In 1990, the newly installed Fijian government passed a new constitution in which both the positions of president and prime minister, as well as the majority (thirty-seven) of the seventy parliamentary seats, would be reserved for those now categorized as "Indigenous Fijians." By 1992, Rabuka was back in power, this time as prime minister. Ironically, it was his government that enacted the 1997 Constitution allowing non-Fijians to hold the position of prime minister. Yet after the 1999 election of Fiji's first "Indian" prime minster, Mahendra Chaudhry, another coup d'etat was carried out in 2000. After another coup in 2006 as well as a declaration of emergency powers in 2009 (which ended in 2010), a new constitution was enacted in 2013. It eliminated all reference to the racialized categories of voting and holding office. In the 2014 elections, Commodore Frank Bainimarama, the leader of the 2006 coup, decisively won. Nonetheless, the percentage of "Indians" in Fiji fell from around 50 percent in 1987 to about 32 percent in the mid-2010s.

Indonesia declared independence from the Dutch Empire in 1945 (which recognized it in 1949). In 1950 the Republic of Indonesia was formed. Indonesia's 1945 Constitution had already made it clear that Indonesia saw control over immigration as evidence of its sovereignty. It began regulating the entry of non-Indonesian Nationals—starting with those categorized as political refugees—in 1956. Because of ongoing struggles for territory and sovereignty between contending forces within Indonesia, its first nationality law was delayed until 1958, however. Once its criteria for obtaining national citizenship were in place, Indonesia began regulating the entry and employment of Migrant workers within the state (see Indonesia 1958). Indonesia's regulation of Nationals and Migrants was not only an international affair, however. Distinctions were made between Indonesian citizens within Indonesian territory. The meaning of "true" Indonesian nationness came to center around the autochthonous claim to *pribumi-ness*—the claim to "originate" from the Indonesian archipelago (Heryanto 1998, 100). *Pribumi*-ness was first postulated by the Dutch imperial state to separate Indigenous-Natives from Migrant-Natives and subordinate both to Dutch rule. Atanu Mohapatra (2014, 43–44) argues that the category *pribumi*, an amalgam of the Javanese prefix *pri*- (person) and the Sanskrit *bhumi* (earth), was a local translation of the Dutch category of Inlanders. This latter category was the third of the three hierarchically ranked groups constructed by the Dutch colonial administration: "Europeans," "Foreign Orientals," and "Inlanders."

Today, those who identify as *pribumi* are imagined as the Indigenous people of the Indonesian nation-state—its Indigenous National-Natives. This autochthonous identity has been mobilized against those people now constituted as Chinese Migrants (the Dutch Empire's "foreign Orientals"). Indonesian citizens racialized as Chinese have been disproportionately attacked in right-wing violence targeting communists in 1965–1967 as well as in May 1998 riots in several cities (Winarnita 2011). Although they are Indonesian citizens, they are nonetheless granted fewer rights than the *pribumi*. They are required to carry identification cards with distinctive numbers and discriminated against in professions other than commerce. Their involvement with any public institution requires extra paperwork and fees, and they are largely shut out from holding government positions (Heryanto 1998, 100–101).

Such forms of discrimination are evident in Cameroon as well. There, the discourse of autochthony targets select Cameroonian citizens seen to be from elsewhere within Cameroon and politically labeled as Migrants in a bid to exclude them from electoral politics. With the reintroduction of multiparty elections in 1990, people claiming autochthonous status in key electoral districts argued that "strangers" to the area were going to "illegitimately" outvote the "true locals." It was argued that these "strangers" ought to be barred from voting (Zenker 2011, 68). One prominent opposition leader, Samuel Eboua, went so far as to say, "Every Cameroonian is an allogène [French for allochthon] anywhere else in the country . . . apart from where his ancestors lived" (in Ceuppens and Geschiere 2005, 390). It did not matter that Cameroon's 1972 Constitution expressly recognized the right of any citizen to reside in any part of the country they wished or that almost all people constituted as Migrants (or *allogènes*) were Cameroon citizens. Today such claims are relevant not only in local elections but in national presidential elections as well. Drawing from French imperial-era distinctions between Indigenous-Natives and Migrant-Natives, President Paul Biya labeled his opponents *allogènes* to delegitimize their claims to political power (Geschiere 2009; Geschiere and Nyamnjoh 2000; Konings and Nyamnjoh 2003; Nyamnjoh and Rowlands 1998).

In Cameroon, such strategies of autochthony were initiated "from above" but were quickly mobilized "from below." Violent demonstrations erupted after the 1996 municipal elections in Cameroon's largest city of Douala, when supporters of the losing party denounced the winners as *allogènes* and attacked them (Geschiere and Nyamnjoh 2000). Their claims were given legislative authority when the ruling Biya regime passed new laws prohibiting the political participation of *allogènes* in regional associations. Supposed *allogènes* were told to "go home" to their "real villages" to vote (Geschiere 2009). Indeed, Bambi Ceuppens and Peter Geschiere (2005, 389) argue that Cameroon "offers a prime example of the effectiveness that autochthony slogans can acquire in national politics." It also offers an example of what they term the "basic insecurity" within autochthony: "[While] it seems to offer a safe, even 'natural' belonging, [it is nonetheless] haunted by a basic insecurity: apprehension about its own authenticity, the need to prove itself by un-masking 'fake' autochthons, that inevitably leads to internal division and violence" (401).

Cameroon also offers a clear example of how the mobilization of a discourse of autochthony represents a further hardening—or limiting—of "national belonging." In such discourses, autochthonous status is far more important than the formal status of national citizenship.

Such processes are under way in Côte d'Ivoire (Ivory Coast), where ideas of autochthony were first introduced by French colonialists in 1893, as well. During the country's 1930s struggles for national liberation, autochthonous discourses were appropriated by those who established l'Association de Défense des Intérêts des Autochtones de Côte d'Ivoire, which expressly worked against the claims made by those the French had defined as *allogènes* (1934). These politics continued with Côte d'Ivoire's independence from France in 1960 and intensified in the late 1980s and early 1990s. In 1993, President Henri Bédié invoked the idea of *Ivortenorité* ("Ivorian-ness") as a way to discredit his main rival for the presidency, Alassane Ouattara, who, in the simultaneously nationalized *and* localized politics of autochthony, had two strikes against him. Ouattara was from the North, and some claimed that his parents came from Burkina Faso. Indeed, Bédié as well as the intellectuals supporting him tried to establish themselves as "super-autochthons" (Marshall-Fratani 2007). Their status as Baule people, they claimed, made members of their group more capable of governing the nation-state than even other recognized autochthons. Such politics continued to intensify. In 1999, in the southwest of Côte d'Ivoire, violent expulsions at the hands of Krumens took place against some 8,000 to 12,000 Burkinabés who had been redefined as "strangers" or *allogènes* (Human Rights Watch 2001). Prefigured by the 1993 mobilization of the discourse of autochthony by Bédié against Ouattara, "leading government officials in Côte D'Ivoire . . . incited a violent xenophobia [mostly against] the largely Muslim north of the country." This political and social environment was called "the new racism" by a 2001 Human Rights Watch report.

The institutionalization of racism within nationality can be seen in the more restrictive citizenship laws in Africa. Liberia has the most restrictive: its 1986 law allows only persons of "Negro descent" to hold citizenship from birth or to naturalize into Liberian citizenship. Sierra Leone also prohibits the naturalization of "non-Negroes." Malawi only grants citizenship from birth to those with at least one parent who is a Malawi national *and* "a person of the African race." Mali also implemented such a preference for children born there with parents who are "of African origin." Algerian citizenship allows persons who have "always been treated as Algerian" (or *possession d'état de national algérien*) but also provides that "nationality of origin" can only be claimed if two generations of one's family were Muslims born in Algeria. Somalia's 1962 Citizenship Law granted Somali nationality only to a person "who by origin, language or tradition belongs to the Somali Nation" and is resident of Somalia. Libya's first Nationality Law of 1954 was replaced in 1980 by a new Nationality Act. Enacted during a period of heightened Arab nationalism, the act held that only people who were both Arab and Muslim (Article 10h)—but excluding Palestinian Arabs, according to Article 3—could naturalize. Ghana also now has racialized criteria for naturalization, allowing persons of the "African diaspora" to become Ghanaian nationals on terms easier than those for persons who are not of "African descent."

National-Native Time: Autochthony and the Re(formations) of National Liberation States

Across Asia and Africa, autochthonous claims to "first human settlement" are augmented by—and sometimes wholly replaced by—distinctions based on who was where when imperial states first colonized a given place (see Ceuppens and Geschiere 2005). We can see the significance of the formation of *National-Native time* across nation-states in Asia and Africa, each place having very long histories of multiple movements and multiple human settlements. In a sense, of course, all claims to autochthony are temporal. However, the claims to National-Nativeness I discuss in this section arise out of particular postcolonial conditions, wherein postcolonial states rely on the colonizers' gaze to count which colonized Natives can be their National-Natives. This is another iteration of the erection of "paper walls." Those people who cannot provide documentary evidence (usually provided by the former colonizing state) of residency in the postcolonial state's territory are classified as allochthonous Migrants. Such classification schemes are enacted with regard to "belonging" within the nation-state's territory as a whole or in certain areas within a nation-state. Secessions of "oppressed nations" claiming a national autochthony of their own out of the territories of former national liberation states result from such temporal strategies of autochthony.

Egypt's first Nationality Code (1926) established autochthony as a criterion for Egyptian nationality by harking back to the late-nineteenth-century Ottoman suzerainty in which some, but not all, Ottoman imperial subjects in Egypt were categorized as "indigenous Egyptians." This was further hardened in 1956 by the new nationality law decreed by President Gamal Abdel Nasser. 1900 was the date by which people had to have been resident in Egypt to qualify for citizenship (Laskier 1995). Article 1 of this law further stipulated that "neither Zionists nor those against whom a judgement has been handed down for crimes of disloyalty to the country or for treason, shall be covered by this provision." Since no definition of who constituted a "Zionist" was offered, these stipulations left all Jewish persons at risk of either being denied Egyptian nationality or of being stripped of their Egyptian nationality.

From one of the older nation-states in Africa to the most recent, we see such an emphasis on an always-already racialized autochthony. The relatively new nation-state of Eritrea (established in 1993) mandates that nationality from birth is only given to a person with a parent "of Eritrean origin," defined as someone resident in what is now Eritrea in 1933. The Democratic Republic of Congo (DRC) only allows nationality to persons who are members of an "indigenous community" present in the DRC on the date of independence (30 June 1960). However, different laws in the DRC allow for the required autochthonous origins to be established at various points: 1885 (the first year that the borders of "Congo" were described), 1908, and 1950. Each includes and excludes certain persons now resident in the DRC. In Swaziland, the 1992 Citizenship Act grants citizenship "by KuKhonta," or "customary" law, which in practice ensures that only "ethnic Swazis" (those defined as Indigenous-Natives by the former imperial state) are able to easily acquire citizenship. The Ivory Coast effectively prevents people said to be lacking in *Ivortenorité* (or "Ivorian-ness") from holding Ivorian nationality.

The Hutu/Tutsi divide in Rwanda is one particularly stark—and genocidal—example of how National-Native time has reified the process by which imperial states separate Indigenous-Natives and Migrant-Natives. Indeed, the 1994 Rwandan genocide is perhaps the most analyzed example of the politics of autochthony in the African context. Carried out by Hutus in the name of their autochthonous rights in Rwanda, Tutsis—defined as *colonizing Migrants*—were attacked and killed in the hundreds of thousands. "Traitorous" Hutus who refused to participate in this genocide were also targeted. The ways that the genocidal attacks against both were normalized have been widely studied (see Boone 2014; Cruvellier 2010; Kabanda 2007; Chrétien 2007; Melvern 2006; LeBor 2006; Amnesty International 2004; Karlsson 2003; Mamdani 2001; Human Rights Watch 1999; Carlsson, Sung-Joo, and Kupolati 1999; Wagner 1999; Gourevitch 1998; Prunier 1995; Newbury 1995; Morrison 1993; Linden 1977).

Such enormous violence is not an anomaly but is part of the present Postcolonial New World Order, the violence of which continues to be normalized. This is evident in the formation of South Sudan, the world's newest state. South Sudan's 2011 secession from Sudan shows the continued salience of a politics of autochthony to ongoing national liberations. It also reveals the importance of enacting policies on citizenship and immigration to ensure processes of national "culling" through deportation of non-Nationals. Here as elsewhere, both are legacies of imperialism. Beginning in 1899, Sudan was technically ruled by a British-Egyptian condominium but was effectively a British colony. From 1924 onward, Britain administered Sudan as two separate provinces: the North, which it defined as Muslim, and the South, which it defined as Christian. Movement between them was controlled by the British. In the mid-1940s, some degree of self-government was extended to Sudan. In 1948 a legislative assembly and an executive council were established in the merger of the two segregated provinces. Legislation defining who was to be recognized as "Sudanese" dates to this time, when the clock for claiming Sudanese nationality was set to 31 December 1897 (just prior to the British takeover). As we will see, this became important a century later, because bordering regions (most notably Darfur) were not considered a part of Sudan in 1897.

Sudan became an independent state in 1956, with its capital, Khartoum, located in the north. From the start there were concerns over marginalization from politicians in the south. Shortly after independence, the Khartoum Parliament passed its 1957 Sudanese Nationality Act, which remained in effect until 1993. Nationality could be acquired by three categories of persons: those who were "Sudanese by descent" (with a domicility date set at 1924, when the British created two separate provinces), "foundlings" (those deserted as infants), and those given permission to naturalize (Articles 5, 6, and 7; see Sudan 1957). Naturalization required males to be domiciled in the state for a minimum of 10 years (Article 8c) and be able to speak Arabic (Article 8c). "Alien" women could only naturalize upon marriage to (and a minimum two years' residence with) a Sudanese national (Article 9). Notably, all naturalized citizens' names would be kept on a separate register (Article 11).

When demands by southern politicians for a federal system were soundly rejected by Khartoum, civil wars between the two formerly segregated British provinces ensued. On 9 July 2011 the Sudanese state was split into the Republic of Sudan and the Republic of South Sudan. Neither state provided people with a real choice as to what their nationality would be. It was presumed that each state had a "natural" makeup along racialized or ethnicized lines and, as such, nationality would be bestowed to those who "belonged" to either the north or the south of the formerly bifurcated colony. Each separated ethnic group was assigned a particular nationality. In the law, one could neither renounce nor contest the nationality one was given, regardless of one's desires, intents, or attachments to the places claimed as the territories of either nation-state.

The (north) Sudanese state passed a new Nationality Law in August 2011 that automatically stripped the citizenship not only of all those who had acquired South Sudanese citizenship but also of anyone it constituted as "southerners," even if their link to South Sudan was a distant relative, such as a single great-grandparent born in what is now South Sudan (Manby 2012, 4). A nine-month (9 July 2011 to 8 April 2012) deadline was established for "southerners" resident in Sudan to legalize their status or else be treated as "illegal" Migrants. By the end of the deadline, an estimated two million people had left Sudan for South Sudan—many of whom had never lived there and were leaving many people and things behind. Meanwhile, approximately 350,000 "southerners" remained in Sudan (UN-OCHA 2012). Now classified as illegal Migrants, they lost their jobs, faced enormous difficulties in keeping their land and properties, and were denied education and medical attention. And, of course, no longer Sudanese National Citizens, they became subject to deportation. A Charter of Voluntary Return, whereby "southerners" in Sudan would move to South Sudan, was signed by the governments of the two new nation-states and endorsed by the African Union (Manby 2012, 34).

However, the state of South Sudan provided no guarantees that persons classified by the Sudanese government as "southerners" would in fact be given citizenship in South Sudan. In the lead up to the day of independence, South Sudan passed a Passports and Immigration Act as well as a Nationality Act on 7 July 2011 to establish its boundaries of national belonging. The definition of who was to be considered a "South Sudanese national" was extremely vague. It was less of a legal status than a racialized one. South Sudanese nationality was attributed on three main criteria: first, to those people able to show that one parent, grandparent, or great-grandparent was born in what was now South Sudan; second, to those who could show that they were members of one of the "indigenous ethnic communities" of South Sudan (of which no list was compiled); and third, to those whose parents or grandparents had been "habitual residents" of what became South Sudan since the independence of Sudan in 1956.

Many people regarded as southerners in Sudan were unable to fulfill any one of the three criteria of being South Sudanese and were denied its nationality. Many people already resident in South Sudan were unable to do so either, for they were unable to provide proof of membership in a South Sudanese "indigenous ethnic community" or show that they had the requisite relatives born in what was now South Sudan. At the same time, the South Sudan Ministry of the Interior announced on 10 April 2012 that all people it considered to be "nationals of the Republic of Sudan are declared foreigners" (in Manby 2012, 4). All so classified would be subject to confiscation of land and property as well as arrest, detention, and deportation as illegal Migrants (Manby 2012, 1). It added that Sudanese nationals resident in South Sudan would have an unspecified period to regularize their status and would be granted temporary stay documents in the meantime. A report by the NGO Refugees International (2012) found that the new South Sudanese state adjudicators had rejected nationality applications in Juba (the new state capital) on the basis of discriminatory and arbitrary decisions. For instance, some persons were denied nationality because they did not look like South Sudanese persons (usually on the basis of their skin not being "dark enough").

Today there are many people who cannot prove definitively that they are either northerners or southerners. Included in this large group are people identified as Kresh, Kara, Yulu, Frogai, and Bigna who live on both sides of the new border (Manby 2012, 7). There are also people who continue to practice a pastoralist livelihood that has them moving between the territories of now two separate nation-states (9). This includes people identified as Rufa'a who, due both to their status as "Arabs" and their "unsettled," nomadic livelihoods, often leaves them without citizenship in either state. Additionally, there are hundreds of thousands of people in both Sudan and South Sudan who are considered Migrants from the region now known as Western Africa— for example, Ngok Dinka, Misseriya Arab, Mbororo, and Falata (a generic term for all Muslims thought to be from West Africa)—who now face grave uncertainty in the places they live. Moreover, all those fleeing the conflicts leading up to (and following) the establishment of two separate states now face enormous bureaucratic hurdles in being declared the nationals of one or the other state and are, thus, at the risk of being expelled.

An even greater threat lurks, however. On 25 December 2011, the Nuer White Army, a newly formed group in South Sudan, issued a statement stating its intention to "wipe out the entire Murle tribe on the face of the earth as the only solution to guarantee long-term security of Nuer's cattle" (Ferrie 2011). On 27 September 2012, a "Four Freedoms" agreement was signed by representatives of both Sudan and South Sudan. Freedom of residence, movement, economic activity, and property rights for nationals of either state living on the territory of the other were to be respected. However, upon its signing, protests erupted in South Sudan centered on the concern that such freedoms would strengthen the power of Sudanese citizens in South Sudan. The similar concern that one group of citizens (or ex-citizens) are major threats to the security of nations is currently being deployed in the attempted "disappearance" of Rohingya people in Myanmar, to which I now turn my attention.

The discourse of autochthony is the normalizing frame for what many observers call the "world's next genocide" in Myanmar, formerly known as Burma (see Brinham 2012; Zarni and Cowley 2014; International State Crime Initiative, Queen Mary University of London 2015). In 1974, Rohingya people,[3] who live primarily in the borderland regions of western Myanmar, were registered as foreigners by the Burmese nation-state. This effectively rendered them stateless.[4] Having denied Rohingya people national citizenship, the current Myanmar government regards them as Migrants with no inherent right to reside in its territories. Consequently, the homes, livelihoods, and lives of Rohingya people have come under increased assault. In 2012, Myanmar constructed approximately sixty-seven camps and moved about 140,000 Rohingya people there. Many observers viewed these camps as nothing less than concentration camps, both because of their biopolitical basis and because of the *calculated* pain suffered by those held captive in them (Motlagh 2014; Fortify Rights 2015; Kristof 2016). The violence against Rohingya people intensified further: from late August 2017 to January 2018, two-thirds of all Rohingya in Myanmar—an estimated 688,000 people—crossed into Bangladesh to flee the raging violence against them, including the systematic raping of women and children (UNHCR 2018). These attacks were led by Myanmar's military forces (see Ibrahim 2018; UNHCR 2018). Rohingya people are simultaneously victims of the growing autochthonization of national citizenship across the world and the paper walls denying them free entry into and rights within nation-states whose citizenship they do not possess. Together this leaves Rohingya people in a highly dangerous situation.

These specifically postcolonial threats to the existence of Rohingya people in Myanmar are legacies of British imperialism. The two coastal areas of what is now Myanmar, including contemporary Tenasserim and Rakhine states (where the majority of Rohingya people have lived) were incorporated as a "minor" province of British India in 1824. The British expanded their rule in 1852 by annexing Lower Burma and again in 1885 when all areas of present-day Myanmar (including Upper Burma) became an administrative part of British India. Given the timing of British colonization, British Burma was governed according to the logic of "indirect rule" colonialism (see chapter 2). Throughout Burma, the British placed people they defined as different from one another in various biopolitical groups. As elsewhere, the British favored certain groups over others. In areas the British classified as Frontier (later Scheduled) Areas—where the majority of "national ethnic minorities" in Myanmar live today, including Chin, Shan, Kachin, and Karenni people—"traditional rulers" were selected to nominally rule over the colonized Natives. On the other hand, in areas classified as "Ministerial Burma," a form of parliamentary home rule (controlled by the British India Office in Calcutta) was established. This is where the majority of people constituted as Bamar (or Burman: speakers of Burmese) lived. The British disadvantaged Bamar people—who now dominate the nation-state of Myanmar—in relation to those groups who today are constituted as either national ethnic minorities or, like the Rohingya, as Migrants.

In the nation-building project preceding and following Burma's declaration of independence in 1948, a conflicted process of both "place-making and claim-staking" ensued (Zarni and Cowley 2014, 697).[5] New national leaders began to sort out who was—and was not—eligible for Burmese nationality. In chapter 2 of Burma's founding constitution (1948), the criterion of "indigenous race" (in Burmese: *Taiyintha*, or the "original children of the soil"), a category first used when Burma was still under British imperial rule, was selected over residency or birth in the new nation-state's territory as the basis of citizenship. Initially, Rohingya people were included as one of the so-called indigenous races and, as such, granted national citizenship rights. Indeed, in these early days of the Burmese nation-state, the government officially had little difficulty in recognizing that Rohingya people lived on both sides of the Burmese–East Pakistan (now Bangladesh) border. As late as 1961, Brigadier Aung Gyi "was emphatic about the indigenous nature of the Rohingya people" (in Zarni and Cowley 2014, 695–696).

However, one of the legacies of British imperialism was a simmering resentment of anyone viewed as "Indian," many but not all of whom had been positioned in a "middle" position in the Burmese province of British India. These people came to be prominent in both commercial activities and in the British security forces and were permitted entry to the parliament set up by the British. Active mobilization against Burmese citizens racialized as Indian began after the 1962 military coup led by General Ne Win and his Burma Socialist Programme Party. One of the junta's first acts was to dissolve Rohingya social and political organizations. This was justified by rhetoric that recast Rohingya people as Migrants from South Asia (either India or East Pakistan–Bangladesh). In 1964, shops and stores owned by people popularly referred to as "Indian" or "Chinese" were targeted by the state for nationalization (Zaw et al. 2001). This succeeded in creating a mass exodus of people in these biopolitical groups out of Burma. Soon thereafter, anti-Rohingya racism intensified and began to be encoded in the law. By 1974, the situation had deteriorated significantly. An Emergency Immigration Act, which mandated that Rohingya people be issued foreign registration cards, effectively took away their Burmese citizenship. In 1978, there were mass expulsions of people the state now represented as illegal migrants. Approximately 250,000 Rohingya people fled, mostly to neighboring Bangladesh. Most were forced to return after Bangladesh refused to accept them and international pressure was applied to Burma to allow them reentry.

In the ensuing international crisis, a new 1982 Burmese Citizenship Law was passed that reemphasized the term *taingyintha* (i.e., "national" or "indigenous races"). General Ne Win, during its framing, portrayed this as necessary for national unity, which, he argued, was necessary for the *ongoing* anticolonial struggle (N. Cheesman 2017, 463). Marrying the British imperial category of colonized Native with the national category of Burmese citizen, he argued, "We, the natives or Burmese nationals, were unable to shape our own destiny. We were subjected to the manipulations of others from 1824 to 4 January 1948. . . . The people in our country [were] comprised of true nationals, guests, issues from unions between nationals and guests or mixed bloods, and issues from unions between guests and guests. . . . This became a problem after independence. The problem was how to clarify the position of guests and mixed bloods. When the problem was tackled, two laws emerged [the Union Citizenship Act of 1948 and Union Citizenship Elections Acts of 1948]" (in Zarni and Cowley 2014, 699). Now, he argued, these laws were no longer sufficient to protect the nation.

The 1982 Citizenship Law (Section 3) made state recognition of a person's *autochthonous* relationship to Burma central to claiming Burmese citizenship. Section 5 stated that "all persons born *taingyintha*, or all persons born of parents both of whom are *taingyintha* are citizens" (in N. Cheesman 2017, 471–472). Significantly, the law deployed National-Native time by declaring that "Kachin, Karenni, Karen, Chin, Burman, Mon, Arakanese, Shan, and other *taingyintha* and ethnic groups who resided in an area of the state as their permanent home anterior to 1185 Myanmar Era or 1823 A.D. are Burmese citizens." It was not a coincidence that the areas where the majority of Rohingya people resided were incorporated into British India in 1824, a year after this deadline. Demand for documentary evidence that privileged a timeframe centering the start of imperial rule resulted in Rohingya people being left off the 1982 list of *taingyintha*. However, for those desperately seeking loopholes, it did not expressly exclude them either (N. Cheesman 2017, 472–473).

After a new military junta took state power in 1988, Rohingya people were, in practice, officially denied Burmese citizenship. Following the 1988 junta, General (now-Chairman) Saw Maung talked about the existence of 135 "national" or "indigenous race" groups, in which Rohingya were not included (N. Cheesman 2017, 478). Not being included as *taingyintha*, which had become a "pre-eminent term of state practice," officially made Rohingya people *Migrants* (472). Throughout Myanmar society, Rohingya people were (and are now) commonly referred to as "Bengali" or "Kalar," both of which have become racist pejoratives. And in keeping with the basic postcolonial condition that nation-states owe little or nothing to people they categorize as Migrants, Myanmar has consistently normalized the persecution of Rohingya by referring to them as "illegal (im)migrants" descended from people arriving either during the time of British rule (i.e., after 1824) or after national independence in 1948, when *jus sanguinis*, in this case having the "blood" of an "indigenous race," was made the basis for national citizenship.

In a 1998 letter to the UNHCR, General Khin Nyunt, secretary of the State Peace and Development Council, declared, "These people [Rohingya] are not originally from Myanmar but have *illegally migrated* to Myanmar because of population pressures in their own country" (in Lewa 2009; emphasis added). President Thein Sein (2011–2016) commonly referred to Rohingya people as "Bengalis" and in 2011 proposed that Rohingya people be "*re*settled" abroad. The representation of Rohingya-as-Migrants intensified as they were increasingly portrayed not only as a threat to peace but also as an *existential threat* to Burmese *taingyintha*-ness. In 2012, Sein declared that most Muslims in Myanmar were a "threat to the peace of the nation" and would be "put in camps and sent abroad" (in Fuller 2012). These camps were built, and approximately 140,000 Rohingya people were forced into them. In this same vein, a 2015 presentation to new army recruits entitled "Fear of Extinction of Race" asserted that "Bengali Muslims [i.e., Rohingya people] . . . infiltrate the people to propagate the religion [of Islam and] aim to increase their population and wipe out the Burmese Buddhists" (in Iyengar 2015).

The use of autochthonous discourses about "national" or "indigenous" races to categorize Rohingya people as Migrants is especially rampant in Rakhine state, where the majority of Rohingya people live. U Oo Hla Saw, general secretary of the state's largest party, the Rakhine Nationalities Development Party (RNDP), proclaimed in 2013 that "this is our native land; it's the land of our ancestors" (in Fuller 2012). When outlining his party's vision, RNDP chairperson and member of Parliament Aye Maung stated, "We need to rebuild the Rakhine State only for the Rakhine who alone are the indigenous on the soil" (in Zarni and Cowley 2014, 694). Responding to questions about the recent pogroms against Rohingya people, the head of a Buddhist monastery in the Rakhine capital of Sittwe, U Pynya Sa Mi, maintained that "the Rakhine people are simply defending their land against immigrants who are creating problems" (in Motlagh 2014). Likewise, the head of an association of young monks in Sittwe, U Nyarna, was quoted as saying that Rohingya were "invaders, unwanted guests and 'vipers in our laps'" (in Fuller 2012). Buddhist monk leader Ashin Htawara encouraged the government to send Rohingya people "back to their native land" (in Hindstrom 2012). The monk leading the economic boycotts and social shunning of Rohingya people gave these reasons for doing so: "The Muslim people are stealing our land and drinking our water and killing our people. They are eating our rice and staying near our houses. So we will separate. We need to protect the Arakan people [another name for Rakhine state]. . . . We don't want any connection to the Muslim people at all" (in Human Rights Watch 2012, 46).

Perhaps the most outspoken person calling for the expulsion of Rohingya people (and other Muslims) from Myanmar is Buddhist monk Ashin Wirathu, the current leader of the violently Islamophobic "969" movement. Calling mosques "enemy bases," Wirathu argues that it is simply impossible for "native Burmese" to live with "Muslim migrants."[6] The theme song of the 969 movement refers to Rohingya people as those who "live in our land, drink our water, and are ungrateful to us." The song's refrain is "We will build a fence with our bones if necessary" (in S. Kaplan 2015). The 969 movement receives support from senior government officials. In 2013, President Sein declared that 969 "is just a symbol of peace" and that Wirathu is "a son of Lord Buddha" (in Marshall 2013). Such sentiments remain common in the current reformist government, including from some members of Aung San Suu Kyi's National League for Democracy (NLD). In contrast, a Yangon representative of the Burmese Muslim Association, Myo Win, likened the 969 movement to the Ku Klux Klan. This is not a far-fetched comparison: in 2013 Wirathu told *The Times* of London that his organization aims to imitate the fascist English Defense League. There is a Facebook page for admirers of both groups: "Myanmar Buddhists Who Support English Defense League" (in R. L. Parry 2013).

The autochthonous discourse raging in Myanmar is not just talk. Rohingya people face systematic abuse—arson, looting, beatings, torture, forced labor, detention, and the arbitrary confiscation of land and property (Human Rights Watch 2000). Along with restrictions on Rohingya people's employment, health care, and education, Myanmar controls whom Rohingya people can marry as well as whether and how many children women can birth (Lewa 2009). This has been devastating for Rohingya women, who often resort to "backstreet" abortions to avoid prosecution from the state for giving birth to children defined as "enemies of the nation." When they try to make a livelihood, Rohingya people encounter organized boycotts against their employment or small businesses. The Young Monks' Association of Sittwe and the Mrauk Oo Monks' Association have both released statements urging "locals" to shun Rohingya people and deny them food and other necessities (Hindstrom 2012). Many people prominently display signs supporting violence against Rohingya people. When non-Rohingya people extend them help and/or solidarity, they too are socially shunned.

In keeping with the segregationist politics of autochthony, Rohingya people have been denied freedom of mobility within Myanmar.[7] They must receive state permission from a local Peace and Development Council chairman to cross township and state boundaries (see Human Rights Watch 2000). Those placed in camps after 2012 are not permitted to leave. Outside of the camps, random identification checks are common, and some Rohingya people have been prosecuted under national security legislation for traveling without permission (Lewa 2009). Additionally, official lists of household members are checked regularly to see if people without permission to be there are present. Rohingya people are also restricted from building or maintaining religious structures (Lewa 2009; J. Taylor and Wright 2012).

Such attempts to disappear Rohingya people from Myanmar demonstrate the veracity of Edward Said's (2000, 176) insight that "in time, successful nationalisms consign truth exclusively to themselves and relegate falsehood and inferiority to outsiders." Indeed, even the name "Rohingya" has been successfully extricated from political discourse in Myanmar. Again, deploying National-Native time, Myanmar officials consistently say things like "The term 'Rohingya' . . . has never existed in the country's history."[8] In 2015, Myanmar imprisoned five men who printed copies of the next year's calendar in which Rohingya were listed as an official "national ethnic group." They were charged with "publishing materials that could damage national security" (Myat 2015). That same year, the NLD, led by Aung San Suu Kyi, won the elections. Suu Kyi also avoids saying the word "Rohingya" and has failed to denounce their persecution (Fisher 2015). The United States Embassy in Myanmar, eager to normalize relationships with this resource-rich nation-state, does not use the term in its official statements either (Kristof 2016).

The removal of Rohingya people from Myanmar is far from being only symbolic. In 2012 the UNHCR (2015) estimated that "violence in Rakhine State forced around 140,000 people to flee their homes." In a Human Rights Watch (2012) report entitled "The Government Could Have Stopped This," eyewitnesses stated that the Myanmar state not only did little to prevent these attacks against Rohingya people or to stem them once they began, but actively participated in acts of rape and murder. Additionally, "witness after witness described . . . how Arakan [or Rakhine] and local security forces colluded in acts of arson and violence against Rohingya in Sittwe and in the predominantly Muslim townships of northern Arakan State" (Human Rights Watch 2012). The following year, the UNHCR (2015) reported that a further "75,000 Muslim residents were violently expelled" from Rakhine state, with a Reuters investigation finding that there was a heavy involvement of Myanmar nationalists in such atrocities (Marshall 2013).

The persecution has intensified since August 2017. From then to January 2018, almost 700,000 Rohingya people fled Myanmar—mostly to Bangladesh, which has set up rudimentary refugee camps to house them. In November 2017, Bangladesh and Myanmar agreed on a deal to return Rohingya people to Myanmar. It stated that rather than being allowed to return to their homes, Myanmar would instead place—and keep—them in camps. A start date of 23 January 2018 was set for these supposedly voluntary movements. However, the plan was put on hold because of both bureaucratic delays and pressure from various groups, including Rohingya people themselves. Bangladesh thus began construction of a camp on a silt island in the Bay of Bengal in which to place Rohingya people under armed guard. An advisor to Bangladesh's prime minister, Sheikh Hasina, stated that they would only be able to leave the island if they wanted to go back to Myanmar or were selected for asylum by a third country (CBC News 2018).

While such negotiations take place, according to most human rights observers, a genocide is taking place in Myanmar. Zarni and Cowley (2014, 686) argue that four out of five acts of genocide as spelled out in Article 2 of the 1948 UN Convention on the Punishment and Prevention of the Crime of Genocide have already taken place in Myanmar: killing members of the group; causing serious bodily or mental harm to members of the group; deliberately inflicting on the group conditions of life calculated to bring about its physical destruction in whole or in part; and imposing measures intended to prevent births within the group.[9] A recent report from the International State Crime Initiative (ISCI 2015) at the Queen Mary University of London concurs. Given that the stated goal of the perpetrators of violence against Rohingya people—both state and nonstate—is to create "Muslim-free" areas, this 2015 report concludes that Rohingya people are in imminent danger of experiencing "mass annihilation."

None of this is *officially* supposed to happen. At the end of WWII, there was an emerging consensus condemning the Nazi Holocaust in Europe. Indeed, preventing mass atrocities was defined as a *founding aim* of the United Nations (see UN 1948). The persecution of Rohingya people also contravenes numerous international conventions governed by the United Nations, many of which were also meant to address the methods the Nazis employed in carrying out the Holocaust. These include Article 15 of the UN's Universal Declaration of Human Rights, which states that "everyone has the right to a nationality" and that "no one shall be arbitrarily deprived of his nationality nor denied the right to change his nationality"; Article 11 of the 1961 UN Convention on the Prevention of Statelessness; Article 7(1) of the UN Convention on the Rights of the Child, which states that every child shall be registered immediately after birth and shall have the right to a name and to acquire a nationality; Article 24(3) of the 1966 UN International Covenant on Civil and Political Rights, which states, "Every child has the right to acquire a nationality"; Article 9 of the 1979 UN Convention on the Elimination of All Forms of Discrimination Against Women (CEADAW), which declares, "(a) States Parties shall grant women equal rights with men to acquire, change or retain their nationality . . . (b) States Parties shall grant women equal rights with men with respect to the nationality of their children"; and Article 5(d)(iii) of the 1965 UN Convention on the Elimination of All Forms of Racial Discrimination, which reads, "States Parties undertake to prohibit and to eliminate racial discrimination in all its forms and to guarantee the right of everyone, without distinction as to race, colour, or national or ethnic origin, to equality before the law . . . [and to] the enjoyment of . . . the right to nationality." Most recently, the UN's Independent International Fact-Finding Mission on Myanmar released a report calling for "an investigation and prosecution of Myanmar's Commander-in-Chief, Senior General Min Aung Hlaing, and his top military leaders for genocide, crimes against humanity and war crimes" (see UNHCR 2018).

Yet the persecution of Rohingya people shows no signs of ending. There is an enormous—and for Rohingya people, a deadly—gulf between postcolonial rhetoric and reality. Like the largely toothless, post-WWI League of Nations "Minority Treaties" agreed to by states (see chapter 4), today's UN Conventions have consistently failed to protect those whom nation-states are determined to exclude, expel, and even exterminate. Hence, even though the UN Special Rapporteur for Human Rights, Tomas Ojea Quintana, agreed with nongovernmental observers that "there are elements of genocide in Rakhine with respect to Rohingya" (in Zarni and Cowley 2014, 682) and a confidential UN Security Council report acknowledged that the situation in Myanmar may very well constitute "crimes against humanity under international criminal law," not only has the UN refused to enact a commission of inquiry to conduct an "urgent, comprehensive and independent investigation" into what is taking place in Myanmar, but there have also been no negative repercussions for Myanmar from other nation-states (in Kristof 2016). The United States and China fully support the so-called reform effort underway and led by Suu Kyi (Zarni and Cowley 2014, 684). This is likely related to their support for both state-run and private capitalist enterprises eager to exploit the estimated "tens of billions of dollars' worth of verified natural gas deposits . . . found in the Bay of Bengal off the coast of Arakan [Rakhine] State" as well as other valuable resources on Myanmar territory.[10] Unsurprisingly, then, anti-Muslim violence is growing and, according to the Yangon representative of the Burmese Muslim Association, Myo Win, "The government isn't stopping it" (in Marshall 2013).

The "slow-burning genocide" (Zarni and Cowley 2014) of Rohingya people in Myanmar is one of many mobilizations of autochthonous discourses in the national liberation states. However, such discourses are prevalent not only in the former colonies but in the former metropoles of imperial states. Analyzing these, I believe, shows us the centrality of a discourse of Nativeness to all national projects. In European nation-states, where the state category of Native was once a category of *subordination*, nationalists increasingly self-identify as Natives or Indigenous peoples in order to elevate their claims above those constituted as Migrants. I therefore move to a discussion of autochthonous movements in Europe, followed by a discussion of the *dual* character of autochthony in the former White Settler colonies, where both those racialized as Whites *and* as Indigenous claim National-Native status.

As discussed in chapters 3 and 4, the nationalization of state sovereignties began in the Americas in the mid to late nineteenth century, while the transformation of European imperial metropoles into contemporary nation-states began with the fall of the various empires after WWI and was only completed in the 1960s when the metropoles of the largest European empires nationalized their sovereignties. In each of these varied historical processes, national sovereignty was premised on a separation of Nationals from Migrants. The making of Nationals was a process not only of making a People, but making them a People *of a place*. Nation-building projects were thus always projects of autochthonization. In the following sections, I discuss how this process has only intensified as anti-immigrant politics have led to a hardening of criteria for national citizenship. The demand to reduce not only the "foreign workforce" but also the "overforeignization" that comes with the coexistence of people associated with the former colonies in the former metropoles of empires is engendering a significant shift to the far right across

Europe. The growing use of autochthonous discourse is part of this shift as it helps to reframe migration as a form of colonization by "foreigners." Across Europe, migrants are increasingly portrayed as "invading" European nation-states and "colonizing" their "indigenous people." Anti-immigrant politics are thus normalized as being nothing more or less than a battle for "national self-determination."

National-Natives of Europe and Their Migrant-Others

The far right in Europe has recently repositioned itself. Its adherents now represent their ideas and activities as centered on defending the Native or indigenous people of Europe and/or the Natives of a given European nation-state. Many political parties situated in the mainstream have followed suit by incorporating autochthonous discourses into their own electoral strategies. The self-identification of Europeans as Natives is an uncanny discursive shift, particularly in the former imperial metropoles. After all, the separation of Europeans and Natives was one of the great, divisive legacies of imperialism. Europeans were *produced* through binary constructions of the essential difference between them and their negatively racialized Native-Others (Stoler 1995). To be European was to be interpellated into imperial projects on the side of the colonizer against the colonized Natives. To be European was to *not* be Native.

The shift to seeing Europeans *as* Natives therefore starkly signals the growing moral authority of autochthonous discourses in politics. It marks a discursive shift wherein claims are made not only on the basis of "Europeanness," "Whiteness," or even one's nationality, but on one's indigeneity to national territory. Here too, this framework is deployed to normalize the *exclusive* claims of those able to claim *National-Nativeness*. And like other autochthonous discourses, in Europe such deployments rest on the exclusion and/or political subordination of Migrants. As more and more Europeans re-imagine themselves to be National-Natives—as the "people of a place"—they see themselves as the only ones with an inherent right to be in the territory of the nation-state. Autochthonous discourses allow people and political parties in Europe to claim that their demands to halt migration and to subordinate, imprison, or expel Migrants are not racist but "only" nationalist. The universal legitimacy of nationalism, along with the growing legitimacy of discourses of indigeneity, allows such demands to appear to be unpolitical.

This is true for marginal parties who are often quite violent at the level of "the street," as well as those with firm command over the apparatuses of violence of the nation-state. On the website of the relatively marginal British National Party (BNP), it was recently stated that "the nationalisms of Europe champion the right of the traditional peoples of Europe to be recognized as the indigenous inhabitants of their lands, and to be accorded the moral right to the special status and right to self-preservation that all native peoples enjoy" (BNP n.d.). On the same website, Donna Treanor, the BNP's London regional secretary, warned that "indigenous" British people were facing "genocide" and "psychological trauma" from immigration and were on their way to becoming "a minority in their own homeland" (BNP n.d.). Likewise, on its website, Germany's neo-Nazi National Democratic Party (NPD), somewhat less electorally marginal, recently electioneered under the slogan, "Money for granny instead of Sinti and Roma." A lead candidate, Udo Voigt, told Reuters, "We say Europe is the continent of white people and it should remain that way." He added, "We want to make sure that even in 50 years' time an Italian, a Frenchman, an Englishman, an Irishman and a German are still recognisable as European and cannot be mistaken for Ghanaians or Chinese" (in Martin 2014). Voigt won a seat in the European Parliament in its 2014 elections, and that year the NPD also held two state assemblies as well as hundreds of seats on local councils.

Somewhat less marginal than the NPD are the Swedish Democrats (*Sverigedemokraterna*), who maintain that "Native Swedish" people are being threatened by "immigrants." In a recent public advertisement campaign, the Swedish Democrats stated that if elected, "native Swedes" would be "welcome back to a Better Sweden" (in Crouch 2014). Not at all marginal is Denmark's Danish People's Party, which argues that it is the state's "moral responsibility to the people of Denmark to keep Denmark Danish." The party's founder, Pia Kjærsgaard, has stated that immigration is neither "natural" nor "welcome" in Denmark (in Milne 2015). In the 2015 general election, it became the second largest party in Denmark, winning almost 22 percent of the electoral vote and becoming a crucial member of the Danish minority government.

More troubling is that by late 2015, far-right parties deploying a discourse of autochthony to make racism and anti-immigration key planks in their campaigns formed the government in Hungary; were a significant part of governments in Switzerland, Greece, Finland, Latvia, and Norway; and were electorally powerful across many European nation-states. The Fidesz party has been in power in Hungary since 2010, when it won a two-thirds majority of seats. Jobbik, a party that is even further to the right than Fidesz, became the second-largest party in Hungary's parliament after winning 20 percent of the vote (Bayer 2017). Concerned that Jobbik would gain political ground, the Hungarian government upped the anti-immigrant ante by erecting razor wire across the Hungary-Serbia border in September 2015 to make the path for people fleeing Syria, Iraq, and Afghanistan more difficult and to demonstrate its concern for "genuine Hungarians" (Szirtes 2015). The razor wire, while largely ineffectual in keeping all people out, allowed Hungary to openly flaunt European Union directives about accepting people seeking refuge and to claim that it was putting Hungarians first.

In March 2016, with tens of thousands of people stranded in Greece (a key first entry point into the European Union), Hungary declared a state of emergency across its national territories. Laszlo Toroczkai, the popular mayor of the Hungarian border town of Asotthalom, normalized the violent attacks against Migrants from both the military and civilian militias by saying, "Migration is just going to lead to bloody conflict" (in Yardley 2016). Shortly thereafter, Hungary's prime minister, Viktor Mihály Orbán, distributed a questionnaire whose questions included these: "Do you agree with the government that instead of allocating funds to immigration we should support Hungarian families and those children yet to be born?" and "Would you support the government placing illegal immigrants in internment camps?" (in Traynor 2015b). By 2016, €16 million in government funds was used to erect billboards with messages such as "Did you know that since the beginning of the immigration crisis the harassment of women has risen sharply in Europe?" (in Gall 2016). Predictably, all this contributed to a worsening environment for anyone not seen as a "genuine Hungarian." The fact that it also enhanced the popularity of political parties deploying such autochthonous discourses was not lost on anyone.

The popularity of such politics has also been evident in Switzerland. During the 2015 Swiss elections, the Swiss People's Party ran under the slogan of *"Masseneinbürgerrung stoppen!"* ("Stop mass naturalizations!"). It was first in the polls, winning 29.4 percent of the vote and 27 percent of parliamentary seats. Its election posters often deployed autochthonous themes, including one showing veiled Muslim women with the question "Where are we living, Baden or Baghdad?" In December 2016, the Swiss Parliament adopted a Federal Act on Foreign Nationals allowing employers to give priority to hiring "native" Swiss over "foreign" workers in parts of the labor market. This agreement also required foreigners seeking a residence permit to show they were truly "integrated" into Swiss society. "Ours First" (*Primi i nostri*) was the Swiss People's Party slogan for the referendum preceding this agreement.

In Greece, the violent, neofascist Golden Dawn Party placed third in the 2015 elections (up from fifth in the 2012 elections and fourteenth in 1996). In doing so, it took 18 parliamentary seats. Its long-time leader, Nikolaos Michaloliakos, marched under the slogan "Out of my country; out of my home" and called Migrants "invaders" of Greece. A Golden Dawn MP, Ilias Panagiotaros, stated that Greece was a "one-race nation," adding, "That is how God fixed earth" (in *60 Minutes* Australia 2014). In Italy in 2018, the Northern League (*Lega Nord* in Italian and since 2018, simply *Lega*, as its demand to separate the North from Italy was dropped) received 17.4 percent of the vote in the national election and became a key partner of the coalition government dubbed by *The Economist* (2018) as the "first all-populist government" in Western Europe.

The *Lega*'s leader, Matteo Salvini, was sworn in as the deputy prime minister and minister of the interior responsible for Italy's immigration policies. Five other members of the *Lega* (plus an independent close to the party) were also made cabinet members. At its founding in 1991, the Northern League used the term "autochthons" to refer to those it imagined as its "own people," while those residents constituted as not of the northern region of Italy were referred to as "allochthons." This included not only non-Italian citizens, particularly Black people, but also "southern Italians." Its anti-immigrant rhetoric was strengthened—and mainstreamed—in 1994, when the Northern League, with 117 deputies and 56 senators, joined the coalition government in alliance with Silvio Berlusconi's right-wing Forza Italia party and were given powerful positions in his cabinet, including deputy prime minister and ministry of the interior. By 2003, Northern League leader Umberto Bossi argued for opening fire on boats of "illegal immigrants" from Africa, whom he described as "bingo-bongos" (in Horowitz 2003). Demonstrating the traveling character of autochthonous discourse, a Northern League party poster in the 2008 election, as described by Aidan Lewis (2008), "displayed a drawing of an American Indian in a feathered headdress, accompanied by the warning: 'They suffered immigration: Now they live in reserves.'" A year later, with another *leghista* minister of the interior, Italy ordered the expulsion of people who had come from Libya to Italy by ship. The *leghista* deputy transport minister publicly declared that Italy needed to protect itself against the "invasion," adding that "this problem could become so unbelievably big that we must ask ourselves if we need to use weapons" (in *Deutsche Welle* 2011).

By June 2018, and in contravention of the International Convention for the Safety of Life at Sea, Salvini refused to allow two boats to dock in Italy: the Aquarius, a rescue ship operated by the NGO SOS Méditerranée with 629 people, and another rescue ship operated by the NGO Lifeline with 224 people. Both ships had rescued people embarking from Libya and trying to cross the Mediterranean to Italy. In August 2018, Salvini turned away yet another boat, this time one carrying 141 people leaving Africa. That same summer, Salvini also called for a "mass cleansing" of migrants, with a focus on Roma people, from "entire parts" of the country. He stated, "We need a mass cleansing, street by street, piazza by piazza, neighbourhood by neighbourhood," adding, "We need to be tough because there are entire parts of our cities, entire parts of Italy, that are out of control" (in Embury-Dennis 2018). In June 2019, the Italian government further decreed that boats bringing Migrants rescued from drowning in the Mediterranean to Italy could be fined up to €50,000 and impounded. As additional boats have been denied entry into Italian ports, it has been reported that "at least 1,150 migrants have died in a year as they attempt to reach Italy from Libya" (Tondo 2019).

The third-largest party in the Flanders region of Belgium, the Vlaams Belang, demands a separate Flemish national sovereignty (see Ceuppens 2006, 147). Its slogans include *Eigen volk eerst* ("One's own people first") and *Baas in eigen land* ("Boss in one's own country"). Its criterion of "nationhood" is one's dutchophone Flemish "ancestry." All others, including Flemish francophones, negatively racialized Belgian citizens, and noncitizens, are considered "allochthons" (Ceuppens and Geschiere 2005, 396). Indeed, such terms are part of the official state language in Flanders. Since 1998, the Flemish administration has officially used these categories, disrupting the idea of a shared Belgian citizenship in the process. Attesting to the racialized character of the discourse of autochthony, all those who are viewed by the state as "non-Western," including Belgian citizens, are categorized as "allochthons," while "western" Migrants are defined as autochthons (Bekers 2009, 61). For the Vlaams Belang, even this is insufficient, because Belgium's "autochthons" include non-dutchophone Flemish.

The Netherlands also officially classifies its residents as either *autochtoons* (people of "Dutch heritage") or *allochtoons* (people of "foreign" birth). Since 1999, *allochtoons* have been further separated into "Western *allochtoons*" and "non-Western *allochtoons*." Indeed, this latter category is *further* divided into first- and second-generation "non-Western allochtoons." The Dutch far-right Party for Freedom (in Dutch, *Partij voor de Vrijheid*, or PVV) has risen rapidly (Yanow and Van der Haar 2013). In 2010, its leader, Geert Wilders, stated that Muslims were trying to "colonise" Holland (Beaumont 2010). Wilders campaigned to defend "Western civilisation as well as Dutch culture," and called for both an end to Muslim immigration and the "repatriation" of all Muslims, including Dutch citizens. In the 2017 elections, the PVV won the second-largest number of votes and gained a further five seats in the legislature (*Economist* 2017).

In Austria, the far-right Freedom Party, whose motto is "Austria first," ran under the slogan *Mehr Mut für unser Wiener Blut* ("More courage for our Viennese blood"). The next rhyming line, "Too many foreigners does no one any good," signaled its main policy of halting all immigration to Austria. It too made significant electoral gains. Norbert Hofer, boasting that his possession of a Glock 9mm gun was the "natural consequence" of immigration, won 46.7 percent of the vote in the December 2016 presidential elections, thus coming closer to becoming head of government than any other far-right party in Central Europe since the end of WWII (Reuters 2016; Foster 2016).

In 2017, the National Front in France also came the closest it had to date to governing. It ran under the autochthonous slogan *Les Francais d'abord* ("First French"). Its leader, Marine Le Pen, with 21.3 percent of the vote, was second in the first round of presidential elections. In the second round, Le Pen, speaking at a rally in the southern port city of Marseille, promised a "moratorium" on immigration as a response to "interlopers from all over the world [who] come and install themselves in our home." She declared that she would make France "more French" and allow "the owner to decide who can come in." The crowd of about five thousand people roared its approval and chanted, "This is our home!" (Nossiter 2017). Le Pen closed the rally by saying, "More and more are coming from the third world, taking advantage of our benefits," adding, "It's a choice of civilization. I will be the president of those French who want to continue living in France as the French do." She won almost 34 percent of the vote.

In Norway, the far-right Progress Party, a part of the governing coalition after the 2013 elections, was the party of Anders Behring Breivik (a member from 1999 to 2006). Breivik is infamous for killing 77 people and injuring 151 in 2011 at a government office in Oslo and at a Labor Party youth camp in order to promote his anti-immigrant politics. Two years after Breivik's murderous rampage, the Progress Party, whose leader, Siv Jensen, argued that a "stealth Islamization of Norway" is taking place, entered into a national governing coalition with the Conservative Party, thereby consecrating a "marriage of neoliberal conservatism and rightwing populism" (Nilsen 2013). This government's goal was to build upon Norwegian, Western, and Christian "traditions" and "cultural heritage."

In Germany, residents viewed as "not German" are divided into categories of *Ausländische Mitbürger* (foreign fellow citizens), *Menschen mit Migrationshintergrund* (persons of migrant background) and *Menschen ausländischer Herkunft* (persons of foreign descent). They exist within the context of ever-proliferating declarations of "the end of multiculturalism." In 2010, German Chancellor Angela Merkel declared that attempts to build a "multicultural" society there had "failed, utterly failed." Laying this "failure" at the feet of Migrants who were not properly "integrating," she prefaced her declaration by saying that at "the beginning of the [19]60s our country called the foreign workers to come to Germany and now they live in our country. We kidded ourselves a while, we said: 'They won't stay, sometime they will be gone,' but this isn't reality" (in M. Weaver 2010). Nonetheless, and largely in response to the displacement of millions of people from the Syrian government's war, Merkel allowed all people seeking asylum to enter Germany while awaiting review of their applications. Between 2015 and 2018, approximately 1.4 million asylum seekers were resident in Germany.

Merkel's actions brought a swift and negative response from much of the electorate and from political parties. By late 2017, the recently formed German far-right party, the Alternative for Germany (*Alternative für Deutschland*, or AfD), won representation in fourteen of the sixteen German state parliaments and ninety-four seats in the Bundestag. It is now Germany's largest opposition party. That year, speaking at a meeting organized by the Europe of Nations and Freedom group in the European Union, Frauke Petry, then-leader of the AfD, condemned the European Union and Merkel for allowing "hundreds of thousands, millions, of mostly illiterate young men from a far and partly violent culture [to] invade our continent" (in Engelhart 2017). Sharing the same stage, Geert Wilders, leader of the Islamophobic and anti-immigrant Dutch Freedom Party, added, "This year [2017] will be the year of the people . . . the year of *liberation*, the year of the patriotic spring" (in Dearden 2017; emphasis added). Joining him, Marine Le Pen, head of France's National Front, declared, "We are experiencing the return of nation-states" (in Geddes 2017).

In the United Kingdom, former British Prime Minister David Cameron also declared in 2011 that the "doctrine of state multiculturalism" had failed. Like Merkel, Cameron held that the <u>central issue was that multiculturalism encouraged "separatism" rather than "integration" from those</u> (many British citizens) <u>constituted as Migra</u>nts. Cameron (2011) argued that "integration" meant "making sure immigrants speak the language of their new home" and "ensuring that people are educated in elements of a common culture and curriculum." He stressed that this "common culture" was one informed by a "British national identity," adding, "It's that identity—that feeling of belonging in our countries that is the key to achieving true cohesion." In February 2012, U.K. Communities Secretary Eric Pickles clarified some of the elements of this shared "British national identity" and how state policies would address them in a government paper entitled "Creating the Conditions for Integration." It stated, "Migrants will be required to speak English, the number of official documents translated into other languages will be reduced and councils will be allowed to hold [Christian] prayers at the start of meetings" (quoted in Walford 2012). At the same time, Cameron's government increased the number of raids at the homes and workplaces of Migrants by 80 percent from 2010 to 2015 with the aim of dramatically increasing the number of deportations (Kleinfeld 2016). This deportation campaign included Theresa May, Cameron's home secretary, who tested a system of "mobile billboard vans" that drove around six London boroughs between 22 July and 22 August 2013 with a large printed message saying, "In the UK illegally? Go home or face arrest" (Travis 2013a). It was part of a wider advertising campaign, which included placing advertisements in eight "minority ethnic" newspapers (Travis 2013a). Labor's shadow home secretary, Yvette Cooper, argued that May was "borrowing the language of the 1970s [fascist] National Front" (in Travis 2013b).

Shortly thereafter, a new political party, the United Kingdom Independence Party (UKIP), was formed and similarly promoted an anti-immigrant agenda. UKIP leader Nigel Farage was a major figure promoting Britain's exit from the EU. His campaign in favor of "Brexit" in the 2016 referendum featured a poster of a column of refugees escaping Syria with the message that the United Kingdom had reached a "breaking point." As British tabloids continuously associated leaving the EU with "taking back our nation," a poll conducted in the last two weeks of the referendum campaign found the main concern of the British electorate was immigration (H. Stewart and Mason 2016). By a slight margin of 51.89 percent, the "leave" side won the referendum. Postreferendum studies show that anti-immigration politics were key to predicting who voted to leave and who voted to stay (Goodwin and Milazzo 2017).

Those targeted as Migrants by the increasingly popular far right in Europe thus include many noncitizens, especially the impoverished and the negatively racialized, as well as both negatively racialized citizens and those not seen as being autochthonous to a particular national *region*. A significant part of this, at least in some nation-states such as Germany and the United Kingdom, is the fact that some negatively racialized people *have* indeed obtained formal national citizenship status. These citizens have gained not insignificant civil rights, including voting and entering state government. Some have also gained some amount of economic power. Thus, for those who see such changes as evidence of "European decline" and see the only place for what Ghassan Hage (2000) has cheekily termed "third world looking people" as either exclusion or formal subordination, the "problem" does not appear to be a *lack* of their assimilation but their *overassimilation*.[11] Possession of formal citizenship, National-Natives argue, does not make someone a member of the nation. Thus, as citizenship has been extended to some Migrant-Others, an autochthonous identity has become a *refuge* as well as a *rampart* from which to attack them.

In these nation-states, as well as in those where Migrants have been purposefully denied nationalized rights and entitlements, the affective response by those who see themselves as the Natives of European nations is a deep and abiding sense of betrayal. A postcolonial melancholy is therefore evident in Europe as well. As elsewhere, it has kept the idea of "national liberation" alive and informed the growing attraction of claims to autochthony. Those imagining themselves as "Europeans" or as "Whites" increasingly claim the status of European-Native in an effort to simultaneously hold on to the imperial privileges of being European while exteriorizing Migrants from extant nation-states. In all cases, the intensification of autochthonous discourses in the nation-states of Europe has resulted in a hardening of ideas about national citizenship and, as I showed in chapter 7, has made citizenship much more difficult to obtain. What is mobilized by far-right and, increasingly, mainstream political parties is the idea that keeping Migrants out—or, at the very least, ensuring their state-enforced "assimilation" into a particular, racialized version of nationness—is necessary for National-Natives to be "sovereign" in "their own land." Claims made on the basis of autochthony further allow claimants to state baldly that they are not racist but simply asserting their "national pride," something all postcolonial subjects are understood as being entitled to. Autochthonous discourses are thus part of the ongoing process of nation building in a Europe only decades away from being the site of imperial metropoles.

The demand that Migrants either "leave" or "assimilate" disavows the structural characteristics of Migrants' social and labor market position within national societies and lays the supposed failures—*and* successes—of Migrants squarely at their own feet, as if their lives are not shaped by the same structural factors affecting the lives of Europeans (R. Miles 1993, 181). This, in turn, naturalizes the existence of the supposedly homogenous and unified nation inhabited by "national capitalists" and "national workers." Claims to European-Nativeness can thus be seen as a continuation of the long-standing practice of denying the *relational* formation of Europe and its Others (Said 1979). More specifically, European autochthony is a deep denial of the formation of Europe *by* its Others. It is also shaped by the deep denial of the massive transformations wrought by postcolonialism—and the refusal to acknowledge that, despite nationalism's promise to the contrary, nation-state power was never meant to be *shared* between ruling and working classes. hmm.

National-Natives of the Former White-Settler Colonies and Their Migrant-Others

In the former White Settler colonies there are *competing* discourses of autochthony.[12] There, two biopolitical groups lay claim to National-Nativeness in order to make claims to national sovereignty and territory: White National-Natives and Indigenous National-Natives. In these once-European colonies and now nation-states, one set of claimants to autochthony are those racialized as "White." Identifying as the heirs of European colonizers, they base their claims to National-Nativeness on the autochthonous principle that they were the *first* to "productively use" (i.e., exploit) both land and labor. As "improvers," they claim to have been the *first* to "civilize" (i.e., bring into the purview of state power) land and people, thus territorializing both and becoming the *first* sovereigns. In short, claims of White National-Nativeness are based on a discourse of White supremacy, one that now depends on a disavowal of its colonial basis. The other claimants to National-Nativeness in the former White Settler colonies are those highly diverse people colonized by European imperial states and defined as the Natives *of* their colonies. Indigenous National-Natives base their claims on the autochthonous principle that they were both the *first inhabitants* and the *first sovereigns* of these territories.

The discourses of White National-Natives and Indigenous National-Natives, each powerful in its own way, are highly asymmetric. The discourse of White National-Nativeness informs the operation of nation-state power and dominates their historiography. While there are numerous and clear challenges to claims that they are the *only* Nationals, White people are still very much regarded as the *center* of each national project. This is evident in the ways that, to paraphrase Ghassan Hage (2000), Whites are the only ones to have the unquestioned authority to worry: worry about national society, worry about the presence of others who may spoil national society, and worry about who gets in and who gets to stay.

The discourse of autochthony deployed by Indigenous National-Natives, on the other hand, has no hold on the dominant structures of any of these nation-states. Nonetheless, their claims to autochthony carry a great *moral* and, sometimes, significant legal weight. Indeed, in the global field of autochthony, writes Bengt Karlsson (2003, 414), "the 'archetypical case' against which indigenousness is to be measured remains that of white settler colonies." This idea was brought home in a 1997 report to the UN's Working Group on Indigenous People (WGIP) by its special rapporteur, Miguel Alfonso Martínez, representing the Cuban government. Martínez (1997, 10–11, para. 77, 80) argued that people attending WGIP meetings from Africa and Asia, unlike those from the Americas, were "ethnic and national minorities [and] [were] not [to] be considered 'Indigenous peoples' in the United Nations context." He argued that the two groups had "intrinsic dissimilarities," which he left undefined (other than to foreground the signing of treaties between colonized people and imperial states in parts of the Americas).

The moral weight granted to Indigenous National-Natives in the former White Settler colonies, in contrast to that granted to people making similar claims in Africa and Asia, rests in the former being seen as continuing the fight for national liberation (see Trask 2000). People claiming indigenous status in Africa (especially) and Asia, on the other hand, are seen to have already gained "their own" sovereignty (Niezen 2003). As a result, Indigenous National-Natives in the former White Settler colonies who demand their own national and territorial sovereignty are seen to be crucial for the task of *completing* the postcolonial project. Increasingly, national courts, deciding on the validity of colonial-era treaties, have ruled in their favor (McHugh 1991). In addition, the 2007 UN Declaration on the Rights of Indigenous People, even though nonbinding, has had some effect on national courts (Wiessner 2008).

Despite the massive dissymmetry between them, then, White and Indigenous discourses of autochthony do have some things in common: people in both biopolitical groups stake an exclusive claim as the rightful *national* sovereigns of the territory in question. As I discuss later, both also view the existence of Migrants as a *barrier* to their obtainment of this goal. Indeed, this third group of people within the former White Settler colonies—neither White nor Indigenous National-Natives, and neither "civilizers" nor first inhabitants—is wholly unable to claim *autochthonous* rights. Indeed, *as* Migrants, they have no claims to sovereignty over the territory in which they live. Instead, they are a People of some other nation and its own sovereign state. They are, in the logics of the Postcolonial New World Order, the "people out of place."

In the following two sections, I discuss the centrality of anti-immigrant politics to the discourses of autochthony employed by White National-Natives and by Indigenous National-Natives. Increasingly, both view Migrants as having "colonized" them. By centering Whiteness as a criterion for national belonging, while simultaneously portraying themselves as the victims of a "flood of Migrants," White National-Natives extend the racist project begun by imperial states. On the other hand, the Indigenous National-Native discourse of autochthony, by dramatically expanding the category of "colonizer" (or "settler colonist") to include non-Whites who were *expressly excluded* from White Settler colonial projects, conflates migration with colonialism. Both are classic postcolonial moves.

White National-Natives and Their Migrant-Others

Claiming a White National-Native identity has a far longer history in the former White Settler colonies than in contemporary European nation-states. In the United States, the autochthonous discourse of Whiteness is what Ronald

Takaki (1993) calls the "Master Narrative of American History." In it, "America" was made by a process in which "Europeans" became less European and more American through their "taming" of the "frontier." The "father of the Master Narrative," Takaki argues, was Frederick Jackson Turner, who developed his "frontier thesis," including a theory of *replacement*, in an influential 1893 speech to the American Historical Association. Speaking just "two years after the Census Bureau announced that Americans had settled the entire continent," Turner posited that, initially, "the wilderness masters the colonist. It finds him a European in dress, industries, tools, modes of travel and thought. It takes him from the railroad car and puts him in a birch canoe. It strips off the garments of civilization, and arrays him in the hunting shirt and moccasin. It puts him in the log cabin of the Cherokee and Iroquois. . . . Before long he has gone to planting Indian corn and plowing with a sharp stick; he shouts the war cry and takes the scalp in orthodox Indian fashion." But, Turner argues, "little by little he transforms the wilderness," and in "a series of Indian wars," the "stalwart and rugged frontiersman takes land from the Indians for white settlement [and the advance of] . . . manufacturing civilization. . . . The outcome is not the Old Europe [but] . . . a new product that is American" (in Takaki 1993, 15). Turner developed his historiographic thesis in a period after the United States had nationalized its sovereignty (i.e., after 1875; see chapter 3), implying that Turner helped to construct *White National-Native* Americans.

Turner's frontier thesis is generally applicable to White national projects of autochthony in other former White Settler colonies, such as Canada, New Zealand, and Australia. The jurisprudence of European imperial states applied the combined principles of *res nullius* and *terra nullius*, wherein anyone or any land designated as "ownerless" was said to lawfully belong to the *first taker*.[15] This allowed imperial states to define themselves as the *first sovereigns* of colonized territories (Anstey 2003). Such acts were part of a powerful imperialist autochthony story, one not reliant on primordialism but on providence. European imperial states claimed they "found" the "New World," because people already living there were seen as simply occupying lands, not possessing territories. Thus, Natives were regarded as lacking sovereignty, over themselves and the land. Colonial dictates mandated that both were thus free to be owned by empire. Such views were significantly reinforced by making Europeanness, and then Whiteness, a "possessive identity" for workers within the shared space of empire, one that gained value in relation to the degraded status of colonized Natives, as well as all Others (Hyslop 1999; Lipsitz 1995). In the process, colonies where European/White workers moved (and were moved) in significant numbers (largely as unfree labor until the nineteenth century) eventually came to be seen by them as *theirs*.

As discussed in chapter 3, it was in the latter part of the nineteenth century that White Settler colonies began to nationalize their sovereignty. Indeed, the social and juridical separation—and elevation—of Whites from all others, a process that had turned these colonies *into* "White Settler" colonies, was also central to transforming some already independent, protoimperialist states in the New World into the world's first nation-states. For example, in the United States from the mid-nineteenth century onward, Whiteness was further used to define who could be a national citizen and who could not. In 1790, its first Naturalization Law (1 Stat. 103) limited naturalizing into U.S. citizenship those who were free, White, and possessing "good character." In 1856, the U.S. attorney general further declared that "Indians" were *subjects* of the United States and could not become naturalized *citizens*.[14] In 1857 the *Dred Scott* decision reemphasized the exclusion of Black people, regardless of whether they were enslaved or free, from citizenship. By 1875, when the United States enacted the Page Act, its first immigration law, the "American nation" was further defined against "coolies" from China and women deemed to be "prostitutes." Both were barred from lawfully entering. As White supremacists well understood, such laws created "segregation on a large scale" (Stoddard 1921, 259). In the process, the United States and other nation-states forged from former White Settler colonies became White "nations."

Together, White supremacy and White nationalism bred nativism with its distrust of influences deemed to be from "outside" and therefore not "native." Powerful movements aimed at ending the movement of people to the United States, such as the mid-nineteenth-century "Know Nothings" (initially called the Native American Party), agitated for limiting both citizenship and appointment to public office to "native-born" Whites. This, they hoped, would consolidate the separation between their Protestant selves and their Catholic others from Ireland and Germany. They enjoyed brief electoral success throughout the mid-1850s (S. Taylor 2000). The U.S. 1924 Immigration Act (see chapters 2 and 3), which established limits to the entry of people arriving from Southern or Eastern Europe for the first time, was designed, in part, in the name of protecting White "Native Americans." The bill's authors—Representative Albert Johnson and Senator David Reed—were "avid readers" of the book *The Passing of the Great Race*, in which prominent eugenicist Madison Grant (1918, 110), warned that the United States was in "great danger" of a "replacement of a higher type by a lower type here in America unless the native American uses his superior intelligence to protect himself and his children from competition with the intrusive peoples drained from the low-est races of eastern Europe and western Asia." Workers who became White were exploited by the White ruling class, but they often joined them in op-posing both the claims of Migrants and those made by their competitors for autochthonous status—Indigenous National-Natives. Thenceforth, people in these latter biopolitical groups would be portrayed by White National-Natives as taking what was exclusively theirs by right of National-Nativeness: jobs, benefits, housing, fish, wildlife, land, and White women.

Today the autochthonous character of White supremacy is evident across the nation-states that were former White Settler colonies. In the United States, the Southern Poverty Law Center (2017b) found a significant increase in White supremacist groups following the presidential election of Donald Trump. Much of their ire, like that of Trump's, targets Migrants. Members of the U.S. National Front, marching at a White Lives Matter rally in Tennessee in October 2017, chanted, "Closed borders, White nation, now we start the deportations!" About six months later, Trump said about undocumented Migrants trying to enter the United States, "These aren't people. These are animals" (in J. H. Davis 2018). At the same time, there are also sizable far-right groups demanding that states disband Native governance councils, abrogate treaties, overturn their legal protections, and further extend the state's expropriation of land currently held in "aboriginal" title (see Southern Poverty Law Center 2018).

Similar White National-Native projects against both Indigenous National-Natives and Migrants exist in the other former White Settler colonies. One of the more far-reaching attacks on Indigenous National-Native people is Aus-tralia's Northern Territory National Emergency Response (NTNERA, or "the in-tervention"). NTNERA was spurred by a 2007 report of the Inquiry into the Pro-tection of Aboriginal Children from Sexual Abuse, which alleged widespread "intra-racial" sexual abuse of Indigenous National-Native children in the Northern Territory, where the majority of residents are categorized as Aborig-inal. Although the report argued that the situation was best handled locally, the Howard government expanded its authority over the Northern Territories (see NTNERA 2007, 234). Calling "the intervention" a "national emergency," Howard (2007) stated that the federal government needed to undertake "a sweeping assumption of power" in response to "extreme social breakdown" so that the state could ensure "social order enforced by legitimate authority." It also sent in the army. The dominant discourses normalizing the interven-tion were "protection" and "civilization." The figure of the Aboriginal child was centered in practices said to transform "failed societies" where there was supposedly "no natural social order of production" into "normal suburbs" (Brough 2007).

Earlier that decade, the Howard government had declared another crisis—a "refugee crisis"—as people arrived to Australian territory from Afghanistan, Iraq, Iran, China, and Vietnam. Government officials consistently represented them as "bogus refugees" attempting to "take advantage of Australians." Framing it as an issue of national sovereignty in the lead-up to the November 2001 election, Prime Minister Howard argued that it was "the fundamental right of this country to protect its borders," adding, "it's about this nation saying to the world we are a generous open hearted people . . . but [that] we will decide who comes to this country and the circumstances in which they come" (in ABC 2001). Howard had stated earlier that those empowered to make such decisions were those Australians in "the mainstream" who represented the "national interest" versus the "vested interests" of those who declared themselves victims of "designer forms of discrimination . . . race, gender and sexual preference" (in Dyrenfurth 2005, 187). For Howard's government, the rightful Australian was the one who embodied the White National-Native.

As he later did against "Aborigines" in the Northern Territories, Howard called out the military and placed the navy in charge of asylum seekers arriving by boat. The Royal Australian Navy was sent to intercept and board any ships thought to be carrying refugees and forcibly transport them to territories redefined as "not-Australian" for the purposes of claiming refugee status (Australia Senate Select Committee 2002, xxi). In 2001, Howard, with Parliament's support, created a new "migration zone," one that removed certain Australian territories, such as Christmas Island, from the definition of Australian territory—all without giving up Australian sovereignty over them. The determination of asylum claims was further politicized and militarized in the 2001 Border Protection Bill, as decision-making powers were shifted from judges to government and military officials.

These two "crises" for the Australian nation-state—the redefinition of "Australian territory" to limit people's claims to asylum and the Northern Territory National Emergency Response—were part of a piece. In both, two biopolitical groups—Indigenous National-Natives and Migrants—were defined by the Australian nation-state as *outside* of the nation and, as such, people to be acted against. The underlying principle informing both was the related discourse of Australia as the place of normatively *White* National-Natives, with the Australian nation-state as a rightful actor defending their territorial homeland.

Arguably, autochthonous discourses are the most readily recognized—and most normalized—when deployed by those constituted as Indigenous National-Natives in the nation-states of the former White Settler colonies (Niezen 2003). Indigenous National-Natives, initially classified by imperial states as the Natives (or "Indians" or "Aborigines") of the colonies, base their claims for national sovereignty on two autochthonous principles: being the *first nations* and the *first sovereigns*. In postcolonial fashion, the claims of Indigenous National-Natives rest upon their being something more than a national minority or ethnic group (see Battiste and Youngblood 2000, 173). This something "more" is *nationhood*, precisely what "minorities" and "ethnic groups" lack in the Postcolonial New World Order.

Thus, it is common for Indigenous National-Native scholars to argue, as Audra Simpson does, that "'Mohawk' and 'nationhood' are inseparable," and that "both are simply about *being*." She continues: "Being is about who you are, and a sense of who you are is arrived at through your relationships with other people—your people. So who we are is tied with what we are: a nation" (in Valaskakis 2005, 214). Taiaiake Alfred concurs: "We have to think of ourselves as nations and act as nations. We really need to develop our own governments." Trying to insulate his claims from critique, Alfred adds, "Anyone who denies our right to exist as nations under our own law on our homelands is a white supremacist in my mind" (in Barrera 2012).

In no small part, Indigenous National-Native claims to nationhood rest on the numerous treaties signed between imperial states (and, later, sometimes by nation-states) and colonized Natives. These treaties are seen as recognition from the colonizing state of their having been "nations" at the time of signing. Today these treaties are referred to as "nation-to-nation relations" between sovereigns. As Donald Fixico (2012, xii; emphasis added) argues in regard to the United States, "Sovereignty, treaties and the trust relationship make American Indians uniquely different than anyone else in the United States because their nations have signed nearly 400 treaties and agreements with the federal government. Due to the international doctrine of law, *sovereigns respect sovereigns in treaty agreements.*" Recent recognition by national courts of prior Native title to territory is regarded by Indigenous National-Natives (and others) as further evidence of their *precolonial*, and *national*, *sovereignty* over territory (Landsman 1988; Macklem 1993; Barker 2005; Biolsi 2005; Moreton-Robinson 2007; Corntassel, Witmer, and Robertson 2008; A. Simpson 2011).

Claims to indigenous nationhood comprise a form of presentism. The existence of political communities imagining themselves as nations is read back into a time when people did not organize themselves as such. This is evident in the 1996 report of Canada's Royal Commission on Aboriginal People (RCAP), which views the nation as "the basic political unit for Aboriginal peoples" not just now, but always (in Cairns 2005, 16). Such presentist arguments are also evident in Audra Simpson's (2014, 26) argument that Mohawk claims to national sovereignty over certain territories held by Canada and the United States are based on Mohawks' being "the world's first people's republic and the first to make a national constitution" in the sixteenth century.

Like much national autochthonous historiography, the significance of such claims lies less in their historic accuracy than in their political importance today. Such claims allow Indigenous National-Natives to be seen as the *first nations*. Specifically, Indigenous National-Native claims to having been national sovereigns *prior* to European colonization enable them to make a competitive claim to being the *first national sovereigns* over the territory in dispute. In Canada, for example, where the term "First Nations" is institutionalized, many of the over six hundred Indian bands now have "nation" in their official titles. Alan Cairns (2005, 16) notes that this "descriptive title" was "most frequently added in the last two decades." Marking this shift, the umbrella organization acting and speaking on behalf of these bands has, since 1982, been named the "Assembly of First Nations." Across the nation-states of the former "White Settler" colonies, Indigenous National-Natives, by forming themselves as nations today, hope to counter White National-Native claims to national sovereignty over territory.

As such, while sometimes deploying radical, anticolonial discourse, Indigenous National-Native nationalist projects do not disrupt a postcolonial world of separate and national territorial sovereigns. They *reproduce* it. Self-defined anarchist Taiaiake Alfred (2005, 266–267), for instance, argues that supposedly distinct and discrete "nations" can and should "move from colonial-imperialist relations to pluralist multinational associations of autonomous peoples and territories that respect the basic imperatives of indigenous cultures as well as preserve the stability and benefits of cooperative confederal relations between indigenous nations and other governments." This vision is, of course, the *core* of the Postcolonial New World Order. Defining oneself as part of a "nation" is the crucial first step for any claim to national sovereignty. Use of—and enthusiastic acceptance of—nationalist discourse also hails Indigenous National-Natives into political projects that construct "Nationals" as a distinct, *genealogically defined* group, indeed, as a "national race" (Balibar 1991c, 43).

Autochthonous discourses calling for the "centering" of Indigenous National-Natives have contributed to the further separation of Natives and Migrants (Lawrence and Dua 2005). Currently this distinction is being more sharply etched into politics in the former "White Settler" colonies. Many scholars and activists alike have dropped the "White" in "White Settler" colonialism altogether and have argued that *anyone* who is not an Indigenous National-Native is a "settler colonist" on "Native land" (Wolfe 1999; Trask 2000; Fujikane and Okamura 2000; Lawrence and Dua 2005).[15] Omitting any reference to the imperial (and national) politics of Whiteness allows for a rereading of the process of human migration as always a process of colonization. The imperial states' historic facilitation of the movement of captive slaves from Africa and "coolie" indentured laborers from Asia, as well as today's movement of people from across the world into the United States, Canada, Australia, or New Zealand, have *all* been refigured as practices of "settler colonialism." A striking example of such a view is found in the argument made by Bonita Lawrence, a Métis scholar, and Enakshi Dua, a self-identified "Asian settler colonist" (2005, 134), who together argue, "[In Canada], people of color are settlers. Broad differences exist between those brought as slaves, currently working as migrant laborers, are refugees without legal documentation, or émigrés who have obtained citizenship. Yet people of color live on land that is appropriated and contested, where Aboriginal peoples are denied nationhood and access to their own lands."

The removal of the White part of "White Settler" colonialism has therefore translated into a special focus being placed on *non-White* Migrants and on their demands for social justice. Indeed, Lawrence and Dua (2005, 122–123) argue that their antiracist praxis "contributes to the active colonization of Aboriginal peoples," indeed that "antiracism is *premised* on an ongoing colonial project" and on "a colonizing social formation" (123, 129–130). Ignoring those who have studied the colonization of people now constituted as Indigenous National-Natives as also acts of racism in Canada (see Maracle 1988; Bolaria and Li 1988; Bourgeault 1989; Abele and Stasiulis 1989; LaRoque 1990; Ng 1993; Bannerji 1995; Backhouse 1999; Mackey 1999), Lawrence and Dua (2005, 128) claim that postcolonial critiques of national liberation strategies or social constructivist critiques of nationhood or nationalisms "contribute to the ongoing delegitimization of Indigenous nationhood" and, thus, to their continued colonization.

The expansion of the term "settler" to include *all* those who can be constituted as Migrants has thus worked to erase the centrality of racism to imperialist practices and separate racism from colonialism (but see James 1963). Patrick Wolfe (in Fujikane and Okamura 2008, back cover) exemplifies such a separation when he says, "The fundamental social divide is not the color line. It is not ethnicity, minority status, or even class. The primary line is the one distinguishing Natives from settlers—that is, from everyone else. Only the Native is not a settler. Only the Native is truly local. Only the Native will free the Native. One is either native or not." Such sentiments are evident in a poem written by self-identified "Native Hawaiian nationalist" Haunani-Kay Trask. She writes,

> Settlers, not immigrants,
>> from America, from Asia.
>>> Come to settle, to take.
>>>> To take from the Native
>>>> that which is Native:
>>>>> Land, water, women,
>>>>>> sovereignty.

> Settlers, not immigrants,
>> bringing syphilis and leprosy,
>>> Jehovah and democracy.
>>>> Settlers, settling
>>>>> our Native Hawai'i,
>>>>>> inscribing their
>>>>>>> lies of discovery,
>>>>>>>> of penury, of
>>>>>>>> victory.

> Settlers, not immigrants.
>> Killing us off,
>>> disease by disease, lie by lie,
>>>> one by one. (Trask 2000, xi)

For Trask, *immigration is conquest*, and Migrants are settler-colonists. Likewise, Audra Simpson (2014, 21) names "the practice of immigration" as one of the ways that "dispossession and occupation" of "indigenous nations" is sustained. She argues that "key to this process of rationalizing dispossession" in the United States and Canada is "the rapid ascent of power for migrants" and their recognition as citizens (25).

Yet, portraying all *non-Indigenous* people as "settlers" assumes that no clear distinction was made between Whites and non-Whites in the "White Settler" colonial projects, nor that any distinction is made between those racialized as White and those racialized as *not* White in today's White National-Native projects. Instead, those whom imperial states (and later nation-states) clearly racialized as undesirable and inferior (e.g., Trask's "Asians" in Hawai'i) are now represented as having been a party to the very projects they were expressly—and juridically—excluded from. Indeed, in the effort to render the experiences of Indigenous National-Natives and Migrants *incommensurable*, the violence done to those who were made into Migrants is rendered as politically unimportant. We see this in self-identified "Asian settler colonist" Candace Fujikane's (2005, 77) assertion:

> Indigenous people are differentiated from settlers by their genealogical, familial relationship with specific land bases that are ancestors to them. One is either indigenous to a particular land base or one is not. Asian Americans are undeniably settlers in the United States because we cannot claim any genealogy to the land we occupy, no matter how many lifetimes Asian settlers work on the land, or how many Asian immigrants have been killed through racist persecution and hate crimes, or how brutal the political or colonial regimes that occasioned Asians' exodus from their homelands.

However, understanding "Asians" to be "settler colonists" is a *territorialized* view of colonialism. In such a view, only those defined (initially by empires) as the Natives of the colony are colonized. All others in the colony are not. This results in seeing people who have been defined as the Natives of colonies elsewhere—in Asia, for instance—as no longer colonized and therefore no longer Natives once they move to another colony. Instead they become Migrants— allochthons from elsewhere; indeed, for a growing number of scholars and activists, their movement out transforms them from being colonized into *colonizers* of other Natives. By conflating migration with colonialism, a discourse of Indigenous National-Native autochthony in the former White Settler colonies thus reproduces an anti-immigrant discourse wherein Migrants become the *cause* of Native dispossession, displacement, and impoverishment.

The understanding of migration-as-colonialization relies on a kind of "methodological nationalism" (Wimmer and Glick Schiller 2002). The argument goes something like this: Indigenous National-Natives comprise the nation and were once sovereign over their national territories, but their sovereignty was usurped by colonizers. Colonization thus consists of a *lack* of national sovereignty by National-Natives. Non-Natives living on these territories can neither be nationals nor sovereigns but are, instead, Migrants. Migrants can be *nothing other than colonists* when on Indigenous National-Native territory that is not their own. Finally, because decolonization is defined as national self-determination, Migrants do not have any legitimate say in such efforts. Instead, they represent barriers to decolonization, especially if Migrants make liberatory claims themselves.

Thus, as with all national autochthonous discourses, the exercise of national sovereignty by Indigenous National-Natives entails the right to define membership in the nation. "We must be the ones who determine who is and who is not a member of our community, based on criteria accepted by our people," declared Ovide Mercredi, a member of the Cree and a former National Chief of Canada's Assembly of First Nations, and Mary Ellen Turpel, a member of the Muskeg Lake Cree Nation and a prominent judge in Canada (in Valaskakis 2005, 231). Affirming this view, Daniel Wildcat, an indigenous studies scholar and Yuchi member of the Muscogee Nation of Oklahoma, adds, "If tribal sovereignty means anything, it means the right of a nation to determine who its members are" (in Valaskakis 2005, 231). Indigenous studies scholar Gail Guthrie Valaskakis (2005, 231) argues that "battles about band membership are grounded in strategies of Native empowerment and struggles articulated to sovereignty, including the recognition of Native bands or tribes as nations that have the legitimate right to determine local membership."

Struggles over membership in indigenous nations are viewed as both an existential issue and a practical issue of allocating rights and resources. Imagined within the framework of nationhood, such views reproduce an antagonism of Indigenous National-Natives to Migrants. Audra Simpson (2014), for example, sees struggles among indigenous people over who should and should not have membership as being of a *different order* than the struggles for rights by Migrants (or "settlers," as she names them). Determining Indigenous National-Native membership is represented as a legitimate matter for nations to decide among themselves, while Migrants' calls for the "right to have rights" are portrayed as an *intrusion* upon indigenous national sovereignty.

However, as we have seen, the making of Migrants is a political process, not a natural one. Today, the upholding of the national right of Indigenous National-Natives to determine membership results in their policing of the borders of their nations. Such ideas are enacted into practices throughout the former "White Settler" colonies (and beyond). In what follows, I briefly discuss two prominent examples: first, the 22 May 1981 adoption of the Kahnawà:ke Mohawk Law and Moratorium on Mixed Marriages by the Mohawks of Kahnawà:ke (in Canada's province of Quebec); second, efforts by the Cherokee Nation to exclude Cherokee Freedmen who are descendants of Black people held as slaves by Cherokees and brought with them on the Trail of Tears to the lands later claimed as Cherokee national territory (T. Miles 2005).

Mohawk and Cherokee National-Natives
and Their Migrant-Others

The Kahnawà:ke Mohawk Law and Moratorium on Mixed Marriages declared that "any Mohawk who married a non-native lost the right to residency, land allotment, land holding, voting, and office-holding in Kahnawà:ke" (in Alfred 1995, 165). The Membership Department of the Kahnawà:ke's Mohawk Band Council further stipulated that "any Mohawk who married a non-native would leave the community," colloquially referred to as the "marry out, get out" rule (see Mohawk Council of Kahnawà:ke 2014). A Mohawk was defined as someone "whose name appeared on the Band list and Reinstatement list and who had 50% or more blood quantum" (in Mohawk Council of Kahnawà:ke 2012). While several evictions of non-Mohawks took place in 1981, a long hiatus ensued until February 2010, when the Mohawk Band Council restarted the practice of issuing eviction letters.

That month, twenty-six letters were sent to "non-Mohawk" people living on the Kahnawà:ke reservation (Magder 2010). When discussing another mailing of eviction letters in 2014, Michael Delisle, grand chief of the Mohawk Council of Kahnawà:ke, argued that permitting non-Mohawks onto the reservation took away space from Mohawks. He stated, "All we are trying to do is preserve, not only culture and language and identity, but who we are as a people, and those days of incorporating others into our society, I won't say is over, but it needs to be controlled by us, and not by outside entities" (in CBC News 2014). Audra Simpson (2014, 9) echoed his case, arguing that any exclusions determined by the Mohawk Nation in Kahnawà:ke stemmed from "their diminished land base" and "the imposition of the Indian Act." She added, "Membership was then [in the 1990s] and still is considered deeply fundamental" to the Mohawks' existence as a nation. It is national membership, she contended, that "affords someone 'the rights that matter': to live on the reserve, to vote if you want in band council or tribal elections, and to be buried on the reservation" (9). In mid-June 2016, an additional twenty eviction letters were sent out to non-Mohawks in Kahnawà:ke. A sign seen at a protest outside the home of a non-Mohawk person during that time read, "Our Lands. Our Rights. Our Blood. Forever" (Shivji 2016).

An April 2018 decision by the Quebec Superior Court overturned the "marry out, get out" rule. Ruling on a complaint filed by sixteen people negatively affected by the membership law who "were exposed to protests, threats and expulsion notices," Justice Thomas Davis stated that the law was discriminatory and violated the Canadian Charter of Rights and Freedoms. Grand Chief Joe Norton responded, "Obviously we maintain the position that matters that are so integral to our identity have no business in outside courts" (in CBC News 2018). However, in June 2018, the Mohawk Council of Kahnawà:ke decided against an appeal.

Basing membership on the racialized criterion of "blood quantum"—a criterion explicitly formulated to reduce the number of people the state recognized *as* Native—has also become the most effective route to limiting membership in Indigenous National-Native nations. In what is now the United States, blood quantum laws dictating that a minimum of 50 percent "Indian blood" was required in order for a person to be recognized as an Indian were first established in the early eighteenth century as part of the general separation of the population along ideas of "race." The U.S. Indian Reorganization Act of 1934 made such requirements ubiquitous. Recently these rules have been used by Indigenous National-Natives in the United States to exclude people previously considered as members. The most infamous of these cases is that of the Cherokee Freedmen.

Following the 1865 emancipation of slaves, an 1866 treaty was signed between the United States and the Cherokees (who reportedly signed under great duress). It stated that freed African slaves once owned by Cherokees and their descendants "shall have all the rights of native Cherokees" (Warrior 2007). In 1893, the United States Dawes Commission was established as part of the government's efforts to break up collective land held by the so-called Five Civilized Tribes (Cherokee, Choctaw, Creek, Chickasaw, and Seminole). It constructed a final roll or list of people recognized by the U.S. government as tribal members.[16] In addition to creating individual allotments of land and dividing monies from the U.S. government's sale of reservation lands to male "heads of households," the Dawes Roll also created different categories of Cherokee membership: "Cherokees by blood," "Cherokees by marriage," "Freedmen," and "Delaware Indians." The Dawes Roll was thus productive of private property, patriarchal relationships, and the racialized idea of "Indian blood" whose lack signified the absence of Indianness.

As historian Daniel Littlefield (in Kellogg 2011) has noted, the Dawes Roll discriminated against those racialized as Black when listing who was—and was not—an "Indian." Cherokee Freedmen with Indian relatives were categorized as Freedmen, while Whites with Indian relatives were categorized as "Cherokee by blood." All of these racialized differences were materialized by making one's eligibility for land allotments and political rights dependent on which category of Cherokee one was placed in. Differences in the size and location of these allotments, as well as differential regulations governing their use, also depended upon these identifications (Sturm 2014, 580).

One of the ways that the United States managed its relationship to "its native people" under federal Indian laws was to grant each tribal council the sovereign right to determine its own citizenry. By the late nineteenth century—precisely the time when the United States was nationalizing its sovereignty (see chapter 2)—the Cherokee had also come to regard themselves as a "nation" and, not unlike the United States, to define their *national* sovereignty as centered on decisions over membership. Thus, as with all communities imagining themselves as a nation, efforts were made to *limit* Cherokee membership. After 1866, Cherokee membership was denied to Black people marrying Cherokees (including Cherokee Freedmen). In 1883, the Cherokee Nation National Council (CNCA) conducted its own census of Cherokees to determine entitlements. Being categorized as "Cherokee by blood" was made a necessary criteria for membership (in *Cherokee Nation v. Nash*, 2017). Such practices fostered a strong sense that being Cherokee was to be a distinct member of a broader "Indian race" and not a member of the separate "race" of Black people (Yarbrough 2007, 129). Thus, despite the fact that the Cherokee Nation did not formally use blood quantum as the basis of tribal citizenship, by the 1970s, very few benefits of membership—such as access to health care clinics, food distribution for the poor, and assistance for low-income homeowners—were available to Cherokees who had less than one-quarter of "Cherokee blood" (Feldhousen-Giles 2008, 189–190). As with other nations, these exclusions were justified on the twin bases of maintaining national "purity" and securing scarce resources. The combined practices of the U.S. government and the Cherokee Nation thus solidified the racialization of Cherokee tribal sovereignty.

In 1983, exclusionary efforts intensified as Cherokee membership was redefined: "Tribal membership is derived only through proof of Cherokee blood based on the [Dawes] Final Rolls" (11 CNCA § 12, as cited in Sturm 2014, 577). Insisting that those enrolled as "Cherokee by blood" were the "real" Cherokees, this redefinition nullified the membership of Cherokee Freedmen. The newly named Cherokee Nation Supreme Court ruled this decision unconstitutional and overturned it on 7 March 2006. It found, "There is simply no 'by blood' requirement in Article III [of the 1975 Cherokee constitution]. There is no ambiguity to resolve. The words 'by blood' or 'Cherokee by blood' do not appear." At the same time, it upheld that "all members of the Cherokee Nation must be citizens as proven by reference to the Dawes Commission Rolls" (JAT-04–09, 13, 3, as cited in Sturm 2014). The court thus upheld the membership of Cherokee Freedmen.

The ruling was immediately rejected by those who believed that only "Indians," and specifically those categorized as "Cherokee by blood," were "true" members of the Cherokee Nation. Days after the court's ruling, Chadwick Smith, principal chief of the Cherokees, called a special election to amend the tribal constitution to exclude all those unable to prove descent from ancestors enrolled as "Cherokees by blood" on the Dawes Rolls. Arguing that the *sovereignty* of the Cherokee Nation was at stake, Smith made it evident that this action was primarily directed at expelling the approximately 2,800 Cherokee Freedmen. With less than one-quarter of registered voters casting a ballot, the amendment was approved by more than three-quarters of the votes. Upon casting her vote in favor of the amendment, Cherokee resident and schoolteacher Phyllis Baker, stated, "We believe in by blood only" (in Previch and Stogsdill 2007). Indigenous studies scholar Robert Warrior (2007), on the other hand, called it a form of "legislated racism." In the ensuing debate, the supposed opposition between antiracism and Indigenous National-Native sovereignty was reinforced. While some decried the Cherokee vote to be nothing more than an act of exclusion driven by racism against the Cherokee Freedmen, others argued that accusations of racism amounted to calls for the termination of "Indian" national sovereignty (see Byrd 2011).

While ignoring the many failures of the U.S. government to honor treaty obligations toward the Cherokee, the U.S. Bureau of Indian Affairs informed the Cherokee Nation that Cherokee Freedmen's citizenship rights could not be revoked under the 1866 treaty signed between the Cherokee and the U.S. government. More than $37 million in Department of Housing and Urban Development funding was suspended. The U.S. Department of the Interior refused to recognize the 2011 election for tribal chief because the Cherokee

Freedmen were denied their treaty right to vote. On 20 August 2017, a U.S. District Court judge ruled against the Cherokee Nation's exclusion of the Cherokee Freedmen. It ruled that "in accordance with Article 9 of the 1866 Treaty, the Cherokee Freedmen have a present right to citizenship in the Cherokee Nation that is coextensive with the rights of native Cherokees." It added, "The Cherokee Nation can continue to define itself as it sees fit but must do so equally and evenhandedly with respect to native Cherokees and the descendants of Cherokee freedmen." Arguing that its decision would not lessen the autonomy of the Cherokee Nation, the court stated, "The Cherokee Nation's sovereign right to determine its membership is no less now, as a result of this decision, than it was after the Nation executed the 1866 Treaty. The Cherokee Nation concedes that its power to determine tribal membership can be limited by treaty." It concluded, "By interposition of Article 9 of the 1866 Treaty, neither has rights either superior or, importantly, inferior to the other. Their fates under the Cherokee Nation Constitution rise and fall equally and in tandem" (*Cherokee Nation v. Nash*, 2017). The Cherokee Nation decided against pursuing an appeal.

Bolivia, Morales, and Indigenous National Sovereignty

From the above discussion, one thing is clear: autochthonous discourses vary greatly across the world. From a generalized understanding that only National-Natives have legitimate and sovereign claims to national territories and everything and everyone therein, to the specific historical conjuncture of each mobilization of autochthonous politics, there is no singular method of placing Natives over Migrants. However, each deployment of autochthony, whether articulated "from above" or "from below," further normalizes the postcolonial politics and social relations of *nationalism*. For these reason, it is worthwhile to examine the use of autochthonous discourses in contemporary Bolivia, which, under the leadership of its first self-identified indigenous president, Evo Morales, is largely regarded as politically progressive. Tangible and positive results for Indigenous people subjugated by centuries of colonialism have indeed been provided by the Morales administration. Therefore, looking at Bolivia allows us to evaluate the politics of autochthony at its supposed best.

Bolivia became independent of the Spanish imperial state in 1825. Its sovereignty, nationalized in the late nineteenth century, was announced by prohibiting people from Asia to enter its territories. Like many other nation-states in the Americas, Bolivia was controlled by those with long-standing, privileged ties—racialized and economic—to the former imperial state. In

2005, Juan Evo Morales Ayma, head of the Movement for Socialism Party (MAS) and a former leader of the coca growers' union, won Bolivia's presidential election. Defying both the United States and the class rule of Bolivian Nationals who owned capital and controlled the nation-state, Morales ran on a platform of land reform, the nationalization of gas and oil resources, and a more equitable distribution of the monies derived from these. He gave special attention to improving the lives of Bolivia's Indigenous people.

While Morales had long employed the *campesino* and *cocalero* materialist discourse of class, it was during his first presidential campaign, in 2005, that he first employed the discourse of "Andean spirituality and culture in an official and a more coherent manner in his rhetoric and political discourse and activism" (Burman 2016, 95). Winning in a political climate in which "social justice, oppression, poverty and colonialism had gradually come to be explained in ethnic, cultural and even racial terms," Morales reformulated a Bolivian nationalism that, he said, would now include "its indigenous people" (95). Following recommendations from an elected Constituent Assembly that many *indianista-katarista*, or Indigenous, organizations had been calling for since the 1990s, Bolivia was renamed the Plurinational State of Bolivia in 2009. Its new constitution recognized thirty-six "nations" within Bolivia (Radhuber 2012).

In 2006 Morales's government undertook what has variously been called a "modest form of nationalization" (see Achtenberg 2012) or even a "neoliberal nationalization" (Kaup 2010) by controlling the commercialization of Bolivian natural gas reserves and becoming the majority shareholder in the state-owned hydrocarbon company, Yacimientos Petrolíferos Fiscales Bolivianos (YPFB). It also increased the taxation rates on hydrocarbon industries. Through these measures, Bolivia achieved better contractual terms with energy companies extracting the substantial reserve of natural gas in its territories. This dramatically increased the state's revenues. Since 2006, Morales's government used the rents gained from the extractive industries to implement cash transfer programs for the elderly, schoolchildren, and pregnant women; to improve infrastructure, including building new schools, hospitals, and domestic gas connections; and to raise the minimum wage. These measures, says Emily Achtenberg (2015a), "markedly improved the living standards of ordinary Bolivians."

The rule of Indigenous "customary law" was also entrenched in much of the electoral system, including guaranteed representation of indigenous people on municipal councils. Alongside Spanish, thirty-six Indigenous languages were declared official. Laws governing coca leaf production were re-written. Institutional attempts to fight corruption were launched. And there was a significant retitling of land. A provision of the 2009 Constitution (Article 403) established *Tierra Comunitaria de Origen*, or "Communal Lands of Origin," later changed to *Territorio Indígena Originario Campesino*, or "Peasant Indigenous Territory." Under it, indigenous collective title to certain territories was extended and guaranteed. By 2016, approximately 20 percent of the land in Bolivia—about twenty million hectares—was so designated (International Work Group for Indigenous Affairs n.d.). Made—and left—impoverished by centuries of imperial state rule and, since the late nineteenth century, Bolivian nation-state rule, Bolivia under Morales provided an appreciable increase in the social, political, and economic status of people once constituted as colonized Natives and who now regard themselves as Indigenous (Pluri) National-Natives.

Alongside numerous accolades, however, have come powerful critiques of the Morales government. These have emanated not only from those seeking to overturn the gains made, but also from those in the very social movements that brought the MAS to power. Having started as the indigenous leader of a movement for "decolonization," Morales has successively sidelined the very people and political organizations that brought him into power. A discourse of criminalizing opposition groups, as well as targeting them for violent action, followed. Indeed, Morales has been able to stay in power because of the formation of new alliances. Morales and the MAS are now supported by agrobusinesses and those who, until recently, were violently racist against indigenous people. Emily Achtenberg (2015a) notes that "politically, Morales's landslide victory [in] October [2014] . . . was based on a newly-configured alliance of rural peasants, small producers and merchants, an emerging urban indigenous entrepreneurial bourgeoisie and elements of conservative elite sectors who have been integrated into the MAS."

Ten years after first being elected president, Morales had formed an "implicit pact with 'productive' elite sectors (including soy, timber, and cattle-ranching interests) who agreed to recognize the legitimacy of the MAS government in exchange for concessions to advance their business model" (Achtenberg 2015a). At the same time, the very state policies that allowed for improvements in both the material and social status of large numbers of indigenous people—programs paid for largely by rents on extractive industries—led to the formation of a new and expanded indigenous bourgeoisie and to an "unprecedented expansion of consumerism" (Achtenberg 2015a). In short, the bourgeoisie, both national and foreign—and a growing proportion of it now indigenous—came to form a significant part of Morales's base of support. While Bolivia's economic minister, Luis Arce, argued that this demonstrated how "everyone has the opportunity to get rich in Bolivia, because today's economy is for everybody" (in Achtenberg 2015a), such policies came at the expense of those whose lives Morales and the MAS had campaigned to improve. The negative consequences of this on working-class Indigenous people, and other direct producers reliant on the use of land, became ever more apparent.

Indeed, Linda Farthing and Benjamin Kohl (2014, 150) argue that MAS's stated political goals of "decolonizing the state, granting territorial autonomy to indigenous peoples, turning Bolivia into a truly plurinational state, and the application of *vivir bien* (living well) . . . to development" have largely "remained at the discursive or rhetorical level." In particular, a key issue of concern is that while indigenous groups have gained title over select collective lands, the Morales government has continued with the former policy of leaving the right to *manage* those lands, including resources on it, with the nation-state. This meant that despite significant opposition, Morales was able to issue Supreme Decree 2366 on 20 May 2015, granting concessions for oil and gas extraction in Bolivia's national parks. The new concessions covered as much as 70 to 90 percent of the parks' area (Achtenberg 2015b). These lands had previously been designated as ecological reserves, a status specifically protected under the 2009 Constitution. Never having nationalized the hydrocarbon sector, Morales now allowed YPFB to enter into partnerships with Brazil's Petrobras, Venezuela's PDVSA, Spain's Repsol, France's Total, and others to exploit the reserves found within national parks.

Two weeks after this decree, Morales approved a plan to build a highway through TIPNIS national park, as well as other lands in the Bolivian Amazon that had previously been collectively titled to Indigenous groups.[17] Built in the name of "territorial integration" and "regional development," this highway was crucial for the profitability of the new concessions to the extraction industries. Indigenous people and environmental organizations both in Bolivia and around the world discovered that despite a self-identified indigenous president who had granted collective indigenous land title and markedly improved the lives of many, the practices of expropriation, exploitation, and ecological destruction continued. Indeed, under Morales, the amount of land conceded to gas and oil companies, much of it under indigenous title, increased dramatically—from 7.2 million acres in 2007 to 59.3 million in 2012 (Achtenberg 2015b).

To date, the opposition organized against both the concessions and the highway has had little effect. Some protesters, including Guaraní people in Takovo Mora who have demanded a right to free, prior, and informed consent regarding oil extraction on their communal lands, were attacked by police (Cregan 2015). Instead, Morales's government has granted new incentives for oil and gas exploration throughout Bolivia. At the time of writing, five more concessions in national parks are in the queue for approval. In addition, the Morales government passed a new law on mining that permitted the diversion of water from *campesino* farms to mining operators. Studies to allow for possible natural gas fracking have been initiated. Much of this was in direct contravention with Bolivia's 2009 Constitution, which established more democratic decision-making processes, especially by indigenous people.

These actions significantly challenged the alliance of indigenous, *campesino*, and urban social movements that were part of the campaign to "decolonize" Bolivia and led to increasingly rancorous disputes between the Morales government and the social movements that swept him into the presidency. Political scientist George Gray Molina notes that Morales redefined these critics of extraction-led economic growth as nothing more than obstacles to the "new productive economy" (in Achtenberg 2015b). Molina further notes that Vice President Alvaro García Linera used the fact that "the Bolivian government's effective take of hydrocarbons taxes and royalties, at 72%, [was] among the highest in Latin America" to reframe hydrocarbon extraction as part of the government's "anti-imperialist strategy" promoting "resource nationalism" (in Achtenberg 2015b). Indeed, he maintained that some of the main beneficiaries of the government's expansion of the extractive industries were indigenous *campesinos*.

This type of argument—that the exploitation of land and labor is an anti-imperialist strategy of decolonization that benefits Indigenous National-Natives—not only points to the *limits* of the nationalist project for land reform and redistribution of wealth, but also *exemplifies* postcolonial governmentality. Kaup (2010, 135) argues, "Bolivia thus provides a case through which to see what is possible and the potential problems that states may face as they attempt to exercise greater control over their development trajectories in an increasingly interconnected global economy." Morales's government improved the lives and the national status of people constituted as Indigenous—no small feat by any measure—but such welfare state measures did not, *could not*, provide an alternative to the postcolonial ruling nexus of nation-state/global capitalism. In particular, says Kaup (2010, 131), "the Morales government's ability to create radical socioeconomic change has been inhibited by the path-dependent trajectories of the policies, contracts, and sociomaterial constraints that surround natural-gas extraction, transport, and use." Thus, while the Bolivian state regained legal control of natural gas in its territory, globally operative extractive corporations continued to extract the majority of the natural gas in Bolivia and exported it for sale in much more profitable markets than exist in Bolivia. In short, Morales failed to end more than five hundred years of the extractivism emblematic of colonialism (Farthing and Kohl 2014).

As a result, there is now a growing gap in income and wealth, as well as growing political divisions in Bolivia. Significantly, these are manifested politically by a growing distinction between indigenous and nonindigenous people. These divisions have become more pronounced as the global price of hydrocarbons has declined and as the Morales government's land reform programs have slowed down. The reliance not only on energy companies but also on industrial agriculture, mining, and timber companies has further marginalized small-scale and subsistence farmers and consequently forced many *campesinos*—indigenous and nonindigenous—into low-wage work (Fabricant and Gustafson 2015). At the same time, divisions between them have deepened. Furthermore, as with extractive industries operating elsewhere, gendered divisions have been exacerbated in Bolivia. Most of the paid work in this sector goes to men, intensifying both the "patriarchy of the wage" and women's dependence on men's as well as the nation-state's cash transfers to them as mothers and wives (see Federici 2004). In this environment of predominantly low-wage work and the practical inability to use land to live, writes Achtenberg (2015a), a conflict "between peasant farmers migrating from the highlands in search of more productive land and lowland Indigenous peoples staking claims" to Indigenous territories has emerged. Morales's response to these growing divisions has been to intensify the discourse of autochthony.

At his January 2015 inauguration, Morales focused on explicitly nationalist themes such as regaining the seacoast from Chile and expanding extractive "development." While there from the start, nationalism took precedence over earlier discourses of redistribution and socialism. Importantly, the nationalist pride being encouraged explicitly deployed a discourse of autochthony. Morales made increasingly conspicuous displays of his indigeneity. The day before the inauguration, he staged a ceremony at the pre-Hispanic ruins of Tiwanaku. In view of thousands, he received a highly ritualized blessing from Andean priests. In January 2016, he celebrated ten years of what he called "indigenous socialist" rule in the Plaza Murillo in La Paz. And at that January 2015 inauguration (his third), Morales stated, "*Aqui no mandan los gringos, aqui mandan los indios*" ("Here native people, not foreigners, govern"). What such rhetoric shows, I believe, is that Bolivia's position in the Postcolonial New World Order is an insurmountable barrier to people's ability to end the twin processes of expropriation and exploitation, the very hallmarks of both imperial-state and nation-state rule. It is also a testament to how autochthonous discourses conceal the failure to achieve decolonization.

CONCLUSION

As the example of Morales's Bolivia and others noted in this chapter show, discursive practices of national autochthony are an integral aspect of the Postcolonial New World Order. From the efforts of imperial states to bifurcate the colonized Natives into Indigenous-Natives and Migrant-Natives from the mid-nineteenth century, to the ascendance of nationalist ideologies in the late nineteenth century (and the nationalization of states throughout the New World), to the successive breakup of one empire after another in the aftermath of WWI and WWII and the subsequent transformation of imperial territory into newfound nation-states, we have witnessed the growing importance of discourses of autochthony in political practice. With the hegemony of the nation form of state power shortly after the end of WWII, discourses of national autochthony are now a normalized way to define membership in political communities the world over. In both the former colonies and the former metropoles, some people have been made a People and believe that it is they who govern themselves. As is the nation itself, this power is understood as part of a cross-class project whose benefits are limited to those who are Natives of the nation. Yet nowhere is everyone living within any given nation-state—either in the Rich or the Poor World—so defined. Instead, within all nation-states are its allochthonous others—*Migrants from elsewhere*. Whether knowing no other home, or whether from the next town over, the next province, or another nation-state altogether, those made into Migrants are represented as usurpers of the always-limited resources of the nation—its land, women, jobs, housing, hospital beds, schools, water, and so on.

An ever-harder definition of national citizenship has ensued, one that has not always neatly aligned with formal national citizenship. Hence, in national-autochthonous politics the world over, the nation-state is portrayed as having been taken over by Migrants. *National-Natives have become the new colonized people* who believe that only a fierce anti-immigrant politics can bring about true national sovereignty. And here we are today: another genocide looms, another crisis for refugees proceeds unchecked, and more and more governments are held by far-right political parties that rage against Migrants while basing their platforms on neoliberal policies. In short, we live in a Postcolonial New World Order in which the polarization of class conflict has been transposed onto the always related politics of racism and nationalism. The question remains, one that many people on the move have asked themselves: Where to from here? In the next chapter, I attempt to answer this vexing question.

9

POSTSEPARATION

Struggles for a Decolonized Commons

We, with our fixation on blood, have forgotten:
bending to a common purpose is more important than arising
from a common place.

—*David Treuer, 2011*

Nationalist rewritings of history remain replete with always glorious pasts and promises of ever-brighter futures despite the fact that postcolonial nation-states have failed to bring about anything resembling the promised peace or prosperity, justice, or liberty demanded by anticolonial movements. Seizing national sovereignty was supposed to be the key to unlocking the door to equality in the geopolitical relationships between nation-states. Within national territory, sovereignty was said to be necessary to ensure that everyone lived with dignity and had the essentials of food, housing, health care, and more. And people were supposed to get their land back. This has not happened. Instead, much old imperialist wine has been repackaged in new national bottles. Global inequalities in a world of nation-states are *worse* than in the Age of Empires. Disparities across *and* within nation-states have grown as practices of expropriation and exploitation have intensified in the Postcolonial New World Order. Recognizing this reality is not an argument for a return of empires but is, instead, a call to reject the postcolonial system of nation-states and build social relationships, social bodies, and practices of social reproduction able to meet liberatory demands. Practicing a politics of postseparation—the refusal to confuse categories of rulers with the people placed within them—is an essential aspect of realizing a decolonization worthy of its name.

We have a long way to go. Samir Amin (2004, 8) noted that there was an increase in "the inequality between peoples from a maximum ratio of two to one around 1800, to sixty to one today." Branko Milanovic (2002, 51) further noted that by the 1990s the income of the wealthiest twenty-five million people in the United States was "equal to [the] total income of almost 2 billion people" in the world. In 2013, eighty-five of the wealthiest people in the world had a combined wealth (about $110 trillion) estimated as equal to that of the bottom 50 percent, or 3.5 billion people (Oxfam 2014). It should come as no surprise that twenty-one of these eighty-five ultrarich people were citizens of the Third World. An additional four were Russian Nationals, and five were Chinese Nationals. State-owned and state-controlled capitalist development—much of it since sold off to private entrepreneurs—has paid off handsomely for an extremely small number of people in these former or nominally communist states.

These abysmal ratios are rapidly becoming even more lopsided. By 2015, the richest 1 percent of people globally possessed more wealth than the *rest of the world combined* (Credit Suisse 2015). And by 2016 it took only *sixty-two* of the world's richest people to possess the same amount of wealth as the bottom half of the world's people (Oxfam 2016a). Yet, the fact that in 2009, it only took an annual personal income of $34,000 to be part of the top global 1 percent shows us just how little wealth is owned by 99 percent of the world's people (Milanovic 2010, 72). Indeed, the continuing growth in disparities between rich and poor people comes not only out of an increase in the wealth of the rich but also because of the increasing immiseration of the poor. The amount of wealth owned by people in the bottom 50 percent in the world has *fallen* by 38 percent—or one *trillion* U.S. dollars—since 2010 (Oxfam 2016a). Milanovic (in McElwee 2014, emphasis added) put these global disparities in even clearer perspective by showing that by the 2000s, "an American having the average income of the *bottom* US decile [was] better-off than *2/3 of [the] world population.*" That is, the "very poorest people in the United States have an income level which is equal to that of the middle class in China or even upper middle class in India" (Milanovic, in McElwee 2014).

What has remained the same, then, in the shift of a world dominated by imperial states to one dominated by national-states is that the most impoverished people in the world remain the source of the wealth of the richest. At an international level, a recent study examining the movement of financial resources between Rich World and Poor World nation-states from 1980 to 2012, including "official development assistance, loans, repayments, debt cancellation, foreign direct investment, portfolio investment, remittances, contributions from religious and charitable organizations, and recorded and unrecorded trade flows," found "sustained and significant *outflows* from the developing world" (Centre for Applied Research 2015, ix). In 2012, $1.3 trillion flowed from Rich World to Poor World nation-states in the form of aid, investment, and income, but almost three times that amount—or $3.3 trillion—flowed in the opposite direction. Yet this is probably an underestimation. Much of this movement remains unrecorded and untaxed (Hickel 2017). This study thus concludes that "developing countries have effectively served as net creditors to the rest of the world" (Centre for Applied Research 2015, xi).

Disparities exist not only between nation-states, however, but also between people with different nationalities. Indeed, in the Postcolonial New World Order, one's *nationality* has become the *greatest* determinant of one's income and wealth. In stark contrast to the situation in the mid-nineteenth century, when the "real income of workers in most countries was similar and low" and when much of the inequality between people in the world could be explained by the differences in income between capitalists and workers, today, the gap between "unskilled workers' wages in rich and poor countries often differ by a factor of 10 to 1" (Milanovic 2011). Milanovic (2011) has thus argued that, today, almost three-quarters of global inequality is due to one's national citizenship.

The resultant effects on people's life spans are significant. Life expectancy remains greatest in nation-states in Europe, followed by Oceania, the Americas, Asia, the former Soviet Union, and, lastly, Africa (Roser 2016). According to statistics from the World Health Organization (WHO 2014), "A boy born in 2012 in a high-income country can expect to live to the age of around 76—16 years longer than a boy born in a low-income country (age 60). For girls, the difference is even wider; a gap of 19 years separates life expectancy in high-income (82 years) and low-income countries (63 years)." In nine sub-Saharan African nation-states (Angola, Central African Republic, Chad, Côte d'Ivoire, Democratic Republic of the Congo, Lesotho, Mozambique, Nigeria, and Sierra Leone), life expectancy for both men and women is less than fifty-five years. Thus, which of the world's nation-states one is a citizen of *matters*. Nationals in a Rich World nation-state are provided with a "citizenship rent" (Milanovic, in McElwee 2014). National citizenship matters because nation-states across this international system limit its obtainment.

Deep disparities exist *within* nation-states as well. This, perhaps above all else, shows the lie of all nationalisms claiming the "nation" to be a unified, cross-class "community." As the share of income going to workers has fallen, compensation to officers of large corporations has grown exponentially. The heads of top U.S. firms garnered an almost 1000 percent increase in salary from 1978 to 2014, translating into a ratio of 303:1 for an average CEO's salary to the average worker's salary (Mishel and Davis 2015). This situation is particularly stark in India, which, along with five Nationals on 2013's global top eighty-five billionaires list, also has approximately one-third of the world's 1.2 billion people living in what the UN calls "extreme poverty" (UN 2014, 9). Indeed, a quarter of the world's malnourished live in India today (UNWFP 2015). This is in no small part due to the fact that in recent years, the largest forced removal of people from their land has taken place in India (Todhunter 2014).

Aside from rejecting methodological nationalism (Wimmer and Glick Schiller 2002) when tabulating wealth between and within nation-states, we must note that it is not "nations" who create wealth but people working within its territories, both Nationals and Migrants alike, who do so. We must also note that "workers" is not a uniform category. Nowhere in the world do women have the same earning power as men do. This "patriarchy of the wage" is a crucial aspect of capitalist social relations, one that *fundamentally* conditions women's subordination to men in all aspects of life (Federici 2004). Moreover, while there are far fewer studies done across nation-states on how racism affects wage earnings, studies in the United States reveal that the racialized wage gap has grown over the past forty years. In 1979, the wage gap between White and Black people (men and women) in the United States was 18.1 percent. In 2015, it grew to 26.7 percent. Accounting for education, experience, metro status, and region of residence, the average hourly wage for White men was 22 percent higher than Black men's and 34.2 percent higher than Black women's. White women, in turn, received 11.7 percent higher wages than Black women (Wilson and Rodgers 2016). Whiteness and maleness thus come with a racialized and gendered rent.

This is evident in the racialized and gendered character of poverty in the United States. An American Community Survey conducted between 2007 and 2011 found that the highest national poverty rates were for American Indians and Alaska Natives at 27 percent, followed closely by African Americans at 25.8 percent (Macartney, Bishaw, and Fontenot 2013). The U.S. Census report for 2014 found that the next-highest poverty rate (at 23.6 percent) was for Hispanics (DeNavas-Walt and Proctor 2015). This was double the 11.6 percent national poverty rate for (non-Hispanic) Whites. Poverty rates closely correlate to life expectancy. American Indians and Alaska Natives had a life expectancy 4.4 years less than that of the national average in the United States, while

Black people fell four years behind the national average (seventy-nine years in 2012).

There are even fewer international studies on the "immigration wage gap," especially with regard to different immigration statuses (from "permanent resident" to "illegal"). However, one U.S.-based study found that in 2000 there was an 18.4 percent wage gap between U.S.-born men and "immigrant men" (i.e., U.S. permanent residents) and that this gap was double what it had been in 1980 (Schmitt and Wadsworth 2006). A recent study comparing the wages of U.S. Nationals identified as Mexican-Americans and Mexican Nationals working in the United States as undocumented Migrants found the wage gap between them had jumped from 11 percent in 1970 to 62 percent in 2000, and that by 2007 it was a whopping 78 percent (Massey and Gentsch 2014). In the United States, and likely elsewhere, undocumented immigration status is a significant factor in dramatically lowering one's wages, showing, once again, that nationality is a significant determinant of inequality in the Postcolonial New World Order.

In the midst of these growing disparities in income and wealth, profits made through capital investments have grown. And nation-states have had something to do with this as well: a large part of higher profits is reduced taxes on capital gains offered by nation-states across the world (and across the political spectrum). In the United States in 1952, the early years of Pax Americana, corporate taxes were 33 percent of tax revenue. By 2013, they were 10 percent (U.S. Bureau of Economic Analysis n.d.). Corporate taxes as a percentage of GDP also dropped dramatically: from 5.9 percent in 1952 to 1.6 percent in 2013. Nation-states have also enabled the richest of their Nationals to hide money in tax shelters. An estimated $7.6 trillion in *individual* wealth—8 percent of the world's total financial wealth (of $95.5 trillion)—lies in globally distributed tax havens (Zucman 2015).

The biggest network of tax havens is controlled by Rich World states, much of it by the City of London. However, it is the Nationals of the national liberation states who own the majority of assets held in these havens, about $4.4 trillion (Centre for Applied Research 2015, 4). In 2014, about 4 percent of the wealth of U.S. Nationals, 4 percent of the wealth of various Asian Nationals, 10 percent of the wealth of European Nationals, 22 percent of the wealth of Latin American Nationals, 52 percent of the wealth of Russian Nationals, and a whopping 57 percent of the wealth of Gulf State Nationals was hidden in tax havens (Zucman 2015). In addition, about 30 percent of the wealth in African nation-states (amounting to about $500 billion)—lies in tax havens (Oxfam 2016b).

An assessment of life in the Postcolonial New World Order thus demonstrates that "national self-determination" is a *farce*. It is a mockery of people's dreams of ending colonialism, a pretense at liberation, a masquerade of self-determination. Life in the Postcolonial New World Order, while full of extravagant promises and mistaken identities, is shaped by the *fundamental inability* of postcolonial nation-states to bring about justice and equality. This is not because they are prevented from doing so by "neocolonialism," but because of the national form of state power. Perhaps it is useful, then, to view postcolonialism through the lens of the end of slavery a century or more earlier. Vijay Prashad puts it this way: "Just as the abolition of slavery advanced the cause of human freedom and yet left the formerly enslaved people in decrepit socioeconomic conditions, so too did national independence move history forward and yet do little for the[ir] everyday dilemmas" (Prashad 2007, 224). Indeed, a more apt analogy is that postcolonialism is to colonialism what coolie-ism was to slavery. As discussed in chapter 3, the "coolie" indentured labor system replaced slavery, but far from producing the freedom that people demanded, coolieism ushered in a system of labor regulation and rule that *shared* many of the material conditions of slavery but was less clearly understood as an affront to liberty. Significantly, coolies were controlled not only by the contracts they were forced to sign as a condition of their movement, but also by new immigration controls.

These controls, implemented hesitatingly and with much consternation in 1835—the year when slave labor relations began to be abolished in British Mauritius—was the beginning of the end of free mobility for imperial subjects *within* the empire. Yet despite being bound by contracts of indenture and despite being governed by new mobility restrictions, coolies were portrayed not only as "free labor" but as "voluntary" Emigrants. Thus, even though coolieism was more like slavery than the "free" labor system it was claimed to be, it was not seen as such by hardly anyone other than the coolies themselves. Indeed, both labor contracts and immigration controls were presented as a solution to slavery and a form of protection of coolies. Perhaps this is why there is not much of a sense of horror about the institution of coolieism. In fact, in the Postcolonial New World Order, the descendants of coolies (and slaves) have often been recast as "settler colonists" (see chapter 8).

The transformation of the world system of states from one dominated by imperial states to one now dominated by nation-states has followed a similar trajectory. Just as many failed to see coolieism as the co-optation of workers' struggles against capitalism, proletarianization, and unfree labor, and saw coolieism as freedom instead, today most fail to see the world of nation-states as having *contained* anticolonial dreams of liberation. Like coolieism, the post-colonial chains that bind workers to capital and to states remain invisible to many. The fact that the Postcolonial New World Order is *a ruling order* is soundly ignored, even while the glaring lack of parity or equality within it is widely documented.

The fact that the very practices denounced as imperialist—expropriation of land, exploitation of labor, and the oppression of the colonized—continue unimpeded in every nationally sovereign state is the truth that is rarely spoken to postcolonial power. Instead, ongoing, indeed *intensifying*, disparities are largely explained in two main ways: as either caused by "neocolonialism" or by the existence of Migrants within National-Native territories. Both work as *alibis* for the obvious failures of nation-states to ensure the conditions for people to thrive. This is perhaps nowhere more important than in the national liberation states, many of which are now seventy years old or more. Here the discourse of "neocolonialism" is most readily deployed to explain why the promises of decolonization were not upheld—and why they are receding ever further from view. In offering a refuge for nationalists, discourses of "neocolonialism" keep the project of "national independence" alive. Indeed, claiming to be fighting colonialism, "neo" or otherwise, is the *governmentality* of the Postcolonial New World Order. So much so that even the quintessential institutions of *postcolonialism*—the IMF, the World Bank, the WTO, and even the EU—are re-presented as *colonial* institutions by nationalists desperate to maintain the illusory promises of home rule.

The continuing significance of movements for "national self-determination," both in extant nation-states and in movements for new national sovereigns, has left us with an understanding of colonialism as nothing more than "foreign rule." Consequently, *decolonization* has become nothing more than "home rule"—the elevation of National-Natives over Migrants. The Postcolonial New World Order has thus been extraordinarily successful in continuing the imperial practices of "define and rule" through the constant evocation of the ideas of autochthony and allochthony. This too has helped to contain anticolonial demands by allowing nationalists of all stripes to make the case that the reason national sovereignty has not yet been realized is the existence of "foreigners" in the nation's territory. The result has been a hardening of nationalism(s) and a resultant increase in anti-immigrant politics. Indeed, anticolonialism has been redefined as anti-immigration, and contenders for political power in Rich and Poor World nation-states bemoan their lack of "national independence." The reason for people's lack of land, lack of a sustainable livelihood, and lack of respect is said to be that *the People* are not yet independent of "foreign rule."

Can we just blame neoliberalism?

The nation-states that replaced former imperial metropoles as well as former colonies play this game, the former more uncannily than the latter.

Yet, as the arguments advanced in this book demonstrate, the nation-state is wholly *incapable* of delivering on the promises of "national self-determination." This is not because it doesn't have *enough* national sovereignty, but because of the global arena in which capitalism operates and because of the relationship between ruling classes and state power. This is glaringly so with regard to national citizenship and immigration controls, which have, from the start, been a response to crises in capitalism. From the first controls against the free movement of coolie workers in the British Empire in the early nineteenth century, to the reorganization of the global political order into postcolonial nation-states, citizenship and immigration controls have done two main things: provide flexible and relatively cheaper labor power and politically separate workers within a world market for labor power. While portrayed as benefiting Citizens by elevating them above Migrants, in reality, citizenship and immigration controls harm all workers. To acknowledge this is to acknowledge the failure of nation-states. To avoid addressing this reality, nation-states endlessly replay the fight against colonialism, for this positions them as the defenders of the nation, rather than the managers of ruling relations. This is why new colonizers have to constantly be produced and why Migrants—the quintessential "people out of place"—can be represented as settler-colonists invading Native nations. The existence of new colonizers normalizes National-Native sovereignty.

Today, Nationals increasingly claim Nativeness as the grounds upon which to make sovereign claims over national territory and the resources in it. This represents a further limiting of the criteria for national membership. While some Migrants are able to become National Citizens, because of the racialized and territorialized grounds for Native standing, it is impossible for Migrants to become National-Natives. Autochthonous discourses across the world of nation-states in Asia to Africa, in Europe to the Americas, and in the Caribbean to Oceania demand sovereign power for Native-Nationals and present Migrants as the barriers to its achievement. This is true for those who believe their "nations" have national sovereignty (even as they see it as under attack), as well as those who see their nations as under the yoke of a foreign sovereign. In this way, postcolonial governmentalities have indeed played upon and strengthened the separations wrought by colonialism.

Across the Postcolonial New World Order, while land, wealth, and power may not be plentiful, *national pride* is. Many of us continue to work for the glory of the nation while raging against our fellow builders defined as Migrants.

More and more, we demand unscalable walls to further enclose ourselves within "national homelands." Yet, until we take into account what we have lost by demanding sovereignty for National-Natives and recognize what we have lost by centering on the glory of the "nation" instead of the glory of the world's builders, we will not realize decolonization. This book, then, is not a lament for imperialism; it is a dirge for nationalism. Only after the death of the national liberation project can we renew our commitment to decolonization.

RECONNECTIONS

How do we get there? In the national form of state power and in the national style of governmentality, citizenship and immigration controls *define* the sovereignty of nation-states. A crucial first step toward decolonization, then, is dismantling the borders between people categorized either as National-Natives or as Migrants and rebuilding our solidarity across—and more importantly *against*—the "nations" and nation-states that depend on these categories for their existence. This is not possible without also dismantling barriers to people's free mobility. Removing constraints against mobility is important because freedom of movement is "historically the oldest and also the most elementary" basis of liberty from state and class rule (Arendt [1968] 1993, 9). A liberatory politics of "no borders" is thus central to our collective liberation from postcolonialism, with its national expropriation of land and labor.

A significant aspect of the governmentality of postcolonialism is the breaking down of solidarity through the erection of national border controls (see Anzaldúa [1987] 1999, 25). This is because there is perhaps nothing more effective in producing a self-identity of National—or in breaking down the solidarity between direct producers of wealth—than the *nationalization of the wage*. Defining jobs, at least "good jobs," as "belonging" to Nationals is an important aspect of how Nationals believe that nations are cross-class communities. We can see this in slogans such as British Labor Prime Minister Gordon Brown's infamous 2007 "British Jobs for British Workers" election campaign, which was used again by the far-right British National Party in the 2010 election (Bridget Anderson 2013, 57). The nationalization of the wage—and the immigration controls necessary for the production of Nationals—maintains the *plausibility* of national projects. Immigration controls, because they operate as a market mechanism that changes the *value* of people according to whether they are Nationals or Migrants, becomes seen as a necessary part of the "citizenship premium." Being Nationals—and not Migrants—is a way of being in the Postcolonial New World Order that allows people to claim (relatively good) waged jobs as theirs.

Yet, as I have shown in chapters 3, 4, and 7, the creation of the global nation-state system is simultaneously the history of the global expansion of capitalist social relations. The world system of nation-states has produced a grossly unequal inter*national* and inter*statal* regime of ruling. Each nation-state, from the most powerful to the least, is reliant on international markets for much-needed financial capital, raw resources and finished commodities, various services, technologies, and, of course, labor. As competition within each of these global markets intensifies, the politics of separation do as well. Thus have national technologies of border controls intersected with technologies of the self to secure a postcolonial governmentality. In making Migrants a despised biopolitical group within nation-states, the value of their labor power is lowered and they are made more "competitive." Thus, anti-immigrant politics only create *more* competition within labor markets nationalized through citizenship and immigration controls. More nationalism leads to more anti-immigration politics, which leads to further cheapening of Migrants, which leads to more competition, which leads to ever more nationalism, more competition, and more cheapened Migrants *ad infinitum*.

At the same time, the national politics of autochthony, while central to the binary of National-Natives and Migrants, do not work for most National-Natives. Not all National-Natives have "national jobs" (i.e., those with the highest economic, social, and cultural capital). Indeed, some have no jobs at all. Further, as Bridget Anderson (2013) notes, in any national project *all* people are judged, policed, and disciplined, including National Citizens. Just as Migrants must prove their value or worth to the nation, so too are National Citizens expected to demonstrate value to the nation vis-à-vis capitalist markets to enjoy "rights" and privileges. Indeed, across the world, most people defined as either National-Natives or Migrants exist in positions of subordination. In this, we can learn from the imperial practices of indirect-rule colonialism, under which groups of Natives differentiated as either the Indigenous-Natives or Migrant-Natives were *defined as separate* in order to ensure that people in *both* groups were kept under the rule of imperial states. Nation-states with their "self-determinate" sovereignty have done no less. Entrenching "define and rule" politics in the distinction between Nationals and Migrants, nation-states subordinate Migrants in both the political community and in the labor market. Yet though the structural subordination of Migrants within nation-states does offer Nationals relative privilege, it does not produce a world of wealth, security, and peace for them either—far from it.

Despite their purported work in protecting National Citizen-workers, citizenship and immigration controls grant greater power to states and capital.

Anti-immigrant politics become especially important not only when capital faces crises of profitability, but also when nation-states face "crises of legitimacy" stemming from their structural inability to protect their Nationals (S. Hall et al. [1978] 2013). Indeed, because the global character of postcolonial power is left unacknowledged, such politics rejuvenate and solidify national projects further. As this postcolonial cycle is repeated, struggles over the political status of Nationals intensify. As we have seen, the result is that Nativeness becomes more essential to National status, resulting in more and more people being categorized as Migrants (even some National Citizens), and Migrants are made into colonizers.

The shrinking of the category of National—the subject of the Postcolonial New World Order—and the concomitant growth in the category of Migrant has worked well for capital and for nation-states. Greater support for immigration controls has furthered the formation of a "national community." By relying on the principle of "internal bonding through external bounding" (Ferrera 2005, 4), nation-state immigration controls have produced supposedly bounded, national societies, in which any destruction of livelihoods, any loss of land, any loss of ability to influence "society" is seen as a betrayal of the national project. Such politics of betrayal produce a search for the one(s) who will restore the glory of the nation—and protect the rights of National-Natives. Immigration controls are thus crucial for producing the kind of people who will support nation-states and support those states' efforts to make the nation great. Simply put, without immigration controls, there would be no nation-states with their national economy, national labor market, and national social entitlements.

Donald Trump (2015) understood this well on the campaign trail when he stated, "A nation WITHOUT BORDERS is not a nation at all. We must have a wall." Nation-states _are wholly reliant on the existence_ of citizenship and immigration controls. Trump uttered this to exalt the nation and normalize its border-making practices. However, we can turn his message on its head. "No borders" leads to "no nations"—and this, I argue, is a good thing indeed. From the start, migrants have been the specter haunting postcolonialism. Migrants _do_ pose a particular kind of existential danger to the idea of national sovereignty and it is this: the very fact of people's mobility calls into question the organization—and segregation—of the world into discrete, demarcated zones of national belonging.

A world without nations and their borders is essential to realizing a world without racism(s). Just as postcolonialism did not end the social relations of colonialism, neither did it end those of racism. In the immediate post-WWII years, along with the discrediting of the imperial form of state power, a particular kind of racism was also rendered reprehensible. From the 1950s, the kind of racism resting on pseudoscientific typologies, the kind that normalized atrocities leading up to and including the fascist holocausts of WWII, was made anathema. People did anything to declare they were *not racists*. However, just as imperial states were replaced by national ones, postcolonialism was also productive of a new, largely normalized, *horizontal* form of racism (Taguieff 1990; Balibar 1991a).

It is best to call this form of racism *postcolonial racism*, because it depended on ideas of distinct and separate "national cultures," each with its own territorial claims. The 1955 International Court of Justice ruling in the Nottebohm case established the international jurisprudence for the distinction between formal Nationals and "true" Nationals by arguing that "nationality is a legal bond having as its basis a social fact of attachment, a genuine connection of existence, interest and sentiments, together with the existence of reciprocal rights and duties" (in Batchelor 1998, 159–160). This became known as the legal principle of *effective nationality*: that formal citizenship in a nation-state is insufficient for an individual to be considered a National of it. Instead, a National must prove a *meaningful connection* to a state in which he or she is a citizen. Informed and mobilized by such nationalist geographies, in the Postcolonial New World Order, nation-states' territories thus became "a space for each race" (Cohen 1997, 75). Postcolonial racism, thus, harnessed previous autochthonizing practices of "define and rule." Nationhood became the new racist typology and Nationals the new "superior race."

In the *nationalist* politics of racialized purity, migration became the route to miscegenation, which this time did not involve the feared mixing of "races" but of "nations." The sentiment that one has lost one's "national identity" is now a basic feature of life in the postcolonies, one eliciting a melancholic and often violent response. Assuming the nation to be unified, whole, and integrated around common national norms, Migrants, because they are from someplace else, are produced as deficient and irreducibly Other. Hence, they become a fundamental threat to nationalists of all political stripes (Schinkel 2013). The question thus ceases being whether Migrants are a problem, but what to do with this problem. Viktor Orbán, the far-right prime minister of Hungary, captured this sentiment well when he claimed that "the Hungarian man . . . does not want to see throngs of people pouring into his country from other cultures who are incapable of adapting and are a threat to public safety, to his job and to his livelihood" (in Traynor 2015a).

Such sentiments are not the exclusive terrain of the far right but are evident in statements by the International Organization for Migration (IOM), one of the main international bodies enforcing border controls today. The IOM, arguing for more intensive management of national borders, portrays human mobility as "gradually eroding the traditional boundaries between languages, cultures, ethnic groups and nation-states" (IOM 2003, 4). Human movement thus is made into a *cause*, not an *effect*, of the rampant crises of the Postcolonial New World Order. As with all racisms, the victims of postcolonial racism are held responsible for the *structural and recurring crises* of postcolonialism—poverty; underemployment and unemployment; dangers of the present; insecurities of the future; feelings of being disrespected, of having no control, of not counting—nationalists have laid all this and more at the feet of those constituted as Migrants. In speaking for the "nation," postcolonial racisms claim to be neither racist nor hierarchical but a reiteration of the "natural" spatial order of national sovereigns.

NO SOVEREIGNS: "UNLORD THOSE THAT ARE LORDED BY YOU"

But what would a world without nations, without borders, without racisms, without people being separately categorized as either National-Natives or Migrants look like?[1] Some might say that a world beyond postcolonialism simply looks like a *more inclusive nation-state*. The thinking goes, since national citizenship is a category that grants people rights, let's move Migrants into the category of National. There are two problems with this approach: First, "national societies" are always closed, although they might be open or closed to different categories of people at different times. Thus, any expansion of national citizenship will hit one limit or another. This is because the existence of immigration controls *define* national sovereignty. Together, national limits to citizenship and to free mobility is what allows nation-states to make both Nationals and Migrants. Second, the idea that making Migrants into citizens resolves the fact of subordination and exploitation assumes that citizens are neither oppressed nor exploited, thus reproducing the quintessential nationalist myth that the bonds of nationhood *transcend* class. They do not. No nation-state is structurally able to counteract the very real limits to equality set by global capitalism.

These obvious limits might then lead some to say that what we need is a postnational state—that is, a state that merely administers its territory without setting any boundaries of state belonging, a state that merely acts as a system of redistribution and protection without demanding adherence to one or another form of identity. Yet, states are much more than administrative institutions. Historically, states emerge when a ruling class is formed. In the process, land is turned into state territory upon which people's labor is exploited. This is an aspect of *each and every form* of state power: monastic, monarchical, imperial, or national. It is through these sorts of relationships, ones that govern people's sense of both time and place, that certain forms of state-mandated identities, such as "race" and nation, arise. Such identities are indeed *state effects*.

This is to say that a world without borders, without racisms, without people being separated into categories of Natives or Migrants, is not a matter of making a slight administrative fix. *It would turn the Postcolonial New World Order upside down.* Current efforts to build such a world would not be the first. Since the world's first sovereigns, the earth's builders have demonstrated a vast practice of the "art of not being governed" (Scott 2009). With every effort at separating the world's builders from one another, a counterresponse was organized. The most effective were those that *broadened* the circle of builders (see Linebaugh and Rediker 2000). The building of the tower of Babel is one mythical example: its builders set out to defy God's claim to be their Lord by collectively erecting a tower to the glory of their self-produced heaven on earth.

With the advent of capitalist social relations some five hundred years ago, struggles to regain a world held in common have not waned (see Hill 1972; Wright and Wolford 2003). Would-be commoners have had aims similar to the people who, in the mid-seventeenth century, called themselves the Diggers. Part of the dispossessed and displaced people living in England, they demanded not only a *return* of the commons stolen from them, but its *expansion* to encompass the whole of the world being taken by capitalists and colonists. In their 1649 manifesto, *The True Levellers Standard Advanced: Or, The State of Community Opened, and Presented to the Sons of Men*, the Diggers demanded for *all people* that,

> we may work in righteousness, and lay the Foundation of making the Earth a Common Treasury for All, both Rich and Poor, That every one that is born in the land, may be fed by the Earth his Mother that brought him forth, according to the Reason that rules in the Creation. Not Inclosing any part into any particular hand, but all as one man, working together, and feeding together as Sons of one Father, members of one Family; not

one Lording over another, but all looking upon each other, as equals in the Creation; so that our Maker may be glorified in the work of his own hands, and that every one may see, he is no respecter of Persons, but equally loves his whole Creation.

Seeking neither territory nor sovereignty but *land* and the ability to enjoy a livelihood on it *without exclusion*, the Diggers and many others since recognized the integral relationship between freedom and mobility. An essential aspect of this freedom/mobility was the ability to change or shift one's identity. The Ranters, another group of seventeenth-century radicals seeking justice from within the rapidly expanding British Empire, refused distinctions of *place*. In their 1650 pamphlet about God, *A Justification of the Mad Crew*, the Ranters argued, "He is in England, France, and Turkey," and therefore, "the people in England, France, and Turkey [must become] one people and one body, for where the one lives there liveth the other also" (in Linebaugh and Rediker 2000, 86).[2]

The builders of the tower of Babel, the Diggers, the Ranters—and many more "motley crews"—all lost. Their loss is indeed our loss. But we do not have to keep losing. We can regain our lands and use our labor for a collective glory. To be successful in our efforts at decolonization, I argue, we need to rethink *what* decolonization means and *whom* it means something to. In this book, I have contested the idea that National-Natives are the protagonists of decolonization with Migrants as their antagonists. I have argued additionally that to further the project of decolonization, we need to disidentify with the postcolonial political categories of National-Native and Migrant. Fundamentally, this requires us to disidentify with being National Citizens.

We can start by acknowledging that the historic and gross injustices done to people captured in both of these state categories are intimately connected to one another. Neither the National-Native nor the Migrant is, in fact, foreign to the other. They have come into being side by side, and they remain inseparable. It is only our disavowal of these relationships that leads to their separation. This book is a call to come together against the Postcolonial New World Order, to allow ourselves the freedom to build a new *worldly* place of our making, one that is held in common so that we can withstand the efforts of future Lords.

I end as I started: with a story of the tower of Babel told from the perspective of its builders. I once again borrow the words of Toni Morrison (1993) to do my work:

The conventional wisdom of the Tower of Babel story is that the collapse was a misfortune. That it was the distraction, or the weight of many languages that precipitated the tower's failed architecture. That one monolithic language would have expedited the building and heaven would have been reached. Whose heaven, she ["an old woman. Blind. Wise"] wonders? And what kind? Perhaps the achievement of Paradise was premature, a little hasty if no one could take the time to understand other languages, other views, other narratives period. Had they, the heaven they imagined might have been found at their feet. Complicated, demanding, yes, but a view of heaven as life; not heaven as post-life.

NOTES

Chapter One

1 "Creation, fall, flood, nations" is a popular refrain regularly recited by staff and students at St. Julian's Church School in Wellow, United Kingdom. Many thanks to Alfreda Barosso Taylor, a former student there, for this information.

2 Throughout this book, I capitalize the political categories of National, Native, Citizen, and Migrant (and their various permutations) to acknowledge that each is a social and political *figure* as well as a category of states. I use the term "Migrant" over "Immigrant" to recognize that the legal meaning of immigrant is associated with having the right of permanent residency in a nation-state. The term "Migrant" thus allows us to talk about the full range of statuses a non-citizen might be given within a nation-state. I use the term "immigrant" when directly quoting its use.

3 The first multilateral treaty on nationality was concluded in 1930 at the Hague Codification Conference. Its basic principle was that each state had the right to establish its own law determining who its nationals are. A number of treaties confirming this were signed after the end of WWII (Hailbronner 2006).

4 As the term "coolie" is a racist term, I place it within quotation marks to signify its being problematized. However, for the sake of easier reading, I will omit these quotation marks from hereon in. Likewise, in subsequent chapters, I will place scare quotes around it the first time it is used only.

5 I use the term "Rich World states" instead of either First World, with its Cold War connotations, or Global North, with its inaccurate geographical designation. Like these other designations, however, it too is a relational term that refers to those nation-states which collectively experience average quality of life indicators and average standards of living well above those of Poor World nation-states.

6 This is true even in free-passage zones, such as the European Union (EU). The EU lifted restrictions against the intra-EU movement of "EU Nationals" with its 1995 Schengen Treaty. However, Schengen simply reorganized the category of "members" and "non-members" of a nascent European "society" by expanding the group of people able to move (relatively) freely and reside lawfully in an EU nation-state other than their own, while constraining the mobility of people at its frontiers. Even so, Schengen is unraveling, as some EU member states reintroduce border controls, while others who are not in the Schengen zone, such as the United Kingdom, increasingly detain EU Nationals in immigration detention centers (see U.K. Home Office 2017). In 2017, France, Malta, Germany, Austria, Denmark, and Sweden "temporarily" reinstated border controls (see European Commission, Migration, and Home Affairs 2017).

7   Organized as a body of nationally sovereign states, the UN had as one of its paramount objectives the establishment of an international regime of laws. As stated in the preamble to the Charter of the United Nations, the objective "to establish conditions under which justice and respect for the obligations arising from treaties and other sources of international law can be maintained" is central to the work of the UN (UN n.d.).

8   Dominion status entailed a form of semi-independence in government, civil service, armed forces, and treasury. Canada gained Dominion status in 1867, Australia in 1900, New Zealand in 1907, Newfoundland in 1907. South Africa also became a Dominion in 1910. Together, they came to be known as the "White Dominions." Nevertheless, under the British Colonial Laws Validity Act of 1865, the British Empire had the power to nullify any laws that contradicted laws passed by the British Parliament. Moreover, the White Dominions lacked the power to pass laws which had extra-territorial effect.

9   I use the term "New World" to designate colonies claimed by various European empires across what is now the Caribbean and the American continents and in the Pacific. My usage follows that of Sylvia Wynter, who in addition to rejecting the colonizers' doctrine of discovery, also argued that, "a New World view of 1492 should seek to reconceptualize the past in terms of the existential reality specific to our [American] continent. It must recognize, as Cuban novelist Alejo Carpentier (1976) indicates, that all the major and hitherto-separated races [sic] of the world have been brought together in the new world to work out a common destiny." She adds that, "this destiny would entail the transformation of our original dominant/ subordinant social structure and its attendant perceptual and cognitive matrices into new ones founded on reciprocal relations" (in Sharma 2015, 164).

Chapter Two

1   Although many believed the partition to be a cynical act of divide-and-rule politics, and even though the division was rescinded and the borderline between the two erased in 1911, the initial partition spurred some Muslims to form an India-wide movement separate from that of Hindus (who dominated the Indian National Congress). Indeed, the 1947 partition of British India was carried out along the lines Curzon first laid out in 1905. Indeed, what came to be East Pakistan was almost indistinguishable from Curzon's "East Bengal."

2   "Zomia" generally refers to the uplands of southern Asia—"from the Vietnamese highlands up into the Tibetan plateau and as far west as Afghanistan"—where "hill peoples" have purposely lived with as little contact with state power as possible, at least until the era of postcolonialism (see Bennett 2009). It was first named "Zomia" by Willem Van Schendel (2002) to challenge official geographical boundaries and proffered an alternative way of understanding the terrain of power in the region.

3   In addition to the two categories of French "citizens" and "subjects," there was a third category of persons within imperial French territory: "French-

administered persons" (*administrés français*) from Togo and Cameroon, who were placed under French control by League of Nations mandate following WWI (Czapliński 1985). An intermediate category of "mixed race" (i.e., those with some "European blood") was developed to account for the widely evident lack of purity within either grouping.

4 Colonization by various European imperial powers began in the late fifteenth century in the Caribbean, the early sixteenth century in Central and South America, the sixteenth to seventeenth centuries in North America and Southern Africa, and the late eighteenth century for Australia, New Zealand, and the Pacific Islands.

5 Such a designation, however, precluded Indians from asserting a separate sovereignty from the United States, as they had earlier been defined as "domestic dependent nations" by Chief Justice John Marshall in 1831 (*Cherokee Nation v. Georgia*).

6 The 1867 British North America Act (BNA) provided the government of Canada with its current federal political structure, its own parliament, and its own justice and taxation systems. However, the BNA remained subject to section 2 of the 1865 British Colonial Laws Validity Act (An Act to Remove Doubts as to the Validity of Colonial Laws, 28 & 29 Victoria, c. 63).

7 Between 1492 and 1820, while approximately ten to fifteen million people from Africa were forcibly brought to the New World, only two million or so people from Europe had made the journey. This only began to change after the abolition of the African slave trade and, even then, only in the 1820s. The Great Migration of the nineteenth century was part of this process.

Chapter Three

1 The English 1533 Statute in Restraint of Appeals had declared "that this realm of England is an Empire" (in Koebner 1953).

2 Tellingly, the full title of the 28 August 1833 act of Parliament abolishing slavery was "An Act for the Abolition of Slavery throughout the British Colonies; for promoting the Industry of the manumitted Slaves; and for compensating the Persons hitherto entitled to the Services of such Slaves." It came into effect on 1 August 1834 (with the exception of both the Colony of the Cape of Good Hope, which was given an extension of four months, and the Colony of Mauritius, which was given an extension of six months). However, on these dates, only enslaved workers below the age of six were actually freed. Slaves laboring as domestics had to "apprentice" for four years, while agricultural slaves had to do so for an additional six years after emancipation. The first set of apprenticeships ended on 1 August 1838, while the system as a whole ended on 1 August 1840 (Carter 1993). Moreover, the 1833 act contained a clause allowing slavery in British India for those producing goods for colonial markets operated by the East India Company. Such slavery was not abolished until the Indian Slavery Act V. of 1843. It was not until provisions of the Indian Penal Code of 1861 that enslavement itself became a criminal offense.

3   Under the 1842 Treaty of Nanking, the British gained direct control over Hong
    Kong, while Canton, Shanghai, Amoy, Fuzhou, and Nigbo were opened up as
    nodes in the British-controlled trade in opium. Between 1868 and 1903, the Brit-
    ish also colonized significant parts of the African continent, including Egypt,
    Zululand, Fante Confederacy, Basutoland, Bechuanaland, Ijebu, Bunyoro, the
    Kingdom of Benin, Ashanti Confederacy, Swaziland, and parts of the Fulani
    Empire.

4   I am deeply indebted to Radhika Mongia's 2007 article for many of the historical
    details of the enactment of immigration controls in British Mauritius.

5   It is likely that enslaved people on Mauritius, transported from various sites on
    the African continent, were considered the natives of Mauritius, because the
    British imagined that Mauritius was a part of Africa.

6   This may have been important since it was not only coolies but also White,
    male workers in the empire's White Settler colonies who were subjected to
    contracts of service. An 1823 United Kingdom Act described its purpose as "the
    better regulations of servants, laborers and work people." This particular act
    influenced employment law in Australia (1845), Canada (1847), New Zealand
    (1856), and South Africa (1856). These acts disciplined employees by requir-
    ing their obedience and loyalty to their contracted employer. Infringements
    of contracts were punishable before a court of law, which often sent people
    to jail under a sentence of hard labor. The 1823 U.K. law was also used against
    workers organizing for better conditions from its inception until several years
    after the first U.K. Trade Union Act of 1871. Between 1858 and 1875 an average
    of 10,000 prosecutions a year took place under the act. Statutes legislating un-
    freedom in England remained in effect until 1875, when criminal sanctions for
    premature departure from a contracted place of employment were eliminated
    (Steinfeld 1991, 115, 160). However, these workers were not made subject to im-
    migration controls until well into the twentieth century.

7   Generally, imperial states enhanced emigration controls during the eigh-
    teenth century amid concerns over shortages of workers in both the
    colonies as well as in the imperial metropoles by regulating and restricting—
    sometimes even prohibiting—emigration. This changed in the nineteenth
    century, as emigration from Europe came to be perceived as a safety valve
    for "surplus populations" displaced from the rural economy and left without
    a livelihood in the urban industrial sectors (see Kritz, Keely, and Tomasi 1981,
    xxii–xxiii).

8   In 1807, the year the British Empire abolished the slave trade, Trinidad was
    the first site to which coolies from China were brought to labor as indentured
    servants (Sookdeo 2000, 22).

9   Canada was following Australia's Commonwealth Parliament, whose very first
    piece of legislation was its Immigration Restriction Act in 1901. Considered the
    start of the "White Australia Policy," this act, however, did not explicitly declare
    that only people racialized as "White," and preferably only "White British,"
    could enter Australia. Instead, the act used an indirect method—the dictation

test—to ensure the exclusion of "undesirables." Demonstrating the circulation of technologies of rule throughout the British Empire, Australia's dictation test was similar to an earlier one established in the British colony of Natal. Its Immigration Restriction Act of 1897 was enacted against British subjects from India. This test was to be administered by an immigration officer in *any* European language of the officer's choice. The new Australian Parliament went this route because of British imperial office pressure to not alienate non-White British subjects.

10 A 1902 Royal Commission to Investigate Chinese and Japanese Immigration into British Columbia had earlier declared that all "Asians" were "unfit for full citizenship . . . obnoxious to a free community and dangerous to the state" (Canada 1902).

11 Canada's Immigration Act of 1910 designated as "Canadian" those British subjects who were born, naturalized, or domiciled in Canada and declared that all other British subjects required permission to land (see Knowles 1997, 85–86). Thus, in contrast to the imperial office's distinction between subjects and aliens, Canada's 1910 Immigration Act created a legal distinction between Canadians and Migrants. Indeed, a separate status of "Canadian national" was to follow in the Canadian Nationals Act of 1921. A Canadian national was a person who was defined as being a Canadian citizen by the 1910 act, but this now included their wives (but not husbands) and children (if fathered by a Canadian national) not yet landed in Canada.

12 In 1798, the Fifth U.S. Congress passed four bills that made up the Alien and Sedition Acts. These were not immigration acts, however. One was the Naturalization Act, which restricted access to U.S. citizenship. The Alien Friends Act allowed for the imprisonment and deportation of non-U.S. citizens deemed to be a threat. The Alien Enemy Act did the same for noncitizens from states the United States was at war with. The Sedition Act criminalized criticism of the federal government deemed to be false.

13 The 1875 Page Act extended the work of California's 1862 Anti-Coolie Act (whose official title was "An Act to Protect Free White Labor Against Competition with Chinese Coolie Labor, and to Discourage the Immigration of the Chinese into the State of California").

14 Specifically, the Page Act prohibited the entry of "any subject of China, Japan, or any Oriental country, without their free and voluntary consent" (US 1875, chap. 141, sec. 2). However, as there were very few subjects other than those of China, its main effect was on Chinese workers.

15 A total of 350,000 workers from China came to the continental (or "mainland") United States between 1840 and 1882 under the U.S. "credit-ticket" system, which embodied many features of the coolie indentured labor recruitment system. U.S. employers loaned money to workers from China for travel costs, to be repaid, with interest, from future wages. Thus, while workers could formally choose whom to work for, they were tied to the lenders until the debt was paid off. It is estimated that on average it took workers seven months to pay off these debts. Moreover, between 1852 and 1887,

approximately 50,000 people from China were recruited to work as coolie indentured laborers in the Kingdom of Hawaii on sugar plantations owned by U.S. investors (Takaki 1983).

16 In 1880, the Burlingame Treaty was amended to suspend—but not wholly prohibit—the entry of people moving from China to the United States. It continued the previous obligation of the United States to protect those who had already entered, however.

17 "Asians" were also excluded from the right to naturalize until the 1940s (Lopez 1997, 44).

18 The only states on the American continents not to nationalize their sovereignty until after WWII were Belize (1981), Guyana (1966), Suriname (1975), and French Guiana (which remains an overseas department of France).

19 The imbrication of local knowledge with archaeological knowledge in the late nineteenth and early twentieth centuries throughout Latin America also helped to shape a "lived memory of the past" and provided a narrative of the supposedly eternal nation that awaited rebirth (Castro-Klarén 2003, 188, 195).

20 There was an 1847 ban on the entry people of the "African race." However, this was not codified into law but was a stipulation of a six-year contract between Colombia and the Company of Panama to build a train track across the Panamanian isthmus, which was part of Colombia until 1903 (see Fitzgerald and Cook-Martin 2014, 356).

21 In 1801, after the French military's withdrawal, Toussaint L'Ouverture declared himself the leader of the sovereign Black state of Saint Domingue and drew up its first constitution (modeled on the French Declaration of the Rights of Man and Citizen). True to the goal of the revolt beginning in 1791, slavery abolition was written into this constitution. Haitian independence from France, however, is usually dated to 1 January 1804, when Jean-Jacques Dessalines declared independence from France (James 1963).

22 I take this from the title of a powerful film by Rob Lemkin (2010) exploring the legitimating discourses employed by the Khmer Rouge in Cambodia in the 1970s.

Chapter Four

1 The 1923 Lausanne Treaty granted the British Empire much of the territories of the Ottoman Empire, including Cyprus (Article 20), Egypt and Sudan (Article 17), and Iraq and Syria (both organized by Article 3). The British Mandate for Palestine was constructed on 24 July 1922 by the League of Nations.

2 Filipinx who had served in the U.S. military, along with their (mostly female) spouses, were exempt from quota restrictions placed at that time.

3 Such discourses were not wholly new, of course, but drew from earlier pogroms and expulsions mandated by monarchical or imperial states. Spain's 1492 expulsion of practicing Jewish people, the 1502 demand that Muslim people either convert to Christianity or leave the territory, and the 1609 expulsion of *Moriscos* (Muslim converts to Christianity), as well as France's seventeenth-century expulsion of Huguenots (Protestants), are classic examples in the formation of

societies correlating with racist ideas of antimiscegenation, this time on the basis of religion.

4   The Allied Powers during WWI were the British Empire; the French Empire; the Kingdoms of Italy, Greece, and Romania; and the Empire of Japan. The United States joined as an "associated power" rather than an official ally.

5   The Turkey-Greece agreement on population transfer was itself modeled on previous partitionings of the declining Ottoman Empire. In 1913, a forced population exchange of persons variously constituted as "Greeks" and "Bulgarians" in the Balkan region was brokered by the Great Powers in the aftermath of the First Balkan War.

6   By the time the 1923 convention was signed, most "Greeks" had already fled because of the nationalist pogroms in Turkey in the last days of the Greco-Turkish war (1919–1922).

7   Sociologically, "majorities" and "minorities" are not about numbers but about one's relationship to power and, crucially, to dominant ideas of national belonging. Consequently, one can be part of the Majority while comprising only a small numerical proportion of the population within a nation-state. Conversely, one can be part of a Minority group even when it is numerically greater.

8   The League of Nations arose as an institutional mechanism in part to manage and ameliorate the exclusions and abuses *inherent* to the expanding nation-state system (see Torpey 2000, 127).

9   For example, neither the signatories to the growing number of Minority Treaties nor the League considered nation-state policies requiring minorities to assimilate to the "national culture" as a violation of minority rights.

10 Many of the laws passed by the Nazis were extensions of previous ones passed by various administrative districts in Germany, including a 1922 law in Baden requiring that all "Gypsies" carry special identification papers and the 1926 Bavarian Law for Combating the Gypsies, Travellers, and Work-Shy that, in an effort to sedentarize Gypsies, prohibited them from "roam[ing] about or camp[ing] in bands." This law also allowed for the imprisonment of Gypsies over sixteen who could not prove regular employment in workhouses for two years. Nazi Germany was not, of course, alone in enacting racialized policies on citizenship. In fascist Italy, the September 1938 Manifesto of Race (*Manifesto della razza*) stripped Jewish and "African" people of their Italian citizenship, nullified and banned marriages between "Italians" and "Jews" or "Africans," and barred "Jews" or "Africans" from positions in government, banking, and education. In addition, the properties of those deemed to be of these "inferior races" became subject to confiscation.

11 This treaty was signed by Belgium, Denmark, France, Norway, the Netherlands, and Switzerland (see League of Nations 1936).

12 This treaty was signed by Belgium, Great Britain and Northern Ireland, Denmark, Spain, France, Norway, and the Netherlands (see League of Nations 1938, 59).

13 Attempting to sanitize his record of killing approximately 12,000 Black people (categorized as "Haitian immigrants") in October 1937, Rafael Trujillo, the

dictator of the Dominican Republic (DR), offered to take 100,000 people from Europe. However, he was only interested in "refugees" racialized as "European" or "White," and for him, Jewishness (but not "Gypsy-ness" or Blackness) was a part of Whiteness. Even so, anticipating their arrival, Trujillo decreed Law 48 (December 1938), which increased the amount of money required to enter the country to five hundred dollars for people of "Mongolian and African races" and for foreigners who were "stateless" (e.g., people fleeing Nazi Germany). German and Austrian Jewish refugees paid almost ninety thousand dollars in revenue to the DR in 1939 alone (M. A. Kaplan 2008).

14 In 1933, most Jewish people lived in urban areas, with approximately one-third living in Berlin (Holocaust Encyclopedia n.d.).

15 Holocaust scholars usually distinguish between concentration camps, first established in 1933 at Dachau when the Nazis came to power, and extermination camps, which began in 1941 (see Fischel 2010; Landau [1992] 2016).

16 In an effort to quell growing anticolonial movements, the British had outlawed new contracts of indenture in British India by 1920. As Kingsley Davis (1951, 104) notes, "The event was hailed as a red-letter day throughout India, where it was regarded as an event paralleling the abolition of slavery nearly a century before."

Chapter Five

1 This is a quote from Article 22 of the League's founding covenant. This covenant asserted the right of the League to determine who was and who was not fit for self-rule. Three separate groups (A, B, and C) of imperial subjects were created on a descending scale of their (League-determined) capacity for self-rule. The main objective of Article 22, written primarily by the United Kingdom and France two months before signing of the 1919 Versailles Peace Treaty, was to formally transfer power over various colonies from the losers of WWI to the victors. Some transferred territories were reclassified as "mandates" under supervision by the League.

2 *Home Rule* was the English title given to Mohandas Karamchand Gandhi's 1909 book, *Hind Swaraj*, in which he argued for Indian nationalism. In using this title, Gandhi borrowed from a mid-nineteenth century use of the term, which according to the Oxford English Dictionary (OED) was used to express, "The government of a colony, dependent country, province, or region by its own citizens; self-government."

3 The IMF defined FDI in 1977 as an "investment that is made to acquire a lasting interest in an enterprise operating in an economy other than that of the investor, the investor's purpose being to have an effective voice in the management of the enterprise" (in Bhalla 2013, 796).

4 The twelve original members of NATO (in alphabetical order) were Belgium, Canada, Denmark, France, Iceland, Italy, Luxembourg, the Netherlands, Norway, Portugal, the United Kingdom, and the United States. Greece and Turkey joined NATO in 1952, while West Germany joined in 1955.

5 The original Warsaw Pact member states (in alphabetical order) were Albania, Bulgaria, Czechoslovakia, East Germany, Hungary, Poland, Romania, and the Soviet Union. Albania withdrew in 1968 and East Germany in 1990. The treaty provided for a unified military command and for the existence of Soviet military units on the territories of the other participating states.

6 The term "state capitalism" has had various usages over the twentieth century, beginning with Tony Cliff's writings for the British Revolutionary Communist Party in 1948 and continuing with the 1969 book *State Capitalism and World Revolution* by C. L. R. James, Raya Dunayevskaya, and Grace Lee Boggs. Its use signals that some nominally "communist" states are best understood as "state capitalist" states because the state owns and controls the means of production while the labor power of workers remains commodified and exploited by the state.

7 In 2001 the SOA was renamed the Western Hemisphere Institute for Security Cooperation (WHINSEC).

8 1944 amendments to the USSR's All-Union Constitution permitted separate branches of the Red Army for each Soviet Republic and allowed for Republic-level commissariats for foreign affairs and defense. These changes enabled them to claim to be de jure independent nation-states in international law. Indeed, the Soviet Republics of Ukraine and Byelorussia were able to join as founding members of the UN General Assembly in 1945, alongside the USSR. While clearly not "independent" of the USSR, but members of the federation of "nationalities" said to comprise the Soviet Union, the Soviet socialist republics were embedded within a *nationality regime*. Through their organization as distinct nations within the USSR, in each people developed a deep structure of feeling of nation-ness that would have enormous consequences when the Soviet Union collapsed and they became "independent" nation-states (Brubaker 1994, 77).

9 The term comes from the Declaration for the Establishment of a New International Economic Order, adopted by the UN General Assembly in 1974, which referenced a range of trade, financial, commodity, and debt-related issues that would be more favorable to the NAM nation-states.

Chapter Six

1 A 19 May 1969 article in the *U.S. News and World Report* referred to "the Man" as a "term for the present system of government" (in Greif 2015, 272).

Chapter Seven

1 In this way, a system of global apartheid does not work to *physically separate* people but to construct Nationals and Migrants as *separate "types" of people* along a hierarchical scale. We would do well to recall that those classified as Black or Coloured in apartheid-era South Africa did not necessarily live apart from Whites. Indeed, they often lived and worked in the homes of those classified as White. However, Black people especially were positioned by the South African nation-state as being citizens of various "Bantustans" and were

thus made noncitizens in South Africa. This was done precisely to deny them national rights in South Africa.

2   An underexamined problem in talking about "Asia" is that what we know as "Europe" has been carved out of it and is considered a separate continent.

3   The GCC nation-states have each attempted reform of their "sponsorship" system to allow "guest workers" to change jobs without permission from their existing employer. These reforms are exceedingly limited, however, largely benefiting those at the higher wage and skill segments of the guest worker labor force (see Hertog 2014, 8). For example, Oman (in 2006), Bahrain (in 2008), Kuwait (in 2009), and the United Arab Emirates (UAE in 2011) reformed their "sponsorship" programs to either abolish (Oman and Bahrain) or relax (Kuwait and UAE) previous requirements that guest workers needed their employer's permission to leave their jobs. These reforms did not effectively change existing *practice*, however. In Bahrain, only 4,271 out of 453,661 guest workers changed employers during the first quarter of 2011, and only 2 percent did so without the consent of their existing employer. Most who did were in the higher wage segment of guest workers (Hertog 2014, 13).

4   Kuwait is the only GCC state with a minimum wage for "migrant workers," but even this is exceedingly low (KD 60, or about $210, per month).

5   Significant numbers of people from Africa and Asia had moved to Europe long before the mid-twentieth century, beginning, of course, with the first peopling of Europe—or, more accurately, Far West Asia (see National Geographic n.d.). For Britain, see Fryer 1984; Ramdin 1987; Holmes 1988; Visram 2015; and Callaway 2015. For France, see Thomas and David 2007. For a world overview, see Cohen 1995.

6   Czarist Russia was an exception to this norm (see Hammar 1990, 42–45).

7   When the New Commonwealth Society was founded in 1932, it was understood to encompass the whole of the British Empire. It was in the 1960s that the term "New Commonwealth" came to designate those nation-states that were former colonies. This naming of negatively racialized people arriving from the former colonies as "New Commonwealth immigrants" emerged through debates about U.K. immigration policy (see Srinivasan 2006).

8   The Aliens Act defined as "undesirable" those aliens who traveled by ship as a "steerage passenger" (the least costly tickets), who were unable to show they could support themselves and their "dependents," those diagnosed with lunacy or idiocy, and people with criminal records (R. Miles 1993, 144). While Jewish people were not specifically included in the list of undesirables, it is evident in the discourse surrounding the passing of the act that they were its primary targets (145).

9   Even so, they *could* face immigration controls if they were deemed to have a mental illness, if they had a criminal record, or if they were said to constitute a national security threat.

10 Uganda, Tanzania, and Kenya used people's lack of national citizenship to advance further anti-Asian policies, insisting that regulations that blocked

noncitizens from certain trades and professions, or those that blocked their free mobility within the state were not racist but merely an enactment of their newfound national sovereignty (Rothchild 1973, 263). They were correct. However, since these same rules did not apply to *nonnationals* racialized as "Black" and "African," such legislation racialized and autochthonized the new nation-states.

11 This criterion was to be applied even in those cases when children would be rendered Stateless because neither the country of their parents' nationality nor Britain would recognize them as its citizen (Blake 1982, 186).

12 This was renamed "British Overseas Territories Citizenship" in 2002.

13 Nevertheless, within French Algeria the French Empire maintained two separate voter rolls: one for those with "French" civil status and another for those of "Muslim" civil status (Cooper 2011).

14 The emigration of people from Europe to North America and Oceania went from 400,000 per year in the early 1950s to less than 100,000 per year by the early 1990s. Concomitantly, annual net immigration into the EU went from 200,000 in the 1980s to over a million people in 1989–1993, before falling again to 640,000 in 1994–1998. This represents more than a tripling of immigration into the EU (Venturini 2004, 13).

15 This is a blog statement by "Fjordman" entitled "Creating a European Indigenous People's Movement" and is from the website of the *Brussels Journal*, published by the Society for the Advancement of Freedom in Europe (SAFE), a Swiss nonprofit organization that bills itself as "the voice of conservatism in Europe."

Chapter Eight

1 Numerous studies of the violence of autochthonous discourses across the African continent have been done. These include violent conflicts of National-Natives against Migrants in the Ivory Coast (Arnaut 2008); Cameroon (Ceuppens and Geschiere 2005); Senegal (Boone 2003); Ghana and neighboring parts of Burkina Faso (Lentz and Somda 2003; Wienia 2003); the Great Lakes Region in Central Africa, including Rwanda-Burundi and Congo's North and South Kivu (Malkki 1995, 63; Willame 1997; Mamdani 2001; Stephen W. Jackson 2003); Sudan, Uganda, Tanzania, Mali, and Zambia (Oppen 2003); Botswana (van Dijk 2003); and South Africa (Comaroff and Comaroff 2001).

2 Kodnani was acquitted of charges in 2018 by the Gujarat High Court.

3 Rohingya is a term currently used by Muslim people who have lived since "time immemorial" in what is now Arakan or Rakhine state in western Myanmar (see Chamey 2007).

4 A 2013 UNHCR country report on Myanmar states that there are 1,185,640 stateless people in Myanmar. Of this, approximately 800,000 to 1,000,000 Muslims (mostly Rohingya people) reside in Rakhine State.

5 I am grateful to Bridget Anderson for drawing my attention to this article.

6   The 969 movement is an effort led by Buddhist monks to persecute Muslims in
    Myanmar with the aim of removing them from "national" territory. It is called
    this after its logo, which displays "969," a numerologically significant sign for
    Burmese Buddhists, along with a chakra wheel and four Asiatic lions repre-
    senting the ancient Buddhist emperor Ashoka. "969" signs are prominently
    displayed on Buddhist homes and businesses to show support for this move-
    ment and opposition to Muslims in Myanmar, particularly Rohingya people.
    The movement was founded by the late Kyaw Lwin, an ex-monk and former
    government official, who was selected by state leaders in 1991 to head its new
    Department for the Promotion and Propagation of the Sasana (or "religion"),
    a unit within the Religion Ministry created by the military junta. Ironically, this
    movement was established by Myanmar's military junta in the aftermath of its
    brutal repression of monks during the 1988 uprising against the dictatorship in
    an effort to redirect their efforts. See Marshall 2013.
7   The restriction of their freedom of movement within Myanmar is based on the
    1940 British Registration of Foreigners Act and Rules.
8   This is part of a statement by H. E. U Wunna Maung Lwin, Myanmar's minister
    for foreign affairs, made at the Twenty-fourth Session of the UN Human Rights
    Council on 13 September 2013 (in Zarni and Cowley 2014, 704).
9   The fifth condition, "forcibly transferring children of the group to another
    group," has not been documented (see UN 1948).
10 Currently, oil and gas transport pipelines are under construction from Rakhine
    State to Yunnan Province in China (see Human Rights Watch 2012, 46).
11 Robert Miles (1993, 173–193) notes that those constituted as Migrants are often
    already well "assimilated" and "integrated" by the institutions of the societies
    they inhabit.
12 In Europe, too, there are competing discourses of autochthony. There are
    people there simultaneously seen as "indigenous" and not European—for
    example, people identifying as Sami, Basque, Nenets, Samoyedic, Komi, and
    Circassian. I have not included a discussion of their deployment of autoch-
    thony, however, because their use of such discourses have not yet carried the
    same political weight as those of Indigenous National-Natives in the former
    White Settler colonies. I hope to devote future research to this topic.
13 The doctrine of *terra nullius* was a legal right granted in the papal bull of Pope
    Urban II in 1095 to European (mostly monarchical) states in claiming land in-
    habited by non-Christians. Later, it was widely deployed by European imperial
    states in the "New World."
14 Select individual Indians, however, continued to be granted U.S. citizenship in
    special circumstances.
15 Jodi Byrd (2011) has deviated from this practice somewhat. She refers to nega-
    tively racialized non-Natives as "arrivants." However, her argument fundamen-
    tally pivots on the separation of Natives and non-Natives, thus reproducing
    most of the tenets of Indigenous National-Native autochthony.

16 There were significant differences in how these five tribes included or excluded their former slaves. The Seminoles were the most inclusive, while the Chickasaws completely excluded them from tribal membership. The Creeks and the Cherokees included Freedmen as members but impeded their political, social, and economic equality with "Indian" Cherokees. In 1979, Muscogee Creek Indian Freedmen also had their membership terminated by the Muscogee (Creek) Nation (see May 1996, 4).

17 TIPNIS is the Isiboro Sécure National Park and Indigenous Territory (*Territorio Indígena y Parque Nacional Isiboro Secure*). These lands were first designated as a national park in 1965 and, in 1990, recognized as an Indigenous territory (formally as Native Community Land) through Supreme Decree 22610. The latter came as a result of pressure from local indigenous people and the broader March for Territory and Dignity organized by the Confederation of Indigenous Peoples of the Bolivian East (Achtenberg 2015b).

Chapter Nine

1 The quote in the heading is from Lawrence Clarkson's pamphlet *A Generall Charge Or, Impeachment of High-Treason in the Name of Justice Equity, against the Communality of England* (London, 1647). Clarkson was perhaps the most well known of the Ranters, a group of people viewed by both the established Church and the English state as a significant threat. Their belief in antinomianism, that everyone was freed from restraints of obeying the Church or the state, along with their rejection of private property, made them dangerous to all existing forms of rule.

2 Linebaugh and Rediker (2000, 86) argue that "in the geographic terminology of the seventeenth century, 'Turkey' signified both the religion of Islam and the continent Africa."

BIBLIOGRAPHY

Abbink, Jon, ed. 2012. *Fractures and Reconnections: Civic Action and the Redefinition of African Political and Economic Spaces: Studies in Honor of Piet J. J. Konings*. African Studies Centre, vol. 5. Münster, Germany: LIT Verlag.

ABC (Australia Broadcasting Corporation). 2001. "Liberals Accused of Trying to Rewrite History." 21 November. Accessed 31 May 2016. http://www.abc.net.au /lateline/content/2001/s422692.htm.

Abele, Frances, and Daiva Stasiulis. 1989. "Canada as a 'White Settler Colony': What about Indigenous and Immigrants?" In *The New Canadian Political Economy*, edited by Wallace Clement and Glen Williams, 240–277. Montreal: McGill-Queen's University Press.

Abella, Irving, and Harold Troper. 1982. *None Is Too Many: Canada and the Jews of Europe, 1933–1948*. Toronto: Lester and Orpen Dennys.

Abella, Irving, and Harold Troper. 1998. "The Line Must Be Drawn Somewhere: Canada and Jewish Refugees, 1933–1939." In *A Nation of Immigrants: Women, Workers, and Communities in Canadian History, 1840s–1960s*, edited by Franca Iacovetta, Paula Draper, and Robert Ventresca, 179–209. Toronto: University of Toronto Press.

Achebe, Chinua. 1958. *Things Fall Apart*. Portsmouth, NH: Heinemann.

Achtenberg, Emily. 2012. "Nationalization, Bolivian Style: Morales Seizes Electric Grid, Boosts Oil Incentives." *Rebel Currents* (blog of the North American Congress on Latin America, NACLA). Accessed 17 March 2018. https://nacla.org/blog /2012/5/10/nationalization-bolivian-style-morales-seizes-electric-grid-boosts-oil -incentives.

Achtenberg, Emily. 2015a. "How Evo Morales's Third Term Will Challenge Bolivia's Social Movements." *Rebel Currents* (blog of the North American Congress on Latin America, NACLA). Accessed 31 May 2016. https://nacla.org/blog/2015 /03/28/how-evo-morales%27s-third-term-will-challenge-bolivia%27s-social -movements.

Achtenberg, Emily. 2015b. "Morales Greenlights TIPNIS Road, Oil and Gas Extraction in Bolivia's National Parks." *Rebel Currents* (blog of the North American Congress on Latin America, NACLA). Accessed 31 May 2016. https://nacla .org/blog/2015/06/15/morales-greenlights-tipnis-road-oil-and-gas-extraction -bolivia%E2%80%99s-national-parks.

Adepoju, Aderanti. 1984. "Illegals and Expulsion in Africa: The Nigerian Experience." *International Migration Review* 18 (3): 426–436.

Agamben, Giorgio. 1998. *Homo Sacer: Sovereign Power and Bare Life*. Stanford, CA: Stanford University Press.

Aglietta, Michel. 1979. *A Theory of Capitalist Regulation*. London: New Left Books.

Agnew, John. 1994. "The Territorial Trap: The Geographical Assumption of International Relations Theory." *Review of International Political Economy* 1 (1): 53–80.

Albright, Madeleine, 2003. *Madam Secretary: A Memoir*. New York: Miramax Books.

Alfred, Gerald R. 1995. *Heeding the Voices of Our Ancestors: Kahnawake Mohawk Politics and the Rise of Native Nationalism in Canada*. Toronto: Oxford University Press.

Alfred, Gerald R. 2005. *Wasase: Indigenous Pathways of Action and Freedom*. Toronto: Broadview Press.

Alfred, Gerald Taiaiake. 2006. "Sovereignty—An Inappropriate Concept." In *The Indigenous Experience: Global Perspectives*, edited by Roger Maaka and Chris Andersen, 322–336. Toronto: Canadian Scholars' Press.

Allen, Theodore William. 1975. *Class Struggle and the Origin of Racial Slavery: The Invention of the White Race*. Hoboken, NJ: Hoboken Education Project.

Allen, Theodore William. 1994. *The Invention of the White Race: The Origin of Racial Oppression in Anglo-America*. Vol. 1. London: Verso.

Aluko, Olajide. 1985. "The Expulsion of Illegal Aliens from Nigeria: A Study in Nigeria's Decision-Making." *African Affairs* 84 (337): 539–560.

Amin, Samir. 1974. *Neo-Colonialism in West Africa*. New York: Monthly Review Press.

Amin, Samir. 1977. *Imperialism and Unequal Development*. New York: Monthly Review Press.

Amin, Samir. 2004. "Globalism or Apartheid on a Global Scale." In *The Modern World-System in the Longue Durée*, edited by Immanuel Wallerstein, 5–30. New York: Paradigm Publishers.

Amnesty International. 2004. "Rwanda: 'Marked for Death,' Rape Survivors Living with HIV/AIDS in Rwanda." 5 April, AFR 47/007/2004. Accessed 20 June 2016. https://www.amnesty.org/en/documents/afr47/007/2004/en/.

Anderson, Benedict, 1991. *Imagined Communities: Reflections on the Origin and Spread of Nationalism*. London: Verso.

Anderson, Bridget. 2013. *Us and Them? The Dangerous Politics of Immigration Control*. Oxford: Oxford University Press.

Anderson, Bridget, Nandita Sharma, and Cynthia Wright. 2009. "Why No Borders?" (editorial). *Refuge: Canada's Journal on Refugees* 26 (2): 5–18.

Anderson, Perry. 2012. "After Nehru." *London Review of Books* 34 (15): 21–36.

Angola. 1978. *Décret No. 13 du 1978, L'entrée et la sortie des étrangers du pays*. 1 February. Accessed 31 July 2016. http://www.refworld.org/topic,50ffbce5220,50ffbce523b,3ae6b4df0,0,,,AGO.html.

Anstey, Peter R., ed. 2003. *The Philosophy of John Locke: New Perspectives*. New York: Routledge.

Anzaldúa, Gloria. (1987) 1999. *Borderlands/La Frontera: The New Mestiza*. San Francisco: Spinsters/Aunt Lute.

Arendt, Hannah. (1951) 1973. *The Origins of Totalitarianism*. New York: Harcourt Brace Jovanovich.

Arendt, Hannah. (1968) 1993. "On Humanity in Dark Times: Thoughts about Lessing." Translated by Clara Winston and Richard Winston. In *Men in Dark Times*, 3–31. New York: Harcourt Brace.

Arghiri, Emmanuel. 1972. *Unequal Exchange: A Study of the Imperialism of Trade*. New York: Monthly Review Press.

Armah, Ayi Kwei. 1968. *The Beautyful Ones Are Not Yet Born*. Boston: Houghton, Mifflin.

Arnaut, Karel. 2008. "Taking the Scales into Account: The Patriotic Movement and the Construction of Autochthon in the Ivory Coast." *Revue Africaine de Sociologie* 12 (2): 69–84.

Asian-African Conference. 1955. *Asia-Africa Speaks from Bandung*. Djakarta, Indonesia: Ministry of Foreign Affairs, Republic of Indonesia.

Atlantic Charter. 1941. U.K.-U.S., 55 Stat. 1603.

Australia Parliament. 2001. *Migration Amendment (Excision from Migration Zone) Act* (September). No. 127. Accessed 1 June 2016. https://www.legislation.gov.au /Details/C2004A00887.

Australia Senate Select Committee on a Certain Maritime Incident. 2002. *Report*. October. Page xxi. Accessed 31 May 2016. https://www.aph.gov.au/binaries /senate/committee/maritime_incident_ctte/report/report.pdf.

Australian Human Rights Commission. 2009. "Bringing Them Home: The Stolen Children Report 1997." Accessed 29 October 2013. https://www.humanrights.gov .au/our-work/aboriginal-and-torres-strait-islander-social-justice/publications /bringing-them-home.

Avalon Project. n.d. "Monroe Doctrine, December 2, 1823." Yale Law School, Lillian Goldman Law Library. Accessed 25 March 2017. http://avalon.law.yale.edu/19th _century/monroe.asp.

Avrich, Paul, ed. 1973. *The Anarchists in the Russian Revolution*. Ithaca, NY: Cornell University Press.

Backhouse, Constance. 1999. *Colour-Coded: A Legal History of Racism in Canada, 1900–1950*. Toronto: University of Toronto Press.

Bajracharya, Rooja, and Bandita Sijapati. 2012. "The Kafala System and Its Implications for Nepali Domestic Workers." Center for the Study of Labor Mobility. Accessed 7 August 2016. http://www.ceslam.org/docs/publicationManagement /Kafala_Nepali_Domestic_Workers_Female_Migration_Eng.pdf.

Baker, Barry. 2011. *World Development: An Essential Text*. Oxford: New Internationalist.

Baker, Houston A., Jr., Teresa Dovey, Rosemary Jolly, and Herbert Deinert. 1995. "Colonialism and the Postcolonial Condition." *Publications of the Modern Language Association of America* 110 (5): 1047–1052.

Balandier, George. 1966. "The Colonial Situation: A Theoretical Approach." In *Social Change: The Colonial Situation*, edited by Immanuel Wallerstein, 34–61. New York: Wiley.

Baldwin, M. Page. 2001. "Subject to Empire: Married Women and the British Nationality and Status of Aliens Act." *Journal of British Studies* 40 (4): 522–556.

Balibar, Étienne. 1991a. "Is There a Neo-Racism?" In *Race, Class, Nation: Ambiguous Identities*, by Étienne Balibar and Immanuel Wallerstein, 17–28. London: Verso.

Balibar, Étienne. 1991b. "The Nation Form: History and Ideology." In *Race, Class, Nation: Ambiguous Identities*, by Étienne Balibar and Immanuel Wallerstein, 86–106. London: Verso.

Balibar, Étienne. 1991c. "Racism and Nationalism." In *Race, Class, Nation: Ambiguous Identities*, by Étienne Balibar and Immanuel Wallerstein, 37–68. London: Verso.

Bangladesh. 1972. *Bangladesh Citizenship (Temporary Provisions) Order* (passed 26 March). Order No. 149. Accessed 15 August 2016. http://www.refworld.org /cgi-bin/texis/vtx/rwmain?page=search&docid=3ae6b51f10&skip=0&query =citizenship&coi=BGD.

Bannerji, Himani. 1995. *Thinking Through: Essays on Feminism, Marxism, and Anti-racism*. Toronto: Women's Press.

Barker, Joanne, ed. 2005. *Sovereignty Matters: Locations of Contestation and Possibility in Indigenous Struggles for Self-Determination*. Lincoln: University of Nebraska Press.

Barrera, Jorge. 2012. "Palmater Backer Blasts Prominent Journalist as "White Supremacist" after Column on AFN Election." *APTN National News*. 16 July. Accessed 15 March 2014. http://aptn.ca/news/2012/07/16/palmater-backer-blasts -prominent-journalist-as-white-supremacist-after-column-on-afn-election/.

Bartosik-Velez, Elise. 2014. *The Legacy of Christopher Columbus in the Americas*. Nashville: Vanderbilt University Press.

Bashford, Alison, and Jane McAdam. 2014. "The Right to Asylum: Britain's 1905 Aliens Act and the Evolution of Refugee Law." *Law and History Review* 32 (2): 309–350.

Batchelor, Carol A. 1998. "Statelessness and the Problem of Resolving Nationality Status." *International Journal of Refugee Law* 10 (1/2): 159–160.

Battiste, Marie, and James Youngblood. 2000. *Protecting Indigenous Knowledge and Heritage: A Global Challenge*. Vancouver: UBC Press.

Bayer, Lili. 2017. "Trading Places on the Hungarian Right." *Politico*. 14 August. Accessed 24 February 2018. https://www.politico.eu/article/hugary-right-wing -trading-places-fidesz-jobbik/.

BBC (British Broadcasting Company). 1971. "UK Restricts Commonwealth Migrants." 24 February. Accessed 12 January 2013. http://news.bbc.co.uk/onthisday /hi/dates/stories/february/24/newsid_2518000/2518513.stm.

BBC (British Broadcasting Company). 2017. "White US Nationalists Chant 'You Will Not Replace Us.'" Accessed 15 August 2017. http://www.bbc.com/news/av/world -asia-40911744/white-us-nationalists-chant-you-will-not-replace-us.

Beaumont, Peter. 2010. "Geert Wilders, the Ultra-right Firebrand, Campaigns to Be Holland's Prime Minister." *The Observer*. 15 May. Accessed 10 February 2016. http://www.theguardian.com/world/2010/may/16/geert-wilders-pvv-holland -netherlands.

Behdad, Ali. 2005. *A Forgetful Nation: On Immigration and Cultural Identity in the United States*. Durham, NC: Duke University Press.

Behrendt, Larissa. 2016. *Finding Eliza: Power and Colonial Storytelling*. St. Lucia: University of Queensland Press.

Beijer, Gunther. 1969. "Modern Patterns of International Migratory Movements." *Migration* 2: 11–59.

Bekers, Elisabeth. 2009. "Chronicling beyond Abyssinia: African Writing in Flanders, Belgium." In *Transcultural Modernities: Narrating Africa in Europe*, edited by Elisabeth Bekers, Sissy Helff, and Daniela Merolla, 57–70. Amsterdam: Rodopi.

Bell, Daniel. 1960. *The End of Ideology*. Vol. 3. New York: Free Press.

Bengio, Ofra, and Ben-Dor Gabriel, eds. 1999. *Minorities and the State in the Arab World*. Boulder, CO: Lynne Rienner.

Bennett, Drake. 2009. "The Mystery of Zomia." *Boston Globe*. 6 December. Accessed 11 November 2017. http://archive.boston.com/bostonglobe/ideas/articles/2009/12/06/the_mystery_of_zomia/.

Bhalla, V. K. 2013. *International Business*. New Delhi: S. Chand Publishing.

Bhatt, Chetan. 2001. *Hindu Nationalism: Origins, Ideologies, and Modern Myths*. Oxford: Berg.

Bigo, Didier. 2008. "Security." In *Foucault on Politics, Security, and War*, 93–114. London: Palgrave Macmillan.

Bilwakesh, Nikhil. 2011. "'Their Faces Were Like So Many of the Same Sort at Home': American Responses to the Indian Rebellion of 1857." *American Periodicals: A Journal of History, Criticism, and Bibliography* 21 (1): 1–23.

Biolsi, Thomas. 2005. "Imagined Geographies: Sovereignty, Indigenous Space, and American Indian Struggle." *American Ethnologist* 32 (2): 239–259.

Birnbaum, Ervin. 2009. "Evian: The Most Fateful Conference of All Times in Jewish History, Part II." *Nativ: A Journal of Politics and the Arts*, February.

Blake, Charles. 1982. "Citizenship, Law, and the State: The British Nationality Act 1981." *Modern Law Review* 45 (2): 179–197.

BNP (British National Party). n.d. "Nationalism—A Definition." Accessed 6 March 2013. http://www.bnp.org.uk/news/national/nationalism-definition.

Bock, Gisela. 1983. "Racism and Sexism in Nazi Germany: Motherhood, Compulsory Sterilization, and the State." *Signs: Journal of Women in Culture and Society* 8 (3): 400–421.

Bolaria, B. Singh, and Peter S. Li. 1988. *Racial Oppression in Canada*. 2nd ed. Toronto: Garamond Press.

Boone, Catherine. 2003. "Decentralization as Political Strategy in West Africa." *Comparative Political Studies* 36 (4): 355–380.

Boone, Catherine. 2014. *Property and Political Order in Africa: Land Rights and the Structure of Politics*. Cambridge: Cambridge University Press.

Bose, Sugata, and Ayesha Jalal, eds. 1998. *Nationalism, Democracy, and Development: State and Politics in India*. Oxford: Oxford University Press.

Boulton, Leanne. 2004. "Native Reserves, Assimilation, and Self-determination: Te Atiawa, the Crown and Settlers, North Taranaki, 1840–1875." MA thesis, University of Canterbury, Christchurch, New Zealand.

Bourgeault, Ron. 1989. "Race, Class and Gender: Colonial Domination of Indian Women." In *Race, Class, Gender: Bonds and Barriers*, edited by J. Vorst, 87–105. Aurora, Ontario: Garamond Press.

Bradley, Megan. 2017. "The International Organization for Migration (IOM): Gaining Power in the Forced Migration Regime." *Refuge: Canada's Journal on Refugees* 33 (1): 97–106.

Braithwaite, Rodric. 2012. "New World Chaos: Review of *Governing the World: The History of An Idea*, by Mark Mazower." *London Review of Books* 35 (2): 33–34.

Brazier, David. 2015. "The Atlantic Charter: Revitalizing the Spirit of the Founding of the United Nations over Seventy Years Past." *UN Chronicle*. May. Accessed 25 July 2015. http://unchronicle.un.org/article/atlantic-charter-revitalizing-spirit-founding-united-nations-over-seventy-years-past/.

Brennan, Timothy. 1997. *At Home in the World: Cosmopolitanism Now*. Vol. 15. Cambridge, MA: Harvard University Press.

Brinham, Natalie. 2012. "The Conveniently Forgotten Human Rights of the Rohingya." *Forced Migration Review* 41: 40.

British and Foreign Anti-Slavery Society (London). (1842) 2014. *Emigration from India, the Export of Coolies, and Other Labourers, to Mauritius*. New York: Cambridge University Press.

Brizuela-Garcia, Esperanza. 2006. "The History of Africanization and the Africanization of History." *History in Africa* 33: 85–100.

Brough, Mal. 2007. "Speech to Parliament: The Northern Territory National Emergency Act 2007." 7 August. Accessed 2 April 2016. http://www.formerministers.dss.gov.au/2929/northern-territory-national-emergency-response-bill-2007-second-reading-speech/.

Brown, Judith M. 1985. *Modern India*. Delhi: Oxford University Press.

Brown, Michael E., and Sumit Ganguly. 1997. *Government Policies and Ethnic Relations in Asia and the Pacific*. Cambridge, MA: MIT Press.

Brown, Wendy. 1995. *States of Injury: Power and Freedom in Late Modernity*. Princeton, NJ: Princeton University Press.

Browne, Thomas. 1646. *Pseudodoxia epidemica, or, Enquiries into Very Many Received Tenents, and Commonly Presumed Truths*. London: printed by T. H. for Edward Dod.

Browning, Christopher R. 1986. "Nazi Resettlement Policy and the Search for a Solution to the Jewish Question, 1939–1941." *German Studies Review* 9 (3): 497–519.

Browning, Christopher, R., with Jürgen Matthaus. 2004. *The Origins of the Final Solution: The Evolution of Nazi Jewish Policy, September 1939–March 1942*. Jerusalem: Yad Vashem, the Holocaust Martyrs' and Heroes' Remembrance Authority.

Brubaker, Rogers. 1994. "Nationhood and the National Question in the Soviet Union and Post-Soviet Eurasia: An Institutionalist Account." *Theory and Society* 23 (1): 47–78.

Brubaker, Rogers. 1996. *Nationalism Reframed: Nationhood and the National Question in the New Europe*. Cambridge: Cambridge University Press.

Brubaker, Rogers. 2010. "Migration, Membership, and the Modern Nation State: Internal and External Dimensions of the Politics of Belonging." *Journal of Interdisciplinary History* 41 (1): 61–78.

Bullard, Nicola, Walden Bello, and Kamal Mallhotra. 1998. "Taming the Tigers: The IMF and the Asian Crisis." *Third World Quarterly* 19 (3): 505–556.

Burman, Anders. 2016. *Indigeneity and Decolonization in the Bolivian Andes: Ritual Practice and Activism*. Lanham, MD: Lexington Books.

Butalia, Urvashi. 2000. *The Other Side of Silence: Voices from the Partition of India*. Durham, NC: Duke University Press.

Buti, Antonio. 2002. "The Removal of Aboriginal Children: Canada and Australia Compared." *University of Western Sydney Law Review* 2 (6): 25.

Buttar, Prit. 2013. *Between Giants: The Battle for the Baltics in World War II*. London: Bloomsbury Publishing.

Byrd, Jodi A. 2011. "'Been to the Nation, Lord, but I Couldn't Stay There': American Indian Sovereignty, Cherokee Freedmen, and the Incommensurability of the Internal." *Interventions: International Journal of Postcolonial Studies* 13 (1): 31–52.

Byrd, Jodi A., and Michael Rothberg. 2011. "Between Subalternity and Indigeneity: Critical Categories for Postcolonial Studies." *Interventions* 13 (1): 1–12.

Cairns, Alan. 2005. *First Nations and the Canadian State: In Search of Coexistence*. Kingston, Ontario: Institute of Intergovernmental Relations, Queen's University.

Callaway, Ewen. 2015. "Europe's First Humans: What Scientists Do and Don't Know." *Nature*. 22 June.

Calvez, Corentin. 1969. "Le problème des travailleurs étrangers." *Journal Officiel de la République Française: Avis et Rapports du Conseil Economique et Social*, no. 7 (March 27): 315.

Cameron, C. R. 1931. "Colonization of Immigrants in Brazil." *Monthly Labor Review* 33 (4): 36–46.

Cameron, David. 2011. "Full Transcript, David Cameron, Speech on Radicalisation and Islamic Extremism, Munich, 5 February 2011." *New Statesman*. Accessed 9 March 2013. http://www.newstatesman.com/blogs/the-staggers/2011/02/terrorism-islam-ideology.

Cameroon. 1968. Loi no. 1968-LF-3 du 11 juin 1968. *Portant code de la nationalité camerounaise*. Accessed 30 July 2016. http://www.refworld.org/cgibin/texis/vtx/rwmain?page=search&docid=3ae6b4d734&skip=0&query=%C3%A9trangers&coi=CMR.

Cameroon. 1997. Loi no. 97/012 du 10 janvier 1997 fixant les conditions d'entrée, de séjour et de sortie des étrangers. *Adoption*. 1997–01–10 | CMR-1997-L-70569. Accessed 30 July 2016.

Campbell, Mavis Christine. 1988. *The Maroons of Jamaica, 1655–1796: A History of Resistance, Collaboration and Betrayal*. Granby, MA: Bergin and Garvey.

Canada. 1876. Indian Act, S.C. RG10, vol. 1923, file 3007.

Canada. 1902. *Report of the Royal Commission to Investigate Chinese and Japanese Immigration into British Columbia*. Archival reference no. R1082–0–0-E.

Canada. 1906. *Immigration Act*, R.S.C.

Canada. 1910. *Immigration Act*, S.C.

Canada. 1921. An Act to Define Canadian Nationals and to Provide for the Renunciation of Canadian Nationality, S.C.

Carens, Joseph, 1995. "Immigration, Welfare, and Justice." In *Justice in Migration*, edited by Warren F. Schwartz, 1–17. Cambridge: Cambridge University Press.

Carlo, Antonio. 1974. "The Socio-economic Nature of the USSR." *Telos* 21: 2–86.

Carlsson, Invar, Han Sung-Joo, and Rufus M. Kupolati. 1999. *Report of the Independent Inquiry into the Actions of the United Nations during the 1994 Genocide in*

Rwanda. Accessed 20 June 2016. http://www.securitycouncilreport.org/atf/cf
/%7B65BFCF9B-6D27-4E9C-8CD3-CF6E4FF96FF9%7D/POC%20S19991257
.pdf.

Carter, Marina. 1993. "The Transition from Slave to Indentured Labour in Mauritius." *Slavery and Abolition* 14 (1): 114–130.

Castles, Stephen. 1995. "How Nation-States Respond to Immigration and Ethnic
Diversity." *New Community* 21 (2): 293–308.

Castles, Stephen. 2006. "Guestworkers in Europe: A Resurrection?" *International
Migration Review* 40 (4): 741–766.

Castles, Stephen, Heather Booth, and Tina Wallace. 1984. *Here for Good: Western
Europe's New Ethnic Minorities.* London: Pluto Press.

Castro-Klarén, Sara. 2003. "The Nation in Ruins: Archaeology and the Rise
of the Nation." In *Beyond Imagined Communities: Reading and Writing the
Nation in Nineteenth-Century Latin America*, 161–195. Baltimore: John Hopkins
University.

Catanach, Ian James. 1970. *Rural Credit in Western India, 1875–1930: Rural Credit
and the Cooperative Movement in the Bombay Presidency.* Berkeley: University of
California Press.

CBC News. 2014. "Mohawks Seek to Remove Non-natives from Kahnawake." 14 August. Accessed 6 June 2016. http://www.cbc.ca/news/canada/montreal/mohawks
-seek-to-remove-non-natives-from-kahnawake-1.2736555.

CBC News. 2018. "'It's Not a Concentration Camp': Bangladesh Defends Plan
to House Rohingya on Island with Armed Police." 22 February. Accessed 23
February 2018. http://www.cbc.ca/news/world/rohingya-bangladesh-island
-concentration-camp-1.4546630.

CEA, U.S. 1967. "Annual Report of the Council of Economic Advisers." *Economic
Report of the President.*

Centre for Applied Research. 2015. "Financial Flows and Tax Havens: Combining
to Limit the Lives of Billions of People." Norwegian School of Economics and
Global Financial Integrity. December. Accessed 17 January 2017. http://www
.gfintegrity.org/wp-content/uploads/2016/12/Financial_Flows-final.pdf.

Centre for Contemporary Cultural Studies. (1982) 2004. *Empire Strikes Back: Race
and Racism in 70's Britain.* London: Routledge.

Cervantes-Rodríguez, Margarita. 2010. *International Migration in Cuba: Accumulation,
Imperial Designs, and Transnational Social Fields.* University Park, PA: Pennsylvania
State University Press.

Cesarani, David. 1987. "Anti-alienism in England after the First World War." *Immigrants and Minorities* 6 (1): 5–29.

Cesarani, David. 1996. "The Changing Character of Citizenship and Nationality in
Britain." In *Citizenship, Nationality, and Migration in Europe*, edited by D. Cesarani
and M. Fulbrook, 67–83. London: Routledge.

Ceuppens, Bambi. 2006. "Allochthons, Colonizers, and Scroungers: Exclusionary
Populism in Belgium." In "Autochthony and the Crisis of Citizenship." Special
issue, *African Studies Review* 49 (2): 147–186.

Ceuppens, Bambi, and Peter Geschiere. 2005. "Autochthony: Local or Global? New Modes in the Struggle over Citizenship and Belonging in Africa and Europe." *Annual Review of Anthropology* 34: 385–407.

Chamey, Michael W. 2007. "Buddhism in Arakan: Theories and Historiography of the Religious Basis of Ethnonyms, Kalaban." PRESS Network. 8 July. Accessed 12 July 2016. http://www.kaladanpress.org/index.php/ scholar-column -mainmenu-36/58-arakan-historical-seminar/718-buddhism-in-arakantheories -andhistoriography-of-the-religious-basis-of-ethnonyms.

Chapman, John. 1987. "The Extent and Nature of Parliamentary Enclosure." *Agricultural History Review* 35 (1): 25–35.

Chatterjee, Partha. 2004. *The Politics of the Governed: Reflections on Popular Politics in Most of the World*. New York: Columbia University Press.

Cheesman, David. 2013. *Landlord Power and Rural Indebtedness in Colonial Sind*. New York: Routledge.

Cheesman, Nick. 2017. "How in Myanmar 'National Races' Came to Surpass Citizenship and Exclude Rohingya." *Journal of Contemporary Asia* 47 (3): 461–483.

Cherokee Nation v. Nash. 2017. 990 F.Supp.2d 1148.

Chinkin, Christine. 1994. "Rape and Sexual Abuse of Women in International Law." *European Journal of International Law* 5 (1): 326–341.

Chrétien, Jean-Pierre. 2007. "RTLM Propaganda: The Democratic Alibi." In *The Media and the Rwandan Genocide*, edited by A. Thompson, 55–61. London: Pluto Press.

Christopher, Emma, Cassandra Pybus, and Marcus Rediker, eds. 2007. *Many Middle Passages: Forced Migration and the Making of the Modern World*. Berkeley: University of California Press.

Churchill, Ward, and Norbert S. Hill Jr. 1979. "An Historical Survey of Tendencies in Indian Education." *Indian Historian* 12(1): 37–46.

Churchill, Winston S. 1942. Speech to the House of Commons. 9 September. Parliamentary Debates, Commons, National Archives of the United Kingdom. CO 323/1848/7322/1942.

Churchill, Winston. 1946. "The Sinews of Peace." Speech at Westminster College, Fulton, Missouri, 5 March. Accessed 29 January 2015. http://www .winstonchurchill.org/resources/speeches/1946–1963-elder-statesman/the -sinews-of-peace.

Cleven, Andrew N. 1925. "Some Plans for Colonizing Liberated Negro Slaves in Hispanic America." *Southwestern Political and Social Science Quarterly* 6 (2): 151–166.

Cliff, Tony. 1988. *State Capitalism in Russia*. London: Bookmarks Publications.

CNN. 2016. "Donald Trump's Full CNN Interview with Jake Tapper." 5 June. Accessed 1 July 2017. http://www.cnn.com/videos/politics/2016/06/03/donald-trump-hillary -clinton-judge-jake-tapper-full-interview-lead.cnn.

Cohen, Robin. 1995. *The Cambridge Survey of World Migration*. Cambridge: Cambridge University Press.

Cohen, Robin. 1997. *Global Diasporas: An Introduction*. London: University College London Press.

Cohn, Bernard S. 1987. *An Anthropologist among the Historians and Other Essays*. Delhi: Oxford University Press.

Cohn, Bernard S. 1996. *Colonialism and Its Forms of Knowledge: The British in India*. Princeton, NJ: Princeton University Press.

Comaroff, Jean, and John L. Comaroff. 2001. "Naturing the Nation: Aliens, Apocalypse, and the Postcolonial State." *Social Identities* 7 (2): 233–265.

Cooper, Frederick. 1996. *Decolonization and African Society: The Labor Question in French and British Africa*. Vol. 89. Cambridge: Cambridge University Press.

Cooper, Frederick. 2005. *Colonialism in Question: Theory, Knowledge, History*. Berkeley: University of California Press.

Cooper, Frederick. 2011. "Alternatives to Nationalism in French Africa, 1945–60." In *Elites and Decolonization in the Twentieth Century*, 110–137. London: Palgrave Macmillan UK.

Cornelius, Wayne A., Takeyuki Tsuda, Philip Martin, and James Hollfield, eds. 2004. *Controlling Immigration: A Global Perspective*. Stanford, CA: Stanford University Press.

Corntassel, Jeff, Richard C. Witmer II, Lindsay Robertson. 2008. *Forced Federalism: Contemporary Challenges to Indigenous Nationhood*. Norman: University of Oklahoma Press.

Coulthard, Glen Sean. 2014. *Red Skin, White Masks: Rejecting the Colonial Politics of Recognition*. Minneapolis: University of Minnesota Press.

Credit Suisse. 2014. *World Wealth Report 2014*. Zurich: Credit Suisse.

Credit Suisse. 2015. "Global Wealth Databook 2015." Accessed 27 December 2016. http://publications.creditsuisse.com/tasks/render/file/index.cfm?fileid =C26E3824-E868-56E0- CCA04D4BB9B9ADD5.

Cregan, Fionuala. 2015. "Rising Tensions in Bolivia over Oil and Gas Exploitation on Indigenous Lands." *IC Magazine* (Center for World Indigenous Studies). 31 August. Accessed 30 June 2016. https://intercontinentalcry.org/rising-tensions -in-bolivia-over-oil-and-gas-exploitation-on-indigenous-lands/.

Crépeau, François. 2003. "The Fight against Migrant Smuggling: Migration Containment over Refugee Protection." In *The Refugee Convention at Fifty: A View from Forced Migration Studies*, edited by Joanne van Selm, Khoti Kamanga, John Morrison, Aninia Nadig, Sanja Spoljar-Vrzina, and Loes van Willigen, 173–185. Lanham, MD: Lexington Books.

Crouch, David. 2014. "The Rise of the Anti-immigrant Sweden Democrats: 'We Don't Feel at Home Anymore, and It's Their Fault.'" *The Guardian*. Accessed 12 February 2016. http://www.theguardian.com/world/2014/dec/14/sweden -democrats-flex-muscles-anti-immigrant-kristianstad.

Crush, Jonathan, and David A. McDonald. 2001. "Introduction to Special Issue: Evaluating South African Immigration Policy after Apartheid." *Africa Today* 48 (3): 1–13.

Crush, Jonathan, and Daniel Tevera. 2010. "Exiting Zimbabwe." In *Zimbabwe's Exodus: Crisis, Migration, Survival*, edited by Jonathan Crush and Daniel Evera, 1–51. Kingston, ON: Southern African Migration Programme (SAMP).

Cruvellier, Thierry. 2010. *Court of Remorse: Inside the International Criminal Tribunal for Rwanda*. Madison: University of Wisconsin Press.

Cull, Nicholas. 1996. "Selling Peace: The Origins, Promotion, and Fate of the Anglo-American New Order during the Second World War." *Diplomacy and Statecraft* 7 (1): 1–28.

Czapliński, Władysław. 1985. "A Note on Decolonization and Nationality." *Verfassung und Recht in Übersee/Law and Politics in Africa, Asia, and Latin America* 18 (3): 329–334.

Dadrian, Vahakn N. 1986. "The Naim-Andonian Documents on the World War One Destruction of the Ottoman Armenians: The Anatomy of a Genocide." *International Journal of Middle Eastern Studies* 18 (3): 311–360.

Daniels, Roger. 2006. "Immigration Policy in a Time of War: The United States, 1939–1945." *Journal of American Ethnic History* 25 (2/3): 107–116.

Davidson, Basil. 1986. "On Revolutionary Nationalism: The Legacy of Cabral." *Race and Class* 27 (3): 21–45.

Davis, Julie Hirschfeld. 2018. "Trump Calls Some Unauthorized Immigrants 'Animals' in Rant." *New York Times*. 16 May. Accessed 18 May 2019. https://www.nytimes.com/2018/05/16/us/politics/trump-undocumented-immigrants-animals.html.

Davis, Kingsley. 1951. *The Population of India and Pakistan*. Princeton, NJ: Princeton University Press.

Dearden, Lizzie. 2017. "Marine Le Pen Claims 'Anglo Saxon World Waking Up' as Europe's Far-Right Parties Meet after Trump Inauguration." *The Independent*. 21 January. Accessed 22 January 2017. http://www.independent.co.uk/news/world/europe/marine-le-pen-national-front-geert-wilders-afd-alternative-germany-koblenz-summit-conference-far-a7539371.html.

De Genova, Nicholas P. 2002. "Migrant 'Illegality' and Deportability in Everyday Life." *Annual Review of Anthropology* 31 (1): 419–447.

Deleuze, Gilles, and Félix Guattari. 1988. *A Thousand Plateaus: Capitalism and Schizophrenia*. London: Bloomsbury Publishing.

Deloria, Philip. 2004. *Indians in Unexpected Places*. Lawrence: University Press of Kansas.

Deloria, Vine, Jr. 1986. "Indian Studies: The Orphan of Academia." *Wicazo Sa Review* 2 (2): 1–7.

DeNavas-Walt, Carmen, and Bernadette D. Proctor. 2015. "Income and Poverty in the United States: 2014." U.S. Census Bureau. September. Accessed 1 February 2017. http://census.gov/content/dam/Census/library/publications/2015/demo/p60-252.pdf.

Deutsche Welle. 2011. "Italian Party Urges Use of Weapons against Refugee 'Invasion.'" 14 April. Accessed 14 February 2016. http://www.dw.com/en/italian-party-urges-use-of-weapons-against-refugee-invasion/a-14988942.

Dhattiwala, Raheel, and Michael Biggs. 2012. "The Political Logic of Ethnic Violence: The Anti-Muslim Pogrom in Gujarat, 2002." *Politics and Society* 40 (4): 483–516.

Dirks, Nicholas B. 2001. "The Ethnographic State." in *Castes of Mind: Colonialism and the Making of Modern India*. Princeton: Princeton University Press, 43–60.

Dirlik, Arif. 1999. "Is There History after Eurocentrism? Globalism, Postcolonialism, and the Disavowal of History." *Cultural Critique* 42: 1–34.

Doty, Roxanne L. 1996. "The Double-Writing of Statecraft: Exploring State Responses to Illegal Immigration." *Alternatives* 21: 171–189.

Dowty, Alan. 1989. *Closed Borders: The Contemporary Assault on Freedom of Movement.* New Haven, CT: Yale University Press.

Draper, Nick. 2007. "'Possessing Slaves': Ownership, Compensation, and Metropolitan Society in Britain at the Time of Emancipation 1834–40." *History Workshop Journal* 64 (1): 74–102.

D'Souza, Rohan. 2003. "Damming the Mahanadi River: The Emergence of Multipurpose River Valley Development in India (1943–46)." *Indian Economic and Social History Review* 40 (1): 82–105.

Duke, David. 2017. "#WhiteGenocide" (Twitter message). 12 March. Accessed 23 May 2017. https://twitter.com/DrDavidDuke/status/841051242658951172.

Duménil, Gérard, and Dominique Lévy. 2005. "The Neoliberal (Counter-) Revolution." In *Neoliberalism: A Critical Reader*, edited by Alfredo Saad-Filho and Deborah Johnston, 9–19. London: Pluto Press.

Dundes, Alan. 1988. *The Flood Myth.* Berkeley: University of California Press.

Dupuy, Alex. 2004. "Class, Race, and Nation: Unresolved Contradictions of the Saint-Domingue Revolution." *Journal of Haitian Studies* 10 (1): 6–21.

Dyrenfurth, Nick. 2005. "Battlers, Refugees, and the Republic: John Howard's Language of Citizenship." *Journal of Australian Studies* 28 (84): 183–196.

Economist. 2017. "Dutch Election Results." 16 March. Accessed 17 March 2017. http://www.economist.com/blogs/graphicdetail/2017/03/daily-chart-10.

Economist. 2018. "The Servant of Two Masters: A Bizarre New Government Takes Shape in Italy." 24 May. Accessed 30 May 2018. https://www.economist.com/europe/2018/05/24/a-bizarre-new-government-takes-shape-in-italy.

Edelman, Lee. 2004. *No Future: Queer Theory and the Death Drive.* Durham, NC: Duke University Press, 2004.

Elkins, David J. 1995. *Beyond Sovereignty: Territory and Political Economy in the Twenty-first Century.* Toronto: University of Toronto Press.

Eltringham, Nigel. 2006. "Debating the Rwandan Genocide." In *Violence, Political Culture and Development in Africa*, edited by Preben Kaarsholm, 66–91. Oxford: James Currey.

Embury-Dennis, Tom. 2018. "Italy's Deputy PM Salvini Called for 'Mass Cleansing, Street by Street, Quarter by Quarter,' Newly Resurfaced Footage Reveals." *Independent.* 21 June. Accessed 7 July 2018. https://www.independent.co.uk/news/world/europe/italy-matteo-salvini-video-immigration-mass-cleansing-roma-travellers-far-right-league-party-a8409506.html.

Emigrants Information Office. 1908. *Handbooks on British Colonies.* London: Darling and Son.

Engelhart, Katie. 2017. "Inside a Meeting of the Minds of Europe's Leading Nationalists." *Macleans.* 21 January. Accessed January 22. http://www.macleans.ca/news/world/inside-a-meeting-of-the-minds-of-europes-most-powerful-nationalists/.

Enloe, Cynthia. 1990. "Bananas, Bases, and Patriarchy." In *Women, Militarism, and War: Essays in History, Politics, and Social,* edited by Jean Bethke Elshtain and Sheila Tobias, 189–206. Lanham, MD: Rowman and Littlefield.

Espeland, Rune Hjalmar. 2011. "Autochthony, Rumor Dynamics, and Communal Violence in Western Uganda." *Social Analysis* 55 (3): 18–34.

European Commission, Migration, and Home Affairs. 2017. "Temporary Reintroduction of Border Control." Accessed 25 June 2017. https://ec.europa.eu/home-affairs/what-we-do/policies/borders-and-visas/schengen/reintroduction-border-control_en.

European Court of Human Rights. 1973. *East African Asians v. UK*—4403/70 ECHR 2. 14 December.

Executive Order 9066. 1942. "Authorizing the Secretary of War to Prescribe Military Areas." 19 February. General Records of the Unites States Government, Record Group 11, National Archives.

Executive Order 13769. 2017. "Protecting the Nation from Foreign Terrorist Entry into the United States." 82 FR 8977. 27 January.

Fabricant, Nicole, and Bret Gustafson. 2015. "Revolutionary Extractivism in Bolivia?" *Rebel Currents* (blog of the North American Congress on Latin America, NACLA). Accessed 31 May 2016. https://nacla.org/blog/2015/03/28/how-evo-morales%27s-third-term-will-challenge-bolivia%27s-social-movements.

Falola, Toyin, and Christian Jennings, eds. 2002. *Africanizing Knowledge: African Studies across the Disciplines.* Piscataway, NJ: Transaction Publishers.

Fanon, Frantz. 1965. *The Wretched of the Earth.* London: MacGibbon and Kee.

Fargues, Phillippe, and Nasra Shah. 2012. "Socio-economic Impacts of GCC Migration." Gulf Research Meeting (25–28 August), Gulf Research Centre, Cambridge University. Accessed 26 June 2014. http://grm.grc.net/index.php?pgid=Njk=&wid=Mjc.

Farthing, Linda, and Benjamin Kohl. 2014. *Evo's Bolivia: Continuity and Change.* Austin: University of Texas Press.

Federici, Silvia. 2004. *Caliban and the Witch: Women, the Body, and Primitive Accumulation.* Brooklyn: Autonomedia.

Feierstein, Danel. 2014. *Genocide as Social Practice: Reorganizing Society under the Nazis and Argentina's Military Juntas.* New Brunswick, NJ: Rutgers University Press.

Feldhousen-Giles, Kristy. 2008. *To Prove Who You Are: Freedmen Identities in Oklahoma.* PhD dissertation. UMI: 3336780. Norman: University of Oklahoma.

Ferrera, Maurizio. 2005. *The Boundaries of Welfare: European Integration and the New Spatial Politics of Social Protection.* Oxford: Oxford University Press.

Ferrie, Jared. 2011. "United Nations Urges South Sudan to Help Avert Possible Attack." *Bloomberg News.* 27 December. Accessed 4 July 2014. http://www.bloomberg.com/news/2011-12-27/united-nations-urges-south-sudan-to-help-avert-possible-attack.html.

Fieldhouse, David Kenneth. 1966. *The Colonial Empires from the Eighteenth Century*. New York: Weidenfeld and Nicolson.

Fiji. 1970. *Fiji Independence Order, Constitution of Fiji 1970*. Accessed 5 September 2016. http://www.constitutionnet.org/files/1970_constitution.pdf.

Fiji. 1971. An Act to Consolidate and Amend the Law relating to Immigration, Acts Nos. 24 of 1971, 40 of 1971.

Fiji. 2013. *Constitution of the Republic of Fiji*. Adoption: 2013-09-07 | FJI-2013-C-94342.

Fischel, Jack. R. 2010. *Historical Dictionary of the Holocaust*. 2nd ed. Lanham, MD: Scarecrow Press.

Fisher, Jonah. 2015. "Aung San Suu Kyi's Party Excludes Muslim Candidates." *BBC News*. 8 September. Accessed 10 September 2015. http://www.bbc.com/news/world-asia-34182489.

Fiskesjö, Magnus. 2006. "Rescuing the Empire: Chinese Nation-Building in the 20th Century." *European Journal of East Asian Studies* 5: 15–44.

Fitzgerald, David Scott, and David Cook-Martin. 2014. *Culling the Masses: The Democratic Origins of Racist Immigration Policy in the Americas*. Cambridge, MA: Harvard University Press.

Fixico, Donald Lee. 2012. *Bureau of Indian Affairs*. Santa Barbara, CA: Greenwood.

Fortify Rights. 2015. "Ethnic Minorities in Myanmar Denied Vote as Aung San Suu Kyi Claims Power." 27 November. Accessed 15 January 2016. http://www.fortifyrights.org/commentary-20151127.html.

Foster, Peter. 2016. "Who Is Norbert Hofer, and Should Europe Be Worried about Him Becoming President of Austria?" *The Telegraph*. 23 May. Accessed 14 July 2016. http://www.telegraph.co.uk/news/2016/05/22/who-is-norbert-hofer-and-should-europe-be-worried-about-him-beco/.

Foucault, Michel. 1977. "Nietzsche, Genealogy, History." In *Language, Countermemory, Practice*, edited by Donald F. Bouchard, translated by Donald F. Bouchard and Sherry Simmon, 139–164. Ithaca, NY: Cornell University Press.

Foucault, Michel. 1978. *The History of Sexuality*. Vol. 1. Translated by Robert Hurley. New York: Random House.

Foucault, Michel. 1991. "Questions of Method." In *The Foucault Effect: Studies in Governmentality*, edited by G. Burchell, C. Gordon, and P. Miller, 73–86. Chicago: University of Chicago Press.

Foucault, Michel. 2003. *Society Must Be Defended: Lectures at the Collège de France, 1975–1976*. Translated by D. Macey. New York: Picador.

France. 1946. *Constitution de la République Française*. 27 October. FRA-1946-C-30703.

Franklin, Cynthia, and Laura Lyons. 2004. "Remixing Hybridity: Globalization, Native Resistance, and Cultural Production in Hawai'i." *American Studies* 45 (3): 49–80.

Fredrickson, George. 1988. *The Arrogance of Race: Historical Perspectives on Slavery, Racism, and Social Inequality*. Middletown, CT: Wesleyan University Press.

Freeman, Gary P. 2015. *Immigrant Labor and Racial Conflict in Industrial Societies: The French and British Experience, 1945–1975*. Princeton, NJ: Princeton University Press.

Freeman, Victoria. 2006. "Attitudes toward 'Miscegenation' in Canada, the United States, New Zealand, and Australia, 1860–1914." *Native Studies Review* 16 (1): 41–69.

Freud, S. 1922. "Mourning and Melancholia." *Journal of Nervous and Mental Disease* 56 (5): 543–545.

Friedländer, Saul. 2009. *Nazi Germany and the Jews, 1933–1945*. New York: HarperCollins.

Friese, Kai. 2015. "India's Great Wall." *Borderlands*. 24 March. Accessed 10 September 2015. https://nplusonemag.com/online-only/online-only/borderlands/.

Fryer, Peter. 1984. *Staying Power: The History of Black People in Britain*. London: Pluto Press.

Fujikane, Candace. 2005. "Foregrounding Native Nationalisms: A Critique of Anti-nationalist Sentiment in Asian American Studies." In *Asian American Studies after Critical Mass*, edited by Kent A. Ona, 73–97. Oxford: Blackwell.

Fujikane, Candace, and Jonathan Y. Okamura, eds. 2000. "Whose Vision? Asian Settler Colonialism in Hawai'i." Special issue, *Amerasia Journal* 26 (2).

Fujikane, Candace, and Jonathan Y. Okamura, eds. 2008. *Asian Settler Colonialism: From Local Governance to the Habits of Everyday Life in Hawai'i*. Honolulu: University of Hawaii Press.

Fuller, Thomas. 2012. "Ethnic Hatred Tears Apart a Region of Myanmar." *New York Times*. 29 November. Accessed 1 December 2012. http://www.nytimes.com/2012/11/30/world/asia/muslims-face-expulsion-from-western-myanmar.html.

Gall, Lydia. 2016. "Hungary's Xenophobic Anti-Migrant Campaign" (dispatch from Human Rights Watch). 13 September. Accessed 15 September 2016. https://www.hrw.org/news/2016/09/13/hungarys-xenophobic-anti-migrant-campaign.

Gandhi, Mohandas K. 1909. *Home Rule*. Phoenix, Natal: International Printing Press.

Gardezi, Hassan N. 1995. *The Political Economy of International Labour Migration*. Montreal: Black Rose Books.

Gardner, Andrew. 2012. "Why Do They Keep Coming? Labor Migrants in the Persian Gulf States." In *Migrant Labor in the Persian Gulf*, edited by Mehran Kamrava and Zahra Babar, 41–58. London: Hurst and Company.

Gatrell, Peter. 2017. "The Nansen Passport: The Innovative Response to the Refugee Crisis That Followed the Russian Revolution." *The Conversation*. 6 November. Accessed 23 December 2017. https://theconversation.com/the-nansen-passport-the-innovative-response-to-the-refugee-crisis-that-followed-the-russian-revolution-85487.

GDP (Global Detention Project). n.d. "Detention Centres." Accessed 16 June 2019. https://www.globaldetentionproject.org/detention-centres/list-view.

Geddes, Duncan. 2017. "Europe Is Waking Up, Le Pen Tells Nationalist Allies." *The Times* (London). 21 January. Accessed 16 May 2019. https://www.thetimes.co.uk/article/europe-is-awakening-le-pen-tells-nationalist-allies-qj6jncdbc.

Geisler, Charles. 2014. "Disowned by the Ownership Society: How Native Americans Lost Their Land." *Rural Sociology* 79 (1): 56–78.

Geschiere, Peter. 2009. *The Perils of Belonging: Autochthony, Citizenship, and Exclusion in Africa and Europe*. Chicago: University of Chicago Press.

Geschiere, Peter. 2012. "The Political Economy of Autochthony: Labour Migration and Citizenship in Southwest Cameroon." In *Fractures and Reconnections:*

Civic Action and the Redefinition of African Political and Economic Spaces, Studies in Honor of Piet J. J. Konings, edited by Jon Abbink, 5:15–35. Münster, Germany: LIT Verlag.

Geschiere, Peter, and Francis Nyamnjoh. 2000. "Capitalism and Autochthony: The Seesaw of Mobility and Belonging." *Public Culture* 12 (2): 423–452.

Giaimo, Cara. 2017. "The Little-Known Passport That Protected 450,000 Refugees." Atlas Obscura, 7 February. Accessed 5 May 2019. https://www.atlasobscura.com /articles/nansen-passport-refugees.

Gilroy, Paul. 1987. *"There Ain't No Black in the Union Jack": The Cultural Politics of Race and Nation*. Chicago: University of Chicago Press.

Gilroy, Paul. 2005. *Postcolonial Melancholia*. New York: Columbia University Press.

Goebel, Michael. 2016. Review of *El oriente desplazado: Los intelectuales y los orígenes del tercermundismo en la Argentina*, by Martín Bergel. *Journal of Latin American Studies* 48 (4): 871–873.

Goldman, Emma. 1935. "There Is No Communism in Russia." The Anarchist Library. Accessed 1 June 2017. https://theanarchistlibrary.org/library/emma -goldman-there-is-no-communism-in-russia.

González-Stephan, Beatriz. 2003. "Showcases of Consumption: Historical Panoramas and Universal Expositions." In *Beyond Imagined Communities: Reading and Writing the Nation in Nineteenth-Century Latin America*, 225–238. Baltimore: John Hopkins University.

Goodwin, Mathew, and Milazzo, Caitlin. 2017. "Taking Back Control? Investigating the Role of Immigration in 2016 Vote for Brexit." *British Journal of Politics and International Relations* 19 (3): 450–464.

Gopal, Priyamvada. 2015. "A Thought for the Fettered." *Open*. 14 August. Accessed 16 August. http://www.openthemagazine.com/article/voices/a-thought-for-the -fettered.

Gottschalk, Peter. 2013. *Religion, Science, and Empire: Classifying Hinduism and Islam in British India*. New York: Oxford University Press.

Goulet, Denis. 1992. "'Development' . . . or Liberation?" In *The Political Economy of Development and Underdevelopment*, 5th ed., edited by Charles K. Wilber and Kenneth P. Jameson, 469–476. New York: McGraw-Hill.

Gourevitch, Philip. 1998. *We Wish to Inform You That Tomorrow We Will Be Killed with Our Families: Stories from Rwanda*. New York: Farrar, Straus, and Giroux.

Goveia, Elsa V. 1960. "The West Indian Slave Laws of the Eighteenth Century." *Revista de Ciencias Sociales* 4 (1): 75–105.

Grant, Madison. 1918. *The Passing of the Great Race or the Racial Basis of European History*. New York: Charles Scribner's Sons.

Greif, Mark. 2015. *The Age of the Crisis of Man: Thought and Fiction in America, 1933–1973*. Princeton, NJ: Princeton University Press.

Guerra, François-Xavier. 2003. "Forms of Communication, Political Spaces, and Cultural Identities in the Creation of Spanish American Nations." In *Beyond Imagined Communities: Reading and Writing the Nation in Nineteenth-Century Latin America*, 3–32. Baltimore: John Hopkins University.

Gulf Research Center. 2016. "GCC: Total Population and Percentage of Nationals and Non-nationals in GCC Countries." In *Gulf Labor Markets and Migration: National Statistics, 2010–2015*. Accessed 7 August 2016. http://gulfmigration.eu/total-population-and-percentage-of-nationals-and-non-nationals-in-gcc-countries-latest-national-statistics-2010–2015/.

Gutman, Yisrael, ed. 1990. *Encyclopedia of the Holocaust*. 4 vols. New York: Macmillan.

Gutman, Yisrael, and Abraham Margaliot, eds. 1999. *Documents on the Holocaust: Selected Sources on the Destruction of the Jews of Germany and Austria, Poland, and the Soviet Union*. Lincoln: University of Nebraska Press.

Hage, Ghassan. 2000. *White Nation: Fantasies of White Supremacy in a Multicultural Society*. New York: Routledge.

Hailbronner, Kay. 2006. "Nationality in Public International Law and European Law." In *Acquisition and Loss of Nationality: Policies and Trends in 15 European Countries*, edited by Rainer Bauböck, Eva Ersbøll, Kees Groenendijk, and Harald Waldrauch, 35–104. Amsterdam: Amsterdam University Press.

Halamish, Aviva. 1998. *The Exodus Affair: Holocaust Survivors and the Struggle for Palestine*. Syracuse, NY: Syracuse University Press.

Hall, Richard C. 2000. *Balkan Wars (1912–1913): Prelude to the First World War*. London: Routledge.

Hall, Stuart, Chas Critcher, Tony Jefferson, John Clarke, and Brian Roberts. (1978) 2013. *Policing the Crisis: Mugging, the State, and Law and Order*. 35th anniversary ed. New York: Palgrave Macmillan.

Hammar, Tomas. 1990. *Democracy and the Nation State: Aliens, Denizens, and Citizens in a World of International Migration*. Aldershot, U.K.: Gower Publishing Company.

Hampshire, James. 2005. *Citizenship and Belonging: Immigration and the Politics of Demographic Governance in Postwar Britain*. Hampshire, U.K.: Palgrave Macmillan.

Handlin, Oscar. 1951. *The Uprooted: The Epic Story of the Great Migrations That Made the American People*. Boston: Little Brown.

Hannah-Jones, Nikole. 2013. "Race Didn't Cost Abigail Fisher Her Spot at the University of Texas." *The Atlantic*. 18 March. Accessed 19 November 2015. http://www.theatlanticwire.com/national/2013/03/abigail-fisher-university-texas/63247/.

Hansen, Randall. 1999. "The Politics of Citizenship in 1940s Britain: The British Nationality Act." *Twentieth-Century British History* 10 (1): 67–95.

Hansen, Randall. 2000. *Citizenship and Immigration in Postwar Britain: The Institutional Origins of a Multicultural Nation*. Oxford: Oxford University Press.

Haque, Shahidul. 2012. "Migration Management Approaches and Initiatives in South Asia." In *Asian Migration Policy: South, Southeast, and East Asia*, edited by Mizanur Rahman and Ahsan Ullah, 155–172. New York: Nova Publishers.

Harris, Bronwyn. 2002. "Xenophobia: A New Pathology for a New South Africa?" In *Psychopathology and Social Prejudice*, edited by D. Hook and G. Eagle, 169–184. Cape Town: University of Cape Town Press.

Harris, Gardiner, and Hari Kumar. 2012. "Stiff Sentence for Former Gujarat Minister." *New York Times*. 31 August. Accessed 28 May 2017. https://india.blogs.nytimes.com/2012/08/31/stiff-sentence-for-former-gujarat-minister/.

Harth, Erica. 2003. *Last Witnesses: Reflections on the Wartime Internment of Japanese Americans*. Basingstoke, UK: Palgrave Macmillan.

Hartman, Saidiya. 2008. *Lose Your Mother: A Journey along the Atlantic Slave Route*. New York: Macmillan.

Harvey, David. 2003. *The New Imperialism*. Oxford: Oxford University Press.

Henning, Sabine, and Bela Hovy. 2011. "Data Sets on International Migration." *International Migration Review* 45 (4): 980–985.

Hepple, Bob A. 1968. "Commonwealth Immigrants Act 1968." *Modern Law Review* 31 (4): 424–428.

Hertog, Steffen. 2014. "Arab Gulf States: An Assessment of Nationalisation Policies." Gulf Labour Markets and Migration No. 1, Gulf Research Centre, p. 5. Accessed 27 June 2014. http://gulfmigration.eu/media/pubs/rp/GLMM%20Research%20new%2024-6-14.pdf.

Heryanto, Ariel. 1998. "Ethnic Identities and Erasure: Chinese Indonesians in Public Culture." In *Southeast Asian Identities: Culture and the Politics of Representation in Indonesia, Malaysia, Singapore, and Thailand*, edited by J. S. Kahn, 95–114. London: I. B. Tauris Publishers.

Hickel, Jason. 2017. "Aid in Reverse: How Poor Countries Develop Rich Countries." *The Guardian*. 14 January. Accessed 17 January 2017. https://www.theguardian.com/global-development-professionals-network/2017/jan/14/aid-in-reverse-how-poor-countries-develop-rich-countries.

Higham, John. (1955) 2002. *Strangers in the Land: Patterns of American Nativism, 1860–1925*. New Brunswick, NJ: Rutgers University Press.

Hill, Christopher. 1972. *The World Turned Upside Down: Radical Ideas during the English Revolution*. London: Temple Smith.

Hindess, Barry. 2000. "Citizenship in the International Management of Populations." *American Behavioral Scientist* 43 (9): 1486–1497.

Hindstrom, Hanna. 2012. "Burma's Monks Call for Muslim Community to Be Shunned." 25 July. Accessed 2 May 2013. http://www.independent.co.uk/news/world/asia/burmas-monks-call-for-muslim-community-to-be-shunned-7973317.html.

Hobsbawm, Eric J. 1990. *Nations and Nationalism since 1780: Programme, Myth, Reality*. Cambridge: Cambridge University Press.

Hobsbawm, Eric, and Terence Ranger, eds. 1983. *The Invention of Tradition*. Cambridge: Cambridge University Press.

Hochschild, Adam. 2006. *Bury the Chains: Prophets and Rebels in the Fight to Free an Empire's Slaves*. Boston: Houghton Mifflin Harcourt.

Holloway, John. 1994. "Global Capital and the National State." *Capital and Class* 52 (spring): 23–50.

Hollywood Reporter. 2015. "While We're in This Nation, We Should Be Speaking English." 3 September. Accessed 9 March 2016. http://www.hollywoodreporter.com/news/donald-trump-speak-english-spanish-820215.

Holmes, Colin. 1988. *John Bull's Island: Immigration and British Society, 1871–1971.* London: Macmillan.

Holocaust Encyclopedia. n.d. "German Jewish Refugees, 1933–1939." Accessed 6 June 2017. https://encyclopedia.ushmm.org/content/en/article/german-jewish-refugees-1933-1939.

Holt, Michael F. 1973. "The Politics of Impatience: The Origins of Know Nothingism." *Journal of American History* 60 (2): 309–331.

Holton, Gerald James. 2005. *Victory and Vexation in Science: Einstein, Bohr, Heisenberg, and Others.* Cambridge, MA: Harvard University Press.

Honig, Bonnie. 2009. *Democracy and the Foreigner.* Princeton, NJ: Princeton University Press.

Hoogvelt, Ankie. 1990. "Debt and Indebtedness: The Dynamics of Third World Poverty." *Review of African Political Economy* 47: 117–127.

Horowitz, Jason. 2003. "A Small Northern Party Has a Sizable Presence in Italian Politics." *New York Times.* 29 December. Accessed 14 February 2016. http://www.nytimes.com/2003/12/29/world/a-small-northern-party-has-a-sizable-presence-in-italian-politics.html.

Howard, John. 2007. "To Stabilise and Protect" (address to the Sydney Institute). 25 June.

Howley, Jacob D. 2006–2007. "Unlocking the Fortress: Protocol No. 11 and the Birth of Collective Expulsion Jurisprudence in the Council of Europe System." *Georgetown Immigration Law Journal* 21:117.

Hugo, Graeme. 2005. "The New International Migration in Asia: Challenges for Population Research." *Asian Population Studies* 1 (1): 93–120.

Human Rights Watch. 1999. "The Rwandan Patriotic Front." Accessed 19 June 2016. https://www.hrw.org/reports/1999/rwanda/Geno15-8-03.htm#P746_238387.

Human Rights Watch. 2000. "Burma/Bangladesh: Burmese Refugees in Bangladesh: Still No Durable Solution." 12 (3). Accessed 24 January 2016. https://www.hrw.org/reports/2000/burma/burmoo5-02.htm.

Human Rights Watch. 2001. "The New Racism: The Political Manipulation of Ethnicity in Côte d'Ivoire." 28 August. Accessed 18 March 2013. http://www.hrw.org/reports/2001/08/28/new-racism-0.

Human Rights Watch. 2012. "'The Government Could Have Stopped This': Sectarian Violence and Ensuing Abuses in Burma's Arakan State." Accessed 1 December 2012. https://www.hrw.org/report/2012/07/31/government-could-have-stopped/sectarian-violence-and-ensuing-abuses-burmas-arakan.

Human Rights Watch. 2015. "Detained, Beaten, Deported: Saudi Abuses against Migrants during Mass Expulsions." 10 May. Accessed 6 November 2015. https://www.hrw.org/report/2015/05/10/detained-beaten-deported/saudi-abuses-against-migrants-during-mass-expulsions.

Human Rights Watch. 2017. "India: 'Cow Protection' Spurs Vigilante Violence." 27 April. Accessed 28 May 2017. https://www.hrw.org/news/2017/04/27/india-cow-protection-spurs-vigilante-violence.

Hussein, Hussein Abu, and Fiona McKay. 2003. *Access Denied: Palestinian Land Rights in Israel*. London: Zed Books.

Hynes, William, David S. Jacks, and Kevin H. O'Rourke. 2012. "Commodity Market Disintegration in the Interwar Period." *European Review of Economic History* 16 (2): 119–143.

Hyslop, Jonathan. 1999. "The Imperial Working Class Makes Itself 'White': White Labourism in Britain, Australia, and South Africa before the First World War." *Journal of Historical Sociology* 12 (4): 398–421.

Iacovetta, Franca, and Mariana Valverde. 1992. *Gender Conflicts: New Essays in Women's History*. Toronto: University of Toronto Press.

Ibrahim, Azeem. 2018. "The Genocide in Burma Continues, yet the International Community Is Still Sitting on Its Hands." *Washington Post*. 7 February.

ILO (International Labour Organization). 1997. *Employment Report 1996/97: National Policies in a Global Context*. Geneva: ILO.

India. 1950. Immigrants (Expulsion from Assam) Act (No. 10), Adoption: 1950–03–01 | IND-1950-L-73553.

India. 1962. Foreigners Law (Application and Amendment) Act (No. 42), Adoption: 1962–11–24 | IND-1962-L-73550.

Indonesia. 1956. Circular Letter of the Prime Minister No. 11/R.I./1956 of 1956 on Political Refugees. 7 September. Accessed 17 August 2016. http://www.refworld.org/cgi-bin/texis/vtx/rwmain?page=search&docid=3ae6b4e918&skip=0&query=foreigner&coi=IDN.

Indonesia. 1958. Circulation Letter from the Minister of Labour (No. 2258 of 1958) on the Execution of Act (No. 3 of 1958) on the Employment of Foreigners, Adoption: 1958-03-19 | IDN-1958-M-39640.

International State Crime Initiative, Queen Mary University of London. 2015. "Countdown to Annihilation: Genocide in Myanmar." Accessed 3 November 2015. http://statecrime.org/state-crime-research/isci-report-countdown-to-annihilation-genocide-in-myanmar/.

International Work Group for Indigenous Affairs. n.d. "Indigenous Peoples in Bolivia." Accessed 21 June 2016. http://www.iwgia.org/regions/latin-america/bolivia.

IOM (International Organization for Migration). 2003. *World Migration Report 2003: Managing Migration—Challenges and Responses for People on the Move*. Geneva: IOM.

IOM (International Organization for Migration). 2013. "Asia and the Pacific." Accessed 17 June 2014. https://www.iom.int/cms/en/sites/iom/home/where-we-work/asia-and-the-pacific.html.

Iriye, Akira, and Pierre Saunier, eds. 2016. *The Palgrave Dictionary of Transnational History: From the Mid-19th Century to the Present Day*. New York: Springer.

Irwin, Graham W. 1977. *Africans Abroad: A Documentary History of the Black Diaspora in Asia, Latin America, and the Caribbean during the Age of Slavery*. New York: Columbia University Press.

Israel. 1950. The Law of Return. Law No. 5710-1950 (5 July). Accessed 12 January 2013. https://www.refworld.org/docid/3ae6b4ea1b.html.

Israel. 1952. Nationality Law. Law No. 5712-1952. Accessed 12 January 2013.
http://www.refworld.org/cgi-bin/texis/vtx/rwmain?page=search&docid
=3ae6b4ec20&skip=0&query=nationality%20law,%201952&coi=ISR.

Israel Ministry of Foreign Affairs. 2013. "Declaration of Establishment of State
of Israel 1948" (14 May). Accessed 10 January 2013. http://www.mfa.gov.il/mfa
/foreignpolicy/peace/guide/pages/declaration%20of%20establishment%20
of%20state%20of%20israel.aspx.

Iyengar, Rishi. 2015. "Burma's Million-Strong Rohingya Population Faces 'Final
Stages of Genocide,' Says Report." *Time*. 29 October. Accessed 9 December 2015.
https://time.com/4089276/burma-rohingya-genocide-report-documentary/.

Jackson, Scott. 1979. "Prologue to the Marshall Plan: The Origins of the American
Commitment for a European Recovery Program." *Journal of American History*
65 (4): 1043–1068.

Jackson, Stephen W. 2003. "War Making: Uncertainty, Improvisation and Involu-
tion in the Kivu Provinces, DR Congo, 1997–2002." PhD dissertation, Princeton
University.

Jaeger, Gilbert. 2001. "On the History of the International Protection of Refugees."
International Review of the Red Cross 83 (843): 727–737.

James, Cyril Lionel Robert. 1963. *The Black Jacobins: Toussaint L'Ouverture and the San
Domingo Revolution*. 2nd ed. New York: Vintage Books.

Jamieson, Ruth. 1999. "Genocide and the Social Production of Immorality." *Theoretical Criminology* 3 (2): 131–146.

Jenkins, Aric. 2017. "Read the Hawaii Judge's Decision Blocking Donald Trump's
New Travel Ban Nationwide." *Time*. 15 March. Accessed 24 May 2017. http://time
.com/4703188/donald-trump-travel-ban-blocked-read-court-decision/.

Jessop, Bob. 1993. "Towards a Schumpeterian Workfare State? Preliminary
Remarks on Post-Fordist Political Economy." *Studies in Political Economy*
40 (spring): 7–39.

Johnson, Chalmers. 1999. "The Developmental State: Odyssey of a Concept." In
The Developmental State, edited by Meredith Woo-Cumings, 32–60. Ithaca, NY:
Cornell University Press.

Jolly, Richard. 2004. *UN Contributions to Development Thinking and Practice*. Vol. 5.
Bloomington: Indiana University Press.

Jones, Reece. 2012. *Border Walls: Security and the War on Terror in the United States,
India, and Israel*. London: Zed Books.

Jureidini, Ray. 2014. "Arab Gulf States: Recruitment of Asian Workers." Gulf Labour
Markets and Migration No. 3, Gulf Research Centre. Accessed 27 June 2014.
http://gulfmigration.eu/media/pubs/exno/GLMM_EN_2014_03.pdf.

Kabanda, Marcel. 2007. "*Kangura*: The Triumph of Propaganda Refined." In *The Media
and the Rwandan Genocide*, edited by A. Thompson, 62–72. London: Pluto Press.

Kagwanja, Peter, and Roger Southall. 2013. *Kenya's Uncertain Democracy: The Electoral
Crisis of 2008*. London: Routledge.

Kandiyoti, Deniz. 1991. "Identity and Its Discontents: Women and the Nation."
Millennium 20 (3): 429–443.

Kapiszewski, Andrzej. 2001. *Nationals and Expatriates: Population and Labor Dilemmas of the GCC States*. Reading, U.K.: Ithaca Press.

Kaplan, Marion A. 2008. *Dominican Haven: The Jewish Refugee Settlement in Sosúa, 1940–1945*. New York: Museum of Jewish Heritage.

Kaplan, Sarah. 2015. "The Serene-Looking Buddhist Monk Accused of Inciting Burma's Sectarian Violence." *Washington Post*. 27 May. Accessed 3 June 2015. https://www.washingtonpost.com/news/morning-mix/wp/2015/05/27/the-burmese-bin-laden-fueling-the-rohingya-migrant-crisis-in-southeast-asia/?utm_term=.500deea3d362.

Karlsson, Bengt G. 2003. "Anthropology and the 'Indigenous Slot': Claims to and Debates about Indigenous Peoples' Status in India." *Critique of Anthropology* 23 (4): 403–423.

Kauanui, J. Kēhaulani. 1999. "'For Get' Hawaiian Entitlement: Configurations of Land, 'Blood,' and Americanization in the Hawaiian Homes Commission Act of 1921." *Social Text* 59 (summer): 123–144.

Kaufman, Will, and Heidi Slettedahl Macpherson, eds. 2005. *Britain and the Americas: Culture, Politics, and History: A Multidisciplinary Encyclopedia*. Santa Barbara, CA: ABC-Clio.

Kaup, Brent Z. 2010. "A Neoliberal Nationalization? The Constraints on Natural-Gas-Led Development in Bolivia." *Latin American Perspectives* 37 (3): 123–138.

Kaur, Amarjit. 2004. "Crossing Frontiers: Race, Migration, and Borders in Southeast Asia." *International Journal on Multicultural Societies* 6 (2): 202–223.

Kazamias, Andreas M. 2009. "Modernity, State-Formation, Nation Building, and Education in Greece." In *International Handbook of Comparative Education*, vol. 22, edited by Robert Cowen and Andreas M. Kazamias, 239–256. New York: Springer Science and Business Media.

Kazimi, Ali. 2004. *Continuous Journey*. Toronto: Peripheral Visions Film and Video Inc.

Kazimi, Ali. 2012. *Undesirables: White Canada and the Komagata Maru: An Illustrated History*. Vancouver: Douglas and McIntyre.

Keil, Charles. 1970. "The Price of Nigerian Victory." *Africa Today* 17 (1): 1–3.

Kellogg, Alex. 2011. "Cherokee Nation Faces Scrunity for Expelling Blacks." National Public Radio. Accessed 3 June 2012. https://www.npr.org/2011/09/19/140594124/u-s-government-opposes-cherokee-nations-decision.

Kennan, George. (1946) 1993. "The Long Telegram." In *Origins of the Cold War: The Novikov, Kennan, and Roberts "Long Telegrams" of 1946: With Three New Commentaries*, edited by Kenneth Martin Jensen, 17–32. Washington, DC: U.S. Institute of Peace Press.

Kennedy, John F. 1963. "Inaugural Address: January 20, 1961." *Journal of Public Law* 12: 235.

Kennedy, John F. 1964. *A Nation of Immigrants*. New York: Harper and Row.

Kesic, Vesna. 2002. "Muslim Women, Croatian Women, Serbian Women, Albanian Women . . ." In *Balkan as Metaphor: Between Globalization and Fragmentation*, 311–322. Cambridge, MA: MIT Press.

Keyfitz, Nathan. 1990. "Alfred Sauvy." *Population and Development Review* 16 (4): 727–733.

Keynes, John Maynard. 1971. *The Collected Writings of John Maynard Keynes*. London: Macmillan.

Khalidi, Walid, and Sharif S. Elmusa. 1992. *All That Remains: The Palestinian Villages Occupied and Depopulated by Israel in 1948*. Washington, DC: Institute for Palestine Studies.

Khan, Mohammad Asghar, ed. 1985. *Islam, Politics and the State: The Pakistan Experience*. London: Zed Books.

Kindersley, Nicki. 2015. "Identifying South Sudanese: Registration for the January 2011 Referendum and Defining a New Nationality." In *Emerging Orders in the Sudans*, edited by Sandra Calkins, Enrico Ille, and Richard Rottenburg, 79–93. Bamenda, Cameroon: Langaa Research and Publishing CIG.

Kinninmont, Jane. 2013. "Citizenship in the Gulf." In *The Gulf States and the Arab Uprisings*, edited by A. Echague, 47–58. Madrid: FRIDE Books.

Klaaren, Jonathan, and Jaya Ramji. 2001. "Inside Illegality: Migration Policing in South Africa after Apartheid." *Africa Today* 48 (3): 35–47.

Kleinfeld, Philip. 2016. "Immigration Raids in London—FOI Data." 2 July. Accessed 12 July 2016. https://medium.com/@PKleinfeld/immigration-raids-in-london-soar-by-80-edfood1e2a5d#.yqxviwm6p,

Knight, Alan. 1990. "Racism, Revolution, and Indigenismo: Mexico, 1910–1940." In *The Idea of Race in Latin America, 1870–1940*, edited by R. Graham, 71–113. Austin: University of Texas Press.

Knowles, Valerie. 1997. *Strangers at Our Gates: Canadian Immigration and Immigration Policy, 1540–1997*. Toronto: Dundurn Press.

Koebner, Richard. 1953. "'The Imperial Crown of This Realm': Henry VIII, Constantine the Great, and Polydore Vergil." *Historical Research* 26 (73): 29–52.

Kohn, Hans, 1961. *The Idea of Nationalism: A Study in Its Origins and Background*. Piscataway, NJ: Transaction Publishers.

Konings, Piet, and Francis Beng Nyamnjoh. 2003. *Negotiating an Anglophone Identity: A Study of the Politics of Recognition and Representation in Cameroon*. Vol. 1. Leiden: Brill.

Krasner, Stephen D. 1995. "Compromising Westphalia." *International Security* 20 (3): 115–151.

Krassowski, Andrzej. (1974) 2011. *Development and the Debt Trap: Economic Planning and External Borrowing in Ghana*. London: Routledge.

Kristeva, Julia. 1993. *Nations without Nationalism*. Translated by L. S. Roudiez. New York: Columbia University Press.

Kristof, Nicholas. 2016. "Myanmar's Peace Prize Winner and Crimes against Humanity." 9 January. Accessed 10 January 2016. http://www.nytimes.com/2016/01/10/opinion/sunday/myanmars-peace-prize-winner-and-crimes-against-humanity.html.

Kritz, Mary M., and Charles B. Keely. 1981. Introduction to *Global Trends in Migration: Theory and Research on International Population Movements*, edited by Mary M.

Kritz, Charles B. Keely, and Silvano M. Tomasi, xiii–xxxi. Staten Island, NY: Center for Migration Studies.

Kritz, Mary M., Charles B. Keely, and Silvano M. Tomasi, eds. 1981. *Global Trends in Migration: Theory and Research on International Population Movements*. Staten Island, NY: Center for Migration Studies.

Kukutai, Tahu. 2011. "Building Ethnic Boundaries in New Zealand: Representations of Maori Identity in the Census." In *Indigenous Peoples and Demography: The Complex Relation between Identity and Statistics*, edited by Per Axelsson and Peter Sköld, 33–54. New York: Berghahn Books.

Kukutai, Tahu. 2013. "The Structure of Urban Maori Identities." In *Indigenous in the City: Contemporary Identities and Cultural Innovation*, edited by Evelyn Joy Peters and Chris Andersen, 311–333. Vancouver: UBC Press.

Kulski, Władysław Wszebór. 1966. *De Gaulle and the World: The Foreign Policy of the Fifth French Republic*. Syracuse, NY: Syracuse University Press, 1966.

Lacina, Bethany, and Nils Petter Gleditsch. 2005. "Monitoring Trends in Global Combat: A New Dataset of Battle Deaths." *European Journal of Population/Revue Européenne de Démographie* 21 (2): 145–166.

Lal, Victor. 1990. *Fiji: Coups in Paradise: Race, Politics, and Military Intervention*. London: Zed Books.

Lambert, Wilfred G. 1969. *Atra-Hasis: The Babylonian Story of the Flood*. Oxford: Clarendon Press.

Landau, Ronnie S. (1992) 2016. *The Nazi Holocaust: Its History and Meaning*. London: I. B. Tauris.

Landsman, Gail. 1988. *Sovereignty and Symbol: Indian-White Conflict at Ganienkeh*. Albuquerque: University of New Mexico Press.

LaRoque, Emma. 1990. "Preface or Here Are Our Voices—Who Will Hear?" In *Writing the Circle: Native Women of Western Canada*, edited by Jeanne Perrault and Sylvia Vance, xv–xxx. Edmonton, AB: Newest Publishers.

Laskier, Michael M. 1995. "Egyptian Jewry under the Nasser Regime, 1956–70." Historical Society of Jews from Egypt. Accessed 9 July 2014. http://www.hsje.org/egypt/egypt%20today/egyptian_jewry_under_the_nasser_.htm#.U7yESKiOAX4.

Lawrence, Bonita, and Enakshi Dua. 2005. "Decolonizing Antiracism." *Social Justice* 32 (4): 120–143.

Layton-Henry, Zig. 2003. "Citizenship and Nationality in Britain." In *Challenging Racism in Britain and Germany*, edited by Zig Layton-Henry and Czarina Wilpert, 60–77. New York: Palgrave Macmillan.

Lazarus, Neil. 2002. "The Politics of Postcolonial Modernism." *European Legacy* 7 (6): 771–782.

League of Nations. 1936. "Provisional Arrangement concerning the Status of Refugees Coming from Germany." League of Nations Treaty Series, vol. 171, no. 3952. 4 July. Accessed 13 June 2015. https://www.refworld.org/docid/3dd8d0ae4.html.

League of Nations. 1938. "Convention Concerning the Status of Refugees Coming From Germany." League of Nations Treaty Series, vol. 192, no. 4461. 10 February. Accessed 13 June 2015. https://www.refworld.org/docid/3dd8d12a4.html.

LeBor, Adam. 2006. *"Complicity with Evil": The United Nations in the Age of Modern Genocide*. New Haven, CT: Yale University Press.

Lee, Chulwoo. 2003. "'Us' and 'Them' in Korean Law: The Creation, Accommodation, and Exclusion of Outsiders in South Korea." In *East Asian Law: Universal Norms and Local Cultures*, edited by Arther Rosett, Lucie Cheng, and Margaret Y. K. Woo, 106–136. New York: RoutledgeCurzon.

Lemkin, Raphael. 1946. "Genocide." *American Scholar* 15 (2): 227–230.

Lemkin, Rob. 2010. *Enemies of the People*. http://enemiesofthepeoplemovie.com/.

Lentz, Carola, and Claude Nurukyor Somda. 2003. *History of Settlement and Interethnic Relations in Burkina Faso*. Paris: KARTHALA Editions.

Lewa, Chris. 2009. "North Arakan: An Open Prison for the Rihingya in Burma." *Forced Migration Review* 32 (April). Accessed 2 September 2012. http://www.fmreview.org/FMRpdfs/FMR32/11–13.pdf.

Lewis, Aidan. 2008. "Italy's Northern League Resurgent." *BBC News*. 17 April. Accessed 27 February 2012. http://news.bbc.co.uk/2/hi/europe/7350691.stm.

Liberia. 1986. *Constitution of the Republic of Liberia*. 6 January. Accessed 31 July 2014. http://www.refworld.org/cgi-bin/texis/vtx/rwmain?page=search&docid=3ae6b6030&skip=0&query=constitution&coi=LBR.

Linden, Ian. 1977. *Church and Revolution in Rwanda*. Manchester: Manchester University Press.

Linebaugh, Peter, and Marcus Rediker. 2000. *The Many-Headed Hydra: Sailors, Slaves, Commoners, and the Hidden History of the Revolutionary Atlantic*. Boston: Beacon Press.

Lipietz, Alain. 1987. *Mirages and Miracles*. London: Verso.

Lipsitz, George. 1995. "The Possessive Investment in Whiteness: Racialized Social Democracy and the "White" Problem in American Studies." *American Quarterly* 47 (3): 369–387.

Liptak, Adam. 2008. "U.S. Prison Population Dwarfs That of Other Nations." *New York Times*. 23 April. Accessed 10 January 2012. http://www.nytimes.com/2008/04/23/world/americas/23iht-23prison.12253738.html.

Liptak, Adam. 2016. "Donald Trump Could Threaten U.S. Rule of Law, Scholars Say." *New York Times*. 3 June. Accessed 17 March 2018. https://www.nytimes.com/2016/06/04/us/politics/donald-trump-constitution-power.html.

Longva, Ann Nga. 2000. "Citizenship in the Gulf States." In *Citizenship and the State in the Middle East: Approaches and Applications*, edited by Nils A. Butenschon, Uri Davis, and Manue lHassassian, 179–197. Syracuse, NY: Syracuse University Press.

Lopez, Ian Haney. 1997. *White by Law: The Legal Construction of Race*. New York: NYU Press.

Lowe, Lisa. 2006. "The Intimacies of Four Continents." In *Haunted by Empire: Geographies of Intimacy in North American History*, edited by Ann Laura Stoler, 191–212. Durham, NC: Duke University Press.

Luard, Evan. 1983. *The Management of the World Economy*. London: Macmillan.

Luibhéid, Eithne. 2002. *Entry Denied: Controlling Sexuality at the Border*. Minneapolis: University of Minnesota Press.

Macartney, Suzanne, Alemayehu Bishaw, and Kayla Fontenot. 2013. "Poverty Rates for Selected Detailed Race and Hispanic Groups by State and Place: 2007–2011." *American Community Survey Briefs*, U.S. Census Bureau. February. Accessed 28 January 2017. http://www.census.gov/prod/2013pubs/acsbr11–17.pdf.

Mackey, Eva. 1999. *The House of Difference: Cultural Politics and National Identity in Canada*. New York: Routledge.

Macklem, Patrick. 1993. "Distributing Sovereignty: Indian Nations and the Equality of Peoples." *Stanford Law Review* 45: 1311–1367.

Madden, Albert Frederick. 1979. "'Not for Export': The Westminster Model of Government and British Colonial Practice." *Journal of Imperial and Commonwealth History* 8 (1): 10–29.

Maddison, Angus. 2001. *The World Economy: A Millennial Perspective*. Paris: Organisation for Economic Co-operation and Development.

Maddison, Angus. 2010. "Statistics on World Population, GDP, and Per Capita GDP, 1–2008 AD." *Historical Statistics* 3: 1–36.

Magder, Jason. 2010. "Kahnawake Community Debates Proposal to Expel 'Non-natives.'" *Montreal Gazette*. 26 May. Accessed 25 May 2017. http://www .pressreader.com/canada/montreal-gazette/20100526/281633891467806.

Malkki, Liisa. 1992. "National Geographic: The Rooting of Peoples and the Territorialization of National Identity among Scholars and Refugees." *Cultural Anthropology* 7 (1): 24–44.

Malkki, Liisa H. 1995. "Refugees and Exile: From 'Refugee Studies' to the National Order of Things." *Annual Review of Anthropology* 24 (1): 495–523.

Mamdani, Mahmood. 2001. *When Victims Become Killers: Colonialism, Nativism, and the Genocide in Rwanda*. Princeton, NJ: Princeton University Press.

Mamdani, Mahmood. 2009. *Saviors and Survivors: Darfur, Politics, and the War on Terror*. New York: Pantheon Books.

Mamdani, Mahmood. 2012. *Define and Rule: Native as Political Identity*. W. E. B. Du Bois Lectures. Cambridge, MA: Harvard University Press.

Manby, Bronwen. 2010. *Citizenship Law in Africa: A Comparative Study*. New York: Open Society Institute.

Manby, Bronwen. 2012. "The Right to a Nationality and the Secession of South Sudan: A Commentary on the Impact of the New Laws." Open Society Initiative for Eastern Africa. Accessed 2 July 2014. http://www.afrimap.org/english/images /report/OSIEA-AfriMAP-Nationality-Sudans-full-EN.pdf.

Manby, Bronwen. 2014. "Trends in Citizenship Law and Politics in Africa since the Colonial Era." In *Routledge Handbook of Global Citizenship Studies*, edited by Engin F. Isin and Peter Nyers, 172–185. London: Routledge.

Manela, Erez. 2007. *The Wilsonian Moment: Self-Determination and the International Origins of Anticolonial Nationalism*. New York: Oxford University Press.

Mann, Gregory. 2009. "What Was the Indigénat? The 'Empire of Law' in French West Africa." *Journal of African History* 50 (3): 331–353.

Maracle, Lee. 1988. *I Am Woman*. Vancouver, BC: Write On Press.

Marchak, Patricia. 1991. *The Integrated Circus: The New Right and the Restructuring of Global Markets*. Montreal: McGill-Queen's University Press.

Marino, Alessandra. 2012. "Writing as Resistance in Postcolonial India." *Open Democracy*. Accessed 1 May 2014. https://www.opendemocracy.net/en/openindia/writing-as-resistance-in-postcolonial-india/.

Marrus, Michael. 1985. *The Unwanted: European Refugees in the Twentieth Century*. New York: Oxford University Press.

Marshall, Andrew R. C. 2013. "Special Report: Myanmar Gives Official Blessing to Anti-Muslim Monks." Reuters. 27 June. Accessed 15 July 2013. http://www.reuters.com/article/us-myanmar-969-specialreport-idUSBRE95Q04720130627.

Marshall-Fratani, Ruth. 2007. "The War of 'Who Is Who': Autochthony, Nationalism, and Citizenship in the Ivorian Crisis." In *Making Nations, Creating Strangers: States and Citizenship in Africa*, edited by S. Dorman, D. Hammett, and P. Nugent, 9–44. Leiden: Brill.

Martin, Michelle. 2014. "German Party Accused of Neo-Nazi Traits Set for EU Parliament." 21 May. Accessed 14 February 2016. http://uk.reuters.com/article/uk-eu-election-germany-neonazis-idUKKBN0E112M20140521.

Martínez, Miguel Alfonso. 1997. "Study on Treaties, Agreements, and Other Constructive Arrangements between States and Indigenous Populations." July. *Final Report to the UN for the "Working Group on Indigenous Peoples."* Geneva: United Nations.

Marx, Karl. 1963. *The Eighteenth Brumaire of Louis Bonaparte*. New York: International Publishers.

Masalha, Nur. 1993. *Is Israel the State of All Its Citizens and "Absentees"?* Haifa, Israel: Galilee Center for Social Research.

Massey, Douglas S., and Kerstin Gentsch. 2014. "Undocumented Migration to the United States and the Wages of Mexican Immigrants." *International Migration Review* 48 (2): 482–499.

Matthews, Roger. 2016. *Doing Time: An Introduction to the Sociology of Imprisonment*. New York: Springer.

Mawani, Renisa. 2010. *Colonial Proximities: Crossracial Encounters and Juridical Truths in British Columbia, 1871–1921*. Vancouver: UBC Press.

Mawani, Renisa. 2015. "Law and Migration across the Pacific: Narrating the *Komagata Maru* outside and beyond the Nation." In *Within and Without the Nation: Canadian History as Transnational History*, edited by Adele Perry, Karen Dubinsky, and Henry Yu, 253–275. Toronto: University of Toronto Press.

Mawani, Renisa. 2018. *Across Oceans of Law: The Komagata Maru and Jurisdiction in the Time of Empire*. Durham, NC: Duke University Press.

May, Katja. 1996. *African Americans and Native Americans in the Creek and Cherokee Nations, 1830s to 1920s: Collision and Collusion*. New York: Garland.

Mbembe, Achille. 2002. "African Modes of Self-Writing." Translated by Steven Rendall. *Public Culture* 14 (1): 239–273.

McAdam, Jane. 2013. "Rethinking the Origins of 'Persecution' in Refugee Law." *International Journal of Refugee Law* 25 (4): 667–692.

McCorquodale, John. 1986. "The Legal Classification of Race in Australia." *Aboriginal History* 10 (1): 7–24.

McDonald, David A., and Jonathan Crush, eds. 2001. *Destinations Unknown: Perspectives on the Brain Drain in Southern Africa*. Pretoria: Africa Institute and Southern African Migrations Project.

McElwee, Sean. 2014. "On Income Inequality: An Interview with Branko Milanovic." Accessed 30 January 2017. http://www.demos.org/blog/11/14/14/income -inequality-interview-branko-milanovic.

McHugh, Paul G. 1991. *The Māori Magna Carta: New Zealand Law and the Treaty of Waitangi*. Toronto: Oxford University Press.

McKeown, Adam. 2004. "Global Migration, 1846–1940." *Journal of World History* 15 (2): 155–189.

McKeown, Adam. 2008. *Melancholy Order: Asian Migration and the Globalization of Borders*. New York: Columbia University Press.

Melvern, Linda. 2000. *A People Betrayed: The Role of the West in Rwanda's Genocide*. London: Zed Books.

Melvern, Linda. 2006. *Conspiracy to Murder: The Rwandan Genocide*. London: Verso.

Menom, Dilip. 2017. "Rethinking the Movement of People." *Independent Online* (IOL). 31 October. Accessed 5 November 2017. https://www.iol.co.za/mercury/news /rethinking-the-movement-of-people-11788118.

Milanovic, Branko. 2002. "True World Income Distribution, 1988 and 1993: First Calculation Based on Household Surveys Alone." *Economic Journal* 112/476 (January): 51–92.

Milanovic, Branko. 2010. *The Haves and the Have-Nots: A Brief and Idiosyncratic History of Global Inequality*. New York: Basic Books.

Milanovic, Branko. 2011. "Global Inequality: From Class to Location, From Proletarians to Migrants." Policy Research Working Paper 5820, World Bank Development Research Group, Poverty and Inequality Team.

Milanovic, Branko, ed. 2012. *Globalization and Inequality*. Cheltenham, U.K.: Edward Elgar.

Milanovic, Branko. 2015. "Global Inequality of Opportunity: How Much of Our Income Is Determined by Where We Live?" *Review of Economics and Statistic* 97 (2): 452–460.

Miles, Robert. 1993. *Racism after "Race Relations."* London: Routledge.

Miles, Robert, and John Solomos. 1987. "Migration and the State in Britain: A Historical Overview." In *"Race" in Britain: Continuity and Change*, 2nd ed., edited by C. Husbands, 75–110. London: Hutchinson.

Miles, Tiya. 2005. *Ties That Bind: The Story of an Afro-Cherokee Family in Slavery and Freedom*. Berkeley: University of California Press.

Mills, Charles W. 1997. *The Racial Contract*. Ithaca, NY: Cornell University Press.

Milne, Richard. 2015. "Sweden Considers Closing the Bridge to Denmark." 3 December. Accessed 9 February 2016. http://www.ft.com/intl/cms/s/0/b2a11dd2-99bd -11e5-bdda-9f13f99fa654.html#axzz3zja6MHP9.

Mingay, Gordon E. 2014. *Parliamentary Enclosure in England: An Introduction to Its Causes, Incidence, and Impact, 1750–1850*. London: Routledge.

Mishel, Lawrence, and Alyssa Davis. 2015. "Top CEOs Make 300 Times More Than Typical Workers." Economic Policy Institute. 21 June. Accessed 1 February 2017. http://www.epi.org/publication/top-ceos-make-300-times-more-than-workers -pay-growth-surpasses-market-gains-and-the-rest-of-the-0-1-percent/.

Mohapatra, Atanu Kumar. 2014. *Vivekananda and Contemporary Education in India: Recent Perspectives*. Delhi: Surendra Publications.

Mohawk Council of Kahnawà:ke, Membership Department. 2012. "Kahnawà:ke Membership Law Project: Communications Package for Community Infor- mation." Accessed 6 June 2016. http://www.kahnawakemakingdecisions.com /promo/KMLBinder1.pdf.

Mohawk Council of Kahnawà:ke, Membership Department. 2014. "History of the Kahnawà:ke Membership Law." September. Accessed 6 June 2016. http://www .kahnawake.com/org/docs/MembershipNewsletterSept4-2014.pdf.

Molavi, Shourideh C. 2009. "Stateless Citizenship and the Palestinian-Arabs in Israel." *Refuge: Canada's Journal on Refugees* 26 (2): 19–28.

Mongia, Radhika Viyas. 1999. "Race, Nationality, Mobility: A History of the Pass- port." *Public Culture* 11 (3): 527–556.

Mongia, Radhika. 2007. "Historicizing State Sovereignty: Inequality and the Form of Equivalence." *Comparative Studies in Society and History* 49 (2): 384–411.

Mongia, Radhika. 2018. *Indian Migration and Empire: A Colonial Genealogy of the Mod- ern State*. Durham, NC: Duke University Press.

Montagu, Ashley. 1972. *Statement on Race: An Annotated Elaboration and Exposition of the Four Statements on Race Issued by UNESCO*. Oxford: Oxford University Press.

Moran, Rachel F. 2003. "Love with a Proper Stranger: What Anti-miscegenation Laws Can Tell Us about the Meaning of Race, Sex, and Marriage." *Hofstra Law Review* 32: 1663.

Moreton-Robinson, Aileen, ed. 2007. *Sovereign Subjects: Indigenous Sovereignty Matters*. Sydney: Allen and Unwin.

Morgensen, Scott Lauria. 2011a. "The Biopolitics of Settler Colonialism: Right Here, Right Now." *Settler Colonial Studies* 1 (1): 52–76.

Morgensen, Scott Lauria. 2011b. *Spaces between Us: Queer Settler Colonialism and Indig- enous Decolonization*. Minneapolis: University of Minnesota Press.

Morris, Benny. 1987. *The Birth of the Palestinian Refugee Problem, 1947–1949*. Vol. 15. New York: Cambridge University Press.

Morrison, Toni. 1993. "Nobel Lecture." Accessed 15 July 2015. http://www.nobelprize .org/nobel_prizes/literature/laureates/1993/morrison-lecture.html.

Motlagh, Jason. 2014. "These Aren't Refugee Camps—They're Concentration Camps, and People Are Dying in Them." *Time*. 17 June. Accessed 15 January 2016. http://time.com/2888864/rohingya-myanmar-burma-camps-sittwe/.

Motomura, Hiroshi. 2006. "Contract and Classical Immigration Law." In *Americans in Waiting: The Lost Story of Immigration and Citizenship in the United States*, 15–37. Oxford: Oxford University Press.

Muñoz, José Esteban. 2009. *Cruising Utopia: The Then and There of Queer Futurity*. New York: NYU Press.

Murray, Charles. 1984. *Losing Ground: American Social Policy, 1950–1980*. New York: Basic Books.

Myat, Bone. 2015. "Five Myanmar Men Arrested, Charged for 'Rohingya Calendar.'" Radio Free Asia. Accessed 6 June 2016. http://www.rfa.org/english/news/myanmar/calendar-11252015140911.html.

Nash, June, and Maria Patricia Fernandez-Kelly, eds. 1983. *Women, Men, and the International Division of Labor*. Albany: State University of New York Press.

National Geographic. n.d. "Continents." Accessed 12 November 2016. http://www.nationalgeographic.com/faq/geography.html.

NBC News. 2015. "Donald Trump's Plan for a Muslim Database Draws Comparison to Nazi Germany" (video clip). 20 November. Accessed 30 November 2015. http://www.nbcnews.com/politics/2016-election/trump-says-he-would-certainly-implement-muslim-database-n466716.

Neocosmos, Michael. 2008. "The Politics of Fear and the Fear of Politics: Reflections on Xenophobic Violence in South Africa." *Journal of Asian and African Studies* 43 (6): 586–594.

New York Times. 1886. "Our Bad Indian Policy." 27 October. P. 9.

Newbury, Catharine. 1995. "Background to Genocide: Rwanda." *Issue: A Journal of Opinion* 23 (2): 12–17.

Ng, Roxana. 1988. *The Politics of Community Services: Immigrant Women, Class and State*. Toronto: Garamond Press.

Ng, Roxana. 1993. "Racism, Sexism, and Nation Building in Canada." In *Race, Identity and Representation in Education*, edited by Cameron McCarthy and Warren Crichlow, 50–59. New York: Routledge.

Ngai, Mae M. 1999. "The Architecture of Race in American Immigration Law: A Re-examination of the Immigration Act of 1924." *Journal of American History* 86 (1): 67–92.

Nicaragua. 1930. Immigration Law. 25 April.

Niezen, Ronald. 2003. *The Origins of Indigenism: Human Rights and the Politics of Identity*. Berkeley: University of California Press.

Nilsen, Alf Gunvald. 2013. "Norway's Disturbing Lurch to the Right." *The Guardian*. 10 September. Accessed 13 February 2016. http://www.theguardian.com/commentisfree/2013/sep/10/norway-lurch-to-right.

Nkrumah, Kwame. 1965. *Neo-colonialism: The Last Stage of Imperialism*. New York: International Publishers.

Noiriel, Gérard. 1996. *The French Melting Pot: Immigration Citizenship and National Identity*. Translated by Geoffroy de Laforcade. Minneapolis: University of Minnesota Press.

Norton, Michael I., and Samuel R. Sommers. 2011. "Whites See Racism as a Zero-Sum Game That They Are Now Losing." *Perspectives on Psychological Science* 6 (3): 215–218.

Nossiter, Adam. 2017. "Marine Le Pen Leads Far-Right Fight to Make France 'More French.'" *New York Times*. 20 April. Accessed 18 May 2017. https://www.nytimes.com/2017/04/20/world/europe/france-election-marine-le-pen.html?_r=0.

Novikov, Nikolai. (1946) 1991. "The Novikov Telegram Washington, September 27, 1946." *Diplomatic History* 15 (4): 527–537.

NTNERA (Northern Territory Board of Inquiry into the Protection of Aboriginal Children from Sexual Abuse). 2007. *Ampa Akelyernemane Meke Mekarle: Little Children Are Sacred*. Darwin, Northern Territory Government. 30 April. Accessed 2 February 2016. https://web.archive.org/web/20070703014641/http://www.nt.gov .au/dcm/inquirysaac/pdf/bipacsa_final_report.pdf.

Nwaubani, Ebere. 2003. "The United States and the Liquidation of European Colonial Rule in Tropical Africa, 1941–1963." *Cahiers d'études africaines* 43 (3): 505–551.

Nyamnjoh, Francis, and Michael Rowlands. 1998. "Elite Associations and the Politics of Belonging in Cameroon." *Africa* 68 (3): 320–337.

Obeng, Letitia. 1977. "Should Dams Be Built? The Volta Lake Example." In "Water." Special issue, *Ambio* 6 (1): 46–50.

OECD (Organization for Economic Co-operation and Development). 2011. "Prison Population." In *OECD Factbook 2010: Economic, Environmental, and Social Statistics*. Accessed 5 February 2012. http://www.oecd-ilibrary.org/sites/factbook-2010.

OED (*Oxford English Dictionary*). s.v. "allochthon (*n.*)." Accessed 17 March 2013. http:// www.oed.com.eres.library.manoa.hawaii.edu/view/Entry/5354?redirectedFrom =allochthon#eid.

OED (*Oxford English Dictionary*). s.v. "allochthonous (*adj.*)." Accessed 17 March 2013. http://www.oed.com.eres.library.manoa.hawaii.edu/view/Entry /5355#eid6666270.

OED (*Oxford English Dictionary*). s.v. "autochthony (*n.*)." Accessed 17 March 2013. http://www.oed.com.eres.library.manoa.hawaii.edu/view/Entry/13391 ?redirectedFrom=autochthony&.

OED (*Oxford English Dictionary*). s.v. "home rule." Accessed 14 June 2010. https://www -oed-com.eres.library.manoa.hawaii.edu/view/Entry/87930?redirectedFrom =home+rule#eid.

OED (*Oxford English Dictionary*). s.v. "indigenous (*adj.*)." Accessed 21 March 2013. http://www.oed.com.eres.library.manoa.hawaii.edu/view/Entry/94474 ?redirectedFrom=indigenous&.

OED (*Oxford English Dictionary*). s.v. "native (*n.*)." Accessed 18 April 2015. http://www .oed.com.eres.library.manoa.hawaii.edu/view/Entry/125303#eid35388283.

Olaniyi, Rasheed. 2008. "The 1969 Ghana Exodus: Memory and Reminiscences of Yoruba Migrants." Working paper, SEPHIS (South-South Exchange Programme for Research on the History of Development.

Opekokew, Delia. 1980. "Indians of Canada Seek a Special Status." *American Indian Journal* 6 (4): 4–10.

Oppen, Achim von. 2003. "Bounding Villages: The Enclosure of Locality in Central Africa, 1890s to 1990s." PhD dissertation, Humboldt University, Berlin.

Osterhammel, Jürgen. 1997. *Colonialism: A Theoretical Overview*. Translated by Shelley L. Frisch. Princeton, NJ: M. Wiener.

O'Sullivan, Christopher D. 2008. *Sumner Welles, Postwar Planning, and the Quest for a New World Order, 1937–1943*. New York: Columbia University Press.

Oxfam. 2014. "Working for the Few: Political Capture and Economic Inequality." Briefing Paper 178, Summary. 20 January. Accessed 5 May 2015. https://www .oxfam.org/sites/www.oxfam.org/files/bp-working-for-few-political-capture -economic-inequality-200114-summ-en.pdf.

Oxfam. 2016a. "An Economy for the 1%: How Privilege and Power in the Economy Drive Extreme Inequality and How This Can Be Stopped." 18 January. Accessed 27 December 2016. https://www.oxfam.org/sites/www.oxfam.org/files/file _attachments/bp210-economy-one-percent-tax-havens-180116-en_0.pdf.

Oxfam. 2016b. "62 People Own the Same as Half the World, Reveals Oxfam Davos Report." 18 January. Accessed 3 February 2016. https://www.oxfam.org/en /pressroom/pressreleases/2016-01-18/62-people-own-same-half-world-reveals -oxfam-davos-report.

Oxfam. 2017. "Just 8 Men Own Same Wealth as Half the World." 16 January. Accessed 16 January 2017. https://www.oxfam.org/en/pressroom/pressreleases /2017-01-16/just-8-men-own-same-wealth-half-world.

Oxfam. 2018. "Reward Work, Not Wealth." Briefing paper. January. Accessed 14 March 2018. https://www.oxfam.org/en/research/reward-work-not-wealth.

Paice, Edward. 2010. *Tip and Run: The Untold Tragedy of the Great War in Africa*. London: Hachette.

Pakistan. 1952. Act to Make Better Provision for Controlling the Entry of Indian Citizens into Pakistan, Adoption: 1952–12–14 | PAK-1952-L-37904.

Pakistan. 1965. The Foreigners (Parolees) Order, Adoption: 1965–11–10 | PAK-1965-R-37908.

Panton, Kenneth J. 2015. *Historical Dictionary of the British Empire*. Lanham, MD: Rowman and Littlefield.

Parker, Kunal M. 2015. *Making Foreigners*. Cambridge: Cambridge University Press.

Parry, Benita. 2004. *Postcolonial Studies: A Materialist Critique*. London: Routledge.

Parry, Richard Lloyd. 2013. "My Cause Is Justified, Says 'Burmese Bin Laden.'" *The Times* (London). 31 May. Accessed 1 July 2013. http://www.thetimes.co.uk/tto /news/world/asia/article3778873.ece.

Pascoe, Peggy. 1990. *Relations of Rescue: The Search for Female Moral Authority in the American West, 1874–1939*. New York: Oxford University Press.

Patnaik, Prabhat. 1993. "The Fascism of Our Times." *Social Scientist* 21 (3/4): 69–77.

Patterson, Orlando. 1982. *Slavery and Social Death: A Comparative Study*. Cambridge, MA: Harvard University Press.

Peil, Margaret. 1974. "Ghana's Aliens." *International Migration Review* 8 (3): 367–381.

Petras, Elizabeth M. 1981. "The Global Labor Market in the Modern World-Economy." In *Global Trends in Migration: Theory and Research on International Population Movements*, edited by Mary M. Kritz, Charles B. Keely, and Silvano M. Tomasi, 44–63. Staten Island, NY: Center for Migration Studies.

Phelan, Marilyn. 2009. "A History and Analysis of Laws Protecting Native American Cultures." *Tulsa Law Review* 45: 45–64.

Pilkington, Edward. 1988. *Beyond the Mother Country: West Indians and the Notting Hill White Riots*. London: IB Tauris.

Plender, Richard, ed. 1988. *International Migration Law*. Vol. 2. Leiden: Martinus Nijhoff.

Plummer, Brenda Gayle. 1997. "Between Privilege and Opprobrium: The Arabs and Jews in Haïti." *Immigrants and Minorities* 16 (1–2): 80–93.

Polanyi, Karl. 1944. *The Great Transformation: The Political and Economic Origins of Our Time*. New York: Farrar and Rinehart.

Porter, Bernard. 1979. *The Refugee Question in Mid-Victorian Politics*. Cambridge: Cambridge University Press.

Potter, George Ann. 1988. *Dialogue on Debt: Alternative Analysis and Solutions*. Washington, DC: Center of Concern.

Potts, Deborah. 2010. "Internal Migration in Zimbabwe: The Impact of Livelihood Destruction in Rural and Urban Areas." In *Zimbabwe's Exodus: Crisis, Migration, Survival*, edited by Jonathan Crush and Daniel Evera, 79–111. Kingston, Canada: Southern African Migration Programme (SAMP).

Potts, Lydia. 1990. *The World Market for Labour Power: A History of Migration*. London: Zed Books.

Powell, Enoch. 1968. Speech for Conservative Association meeting, Birmingham. 20 April. Accessed 3 June 2014. http://www.telegraph.co.uk/comment/3643823/Enoch-Powells-Rivers-of-Blood-speech.html.

Powell, Enoch. 1969. "Immigration." In *Freedom and Reality*, 254–257. New Rochelle, NY: Arlington House.

Prashad, Vijay. 2007. *The Darker Nations: A People's History of the Third World*. New York: New Press.

Prebisch, Raul. 1962. "The Economic Development of Latin America and Its Principle Problems." *Economic Bulletin for Latin American* 7 (1): 1–12.

Previch, Chad, and Sheila Stogsdill. 2007. "Cherokee Nation Votes to Remove Descendants of Freedman." *The Oklahoman*. 3 March. Accessed 9 June 2016. http://newsok.com/article/3021650.

Proshansky, Harold M., Abbe K. Fabian, and Robert Kaminoff. 1983. "Place-Identity: Physical World Socialization of the Self." *Journal of Environmental Psychology* 3:57–83.

Prunier, Gérard. 1995. *The Rwanda Crisis: History of a Genocide*. New York: Columbia University Press.

Radhuber, Isabella M. 2012. "Indigenous Struggles for a Plurinational State: An Analysis of Indigenous Rights and Competences in Bolivia." *Journal of Latin American Geography* 11 (2): 167–193.

Rahman, Mahbubar, and Willem van Schendel. 2003. "'I Am Not a Refugee': Rethinking Partition Migration." *Modern Asian Studies* 37 (3): 551–584.

Rahman, Mizanur, and Lian Kwen Fee. 2012. "Recruiting Migrant Labor in Asia: Interplay between Institutions and Networks." In *Asian Migration Policy: South, Southeast, and East Asia*, edited by Mizanur Rahman and Ahsan Ullah, 251–270. New York: Nova Publishers.

Ramdin, Ron. 1987. *The Making of the Black Working Class in Britain*. Aldershot: Gower.

Rathzel, Nora. 1994. "Harmonious Heimat and Disturbing Auslander." In *Shifting Identities and Shifting Racisms*, edited by K. K. Bhavani and A. Phoenix, 81–98. London: Sage.

Rediker, Marcus. 2007. *The Slave Ship: A Human History*. New York: Penguin.

Reed, David. 1924. "America of the Melting Pot Comes to End." *New York Times* 27 April. P. 3.

Reff, Daniel T. 1991. "Disease Depopulation and Culture Change in Northwestern New Spain 1518–1764." Accessed 3 November 2013. http://www.popline.org/node /326367.

Refugees International. 2012. "South Sudan Nationality: Commitment Now Avoids Conflict Later." 25 May. Accessed 4 July 2014. http://www.refintl.org/policy/field -report/south-sudan-nationality-commitment-now-avoids-conflict-later.

Reich Main Security Office. 1941. "Order Banning the Emigration of Jews from the Reich." Yad Vashem Archives, TR-3/1209. Jerusalem: Shoah Resource Center, International School for Holocaust Studies.

Reséndez, Andrés. 2016. *The Other Slavery: The Uncovered Story of Indian Enslavement in America*. Boston: Houghton Mifflin Harcourt.

Reuters. 2016. "Austrians Roundly Reject Far Right in Presidential Election." 4 December. Accessed 5 December 2016. http://www.reuters.com/article/us-austria -election-idUSKBN13S0W0.

Richards, Eric. 1985. *A History of the Highland Clearances*. Dundee, U.K.: Croom Helm.

Richmond, Anthony H. 1994. *Global Apartheid: Refugees, Racism, and the New World Order*. Don Mills, ON: Oxford University Press.

Ridgway, Whitman H. 2011. "A Century of Lawmaking for a New Nation: US Congressional Documents and Debates, 1774–1875." http://memory.loc.gov/ammem /amlaw/lawhome.html. Washington, DC: Library of Congress.

Rifkin, Mark. 2009. "Indigenizing Agamben: Rethinking Sovereignty in Light of the 'Peculiar' Status of Native Peoples." *Cultural Critique* 73 (Fall): 88–124.

Riley, Eileen. 1991. *Major Political Events in South Africa, 1948–1990: Facts on File*. New York: Oxford University Press.

Rodney, Walter. 1974. *How Europe Underdeveloped Africa*. Washington: Howard University Press.

Roediger, David R. 1999. *The Wages of Whiteness: Race and the Making of the American Working Class*. London: Verso.

Roser, Max. 2016. "Life Expectancy." OurWorldInData.org. Accessed 28 January 2017. https://ourworldindata.org/life-expectancy/.

Rothchild, Donald. 1973. *Racial Bargaining in Independent Kenya: A Study of Minorities and Decolonization*. London: Oxford University Press for the Institute of Race Relations.

Ruggiero, Renato. 1996. "Beyond Borders: Managing a World of Free Trade and Deep Interdependence." Address by the director general of the World Trade Organization to the Argentinian Council on Foreign Relations in Buenos Aires. WTO Press Release No. 55. 10 September.

Rürup, Miriam. 2011. "Lives in Limbo: Statelessness after Two World Wars." *Bulletin of the German Historical Institute* (Washington, DC) 49: 113–134.

Rushforth, Brett. 2003. "'A Little Flesh We Offer You': The Origins of Indian Slavery in New France." *William and Mary Quarterly* 60 (4): 777–808.

Rwanda. 1963. Loi du 15 octobre 1963 relative à la police de l'immigration et aux conditions d'entrée et de séjour des étrangers dans la République rwandaise. Adoption: 1963-10-15 | RWA-1963-L-59912. Accessed 1 July 2015.

Rygiel, Philippe. n.d. "The Exclusion of Foreigners during the Interwar Period: How the Term and the Procedure Were Used." Accessed 20 April 2013. http://barthes.ens.fr/clio/revues/AHI/articles/english/rygeng.html#note6.

Sack, Robert D. 1983. "Human Territoriality: A Theory." *Annals of the Association of American Geographers* 73 (1): 55–74.

SAFE (Society for the Advancement of Freedom in Europe). 2008. "Brussels Journal." 6 April. Accessed 3 April 2013. http://www.brusselsjournal.com/node/3153.

Said, Edward. 1979. *Orientalism*. New York: Vintage.

Said, Edward. 1990. "On Jean Genet's Late Works." *Grand Street* 36:9.

Said, Edward. 1993. *Culture and Imperialism*. New York: Vintage Books.

Said, Edward. 2000. *Reflections on Exile and Other Essays*. Cambridge, MA: Harvard University Press.

San Juan, Epifanio, Jr. 2002. *Racism and Cultural Studies: Critiques of Multiculturalist Ideology and the Politics of Difference*. Durham, NC: Duke University Press.

Saranillio, Dean Itsuji. 2013. "Why Asian Settler Colonialism Matters: A Thought Piece on Critiques, Debates, and Indigenous Difference." *Settler Colonial Studies* 3 (3–4): 280–294.

Sartre, Jean-Paul. (1964) 2001. *Colonialism and Neocolonialism*. Translated by Azzedine Haddour, Steve Brewer, and Terry McWilliams. London: Routledge.

Sassen, Saskia. 1988. *The Mobility of Labor and Capital: A Study in International Investment and Labor Flow*. Cambridge: Cambridge University Press.

Sassen, Saskia. 1991. *The Global City: New York, London, Tokyo*. Princeton, NJ: Princeton University Press.

Sauvy, Alfred. 1946. "Evaluation des Besoins de l'immigration Française." *Population* 1 (January–March): 91–98.

Schaeffer, Robert K. 2003. *Understanding Globalization: The Social Consequences of Political, Economic, and Environmental Change*. Lanham, MD: Rowman and Littlefield.

Scharpf, Fritz W. 2000. "Economic Changes, Vulnerabilities, and Institutional Capabilities." In *Welfare and Work in the Open Economy: From Vulnerability to Competitiveness*, 21–124. Oxford: Oxford University Press.

Schinkel, Willem. 2013. "The Imagination of 'Society' in Measurements of Immigrant Integration." *Ethnic and Racial Studies* 36 (7): 1142–1161.

Schmitt, John, and Jonathan Wadsworth. 2006. "Changing Patterns in the Relative Economic Performance of Immigrants to Great Britain and the United States, 1980–2000." Centre for Economic Performance, Working Paper No. 1422. Washington, DC: Center for Economic and Policy Research. 2 April. Accessed

16 January 2017. http://cepr.net/publications/reports/changing-patterns-in-the
-relative-economic-performance-of-immigrants-to-great-britain-and-the-us.

Scott, James C. 1998. *Seeing Like a State: How Certain Schemes to Improve the Human Condition Have Failed*. New Haven, CT: Yale University Press.

Scott, James C. 2009. *The Art of Not Being Governed: An Anarchist History of Upland Southeast Asia*. New Haven, CT: Yale University Press.

Scott, James C. 2017. *Against the Grain: A Deep History of the Earliest States*. New Haven, CT: Yale University Press.

Segatti, Aurelia. 2006. "Reforming South African Immigration Policy in the Postapartheid Period (1990–2010)." In *Contemporary Migration to South Africa: A Regional Development Issue*, edited by A. Segatti and L. B. Landau, 31–66. Paris: Agence française de développement.

Şeker, Nesim. 2013. "Forced Population Movements in the Ottoman Empire and the Early Turkish Republic: An Attempt at Reassessment through Demographic Engineering." *European Journal of Turkish Studies* 16: 1–16.

Sen, Amartya. 1983. "Development: Which Way Now?" *Economic Journal* 93 (372): 745–762.

Sentencing Project. 2016. "Criminal Justice Facts." Accessed 4 May 2017. http://www
.sentencingproject.org/criminal-justice-facts/.

Sentencing Project. 2017. "Immigration and Public Safety Fact Sheet." Accessed 5 May 2017. http://www.sentencingproject.org/wp-content/uploads/2017/04
/Immigration-and-Public-Safety-Fact-Sheet.pdf.

Servan-Schreiber, Jean-Jacques. 1971. *The American Challenge*. Translated by Ronald Steel. New York: Avon.

Sharma, Nandita. 2006. *Home Economics: Nationalism and the Making of "Migrant Workers" in Canada*. Toronto: University of Toronto Press.

Sharma, Nandita. 2008. "Citizenship and the Disciplining of (Im)migrant Workers in the United States." In *Refugees, Recent Migrants, and Employment: Challenging Barriers and Exploring Pathways*, edited by Sonia McKay, 110–128. London: Routledge.

Sharma, Nandita. 2011. "Canadian Multiculturalism and Its Nationalisms." In *Home and Native Land: Unsettling Multiculturalism in Canada*, edited by May Chazan, L. Helps, A. Staley, and S. Thakkar, 85–101. Toronto: Between the Lines.

Sharma, Nandita. 2015. "Strategic Anti-essentialism: Decolonizing Decolonization." In *Sylvia Wynter: On Being Human as Praxis*, edited by Katherine McKittrick, 164–182. Durham, NC: Duke University Press.

Sharma, Nandita, and Cynthia Wright. 2009. "Decolonizing Resistance, Challenging Colonial States." *Social Justice* 35 (3): 120–138.

Shear, Michael D. 2011. "Obama Releases Long-Form Birth Certificate." *New York Times*. 27 April. Accessed 24 May 2017. https://thecaucus.blogs.nytimes.com/2011
/04/27/obamas-long-form-birth-certificate-released/?_r=0.

Shils, Edward. 1955. "The End of Ideology?" *Encounter* 5 (5): 52–58.

Shiva, Vandana. 1997. *Biopiracy: The Plunder of Nature and Knowledge*. Toronto: Between the Lines.

Shiva, Vandana. 2011. "The Great Land Grab: India's War on Farmers." Al Jazeera. Accessed 31 December 2014. http://www.aljazeera.com/indepth/opinion/2011/06 /2011671175666798.html.

Shivji, Salimah. 2016. "Mohawk Council of Kahnawake Hands Out More Eviction Letters." CBC News Montreal. Accessed 25 May 2017. http://www.cbc.ca/news /canada/montreal/mohawk-kahnawake-marry-out-stay-out-eviction-notice-1 .3658202.

Shohat, Ella. 1997. "The Narrative of the Nation and the Discourse of Moderniza- tion: The Case of the Mizrahim." *Critique: Journal for Critical Studies of the Middle East* 6 (10): 3–18.

Shraga, Daphna, and Ralph Zacklin. 1994. "The International Criminal Tribunal for the Former Yugoslavia." *European Journal of International Law* 5:360–380.

Siemaszko, Zbigniew Sebastian. 1991. "The Mass Deportations of the Polish Population to the USSR, 1940–1941." In *The Soviet Takeover of the Polish Eastern Provinces, 1939–41*, edited by K. Sword, 217–235. London: Palgrave Macmillan.

Silverman, Maxim. 2002. *Deconstructing the Nation: Immigration, Racism, and Citizen- ship in Modern France*. London: Routledge.

Simpson, Audra. 2011. "Settlement's Secret." *Cultural Anthropology* 26 (2): 205–217.

Simpson, Audra. 2014. *Mohawk Interruptus: Political Life across the Borders of Settler States*. Durham, NC: Duke University Press.

Simpson, John Hope. 1938. "The Refugee Problem." *International Affairs*, September, 607–628.

Simpson, Leanne Betasamosake. 2013. *Islands of Decolonial Love*. Winnipeg: Arbeiter Ring Publishing.

Sinha, Shreeya, and Mark Suppes. 2014. "Timeline of the Riots in Modi's Guja- rat." *New York Times*. 6 April. Accessed 28 May 2017. https://www.nytimes.com /interactive/2014/04/06/world/asia/modi-gujarat-riots-timeline.html?_r=0# /#time287_8514.

60 Minutes Australia. 2014. "Greek Tragedy." 10 April. Accessed 19 August 2014. https://www.youtube.com/watch?v=M4pjyiPeBz4.

Sjöberg, Tommie. 1991. *The Powers and the Persecuted: The Refugee Problem and the Intergovernmental Committee on Refugees (IGCR) 1938–1947*. Lund, Sweden: Lund University Press.

Sluman, Norma, and Jean Cuthand Goodwill. 1982. *John Tootoosis: Biography of a Cree Leader*. Ottawa: Golden Dog Press.

Smith, Dorothy. 1990. *The Conceptual Practices of Power: A Feminist Sociology of Knowl- edge*. Toronto: University of Toronto Press.

Soederberg, Susanne. 2005. "The Rise of Neoliberalism in Mexico: From a De- velopmental to a Competition State." In *Internalizing Globalization: The Rise of Neoliberalism and the Decline of National Varieties of Capitalism*, edited by Susanne Soederberg, Georg Menz, and Philip Cerny, 167–182. Basingstoke: Palgrave Macmillan UK.

Song, Jing. 2012. "UNHCR Honoured by Bangladesh for Helping Millions in 1971 Con- flict." 27 March. Accessed 15 August 2016. http://www.unhcr.org/4f71c0e46.html.

Sookdeo, Neil. 2000. *Freedom, Festivals, and Caste in Trinidad after Slavery: A Society in Transition*. Bloomington, IN: Xlibris.

South Africa. 2002. Immigration Act (No. 13). 2002–05–31 | ZAF-2002-L-62432.

South Sudan. 2011a. The Nationality Act. 7 July. Accessed 27 November 2016. http://www.refworld.org/cgi-bin/texis/vtx/rwmain?page=search&docid=4e94318f2&skip=0&query=nationality%20law&coi=SSD.

South Sudan. 2011b. Passports and Immigration Act. 7 July. Accessed 27 November 2016. http://www.refworld.org/docid/4e9432652.html.

South Sudan, Ministry of the Interior. 2012. "Status of Sudanese Nationals in the Republic of South Sudan" (press release). 10 April.

Southern African Migration Project. 2008. *The Perfect Storm: The Realities of Xenophobia in Contemporary South Africa*. Migration Policy Series No. 50. Kingston, ON: Southern African Migration Programme (SAMP).

Southern Poverty Law Center. 2017a. "Stephen Bannon Has No Business in the White House." Accessed 23 May 2017. https://www.splcenter.org/stephen-bannon-has-no-business-white-house.

Southern Poverty Law Center. 2017b. "2016: The Year in Hate and Extremism." Accessed 11 March 2016. https://www.splcenter.org/sites/default/files/ir160-spring2016-splc.pdf.

Southern Poverty Law Center. 2018. "2017: The Year in Hate and Extremism." Accessed 28 February 2018. https://www.splcenter.org/fighting-hate/intelligence-report/2018/2017-year-hate-and-extremism.

Spivak, Gayatri. 1994. "In a Word: Interview." By Ellen Rooney. In *The Essential Difference*, edited by Naomi Schor and Elizabeth Weed, 151–184. Bloomington: Indiana University Press.

Spivak, Gayatri Chakravorty. 1999. *A Critique of Postcolonial Reason: Toward a History of the Vanishing Present*. Cambridge, MA: Harvard University Press.

Spivak, Gayatri Chakravorty. 2014. "General Strike." *Rethinking Marxism* 26 (1): 9–14.

Srinivasan, Krishnan. 2006. "Nobody's Commonwealth? The Commonwealth in Britain's Post-imperial Adjustment." *Commonwealth and Comparative Politics* 44 (2): 257–269.

Stahl, Charles W. 2003. "International Labour Migration in East Asia: Trends and Policy Issues." In *Migration in the Asia Pacific: Population, Settlement and Citizenship Issues*, edited by Robyn R. Iredale, Charles Hawksley, and Stephen Castles, 29–54. Cheltenham, U.K.: Edward Elgar Publishing.

Stasiulis, Daiva, and Nira Yuval-Davis. 1995. *Unsettling Settler Societies: Articulations of Gender, Race, Ethnicity, and Class*. London: Sage.

Steinfeld, Robert J. 1991. *The Invention of Free Labour: The Employment Relation in English and American Law and Culture, 1350–1870*. Chapel Hill: University of North Carolina Press.

Stewart, Heather, and Rowena Mason. 2016. "Nigel Farage's Anti-migrant Poster Reported to Police." *The Guardian*. 16 June. Accessed 21 July 2016. https://www.theguardian.com/politics/2016/jun/16/nigel-farage-defends-ukip-breaking-point-poster-queue-of-migrants.

Stewart, Neil. 1951. "Divide and Rule: British Policy in Indian History." *Science & Society* 1 (January): 49–57.

Stiglitz, Joseph. 2006. "Civil Strife and Economic and Social Policies." *Economics of Peace and Security Journal* 1 (1): 6–9.

Stockton, Kathryn Bond. 2009. *The Queer Child, or Growing Sideways in the Twentieth Century*. Durham, NC: Duke University Press.

Stoddard, Lothrop. 1921. *The Rising Tide of Color against White World-Supremacy*. New York: Charles Scribner's Sons.

Stoler, Ann Laura. 1995. *Race and the Education of Desire: Foucault's History of Sexuality and the Colonial Order of Things*. Durham, NC: Duke University Press.

Sturgis, Amy H. 2007. *The Trail of Tears and Indian Removal*. Westport, CT: Greenwood.

Sturm, Circe. 2014. "Race, Sovereignty, and Civil Rights: Understanding the Cherokee Freedmen Controversy." *Cultural Anthropology* 29 (3): 575–598.

Sudan. 1957. Sudanese Nationality Act 1957. Accessed 3 July 2014. http://www.refworld.org/docid/3ae6b56718.html.

Sudan. 1960. Passports and Immigration Act (No. 40). Adoption: 1960–11–15 | Date of entry into force: 1960-11-15 | SDN-1960-L-49364.

Sudarkasa, Niara. 1979. "From Stranger to Alien: The Socio-Political History of the Nigerian Yoruba in Ghana, 1900–1970." In *Strangers in African Societies*, edited by W. A. Shack and E. P. Skinner, 141–168. Berkeley: University of California Press.

Sutcliffe, Bob. 2001. "Migration and Citizenship: Why Can Birds, Whales, Butterflies, and Ants Cross International Frontiers More Easily Than Cows, Dogs, and Human Beings?" In *Migration and Mobility: The European Context*, edited by Subrata Ghatak and Anne Showstack Sassoon. New York: Palgrave.

Swissinfo.ch. 2016. "Ticino Initiative Prioritising Locals for Jobs Declared Valid." 26 January. Accessed 9 February 2016. http://www.swissinfo.ch/directdemocracy/cross-border-workers_ticino-initiative-prioritising-locals-for-jobs-declared-valid/41920212.

Szirtes, George. 2015. "Hungary Has Been Shamed by Viktor Orbán's Government." *The Guardian*. 16 September. Accessed 29 May 2017. https://www.theguardian.com/commentisfree/2015/sep/16/hungary-shamed-viktor-orban-refugee-hungarian-serbian.

Taguieff, Pierre-André. 1990. "The New Cultural Racism in France." *Telos* 83: 109–122.

Takaki, Ronald. 1983. *Pau Hana: Plantation Life and Labor in Hawaii*. Honolulu: University of Hawaii Press.

Takaki, Ronald. 1993. *A Different Mirror: A History of Multicultural America*. Boston: Little, Brown.

Takaki, Ronald. 1998. *Strangers from a Different Shore: A History of Asian Americans*. Boston: Little, Brown.

Tate, Merze, and Fidele Foy. 1965. "Slavery and Racism in South Pacific Annexations." *Journal of Negro History* 50 (1): 1–21.

Taylor, Jerome, and Oliver Wright. 2012. "Burma's Rohingya Muslims: Aung San Suu Kyi's Blind Spot." *The Independent*. 20 August. Accessed 2 May 2013. http://www .independent.co.uk/news/world/asia/burmas-rohingya-muslims-aung-san-suu -kyis-blind-spot-8061619.html.

Taylor, Steven. 2000. "Progressive Nativism: The Know-Nothing Party in Massachusetts." *Historical Journal of Massachusetts* 28 (2): 167–185.

Thomas, Dominic, and Richard David. 2007. *Black France: Colonialism, Immigration, and Transnationalism*. Bloomington: Indiana University Press.

Thompson, Dorothy. 1938. "Refugees: A World Problem." *Foreign Affairs* 16 (3): 375–387.

Thornton, Russell. 1980. "Recent Estimates of the Prehistoric California Indian Population." *Current Anthropology* 21 (5): 702–704.

Tinker, Hugh. 1974. *A New System of Slavery: The Export of Indian Labour Overseas, 1830–1920*. London: Oxford University Press.

Toal, Gerard, and Carl T. Dahlman. 2011. *Bosnia Remade: Ethnic Cleansing and Its Reversal*. New York: Oxford University Press.

Tobias, John L. 1976. "Protection, Civilization, Assimilation: An Outline History of Canada's Indian Policy." *Western Canadian Journal of Anthropology* 8: 13–20.

Todhunter, Colin. 2014. "War, Economic Catastrophe, and Environmental Degradation: Under the Guise of Progress and Development." *Global Research*. 27 April. Accessed 30 May 2017. http://www.globalresearch.ca/war-economic -catastrophe-and-environmental-degradation-under-the-guise-of-progress-and -development/5379424.

Tomlinson, Matt. 2004. "Perpetual Lament: Kava-Drinking, Christianity, and Sensations of Historical Decline in Fiji." *Journal of the Royal Anthropological Institute* 10 (3): 653–673.

Tondo, Lorenzo. 2019. "Italy Adopts Decree That Could Fine Migrant Rescuers up to €50,000." *The Guardian*. 15 June. Accessed 17 June 2019. https://www .theguardian.com/world/2019/jun/15/italy-adopts-decree-that-could-fine -migrant-rescue-ngo-aid-up-to-50000.

Torpey, John. 1998. "Coming and Going: On the State Monopolization of the Legitimate 'Means of Movement.'" *Sociological Theory* 16 (3): 239–259.

Torpey, John. 2000. *The Invention of the Passport: Surveillance, Citizenship, and the State*. Cambridge: Cambridge University Press.

Trans-Atlantic Slave Trade Data Base. 2013. Accessed 2 June 2015. http://www .slavevoyages.org.

Trask, Haunani-Kay. 2000. "Settlers, Not Immigrants." *Amerasia* 26 (2): xi.

Travis, Alan. 2013a. "Tory Immigration Language 'Like National Front of 1970s.'" *The Guardian*. 25 September. Accessed 28 February 2018. https://www.theguardian .com/uk-news/2013/sep/25/tory-immigration-language-national-front-yvette -cooper.

Travis, Alan. 2013b. "'Go Home' Vans Resulted in 11 People Leaving Britain, Says Report." *The Guardian*. 31 October. Accessed 28 February 2018. https://www .theguardian.com/uk-news/2013/oct/31/go-home-vans-11-leave-britain.

Traynor, Ian. 2015a. "Brussels Plans Migration Centres Outside EU to Process Asylum Applications." *The Guardian*. 5 March. Accessed 7 March 2015. http://www.theguardian.com/world/2015/mar/05/european-commission-third-country-immigrant-processing-centres.

Traynor, Ian. 2015b. "Hungary PM: Bring Back Death Penalty and Build Work Camps for Immigrants." *The Guardian*. 29 April.

Treanor, Donna. 2013. "Question Time for Patriots—London." 3 January. Accessed 6 March. https://bnp.org.uk/bnp-tv/.

Treuer, David. 2011. "How Do You Prove You're an Indian?" *New York Times*. 20 December.

Truman, Harry S. 1947. "President Harry S Truman's Address before a Joint Session of Congress, March 12." The Avalon Project of the Yale Law School, Lillian Goldman Law Library. Accessed 21 October 2014. http://avalon.law.yale.edu/20th_century/trudoc.asp.

Trump, Donald J. 2015. "Donald J. Trump Statement on Preventing Muslim Immigration." 7 December. Accessed 6 June 2016. https://www.donaldjtrump.com/press-releases/donald-j.-trump-statement-on-preventing-muslim-immigration.

Tuan, Yi-Fu. 1977. *Space and Place: The Perspective of Experience*. Minneapolis: University of Minnesota Press.

Turner, Michael Edward. 1980. *English Parliamentary Enclosure: Its Historical Geography and Economic History*. Hamden, CT: Archon Books.

Tyner, James A. 1999. "The Geopolitics of Eugenics and the Exclusion of Philippine Immigrants from the United States." *Geographical Review* 89 (1): 54–73.

Uganda. 1969. Legislation on Immigration Control Board. 2 April. Accessed 31 July 2016. http://www.refworld.org/docid/3ae6b4d244.html.

Ullah, Ahsan. 2012. "Changing Migration Policies in Hong Kong: An Efficacy Analysis." In *Asian Migration Policy: South, Southeast, and East Asia*, edited by Mizanur Rahman and Ahsan Ullah, 83–98. New York: Nova Publishers.

Ullah, Ahsan, and Mizanur Rahman. 2012. "Introduction, Migration Policy: Theoretical and Conceptual Issues." In *Asian Migration Policy: South, Southeast, and East Asia*, edited by Mizanur Rahman and Ahsan Ullah, 1–17. New York: Nova Publishers.

U.K. (United Kingdom). 1807. Abolition of the Slave Trade Act. 47 Geo 3 Sess 1 c 36.

U.K. (United Kingdom) Home Office. 2017. "National Statistics: Detention." 23 February. https://www.gov.uk/government/publications/immigration-statistics-october-to-december-2016/detention.

U.K. (United Kingdom) Parliament. n.d. "Enclosing the Land." Accessed 23 November 2017. http://www.parliament.uk/about/living-\heritage/transformingsociety/towncountry/landscape/overview/enclosingland/.

UN (United Nations). n.d. "Minorities, the United Nations, and Regional Mechanisms." Pamphlet No. 1. Office of the High Commissioner for Human Rights. Accessed 3 January 2013. http://www.ohchr.org/en/issues/minorities/pages/minoritiesguide.aspx.

UN (United Nations). 1945. *Charter of the United Nations*. 26 June. 1 UNTS XVI.

UN (United Nations). 1947. Resolution 181 (II). Resolution Adopted on the Report of the Ad Hoc Committee on the Palestinian Question. Accessed 23 November 2015. https://www.un.org/en/ga/search/view_doc.asp?symbol=A/RES/181(II)

UN (United Nations). 1948. Treaty No. 1021. Convention on the Prevention and Punishment of the Crime of Genocide (adopted by the General Assembly of the United Nations on 9 December 1948). Accessed 2 October 2014. https://treaties.un.org/doc/Publication/UNTS/Volume%2078/volume-78-I-1021-English.pdf.

UN (United Nations). 1951. "Measures for the Economic Development of Under-developed Countries." Report commissioned by the Secretary-General of the United Nations. United Nations, Department of Economic Affairs.

UN (United Nations) General Assembly. 1951. "General Progress Report and Supplementary Report of the United Nations Conciliation Commission for Palestine." 23 August. Accessed 5 May 2013. http://unispal.un.org/unispal.nsf/b792301807650d6685256cef0073cb80/93037e3b939746de8525610200567883?OpenDocument.

UN (United Nations) General Assembly. 1960. Resolution 1514. Accessed 1 June 2014. http://www.un.org/en/ga/search/view_doc.asp?symbol=A/RES/1514%28XV%29.

UN (United Nations) General Assembly. 1965. "International Convention on the Elimination of All Forms of Racial Discrimination." United Nations Treaty Series 660.

UN (United Nations) Security Council. 1992. "Interim Report of the Commission of Experts Established Pursuant to Security Council Resolution 780." UN Doc. S/25274 (1993), Annex I, para. 56.

UN (United Nations) Department of Economic and Social Affairs. 2013a. *International Migration Policies: Government Views and Priorities*. Accessed 2 March 2015. http://www.un.org/en/development/desa/population/publications/pdf/policy/InternationalMigrationPolicies2013/Report%20PDFs/z_International%20Migration%20Policies%20Full%20Report.pdf.

UN (United Nations) Department of Economic and Social Affairs, Population Division. 2013b. *International Migration Policies: Government Views and Priorities*. Report coauthored by Lina Bassarsky, Yumiko Kamiya, Julia Ferre, Victor Gaigbe-Togbe, and Vinod Mishra. ST/ESA/SER.A/342. New York: United Nations.

UN (United Nations). 2014. *The Millennium Development Goals Report 2014*. New York: United Nations. Accessed 8 September 2015. https://www.un.org/millenniumgoals/2014%20MDG%20report/MDG%202014%20English%20web.pdf.

UNHCR (United Nations High Commissioner for Refugees). 2013. "2013 UNHCR Country Operations Profile—Myanmar." Accessed 2 May 2013. http://www.unhcr.org/pages/49e4877d6.html.

UNHCR (United Nations High Commissioner for Refugees). 2015. "UNHCR Country Operations Profile—Myanmar." Accessed 22 January 2016. http://www.unhcr.org/pages/49e4877d6.html.

UNHCR (United Nations High Commissioner for Refugees). 2016. "2015 Global Trends: Forced Displacement in 2015." Accessed 2 December 2016. http://www.unhcr.org/en-us/statistics/unhcrstats/576408cd7/unhcr-global-trends-2015.html.

UNHCR (United Nations High Commissioner for Refugees). 2018. "Operational Update: Bangladesh." January 23–February 5. Accessed 9 February 2018. https://data2.unhcr.org/en/documents/details/61917.

UNICEF (United Nations Children's Emergency Fund). n.d. "The 1960s: Decade of Development." Accessed 23 June 2015. https://www.unicef.org/sowc96/1960s.htm.

UN-OCHA (United Nations Office for the Coordination of Humanitarian Affairs). 2012. Sudan Humanitarian Update, Third Quarter. Accessed 4 July 2014. http://reliefweb.int/sites/reliefweb.int/files/resources/Full_Report_4398.pdf.

UNWFP (United Nations World Food Programme). 2015. "India: Overview." Accessed 21 September 2015. https://www.wfp.org/countries/wfp-innovating-with-india/overview.

United States. 1803. An Act to Prevent the Importation of Certain Persons into Certain States, Where, by the Laws Thereof, Their Admission Is Prohibited. The Avalon Project of the Yale Law School, Lillian Goldman Law Library. Accessed 29 June 2017. http://avalon.law.yale.edu/19th_century/sl003.asp.

United States. 1807. Act Prohibiting Importation of Slaves. 2 Stat. 426, 2 March.

United States. 1831. *Cherokee Nation v. Georgia* 30 U.S. (5 Pet.) 1.

United States. 1875. Page Act. 18 Stat. 477, 3 March.

United States. 1889. *Chae Chan Ping v. United States.* 30 U.S. 581.

United States. 1924. Indian Citizenship Act, 43 Stat. 253. 2 June.

United States. 1947. National Security Act. Accessed 26 October 2014. http://research.archives.gov/description/299856.

U.S. Bureau of Economic Analysis. n.d. "Corporate Profits after Tax (without IVA and CCAdj)." Retrieved from FRED, Federal Reserve Bank of St. Louis. Accessed 30 January 2017. https://fred.stlouisfed.org/series/CP.

U.S. Office of War Information. n.d. *The Atlantic Charter.* Washington, DC: Division of Public Inquiries.

Urry, John. 2000. *Sociology beyond Societies: Mobilities for the Twenty-first Century.* London: Routledge.

USA Today. 2017. "Read the Federal Judge's Ruling on Trump's Immigration Ban." 4 February. Accessed 24 May 2017. https://www.usatoday.com/story/news/2017/02/04/read-washington-judges-ruling-trumps-immigration-ban/97484850/.

Valaskakis, Gail Guthrie. 2005. *Indian Country: Essays on Contemporary Native Culture.* Waterloo, Canada: Wilfred Laurier Press.

Van Dijk, Rijk. 2003. "Localisation, Ghanaian Pentecostalism, and the Stranger's Beauty in Botswana." *Africa* 73 (4): 560–583.

Van Hear, Nicholas. 1993. "Mass Expulsion of Minorities: An Overview." *Journal of Refugee Studies* 6 (3): 274–285.

Van Schendel, Willem. 2002. "Geographies of Knowing, Geographies of Ignorance: Jumping Scale in Southeast Asia." *Environment and Planning D: Society and Space* 20 (6): 647–668.

Vargas, Manuel. 2000. "Lessons from the Philosophy of Race in Mexico." *Philosophy Today* 44: 18–29.

Veit, Peter. 2018. "Brief: History of Land Conflicts in Kenya." Focus on Land in Africa. Accessed 2 January 2019. http://www.focusonland.com/fola/en/countries/brief-history-of-land-conflicts-in-kenya/.

Venturini, Alessandra. 2004. *Postwar Migration in Southern Europe, 1950–2000: An Economic Analysis*. Cambridge: Cambridge University Press.

Veracini, Lorenzo. 2010. *Settler Colonialism: A Theoretical Overview*. Basingstoke, U.K.: Palgrave Macmillan.

Veracini, Lorenzo. 2011. "Introducing: Settler Colonial Studies." *Settler Colonial Studies* 1 (1): 1–12.

Visram, Rozina. 2015. *Ayahs, Lascars, and Princes: The Story of Indians in Britain 1700–1947*. London: Routledge.

Vonk, Olivier Willem. 2014. *Nationality Law in the Western Hemisphere: A Study on Grounds for Acquisition and Loss of Citizenship in the Americas and the Caribbean*. Leiden: Martinus Nijhoff.

Vozella, Laura. 2017. "White Nationalist Richard Spencer Leads Torch-Bearing Protesters Defending Lee Statue." 14 May. Accessed 23 May 2017. https://www.washingtonpost.com/local/virginia-politics/alt-rights-richard-spencer-leads-torch-bearing-protesters-defending-lee-statue/2017/05/14/766aaa56-38ac-11e7-9e48-c4f199710b69_story.html?utm_term=.b9e1eafdd19c.

Wagner, Michele D. 1999. "The War of the Cachots: A History of Conflict and Containment in Rwanda." In *Enfermement, prison et chatiments en Afrique*, edited by Florence Bernault, 473–505. Paris: Karthala.

Walford, Charles. 2012. "'We Need Community Cohesion': Ministers' Pledge to End Era of Multiculturalism by Appealing to 'Sense of British Identity.'" *Daily Mail Online*. 21 February. Accessed 6 March 2013. http://www.dailymail.co.uk/news/article-2104049/Eric-Pickles-signals-end-multiculturalism-says-Tories-stand-majority.html.

Wallerstein, Immanuel. 2005. "After Developmentalism and Globalization, What?" *Social Forces* 83 (3): 1263–1278.

Walters, William. 2010. "Deportation, Expulsion, and the International Police of Aliens." In *The Deportation Regime: Sovereignty, Space, and the Freedom of Movement*, edited by Nicholas De Genova and Nathalie Peutz, 69–100. Durham, NC: Duke University Press.

Wang, Amy B. 2017. "One Group Loved Trump's Remarks about Charlottesville: White Supremacists." *Washington Post*. 13 August. Accessed 15 August 2017. https://www.washingtonpost.com/news/post-nation/wp/2017/08/13/one-group-loved-trumps-remarks-about-charlottesville-white-supremacists/?utm_term=.aefc46b1bfbb.

Ward, Kerry. 2015. "Comparing Abolition across the Indian Ocean," paper given in the History Department, University of Hawaii at Manoa. 2 October.

Ward, Sakej. 2016. "Decolonizing the Colonizer." 13 January. Accessed 15 January 2016. http://www.realpeoplesmedia.org/news/2016/1/13/sakej-ward

-decolonizing-the colonizer?utm_source=Real+Peoples+Media++Weekly+
Newsletter&utm_campaign=744263c227- RSS_EMAIL_CAMPAIGN&utm_
medium=email&utm_term=0_a52e031fab-744263c227-46883993.

Warrior, Robert. 2007. "Cherokees Flee the Moral High Ground over Freedmen." *News from Indian Country*. 7 August. Accessed 12 June 2016. http://
indiancountrynews.net/index.php/news/119-editorialletters/1106-cherokees-flee
-the-moral-high-ground-over-freedmen.

Washington Post. 2015. "Donald Trump Announces a Presidential Bid." 16 June. Accessed 5 June 2016. https://www.washingtonpost.com/news/post-politics/wp
/2015/06/16/full-text-donald-trump-announces-a-presidential-bid/.

Watenpaugh, Keith David. 2010. "The League of Nations' Rescue of Armenian
Genocide Survivors and the Making of Modern Humanitarianism, 1920–1927."
American Historical Review. December. Pp. 1315–1339.

Weaver, Frederick Stirton. 2000. *Latin America in the World Economy: Mercantile Colonialism to Global Capitalism*. Boulder, CO: Westview.

Weaver, Matthew. 2010. "Angela Merkel: German Multiculturalism Has 'Utterly Failed.'"
The Guardian. 17 October. Accessed 2 March 2013. https://www.theguardian.com
/world/2010/oct/17/angela-merkel-german-multiculturalism-failed.

Webb, James. 1951. Progress Reports in Foreign Relations of the United States,
National Security Affairs; Foreign Economic Policy, Volume I, S/S–NSC Files,
Lot 63 D 351, NSC 104. USA Office of the Historian. Accessed 2 May 2013. https://
history.state.gov/historicaldocuments/frus1951v01/d383.

White House Press Office. 2017. "Executive Order Protecting the Nation from
Foreign Terrorist Entry into the United States." 27 January. Accessed 30 January 2017. https://www.whitehouse.gov/the-press-office/2017/01/27/executive-order
-protecting-nation-foreign-terrorist-entry-united-states.

WHO (World Health Organization). 2014. "World Health Statistics 2014" (news release). Accessed 30 January 2017. http://www.who.int/mediacentre/news/releases
/2014/world-health-statistics-2014/en/.

Wienia, Martijn. 2003. *The Stranger Owns the Land but the Land Is for Us! The Politics of
a Religious Landscape in Nanun, Northern Ghana*. Leiden: Institute for Social and
Cultural Studies.

Wiessner, Siegfried. 2008. "Indigenous Sovereignty: A Reassessment in Light of
the UN Declaration on the Rights of Indigenous People." *Vanderbilt Journal of
Transnational Law* 41: 1141.

Willame, Jean-Claude. 1997. *Banyarwanda et Banyamulenge: Violences ethniques et ges-
tion de l'identitaire au Kivu*. Paris: L'Harmattan.

Willen, Sarah S. 2010. "Citizens, 'Real' Others, 'Other' Others." In *The Deportation
Regime: Sovereignty, Space, and the Freedom of Movement*, edited by Nicholas De
Genova and Nathalie Peutz. Durham, NC: Duke University Press.

Williams, Raymond. 1961. *The Long Revolution*. London: Chatto and Windus.

Wilson, Valerie, and William M. Rodgers III. 2016. "Black-White Wage Gaps Expand
with Rising Wage Inequality." Economic Policy Institute. 20 September. Ac-

cessed 16 January 2017. http://www.epi.org/publication/black-white-wage-gaps
-expand-with-rising-wage-inequality/#epi-toc-7.

Wimmer, Andreas, and Nina Glick Schiller. 2002. "Methodological Nationalism
and Beyond: Nation–State Building, Migration, and the Social Sciences." *Global
Networks* 2 (4): 301–334.

Winarnita, Monika Swasti. 2011. "The Politics of Commemorating the May 1998
Mass Rapes." *RIMA: Review of Indonesian and Malaysian Affairs* 45 (1/2): 133–164.

Winckler, Onn. 1997. "The Immigration Policy of the Gulf Cooperation Council
(GCC) States." *Middle Eastern Review* 33 (3): 480–493.

Wolfe, Patrick. 1994. "Nation and Miscegenation: Discursive Continuity in the Post-
Mabo Era." *Social Analysis: The International Journal of Social and Cultural Practice*
36:93–152.

Wolfe, Patrick. 1997. "Should the Subaltern Dream? Australian Aborigines and the
Problem of Ethnographic Centriloquism." In *Cultures of Scholarship*, edited by
S. C. Humphries, 57–96. Ann Arbor: University of Michigan Press.

Wolfe, Patrick. 1999. *Settler Colonialism and the Transformation of Anthropology: The
Politics and Poetics of an Ethnographic Event*. London: Cassell.

Wolfe, Patrick. 2006. "Settler Colonialism and the Elimination of the Native." *Journal of Genocide Research* 8 (4): 387–409.

Wood, Ellen Meiksins. 2002. *The Origin of Capitalism: A Longer View*. London: Verso.

Wordie, J. Ross. 1983. "The Chronology of English Enclosure, 1500–1914." *Economic
History Review* 36 (4): 483–505.

World Bank. 2014. "China Overview." Accessed 17 June 2014. http://www.worldbank
.org/en/country/china/overview.

World Bank. 2018. "Record High Remittances Sent Globally in 2018." Accessed 12
November 2018. https://www.worldbank.org/en/news/press-release/2019/04/08
/record-high-remittances-sent-globally-in-2018

Wright, Angus, and Wendy Wolford. 2003. *To Inherit the Earth: The Landless Movement and the Struggle for a New Brazil*. Oakland, CA: Food First Books.

Wyman, David S. 1968. *Paper Walls: America and the Refugee Crisis, 1938–1941*. Amherst,
MA: University of Massachusetts Press.

Wyman, David S. 1992. "The Abandonment of the Jews." In *The Holocaust: Problems
and Perspectives of Interpretation*, edited by Donald L. Niewyk, 216–228. Lexington, MA: D. C. Heath.

Wynter, Sylvia. 1995. "1492: A New World View." In *Race, Discourse, and the Origin of
the Americas: A New World View*, edited by Vera Lawrence Hyatt and Rex Nettle-
ford, 5–57. Washington, DC: Smithsonian Institution Press.

Yanow, Dvora, and Marleen Van der Haar. 2013. "People Out of Place: Allochthony
and Autochthony in the Netherlands' Identity Discourse—Metaphors and
Categories in Action." *Journal of International Relations and Development* 16 (2):
227–261.

Yarbrough, Fay A. 2007. *Race and the Cherokee Nation: Sovereignty in the Nineteenth
Century*, Philadelphia: University of Pennsylvania Press.

Yardley, Jim. 2016. "The Breaking Point." *New York Times Magazine*. 20 December. P. 42.

Yiftachel, Oren. 2002. "Territory as the Kernel of the Nation: Space, Time, and Nationalism in Israel/Palestine." *Geopolitics* 7 (2): 215–248.

Yuval-Davis, Nira, and Floya Anthias, eds. 1989. *Woman, Nation, State*. London: Macmillan.

Zarni, Maung, and Alice Cowley. 2014. "The Slow-Burning Genocide of Myanmar's Rohingya." *Pacific Rim Law and Policy Journal* 23 (3): 681–752.

Zaw, Aung, David Arnott, Kavi Chongkittavorn, Zunetta Liddell, Kaiser Morshed, Soe Myint, and Thin Thin Aung. 2001. "Challenges to Democratization in Burma: Perspectives on Multilateral and Bilateral Responses." Report for the International Institute for Democracy and Electoral Assistance (Stockholm, Sweden). Accessed 13 July 2016. http://www.idea.int/asia_pacific/myanmar /upload/challenges_to_democratization_in_burma.pdf.

Zenker, Olaf. 2011. "Autochthony, Ethnicity, Indigeneity and Nationalism: Time-Honouring and State-Oriented Modes of Rooting Individual-Territory-Group Triads in a Globalizing World." *Critique of Anthropology* 31 (1): 63–81.

Zinyama, Lovemore. 2002. "Cross-Border Movement from Zimbabwe to South Africa." In *Zimbabweans Who Move: Perspectives on International Migration in Zimbabwe*, Southern African Migration Project, Series No. 25. Kingston, Canada: Southern African Migration Programme (SAMP).

Zolberg, Aristide. 1981. "International Migration in Political Perspective." In *Global Trends in Migration: Theory and Research on International Population Movements*, edited by Mary M. Kritz, Charles B. Keely, and Silvano M. Tomasi, 3–27. Staten Island, NY: Center for Migration Studies.

Zolberg, Aristide. 1997. "The Great Wall against China: Responses to the First Immigration Crisis, 1885–1925." In *Migration, Migration History, History: Old Paradigms and New Perspectives*, edited by Jan Lucassen and Leo Lucassen, 291–315. New York: Peter Lang.

Zucman, Gabriel. 2015. *The Hidden Wealth of Nations: The Scourge of Tax Havens*. Translated by Teresa Lavender Fagan. Chicago: University of Chicago Press.

INDEX

Page numbers in italics refer to tables.

Abbink, Jon, 44
Abolition of the Slave Trade Act
    (Britain, 1807), 69
Aboriginal Protection Boards (APBs,
    Australia), 51–52
"Aborigines," 12, 46, 211; Australia, 51–52,
    249–50; definition, 51
Aborigines Protection Act (Australia,
    1869), 51
Achtenberg, Emily, 261, 265
Adepoju, Aderanti, 176
African colonies, 23–27, 32, 46, 49,
    53–54, 176. See also Algeria; "coolie"
    system; Darfur (Sudan); Sudan
African states, 23–24, 27, 43; "African-
    ization" policies, 192–93, 215–16;
    Asian citizenship controls in, 178,
    192, 215–16; citizenship and immigra-
    tion controls, 176–85, 182–84, 215–21;
    expulsions and exclusions, 214–21;
    nationalized sovereignty, 181, 184–85;
    national liberation states, 156–59,
    176. See also national liberation states;
    South Sudan
Afro-Asian Conference (Bandung Con-
    ference, 1955), 17–18, 138–40, 143
Agamben, Giorgio, 65
Akinsanya, Adeoye, 184
Alfred, Taiaiake, 250, 251
Algeria, 44, 195–97, 220–21
Alien Registration Act (United States,
    1940), 110
"aliens," 92–95. See also "illegal aliens"
Aliens Act (Britain, 1905), 92, 187,
    294–95n8

Aliens Control Act (South Africa, 1991),
    178–79
Aliens Order (Britain, 1920), 95
Aliens Restriction Act (Britain, 1919), 95
Allied Powers, World War I, 99, 124
Allies, World War II, 27, 107–8
All India Congress Party, 40
allochthons, 123, 204; African states,
    185, 219; allochtoons, 239; allogènes,
    219–20; in European far right rhe-
    toric, 238–39; Migrants/Migrant-
    Natives as, 13, 23, 40–41, 64, 88, 207;
    migration story invented for, 98
Alternative for Germany party (AfD),
    241
American Colonization Society (ACS),
    177
American Export-Import Bank, 146
American Historical Association, 246
American Indian Religious Freedom
    Act of 1978, 54
Americas, 26; asylum refused to Nazi
    targets, 108; independent states,
    80–82; racialized immigration laws,
    82–85, 97. See also Latin America
Amichai, Yehuda, 62
Amin, Idi, 10, 216
ancestry and genealogy, claims to,
    42–43, 49, 114, 164, 206; Indigenous
    National-Natives and Migrant-
    Others of, 251–54; Joseonin Dynasty,
    173–74
Anderson, Benedict, 3, 28, 80
Anderson, Bridget, 5, 94, 149, 190,
    194, 277

Anderson, Perry, 154

anticolonial movements, 18, 40, 143–44, 196, 208

anticommunism, 133–36, 150–51

antimiscegenation, logic of, 48–49, 78, 88; applied to nations, 279; Indigenous National-Natives, 256–56; Nazi Germany, 106; population transfers and, 101

antiracist praxis, 252, 259

apartheid, 195; global, 28–29, 115–16, 164, 293n1 (chap. 7); South Africa, 178–79, 293n1 (chap. 7)

Arce, Luis, 263

Archaeological Resources Preservation Act of 1979 (United States), 54

Arendt, Hannah, 16, 18, 65, 101–2

Armah, Ayi Kwei, 159–60

Armenians, 95, 99, 103

Asian colonies, 23–27, 32, 46, 49, 53. See also "coolie" system; India

Asian Exclusion Act (United States), 49

Asians: African state policies against, 10, 294n10; as "settler colonists," 11, 254

Asian states, 294n2; citizenship and immigration controls, 168–74; closed to nonsubjects, World War II, 27; direct- and indirect-rule practices in, 23–24. See also national liberation states

Asia-Pacific zone, 93–94, 96

Assembly of First Nations, 251

assimilationist discourse, 52, 85, 241–43, 291n9; indirect-rule colonialism and, 24, 28, 45–46, 49–53, 59

Atlantic Charter (1941), 15–16, 118–20, 125

Auden, W. H., 90

Australia, 45, 51–52, 109, 248–49, 288n9

Austria, 239–40

Austro-Hungarian Empire, 26, 91, 95, 98, 105

autochthonous discourses, 21–23, 29–30, 32–34, 60, 164; across political spectrum, 12–13, 20, 33, 204, 207–8, 279–80; African states, 179, 185; always-already racialized, 116, 222; Asian states, 173; Bolivia and, 260–66; competing, 243–45; as defensive, 22, 160; as depoliticizing, 209; economic autochthonization, 145; in Europe, 40–41, 234–43; expulsion and, 165, 212, 214–21, 224–25; failure of national liberation project and, 160; "German-ness," 106; historical specificity of variants, 207–9; indigeneity as first principle, 208–9; by Indigenous National-Natives, 244–45; indirect-rule colonialism and, 40–44; Migrant produced by, 13, 34; national autochthonies/autochthons, 7–14, 86–89; National-Native time, 221–25; national self-determination and, 122–23; nation-state foundations and, 64, 98; Nativeness essentialized, 12–13, 26, 98, 278; nativism and, 12, 28, 88, 179, 185, 247; neocolonialism and, 156–57; Other produced by, 8, 206, 212; population exchanges and, 100–101; *pribumi*-ness, 218–19; United Kingdom, 191–93. See also ancestry and genealogy, claims to

autochthons: Indigenous-Natives as, 23, 40, 54, 164, 207, 296n15; National-Natives as, 13, 64, 86, 88, 98, 191–92, 203–4, 210; "real autochthones," 44; "super-autochthons," 220; White National-Natives as, 24–25; Whites as, 58–59, 86

Axis powers, 15

Aye Maung, 229

Babel, Tower of, 1–2, 22, 281–83

Bainimarama, Frank, 218

Baker, Phyllis, 259

Balibar, Étienne, 3, 64

Balkans, 99, 104, 112, 291n5

Balkan Wars (1912–1913), 114

Bamar people (Burman), 227

Bangladesh, 213; Rohingya people as refugees in, 9, 226, 227, 232

banishment legislation, 67

"barbaric" peoples, 5, 42–43

Bavadra, Timoci Uluivuda, 217

The Beautiful Ones Are Not Yet Born (Armah), 159

Bédié, Henri, 220

being, 250

Belgium, 239

belonging, 10, 13, 25–26, 40, 43, 58, 164–65; employment and, 166; national, 4, 7–8, 25, 61–62, 88, 100–101, 160, 202, 212–13, 220–21, 224, 245, 278, 291n7; National-Native time and, 221; "natural," 23, 37, 61; population transfers and, 100–101; racialized, 69

Berlusconi, Silvio, 238

Bharatiya Janata Party (BJP), 213–14

Bhatt, Chetan, 213

biopolitics, 14, 20–21; of citizenship and immigration controls, 4–7, 64, 203; developmentalism's role in, 30; homecomings, imagination of, 26–27; of indirect rule, 37; National-Natives, competing groups, 243–45; of separation, 14, 20, 206

Birnbaum, Ervin, 108, 109

Biya, Paul, 219

Black Homelands Citizenship Act (South Africa, 1970), 178

Black people, enslaved, 25, 54–55

Black people, entry denied to in Americas, 83–86

Black people, United States, 48–50

Blair, Frederick, 109, 111

"blood," 4, 23, 24, 36, 43, 114; Australia, 52; British citizenship and, 191, 194; Indigenous National-Native views, 256–59; *jus sanguinis*, 173, 174, 229; Mexico, 84–85; Nazi Germany, 106–7; New Zealand, 52–53; shared ancestor fantasy, 164; Turkey, 101; United States, 48–50

Bock, Gisela, 87

Bolívar, Simón, 81

Bolivia, 33, 83, 207, 260–66, 297n17

Border Patrol, U.S., 96

borders, 163; 100 million people displaced by nation-state formation, 114; in Deluge story, 1–2; guarding of as virtue, 4; increased technologies for defense of, 202; "paper walls," 27, 70, 217, 221, 226; racialized, 88; "remote control" of, 92, 96. *See also* passports

Bossi, Umberto, 238

bourgeoisie, national, 18, 30, 139–40, 152–55

Bracero Program (United States), 200

Braithwaite, Rodric, 146

Brazil, Empire of, 83

Brecht, Bertold, 104–5

Breivik, Anders Behring, 240

Bretton Woods Agreement, 125

Bretton Woods institutions, 17, 29–30, 123, 125–28, 140, 148; foreign direct investment (FDI), 130; Soviet Union and, 130–33; Third World response to, 139, 153

Brexit, 242

Britain: alien registration cards, 92–93; Americas and, 1840s, 81–82; Anglo-American loan, 121, 125; Atlantic Charter and, 15–16, 118–19, 125; "crime crisis," 159–60; duality of subject and alien, 93; German Nationals forcibly repatriated, 95; "imperial century" (1815 to 1914), 70; interwar period, 95–96; labor relation of slavery maintained, 69; from metropole to nation-state, 185–95; nationalization of sovereignty, 32, 121–22, 187, 191, 195; under Nazi siege, 15; World War II and, 118–19. *See also* United Kingdom

British Empire, 3, 36, 168, 187, 206–7; Arabs, racialization of, 43; asylum refused to Nazi targets, 108; Canadian

British Empire (cont.)
   immigration policy and, 26; decline
   of, 118, 136; enclosure of common
   lands, 57; free trade strategy, 81–82;
   immigration within regulated, 65;
   Indian Rebellion of 1857 and, 7–8, 23,
   39; during interwar years, 91; London
   Office, 26, 54, 75, 77; Mauritius, immigration controls against "coolies," 25,
   63; Ottoman Empire incorporated
   into, 99; resistance to colonization,
   37; U.S. involvement in end of, 121;
   White settler colonies, 23
British India: abolition of slavery (1843),
   70, 206–7; Burma/Myanmar and
   British biopolitics, 226–29; censuses,
   39; limited access to credit and
   wages, 144; Natives of barred from
   United States, 94; partition of, 28, 40,
   100; subjects of denied entrance to
   Canada, 76–77
British Nationality Acts (BNA): 1948,
   187–88, 191, 194; 1981, 193–94
British Nationality and Status of Aliens
   Act (1914), 77, 95
British National Party (BNP), 235–36
Britishness, 93
British North America Act (1867), 50,
   287n7
British Protected Person status, 190
British Raj, 39, 40
British Slavery Abolition Act of 1833, 63,
   69, 287–88n2
British South Africa Company, 180
British Sterling Bloc, 121
British White Dominions, 27, 46, 50,
   286n8, 287n5; emigration to from
   United Kingdom, 188–89; as Old
   Commonwealth, 188, 192; Southern
   Rhodesia, 180–81
Brown, Gordon, 276
Brown, Wendy, 209
Browne, Thomas, 41
Brubaker, Rogers, 21

Buddhist monks (Myanmar), 9, 207,
   229–30, 296n6
Bulgaria, 99
Bureau of Indian Affairs (BIA), 47, 259
Burlingame Treaty (China/United
   States, 1868), 79, 290n16
Burma, 124, 226. See also Myanmar
   (formerly Burma)
Burman, Anders, 261
Byrnes, James, 132

Cairns, Alan, 251
Cakobau, George, 217
Callaghan, James, 192
Calvez, Corentin, 197
Cameron, David, 241
Cameroon, 219–20
Canada, 45; asylum refused to Nazi
   targets, 109; Chinese Immigration
   Act, 77, 79; Citizenship Act (1946), 187;
   First Nations National-Natives, 207;
   guest workers, 199; immigration controls, 26, 76–77, 110–11; Indian Citizenship Act (U.S.) and, 50; Komagata Maru
   incident, 76–77; labor immigration,
   166; Mohawk Indigenous-National
   Natives, 33, 250, 251, 256, 260; nationalization of sovereignty, 76–77
Canadian Charter of Rights and
   Freedoms, 257
Canning, George, 82
capital: freed by postcolonialism, 15, 29;
   markets, forcible creation of, 121–23;
   mobility rights of, 6, 116; national, 123;
   as tool for self-determination, 144–45
capitalism, 18–19, 114; Americas and,
   82; Atlantic slave trade and, 67–69;
   crises of, 19, 30–31, 141, 148–49, 153,
   275; currency, convertibility of, 121;
   depoliticization of, 30, 145; emergence of, England, 66; "free international trade," 126–28; gendered, 68;
   self-determination and, 119–23, 128;
   United States and, 119–23, 126–27

capitalist system, 6, 15, 17, 20
Carens, Joseph, 202
Castles, Stephen, 199
Central African Federation (CAF), 180
Central Treaty Organization, 140
Cesarani, David, 191
Ceuppens, Bambi, 219
Chae Chan Ping v. United States, 79
Chaudhry, Mahendra, 218
Cherokee Freedmen, 256, 257–60, 297n16
Cherokee Indigenous-National Natives,
  33, 256–60
Cherokee Nation National Council
  (CNCA), 258
China, USSR and, 136–37
Chinese, 15, 63, 77–79, 83–84, 289n15;
  Indonesia and, 218–19
Chinese Exclusion Act (United States,
  1882), 78–79
Chinese Immigration Act (Canada,
  1923), 77, 79
Churchill, Winston, 15, 113, 118, 125, 132
Chuter Ede, James, 190
Citizens, 4; French categories, 44; of
  "independent" nation-states, 19; in-
  terred, World War II, 110–11; moved to
  Migrant category, 12; non-Native, 54,
  212, 255–56, 296n15. *See also* National
  Citizens
citizenship: hierarchy of, 94, 149, 203;
  as "hollowed out," 33; Migrants
  denied, 4; permitted only to free
  Whites, 69; as significant factor in
  life chances and expectancy, 32, 165,
  270. *See also* non-Native citizens
citizenship controls, 3, 163–204; African
  states, 176–85, 182–84, 215–21; Asia,
  168–74; belonging and, 164–65;
  biopolitics of, 4–7, 64, 203; disparities
  enforced by, 29; globalization of, 33,
  115; Myanmar, 227; postcolonialism
  and, 123; Rich World states, 199–201
citizenship premium, 32, 165, 203,
  270, 276

Citizen workers, 6, 175–76
"civilizations," as effect of state power,
  60, 66
"civilizing" of Natives, 24, 38, 47, 54
civil rights insurgency, 1960s, United
  States, 58
classed relations, 29, 37, 92; *campesino*
  and *cocalero* materialist discourse,
  261; classes turned into masses, 18,
  22; cross-class solidarity, discourse
  of, 5, 22, 138; neoliberalism increases
  disparities, 31–32, 151–53; Washington
  Consensus and, 30–31
"cleansing," 181, 238–39; "ethnic," 10
Clearing Union (CU) proposal, 129
Code de l'indigénat (France, 1881), 44
Code of Nationality (France, 1945),
  195
Cohen, Robin, 279
Cohn, Bernard S., 39
Cold War, 17, 29–30, 123; establishment,
  132–37; exploitation and expropriation during, 131–32; proxy wars,
  137; Third World nation-states as
  alternative to, 17, 138–40; as three
  international alliances, 141. *See also*
  developmentalism
collective endeavors, 1–2, 21–22, 204,
  208; National-Natives and Migrants
  as cotemporal/cospatial/coproduc-
  tive, 204; shared political project, 22,
  34–35; working class, separation of,
  56–57
colonialism, 7–8; direct-rule and
  indirect-rule forms, 23; as existence
  of Migrants in "nation," 11; operation
  of through Natives, 36–37; redefined
  in postcolonial discourse, 208; Wilsonian doctrine of self-rule and, 15–16.
  See also indirect-rule colonialism;
  neocolonialism
colonization, migration conflated with,
  11–12, 33, 252–55
Columbus, Christopher, 55, 56, 66

Cominform (Information Bureau of the Communist and Workers' Parties), 132, 135

common law, enslaved people outside of, 68–69

commons, 1–2, 34–35, 209, 281–82

Commonwealth Immigrants Act (Britain, 1962), 187, 190–91

Commonwealth Immigrants Act (Britain, 1968), 192–93

communalism, 40, 214

communism, 139–40

Communist People's Liberation Army (Red Army), 136–37

competition, 6, 29, 31–32; among groups of Natives, 24, 61

"competition state," 141

concentration camps: Jewish people transported to, 109, 292n15; permanent detainment in, 231–32; Rohingya people moved to, 9, 226, 229. *See also* death camps

consciousness, territorialization of, 114–15

Conservative Party (Norway), 240

Conservative Party Conference (United Kingdom), 193–94

"constraint, logic of," 5, 25–26, 78, 105

containment: of postcolonial demands for decolonization, 14–21, 28–29, 117, 122, 273–74; Truman Doctrine, 133

Convention Concerning the Exchange of Greek and Turkish Populations (1923), 99–100

Convention concerning the Status of Refugees Coming from Germany (League of Nations, 1938), 107

Convention People's Party (Ghana), 157

"coolie" system, 5, 63, 69–70, 86, 174, 206–7, 247, 285n4; collapse of, 115; immigration controls, making of, 71–77; immigration controls as "protection," 25–26; slavery replaced by, 70–71, 273; in White Settler colonies, 46. *See also* indentured labor

Cooper, Yvette, 242

Cornelius, Wayne A., 171

corporatism, 152

Council for Mutual Economic Assistance (COMECON), 131, 135

"country reports," 127

Cowley, Alice, 226, 234

creoles, aristocratic, in Americas, 80–81

Crépeau, François, 202

crimes against humanity, 233

criminalization, 78, 107, 109, 159–60, 202

crisis: "crime crisis," 159–60; "crises of capitalism," 19, 30–31, 141, 148–49, 153, 275; as excuse for immigration control, 91–92; mobility pathologized as, 64, 88, 108

Croizat, Ambroise, 196

cross-class relations, 266; solidarity, discourse of, 5, 22, 138; Whites, groups of, 46, 58; within-nation disparities, 270–71

Crush, Jonathan, 180–81

currency, 121, 126, 139, 148

Czechoslovakia, 132

Danish People's Party, 236

Darfur (Sudan), 9, 43, 223

Davidson, Basil, 163

Davis, Kingsley, 292n16

Davis, Thomas, 257

Dawes Allotment Act (United States, 1887), 48

Dawes Rolls (United States), 48, 257–59

death camps, Nazi, 27, 109–10

death rates, 55–56, 67

debtor states, 127, 149–50

"decolonial love," 13

decolonization: anti-immigrant politics seen as essential to, 206; collective and cooperative project for, 34–35; as economic autochthonization, 145; expropriation and exploitation not resolved, 121–24, 128, 142, 260–66; as future-oriented, 30–31, 154–57; as

"home rule," 274; Migrants as barriers to, 254–55; nationalization of
states as constraint on, 122; national
self-determination and, 117–23; not
achieved by national liberation, 212;
postcolonialism as containment
of demands for, 14–21, 28–29, 117,
122, 273–74; property rules and, 42.
See also African states; Asian states;
national liberation movements;
national liberation states
"define and rule," 35, 38, 54, 212, 247, 255,
274, 276
definition, 23, 35, 38, 46, 54; of "Aborigines," Australia, 52; of "Indians,"
United States and Canada, 48, 51; of
Whiteness, 80
Deleuze, Gilles, 41
Delisle, Michael, 256
Democratic Republic of Congo (DRC),
222
"denaturalization," 100
Denmark, 236
deportation. *See* expulsion; population
exchanges/transfers
developmentalism, 18, 29–30, 142–63;
conceptual arsenal of, 145–46; exploitation and expropriation normalized,
145; as future-oriented, 30–31, 154–57;
"improvement," rhetoric of, 57, 145–
46; "national development" rhetoric,
156–57; postcolonial schemes for,
143–47; preservationist discourse, 54;
science and technology, rhetoric of,
145; United Nations and, 146–47; as
weapon of the strong, 143. *See also*
Postcolonial New World Order
Diggers, 281–82
Dirks, Nicholas, 42
displacement, 14, 28, 206, 241, 254; due
to development projects, 145–46,
157–58; making of migrants, 65–67;
nation-state formation and, 101–4,
107, 113–14

divide et impera policy, 37
Dominican Republic (DR), 85, 108,
291n13
Doty, Roxanne, 68
Dred Scott decision (1856), 49, 247
Dua, Enakshi, 252
Dutch, 239
Dutch Empire, 44, 218

East Asia, 151–53
Eastern Bloc, 131–32, 135
East India Company, 38, 70
Eboua, Samuel, 219
Economic Commission of Africa, 176
Ecuador, 83
effective nationality, 279
Egypt, 221–22
electoral politics, 40, 219
elimination, logic of, 55–56
El Salvador, 83
emigration controls, 63, 72–74, 288n7,
295n14; Asia, 167–68; Nazi Germany,
107, 109–10. *See also* immigration
controls
Empire Windrush (ship), 189
emplacement, 28, 33, 65, 164, 165; mid-
nineteenth century processes, 37, 40
enclosure of common lands, 57
"enemies of the People," 89, 97–98,
114; Nazi Germany, 105–6, 109–10;
Rohingya labeled as, 230–31
English Defense League, 230
Enloe, Cynthia, 22
environmental issues, 263
environment of life, 6
Eritrea, 222
essentialization, 22, 41; first principles,
208–9; of Nativeness, 12–13, 26, 98,
278; racism as technology of separation, 58
"ethnic cleansing," 10
"ethnic nations," 64
"ethnographic state," 42
eugenics, 247

Europe: Age of Migration, 112–13; autochthonous discourse, present-day, 234–43; citizenship extended to some Migrant-Others, 242; European-Natives, 201, 242; guest workers post–World War II, 199; "Migrant invasions," 10; movement of people into, 201; "multiculturalism," said to have failed, 240–41; nation-state formation, 26; "overforeignization" discourse, 201, 234; postcolonial melancholia in, 242; White National-Natives, 207, 211, 235–43; Whiteness as non-Native, 235

European Court of Human Rights, 193

European Economic Community (EEC), 129, 193, 197–98, 200

European empires, 23, 36; autochthonous discourses used to separate, 40–41. *See also* British Empire; French Empire

European/Native binary, 33, 36

European Parliament, 236

Europeans, as Natives, 201, 242

European subsidiaries of U.S. companies, 129

European Union (EU), 200–201, 237, 285n6

European Voluntary Worker (EVW) Scheme, 188

Europe of Nations and Freedom group, 241

Évian Accords (1962), 197

Évian Conference (League of Nations, 1938), 107–8, 109

Executive Order 9066 (United States, 1942), 110

exit controls, 5–6, 65–66, 72, 78, 92, 187

exploitation and expropriation: anticolonial fight for, 144; Bolivia, 260–66; during Cold War, 131–32; development and, 147; expansion of in Postcolonial New World Order, 15, 28–29, 121–22, 163; global capitalist system increases, 31; imperialism equated with, 145; labor exploitation, logic of, 55–56; land taken for development, 18–19, 57; normalization of, 124–25, 145; postcolonial, 121–23; superexploitation, 166, 174; United States' involvement in, 15–16, 121–22, 128–30

expulsion, 10, 27, 64–65, 84, 98–101, 185; African states, 176; of Armenians, 95, 99; autochthonous discourses and, 165, 212, 214–21, 224–25; GCC states, 174–75; interwar period, 95; from metropole, 197; from Myanmar, 227; Nazi Germany and, 27, 107; from United Kingdom, 241–42; from United States, 200; United States and, 110, 200; World War II, 110–13; World War II–era, 103, 111–13. *See also* population exchanges/transfers; repatriation

exterminations, 10, 27, 97, 109–10. *See also* genocides

"facilitation, logic of," 5, 25–26, 66, 105, 188, 195

Farage, Nigel, 242

Far East, 128

Farthing, Linda, 263

fascism, 27, 105–7, 186; of Hindutva organizations, 213–14

Federal Republic of Central America, 81, 83

Fidesz party (Hungary), 236

Fiji, 10, 216–18

"Finnish Karelians," 112

First Indochina War (1946–1954), 196

first nations, 250–51

first principles, 208–9

first sovereigns, 10, 244, 246, 250

First World, 20, 31, 126–27, 199; welfare capitalism, 148–49

Five Civilized Tribes (Cherokee, Choctaw, Creek, Chickasaw, and Seminole), 257, 295n16

Five Principles (Non-Aligned Movement), 139

Fixico, Donald, 250
Flanders, 239
foreign direct investment (FDI), 130
Foreigner, 82–83, 92–93; European discourse of, 234–35; National, binary with, 30–31, 64, 98, 123, 145; neocolonialist rhetoric of, 156–57
Forza Italia party, 238
Foucault, Michel, 92, 202, 209
Fourteen Points speech (Wilson, 1918), 118
France: far right parties, 240; French Empire, 3, 44, 195, 198, 286–87n3; immigration controls, World War I–era, 93; interwar period, 96; from metropole to nation-state, 185–87, 195–98; nationalization of sovereignty, 32, 121–22; under Nazi occupation, 15; temporary work permits, 196; Third Estate, 138
Franco-Algerian Accord (1964), 197
Freedom Party (Austria), 239–40
free labor, invention of, 68
"free market," 151
"Free World," 131, 141, 143
French Empire, 3, 44, 195, 198, 286–87n3
French National Immigration Office (ONI), 195
Friedländer, Saul, 27
Front de Libération Nationale (FLN, Algeria), 196
frontier thesis, 246
Fujikane, Candace, 254
Fyfe, Maxwell, 188

Gaitskell, Hugh, 190–91
Gandhi, Mohandas Karamchand, 292n2
Gatrell, Peter, 104
Gaulle, Charles de, 196
General Agreement on Tariffs and Trade (GATT), 17, 20, 30, 126, 127–28
Genesis, King James Version, 1–2
genocides: Armenian, 95, 99; Myanmar (formerly Burma), 9, 232–34; Rwandan, 1994, 9–10, 185, 222

German Empire, 26–27, 91, 95, 105
"Germans," expulsion of, 113, 186
Germany: far right parties, 240–41; "guest workers," 186; immigration control, pre–World War I, 93
Germany, Nazi: Allied immigration control and, 107–8; asylum refused to targets of, 108–10, 186–87; emigration from prevented, 109–10; Herrenvolk ("master race"), 106; Holocaust, 91, 109, 232–33; Reich Citizenship Law, 27
Geschiere, Peter, 219
Ghana, 157–58, 215, 221
Gilroy, Paul, 19, 31, 154
Glick Schiller, Nina, 255, 271
global capitalism, 31–32; international institutions of, 16–17, 20, 29–30; labor markets, 6, 32; national economies exist within, 31; postcolonialism as governmentality of, 20; reorganized by nation form of state power, 22. See also Bretton Woods institutions; United Nations (UN)
glory, concept of, 5, 12, 18, 268, 275–76, 278, 281–82
Golden Dawn Party (Greece), 237–38
Göring, Hermann, 107
Goulet, Denis, 147
governmentality, 88, 165–66; contemporary mode of ruling relations, 13; Nationals privileged over Migrants, 165; postcolonial, 3, 6, 13, 14, 20–21, 23–24, 34, 38, 122–23, 154, 161, 201, 208, 261, 264, 274–77; of protection, 38–39, 44–45, 47, 53, 63. See also indirect-rule colonialism; Native authorities; "protection"
"The Government Could Have Stopped This" (Human Rights Watch), 231–32
Government of India Act (1858), 38
Gramsci, Antonio, 159
Gran Colombia (Great Colombia), 81
Grant, Madison, 97, 247

Grant, Ulysses S., 47
"Great Migration" from Europe, 58, 287n8
Greco-Turkish "population exchanges," 91
Greco-Turkish War (1919–1922), 99
Greece, 99–100, 103, 136, 237
Greek Civil War (1946–1949), 136
Greek Communist Party (National Liberation Front), 136
Griffiths, James, 189
gross national product (GNP), 29–30
Guaraní people (Bolivia), 263–64
Guatemala, 84
Guattari, Félix, 41
guest workers, 186, 199–200
Gulf Cooperation Council (Cooperation Council for the Arab States of the Gulf, GCC), 171–72, 174–76, 294n3
Gyi, Aung, 227
"Gypsies," 83, 97, 107, 291n10

Hage, Ghassan, 242, 244
Haiti, 85, 86, 290n21
Hall, Stuart, 159–60
Hasina, Sheikh, 232
Hawai'i, 94, 253
Henry VIII, 66
Hertog, Steffen, 175
"hill people," 42–43
Hindess, Barry, 167
Hindus, 39–40, 212–14
Hindutva ("Hindu-ness") movement, 213–14
Hirakud Dam (India), 145
Hispaniola, 85
Hitler, Adolf, 107
Hlaing, Min Aung, 233
Hobsbawm, Eric, 105
Hofer, Norbert, 240
Holland, 239
Holocaust, 91, 109, 232–33
"homecomings," 26–27, 99, 114, 214

homelands, 10, 45, 102, 113–14, 157, 164, 276; emplacement and displacement, 28, 113; Indigenous National-Natives and, 250, 254; Nationals as "native" to, 64–65; Nazi Germany and, 106; state territories as exclusive to a People, 4, 26–28, 65, 97–98; White Settler colonies as, 45–46
home rule, 292n2. See also national sovereignty (home rule)
Hong Kong, 172, 194
Hoogvelt, Ankie, 150
horizontal system, rhetoric of, 4, 5, 29
Howard, John, 248–49
Hugo, Graeme, 173
Human Rights Watch, 231
Hungary, 236
Hungary-Serbia border, 236–37
Hutus (Rwanda), 10, 207, 222

identity, 36, 42; "Aryan," 106; "Indian," state category of, 48; as state-issued, 104; territorialization of, 37–38, 40–41, 43, 123, 142, 203, 209–10
"illegal aliens," 79, 173, 175, 181, 203; far right European rhetoric of, 237–38; Rohingya as, 229; wage gaps, 272
imagined national community, 26–27
Immigrant Worker category, 93
Immigration Act (Canada, 1910), 77
Immigration Act (Johnson-Reed Act) (United States, 1924), 49–50, 69, 96, 247
Immigration Act (United Kingdom, 1971), 193
Immigration Act (United States, 1917), 93–94
Immigration and Nationality Act (United States, 1965), 97
immigration controls, 3, 90–116, 164, 191–92; African states, 176–85, 182–84; Asia, 168–74; biopolitics of, 4–7, 64, 203; Canada, racist restrictions, 26, 65; Canada and United States

compared, 76–80; "coolies" and, 25, 63, 72–73; "coolie" system and making of, 71–77; as federal jurisdiction, 79; gendering of, 77–78, 79; globalization of, 32–33, 91, 109, 114–15, 165, 202; international system of states and, 91, 109; interwar years, 95–98; literacy tests, 93–94; making of Minorities, Refugees, and Stateless, 101–10; national sovereignty made through, 80–86; plenary power doctrine, 79; population exchanges, expulsions, and exterminations, 98–101; postcolonialism and, 123; post-war expansion of, 27–28; "temporary" restrictions made permanent, 91–92, 95–96, 186; "timelessness" of, 114; United States as early adopter of, 15, 289n12; World War I–era, 91–95; World War II–era, 110–13. See also emigration controls; expulsion; population exchanges/transfers
immiseration of workers, 19, 88, 141, 154, 161, 269
immobility, 5, 23, 46–47, 51–52, 86, 174–75. See also immigration controls
imperialism, 40–61, 287n4; Atlantic slave trade and, 67–69; categorization of Natives, 36–39; end of, 91, 98, 119; European/Native binary, 33, 36; exit controls, 5–6, 65–66, 72, 78, 92, 187; Gran Colombia (Great Colombia), 81; legacy of, 7–9, 13, 22, 23, 36, 88, 166; mobility in, 5, 54–55, 65, 94–95; nationalisms as legacy of, 7–8, 88; nationality as distinction of, 118; National-Natives' legal and moral authority derived from, 33; Postcolonial New World Order as continuation of, 19–20, 124, 243; violence transferred to nation-state form, 14–15, 97–98; Wilsonian doctrine of self-rule and, 15–16. See also "coolie" system; indirect-rule colonialism

imperial-state, 2, 4–5; "logic of facilitation," 5, 25–26, 66, 105, 188, 195
imperium sine fine (empire without end), 5
import-substitution policies, 18–19
"improvement," rhetoric of, 57, 145–46
indentured labor, 5, 25, 46, 57, 63, 288n6, 292n16. See also "coolie" system
"independence," 8
India, 33; forced removal of people, 271; Hindu National-Natives, 207; Hindutva ("Hindu-ness") movement, 213–14; partition of British India, 28, 40, 100, 113, 212, 286n1; poverty, 168, 171, 271
Indian Act (Canada, 1876), 50–51
Indian Appropriations Acts (United States, 1851, 1871), 47
Indian Citizenship Act (United States, 1924), 49–50
Indian Councils Act (Morley-Minto reforms) (1909), 40
"Indianness," racialized construction of, 48
Indian Rebellion of 1857, 7–8, 23, 39, 60, 63
Indian Removal Act (United States, 1830), 47
Indian Reorganization Act (United States, 1934), 48
Indian Reorganization Act of 1934, 257
"Indians"/Natives: "Aborigines," Australia, 51–52; Canada, 50–51; definitions, 48, 51; economic participation denied to, 51; enslaving of, 55–56; population decline, 55–56; precolonial territories, 50; United States, 46–50
Indian Tribal National-Natives, 207
Indigenato Code (Portuguese Empire, 1899), 45
indigeneity, 8, 13, 21, 40–41, 160, 208, 218–22, 227, 235–36, 265–66; South Africa, 179–80
indigenismo, 84–85
"indigenization," 214–15

indigenous, as term, 40

Indigenous National-Natives, 10–11, 210–11, 213; Bolivia, 260–66; as first inhabitants and first sovereigns, 10, 250; first nations and nationhood concept, 250–51; membership struggles, 255–56; Migrant-Others of, 250–56; Migrant-Others of Mohawk and Cherokee, 33, 256–60; moral weight of autochthonous discourses, 244–45; Postcolonial New World Order influences discourse of, 251–52; racialization and, 255–60

Indigenous-Natives: as autochthons, 23, 40–41, 54, 164, 207, 296n15; as emplaced, 40, 45, 164; in European imperialism, 36; Europeans as, 235–43; as mobile, 42–43; as natured, 8, 41, 164; "protection" of by segregating, 23–24; sovereignty of, 250–51; special constitutionally granted rights, 11; stasis of, 23, 41, 144; treaties with, 46–47, 245. *See also* "protection"

indirect-rule colonialism, 23–24, 36–61, 207; "advisers," 42; Australia, 50, 51–52; Canada, 50–51; definition, 23, 35, 38, 48; distinction between Natives and Migrants, 38–45; immigration controls based on, 64; Indigenous-Natives emplaced, 40; "law and custom" court system, 36–38; legacy of in present day, 45, 226–27; major institutions of, 36–37; Migrants displaced, 40; New Zealand, 50, 52–53; precolonial institutions under, 42–43; "protection" as governmentality of, 25–26, 38–39; repackaged, 206, 212, 268; shift to from direct rule, 36; "traditional" people "protected" by, 25–26, 39, 44–45; United States, 46–50

Indonesia, 218

industrialization, 18–19

inequality, global scale, 28, 32, 115–16, 155, 203, 268–70; immigration wage gap, 272; patriarchy of the wage and, 265, 271

inheritance, 3

Inquiry into the Protection of Aboriginal Children from Sexual Abuse, 248

"integration," 241

Intergovernmental Committee on Refugees (ICR, League of Nations), 107

Intergovernmental Conference on Identity Certificates for Russian Refugees, 103

International Bank for Reconstruction and Development (IBRD), 126, 146

International Convention for the Safety of Life at Sea, 238

International Court of Justice, 279

International Development Association, 126

International Finance Corporation proposal, 146

international law, 4, 16, 125, 250, 286n7

International Monetary Fund (IMF), 17, 20, 30, 126–27, 149–50

International Organization for Migration (IOM), 173, 280

International State Crime Initiative (ISCI), 232

Inter-Parliamentary Union conference (Stockholm, 1921), 105

interwar period, 84, 88, 95–98, 108, 114, 118, 148, 168; France and immigration control, 195; Minorities as Migrants, 102; Nazi German laws, 104–6; new nation-states, 16, 27, 90–91; protectionism, 105, 127; stage set for Postcolonial New World Order, 89, 91

Ireland, 67, 188, 191

Iriye, Akira, 127

irredentism, 102

Israel, 28, 100

Italy, 93, 196, 238–39, 291–92n10

Iturbide, Agustín de (Agustín I of Mexico), 81

Ivory Coast (Côte d'Ivoire), 220, 222

Jamaica, 189

Japan, 111, 128, 132

Japanese-Americans, 110–11

jealousy: in Genesis, 1–2; immigration control as, 4, 105, 109, 112

Jensen, Siv, 240

Jessop, Bob, 33

Jewish people, 28, 91, 290n3; asylum refused to, 108–10; British restrictions on entry, 92; criminalization of by Nazis, 107, 109; in Egypt, 221–22; Mexico bars entry to, 97; Nazi German laws against, 106–7; United States bars entry to, 96

Jobbik party (Hungary), 236

Johnson, Albert, 247

Johnson, Chalmers, 151

Jones, Arthur Creech, 189

Joseonin Dynasty, 173–74

jus sanguinis ("right of blood"), 173, 174, 229

jus soli ("right of the soil"), 173, 194

A Justification of the Mad Crew (Ranters), 282

kafala (sponsorship) system, 174–76

Kahnawà:ke Mohawk Law and Moratorium on Mixed Marriages, 256–57

Karimuddin, Kazi Syed, 145

Karlsson, Bengt, 244

Kaup, Brent Z., 264–65

Kennan, George, 132–34

Kennedy, John F., 146, 147

Kenya, 216

Kenyatta, Jomo, 216

Keynes, John Maynard, 129

King, Mackenzie, 77

Kinninmont, Jane, 174

Kjarsgaard, Pia, 236

Klaaren, Philip, 179

Know Nothings (Native American Party), 247

Kodnani, Mayaben, 213–14

Kohl, Benjamin, 263

Kohn, Hans, 64

Komagata Maru (passenger ship), 76–77

Korean peninsula, 136–37

Krassowski, Andrzej, 157–58

Kristallnacht pogrom (Germany), 109

Ku Klux Klan, 230

Kukutai, Tahu, 52–53

Kyi, Suu, 234

labor: European, in White Settler colonies, 55–57; free labor, invention of, 68; immiseration of workers, 19, 88, 141, 154, 161, 269; international labor movement, 133; intimidation and deportation of, 200; precarious workers, 32; immiseration of, 19, 88, 141, 154, 161, 269; racialized division of, 69. *See also* indentured labor; slavery

labor exploitation, logic of, 55–56

labor markets, 18–19, 32, 57, 93; exploitation strengthened, 6

labor unions, 78, 130, 196

land, expropriation of, 18–19, 31, 57, 148

Latin America, 137, 150, 290n20. *See also* Americas

Laurier, Wilfrid, 76–77

Lausanne Convention (1923), 99–100

Lausanne Treaty (1923), 99, 290n1

"law and custom" court system, 36–38

Law for the Protection of German Blood and German Honor (Germany), 106

Lawrence, Bonita, 252

League of Nations, 15, 117–18, 291n8, 292n11; colonialism, view of, 118; Évian Conference, 107–8, 109; Minority Treaties, 16, 101–2, 210, 233, 291nn9–10; Paris conference, 105; Refugees and, 103

Lecocq, Baz, 44

Le Pen, Marine, 240, 241

Lester, Lord, 192–93

Lewis, Aidan, 238

"liberated nations," 138
Liberia, 177, 220
Libya, 221
life expectancy, 270, 271–72
Lifeline (NGO), 238
Lincoln, Abraham, 83
Linebaugh, Peter, 57
Linera, Alvaro García, 264
Lipsitz, George, 57
literacy tests, 93–94, 178, 216, 288n9
Littlefield, Daniel, 258
"logic of constraint," 5, 25–26, 78, 105, 112
"logic of facilitation," 5, 25–26, 66, 105, 112, 188, 195
London, tax havens, 272
Luibhéid, Eithne, 78

Malawi, 220
Malaysia, 172
Malcolm X, 142
Mali, 220
Mamdani, Mahmood, 38
Maori (New Zealand), 52–53
Mara, Kamisese, 217
market society, 105
maroon societies, 35, 43
marriage: antimiscegenation, logic of, 48–49, 78, 88, 101, 106; outlawed between Migrants and National Citizens, 168
Marshall Plan, 130; funds, 17, 121, 128
Martínez, Miguel Alfonso, 244
Marx, Karl, 201
Marxism, 133
massacres, 56, 95, 213–14
masses, classes turned into, 18, 22
"Master Narrative of American History," 246
Maung, Saw, 229
Mauritius, 25, 63, 287n2, 288n5
Mauritius Ordinances (1835), 25, 65
May, Theresa, 242
McCorquodale, John, 52
Mercredi, Ovide, 255

Merkel, Angela, 240–41
Mesopotamian alluvium, 60
metaphysical worldviews, 209
methodological nationalism, 255, 271
metropoles, 6, 19, 115; Britain, 185–95; France, 93, 185–87, 195–98; migration to, postcolonial, 166–67; nationalized sovereignty of, 3, 8, 59, 185; unrestricted movement into, 27, 93, 186–87, 195; World War II–era, 93–95
Mexican Empire, 81
Mexico: Bracero Program and, 200; immigration laws, 84–85, 97
Michaloliakos, Nikolaos, 237
Middle East, 113
Migrant-Natives: as allochthons, 13, 23, 40–41, 63–64, 88, 207; in European imperialism, 36; as mobile, 23; as "modern," 39, 42; over Indigenous-Natives, 45; as placeless, 41–42; as sedentarized, 42–43; as settlers, 8
Migrant-Others: of European National-Natives, 235–43; of Indigenous National-Natives, 250; of National-Natives, 13, 33, 161, 215, 243–45
Migrants: as allochthons, 13, 23, 40–41, 64, 88, 207; as always-already foreign, 65; autochthonous discourse as productive of, 13, 34; Black people, enslaved, 25, 54–55; classed character of, 6, 31; as "colonizers," 7–8, 10–11, 14, 31, 33, 45, 59, 141, 192–93, 201, 203–4, 207, 252–55; as co-National Citizens, 207; demonization of, 8, 204, 208, 248; deportability of, 6, 9; end of slavery as origin of, 63; legally substandard status, 4, 167, 245; making of by nationalism, 65–67; Minorities as, 102; nation-states absolved of responsibility for, 16; as negative others of National-Natives, 13, 33, 161, 215; New Commonwealth, 186, 188–91; no lawful claims permitted, 11–12; non-White, as threat to White

National-Natives, 11; normalization of
violence and, 91; as Others, 4, 235–43;
as "people out of place," 6, 8, 13–14,
21; as problem, 31, 64, 123, 279–80;
proliferation of categories, 115, 165;
Rohingya people as, 227, 229; settler/
colonists as, 11; as social category,
12; subordination of, 13, 166, 172, 178,
234–35, 280; Tutsis as, 10. *See also*
Migrant-Natives; Migrant Workers;
non-Nationals
Migrant Workers, 6, 93; Asia, 168; Britain,
interwar period, 95; "coolie" system
replaced by, 115; in Far East, 152; as
labor market category, 166; remittances, 167, 173, 175–76, 203; Rich World
recruitment of, 32; South Africa, 179;
temporary workers, 166, 196
migration: colonization conflated with,
11–12, 33, 252–55; from less developed
nation-states to developed ones,
166–67; post–World War II, 16
migration story, invention of, 98
Milanovic, Branko, 269
Miles, Robert, 191, 204
military-industrial complex, 17, 29, 121,
123, 140
Ministry of International Trade and
Industry (MITI, Japan), 128
Minorities, 64–65, 101–2, 173, 210, 291n7,
291nn9–10
Minority Treaties (League of Nations),
16, 101–2, 233, 291nn9–10
mobility, 4–6, 63–64, 71–77; of capital,
6, 31, 116, 203; as deviant, 164; eons
of reimagined as national security
threat, 65, 79; from Europe to Americas, 82; exit controls, 5–6, 65–66,
72, 78, 92, 187; five thousand years
of attempts to control, 60; imperialism and, 5, 25, 45, 54–55, 60, 65, 86,
94–95; large-scale migrations, 70, 95,
98, 148, 185–86, 195–97; of Migrant-
Natives, 23, 41–42; nationality and,

165; nation-states and, 26–28, 31,
34, 82; pathologized as "crisis," 64,
88, 108; of workers, 67; World War
I–era, 94–95, 99. *See also* immigration
controls; indirect-rule colonialism;
"people out of place"
mobility premium, 165
modernization, rhetoric of, 18, 30, 143–
44, 146. *See also* developmentalism
Modi, Narendra, 213–14
Mohapatra, Atanu, 218
Mohawk Indigenous-National Natives,
33, 250, 251, 256–60
Molina, George Gray, 264
Molotov Plan, 131
Monetary and Financial Conference
(UN, 1944), 17
Monetary and Financial Conference
(United Nations, 1944), 125–26
Mongia, Radhika, 5, 25–26, 66, 70,
105, 112
Monroe, James, 81
Monroe Doctrine, 81
Montenegro, 99
Morales, Evo, 33, 260–66
Morley, John, 40
Morrison, Toni, 2, 205, 282–83
"most favored nation status," 127
Movement for Socialism Party (MAS,
Bolivia), 260, 262–63
Mugabe, Robert, 180
multilateral free trade agreements, 127
Muslims, 9, 39–40, 213, 220; European
rhetoric against, 239, 240
mutually assured destruction (MAD),
137
Myanmar (formerly Burma), 33, 124,
207; 969 movement, 230, 296n6;
genocide in, 9, 173, 232–35; Rohingya
people, 9, 173, 225–35; *taingyintha*
("national/indigenous" races), 228–29

Nansen, Fridtjof, 103
Nansen passports, 103–4

Nasser, Gamal Abdel, 138, 221
Natal, British colony of, 177–78
"national capitalists," 124, 139, 144–45, 243
National Citizens, 19, 26, 80, 125, 148–49, 164, 207. *See also* Citizens
national citizenship, 26, 80, 114, 148, 280. *See also* Citizens; citizenship; citizenship controls; National Citizens
"national community," 278
national culture, 171, 174, 279, 291n9
National Democratic Party (NPD, Germany), 236
National Front (France), 240
National Historic Preservation Act of 1966 (United States), 54
nationalisms, 13, 260; decolonization as, 117; exploitation and expropriation normalized by, 124–25; as future-oriented, 30–31, 154–57; hardening of, 7, 9, 20, 26, 33, 154, 206, 221, 266, 274; as legacy of imperialism, 7–8, 45, 76, 88; Migrants made by, 65–67; Minorities and, 102; as new religion, 2–3; New World, 80–82; truth claims, 208–9, 231, 274. *See also* interwar period
nationality, 65, 285n3; effective, 279; as imperial distinction, 118; as international barrier, 28
Nationality and Status of Aliens Act (Britain, 1914), 77, 92–93, 95
national liberation movements, 7–11, 18; as capitalist crisis-fixing strategy, 153; containment of decolonization demands, 28–29; preservation discourse and, 54
national liberation states, 11; autochthonous discourses in, 122–23, 210, 212; coup d'etats, 10, 216–17; developed *against* people, 159; developmentalism linked to, 30, 144–45; exploitation and expropriation in, 18–19, 157; kleptocracies, 150; postin-

dependence literary works, 158–59; repressive use of state power, 150–51. *See also* African states; Asian states; Third World
National Majorities, 101, 102
National Minorities, 27, 64–65, 101–2
National-Natives, 6–8, 26, 33, 80, 206, 276; African states, 185; as autochthons, 13, 64, 86, 88, 98, 191–92, 203–4, 210; claimed to be incapable of living in same political community, 100–101; as "colonized," 156–57; competing biopolitical groups, 243–45; of Europe, Migrant-Others and, 235–43; of former White Settler colonies, 243–45; hierarchy of, 276; India, 213–14; *mestizo* Mexicans, 85; Migrant-Others of, 13, 33, 161, 215, 243–45; Migrants said to colonize, 7, 8, 10, 14, 31; of Myanmar, 226–35; as "people of a place," 13, 21, 86, 209; as "People without history," 26, 40–41, 209; postcolonial melancholia and, 154–60; Stateless as negative counterpart to, 105; wage nationalization and, 116, 165; White Supremacist, 210–11. *See also* Indigenous National-Natives; Nationals; White National-Natives
National-Native time, 221–25, 231
National Origins Act (United States), 49
National Park Service's Tribal Preservation Program (United States), 54
"national pride," 243, 275–76
"national race," 64, 107, 252
Nationals, 3, 26; developmentalism, 30; Foreigners, binary with, 145; horizontal sameness, 5; immigration control benefits to, 114–15; immigration laws and, 64; as native to "homelands," 64–65; as "people of a place," 4, 6, 13; "true," 7. *See also* Indigenous National-Natives; National-Natives

national security threats, discourse of, 123, 177, 279–80; Cold War era, 134; "crime crisis," 159–60; mobility reimagined as, 65, 79; Myanmar, 231; refugees and, 102; South Africa, 179; Third World, 140, 151

National Socialist German Workers' Party (Nazis), 27, 91, 105–6

national sovereignty (home rule), 5, 7–8, 10, 20, 28–29, 64, 113–14; Britain, 32, 121–22; Canada, 76–77; decolonization and, 124; development seen as essential to, 144; of metropoles, 3, 8, 59, 185; National-Native right to, 13; nation-state system and, 117; racialized, 76–84; state sovereignty, nationalization of, 3, 5, 8, 20, 113–14; "undesirable immigrants" and, 76, 80, 84; United States, 78–80

"national workers," 139, 145, 167, 243

nationness, 13, 28, 78, 97, 99, 114, 218, 243, 293n8

nation-states, 3–4, 62–89; 100 million people displaced in Europe by formation of (1912–1968), 114; absolved of responsibility for Migrants, 16; classes said to be unified, 5, 18; communitarian basis, 101; cross-class solidarity, discourse of, 5, 22, 138; failures not acknowledged, 160; historically distinguished by immigration controls, 4–5; as inheritance, 4; interwar period, 63–64, 91; as invention, 3; "logic of constraint," 5, 25–26, 78; as model for political community, 161–62; New World origins of, 80–86; non-Nationals in, 64; Ottoman imperial metropole becomes Turkey, 99; proliferation of, 6, 88, 91, 99, 113–14, 201, 213, 221; racist and sexist underpinnings of, 4, 29, 77–80; reversal of imperial order, 5; support for across political spectrum, 12–13, 20, 33, 204; violence of, 14–15

nation-state system, 6, 8, 202–3, 210; hegemony of, 130; as hierarchical, 124, 156, 203; making of, 26, 117–23; as unjust, 124, 164

Native American Graves Protection and Repatriation Act of 1991 (United States), 54

Native authorities, 8, 36–37, 39, 41

Nativeness: essentialization of, 12–13, 26, 98, 278; European discourse of, 234–35, 243–44, 248; as first principle, 160–61; White claims to, 58–59, 234–35, 243–44, 248

Native-Others, 235

Native Reserves Act (New Zealand, 1856), 52

Natives: civilizing mission for, 24, 38; class rhetoric of, 138; competing groups of, 24, 61; divided into categories, 7–8, 36–39; European National-Natives, 235–43; European-Natives, 36, 201, 242; "Indians," United States, 46–50; as Migrants, 63; as "non-workers," 55; as "resources," 37; as subjugated category, 33 (see also Indigenous National-Natives); in White settler colonies, 23–24. See also "Indians"/Natives; Indigenous National-Natives; Migrant-Natives; National-Natives; White National-Natives; White Supremacist National-Natives

Native schools, 24, 53. See also schools, "residential"

nativism, 12, 28, 82, 88, 179, 185, 247

naturalization, 93, 110–11, 171, 176, 193

Nazi Germany. See Germany, Nazi; National Socialist German Workers' Party (Nazis)

Nehru, Jawaharlal, 138–39, 145, 157

Neocolonialism: postcolonialism renamed as, 19, 141, 154–56; rhetoric of, 13–14, 15, 31, 116, 154–60, 273, 274

Neo-colonialism: The Last Stage of Imperialism (Nkrumah), 156

Neocosmos, Michael, 179–80
neoimperialism, 116, 141, 154
neoliberalism, 6, 33; Bolivia and,
    261–64; politically mature, 149, 151–53;
    Washington Consensus, 30–31,
    148–51, 153; welfare capitalism rolled
    back, 148–49
Netherlands, 239
New Commonwealth Migrants, 186,
    188–91
Newfoundland, 46
New World, 45, 286n9; as origin of
    nation-state, 80–86
New Zealand, 45, 52–53
Nilsen, Alf Gunvald, 240
Nkrumah, Kwame, 138, 156–57, 215
Non-Aligned Movement (NAM), 138–39,
    156; developmentalism and, 143,
    145–46, 293n9
noncitizens. See citizenship controls;
    Migrants
nonhuman animals, as Native, 37
non-Nationals, 64–65, 105–6, 115, 164,
    176, 207, 223; defense of nation
    against, 161; under postcolonialism,
    123. See also Foreigner; Migrants
non-Native citizens, 54, 212, 255–56,
    296n15
North Atlantic Treaty Organization
    (NATO), 132
Northern League party (Lega, Italy), 238
Northern Territory National Emer-
    gency Response (NTNERA, Australia),
    248–49
Norton, Joe, 257
Norway, 240
Nottebohm case (International Court
    of Justice, 1955), 279
Novikov, Nikolai, 132, 134–35
Nu, U, 124
nuclear annihilation, threat of, 137
Nuer White Army, 225
Nuremberg Racial Laws (Germany,
    1935), 106

Nwaubani, Ebere, 119
Nyarna, U, 230
Nyunt, Khin, 229

Obote, Milton, 216
Office of Indian Trade (United States,
    1806), 47
Office of the High Commissioner for
    Refugees (League of Nations), 103
oil shocks (1973–1974), 200
Oo Hla Saw, U, 229
"Open Door" policy (United States),
    119–20
Operation Wetback (1954), 200
Orbán, Viktor Mihály, 237, 279–80
Organization for European Economic
    Co-operation (OEEC), 130
Organization of African States (OAS),
    Charter of, 156
Organization of African Unity refugee
    conventions, 179
origins, 41, 164, 209–10
Others. See Migrant-Others; Migrants
Ottoman Empire, 26, 91, 95, 98–100, 174,
    221, 290n1, 291n5
Ouattara, Alassane, 220
"overforeignization," 201, 234

Page Act (United States, 1875), 15, 63,
    77–78, 80, 93, 247, 289nn13–14
Pakistan, 212–13; jus soli, 173
Pakistan (East and West), 28, 40, 100, 113
Palestine, 100, 108, 134
Palestinians, 28, 113
Panagiotaros, Ilia, 237–38
"paper walls," 27, 70, 217, 221, 226
Parker, Kunal, 68
Party for Freedom (Partij voor de Vrijheid,
    Netherlands), 239, 241
The Passing of the Great Race (Grant),
    247–48
passports, 66, 92–95, 104–5, 163–64,
    168; Nansen, 103–4. See also borders
pastoralists/nomads, 225

Patnaik, Prabhat, 214

patriality, 192–93, 195

Pax Americana, 128–32, 272

penal transport, 67

People, 4, 8, 16, 19–20, 26–28, 88; "enemies of," 89, 97–98, 105–6, 114; exploitation and expropriation normalized in name of, 124–25; identified by nation-state, 163–64; League of Nations view, 118; postcolonialism and, 123

"people of a place," 4, 6, 13–14, 60, 86, 114, 160, 209; 1604 designation of Natives as, 37, 57; under imperialism, 23; in international law, 16; under postcolonialism, 123

"people out of place," 6, 13–14, 60, 114, 245; under imperialism, 23, 40; in international law, 16; Minorities as, 102; population transfers, 98–101; under postcolonialism, 123. *See also* Migrants

permanent residency, 166, 171–74, 179, 181, 200, 203, 285n2

Petry, Frauke, 241

Petty, William, 67

Philippine Independence Act (1934), 97

Philippines, 290n2, 96–97

plantation economies, 66, 69

plenary power doctrine, 79

Plender, Richard, 93

pluralism, legal, 44

Poland, 111, 131

Polanyi, Karl, 105

Policing the Crisis (Hall, et al.), 159–60

political categories, 21

political communities, 26, 105, 161–62, 277; reimagining of, 5, 7, 86–87; separation of National-Natives, 100–101; of workers, 153

"political nations," 64

political spectrum, 12–13, 20, 33, 204, 207–8, 279–80; far right, shift to, 234–35

la politique des races, 44

Ponty, William, 44

Poor World nation-states, 20, 116, 165, 203, 266, 274, 285n5; outflows to Rich World countries, 269–70

population exchanges/transfers, 14, 28, 91, 95, 98–101, 103, 114, 198, 291n5; "Germans," expulsion of, 113, 186; India and Pakistan, 113; Nazi Germany, 107; World War II, 111–13. *See also* expulsion; repatriation

"populations," 98, 122, 167

Portuguese Empire, 45, 80, 83, 176

possessive individualism, 18

postcolonialism, 3; as ascendency of national form of state power, 14–15; capital freed by, 15, 29; as containment of demands for decolonization, 14–21, 28–29, 117, 122; international political institutions of, 16–17, 20, 29–30; nations-state form reliance on, 137; United States, influence on, 115–16. *See also* Postcolonial New World Order

postcolonial melancholia, 14, 19–20, 31, 154–60, 242

Postcolonial New World Order, 3; capital investments, mobility of, 6, 116; centrality of the Native/ Migrant binary to, 25, 211–12, 234, 245, 252–53; conflation of migration with colonialism, 11–12; consolidation of, 153; declarations of independence and implementation of controls, by geographic area, 168–85, *169–71, 182–84*; expropriation and exploitation, expansion of, 15, 28–29, 121–22; governmentality of, 4–6, 122–23, 276; as hierarchical, 29, 124, 140–41, 156, 203; horizontal system rhetoric, 4, 5, 29; imperialism not divergent from, 19–20; Indigenous National-Native discourse influenced by, 251–52; inequality on global scale, 23, 32,

Postcolonial New World Order (cont.)
115–16, 155, 203, 265, 268–72; key
historical developments, 20–21; Migrants have no lawful claims, 11–12;
new modes of managing populations, 28–29; normalization of, 4,
6, 13, 275; rejection of, 35; as ruling
order, 274; shifts in categorical
definitions, 59; structural characteristics, 11–12, 32, 61, 125, 154, 161,
174, 243, 277–80. *See also* citizenship
controls; decolonization; developmentalism; immigration controls;
postcolonialism
postcolonial racism, 4–5, 279–80
postcolonial theory, 13, 159–60
postnational state, 281
postseparation, 34–35, 268–69
Potsdam Agreement, 113
Potsdam Conference (1945), 132
Potts, Lydia, 69
Powell, Enoch, 192–93
Prashad, Vijay, 138, 144–45, 153, 273
presentism, 251
preservation, discourse of, 54
President's Council of Economic Advisers 1967 annual report, 147
Preventive Detention Act (Ghana), 157
pribumi-ness, 218–19
"primitive accumulation," 57
privatization, 66, 149, 269
Progress Party (Norway), 240
proletarianization, 67, 86, 122, 155
proletarian movements, 86–87, 144
property rules, 41–42
"prostitutes," legislation against, 78, 247
"protection," 23–26, 38–39; imperial
forms, 38–39, 46–52; of Minorities,
101–3; nation-state form and, 65,
80, 105; of Natives/Indians, United
States, 46–48; New Zealand, 52; of
Stateless, 105; of "traditional" people,
25–26, 39, 44–45; in White Settler
colonies, 46–48

providence, 246
Provisional Arrangement concerning
the Status of Refugees Coming from
Germany (League of Nations, 1936),
107
pseudopsychological discourse, 133, 143
Puerto Rica, 80
Pynya Sa Mi, U, 229–30

Quintana, Tomas Ojea, 233

Rabuka, Sitiveni, 217
Racial Integrity Act (Virginia, 1924),
49, 50
racialization, 114; of Arab-ness, 43; asylum refused due to, 108–9; Europe,
present-day, 235–43; exclusion from
White Settler colonial project, 11; of
geographies, 4, 37, 41, 45, 60, 94; of
immigration controls, 76–89; Indigenous National-Natives and, 255–60;
of "origins," 209–10; of slaves, 68; of
temporalities, 41, 45. *See also* "blood"
"racial purity," 64
racism: Asian immigration policies, 172;
British immigration control, 189–90;
in Canada, 76–77; categorization of
Natives into types, 39; French immigration controls, 197; horizontal, 279;
postcolonial, 4–5, 279–80; segregation, project of, 23–24; separation,
shift to, 204; "settler colonialism"
erases, 252–53; as technology of
separation, 58. *See also* postcolonial
racism
Raison, Timothy, 193–94
Rajaratnam, Sinnathamby, 151
Rakhine Nationalities Development
Party (RNDP), 229
Ramji, Jaya, 179
Ranters, 282, 297n1
rape, 10, 113, 226
Rashtriya Swayamsevak Sangh (RSS), 213
la Raza Cósmica, 85

"Reagan Doctrine," 150–51
"receiving" nation-states, 167–68
Rediker, Marcus, 57, 67
Reed, David, 247
Refugees, 27, 102–3; asylum, refusal of,
    108–10, 186–87, 238–39; in Australia,
    249; Rohingya people, 9, 226–27; in
    South Africa, 179; Syrian, 241–42.
    See also Stateless
Reich Central Office for Jewish Emigra-
    tion (Nazi Germany), 107
Reich Citizenship Law (Germany, 1935),
    106
religion, 2–3, 39–40, 100, 290n3
remittances, 167, 173, 175–76, 203
"remote control," 92, 96
Renton, David, 191
repatriation, 95, 198, 202, 211. *See also*
    expulsion; population exchanges/
    transfers
replacement, theory of, 246
Reséndez, Andrés, 55–56, 66
"reserved" land/reservations, 23–24,
    60, 238; Australia, 51–52; Canada, 50;
    New Zealand, 52–53; United States,
    46–48
Resettlement Law (no. 2510) (Turkey,
    1934), 101
resistance: autochthonous discourse
    used, 208; British riots against non-
    Whites, 191; civil rights insurgency,
    United States, 58; to colonization,
    36–37, 196; GCC states, 175; "IMF
    riot," 150; job actions, aliens barred
    from, 95–96; proletarian movements,
    86–87. *See also* national liberation
    movements
res nullius, 246
Resolution 1514, the Declaration on the
    Granting of Independence to Colo-
    nial Countries and Peoples (Declara-
    tion on Decolonization) (1960), 124
revanchism, 102
Rhodes, Cecil, 180

Rhodesia, 180
Richmond, Anthony, 115
Rich World nation-states, 6, 20, 116, 155,
    266, 274, 285n5; citizenship and immi-
    gration controls, 199–201; citizenship
    premium, 32, 165, 203, 270, 276; guest
    workers, 186, 199–200; Migrant Work-
    ers recruited, 32, 165; Poor World
    outflows to, 269–70
"right to have rights," 65, 102, 115, 255
Rohingya people, 9, 173, 225–35, 295n3,
    296n6; atrocities against, 230–31; as
    Migrants, 227, 229
Roman Empire, 5
Roosevelt, Franklin Delano, 15, 110,
    119, 126
Royal Commission on Aboriginal
    People (RCAP, Canada), 251
ruling relations, 13, 25, 155–56, 275, 281
rural economy, destruction of, 18, 31,
    144, 148
Rürup, Miriam, 104
Russian Empire, 26, 91, 95, 98; pogroms
    against Jewish people, 92
Russian Revolution (1917), 103
Rwandan Genocide (1994), 9–10, 185, 222

Sack, Robert, 3
Said, Edward, 36, 145, 163, 231
Salvini, Matteo, 238–39
sameness, 5, 39, 209–10, 212–13
Saudi Arabia, 175
Saunier, Pierre, 127
Sauvy, Alfred, 138, 195
"Save Darfur" movement, 9
Schengen Treaty (1995), 285n6
schools, "residential," 24, 53
science and technology, rhetoric of, 145
"scientific racism," 48, 78
Scott, James, 5, 42–43, 66, 122, 281
Scott Act (United States, 1888), 79
Second World, 31, 148
Sein, Thein, 229, 230
"self-barbarianization," 43

self-determination, 15–16, 33, 156; Atlantic Charter and, 118–20; autochthonous discourse and, 122–23; capital as tool for, 144–45; capitalism and, 119–23, 128; as farce, 273; national, 4, 13, 117–23; United Nations Charter, 17, 20, 29, 102. *See also* decolonization; national liberation states
self-rule, Wilsonian doctrine of, 15–16
"selling out," 153, 158
Sen, Amartya, 147
"sending" nation-states, 167–68
separation, 2, 13–14, 23–24, 32, 230, 234, 266; apartheid, global, 28–29, 115–16, 164, 293n1 (chap. 7); biopolitics of, 14, 20, 206; electorates divided, 40; hardening and expanding of, 20, 165, 266; "Indian" state-mandated categories, United States, 48–49; Indigenous National-Natives and Migrant-Others of, 251–52; of Indigenous-Natives and Migrant-Natives, 8, 36; of National-Natives and Migrants, 8–9; racialized and gendered, 67; shared identification, destruction of, 86–87, 114; shift from racism to, 204
Serbia, 99
Servan-Schreiber, Jean-Jacques, 129
servitude, attributed to Natives, 37
"settler colonists," 11, 55, 252–53, 273
Sewell, Henry, 52
shared identification, 86–87, 114–15
Shohat, Ella, 18
Sierra Leone, 220
Sieyes, Emmanuel Joseph, 138
Simpson, Audra, 250, 251, 253–54, 255, 256–57
Singapore, 151, 168
slavery, 25, 46, 86, 287n8; abolition movement, British, 25, 63, 65, 273, 287–88n2; "aliens," enslaved people as, 68–69; Atlantic slave trade, 67–69; Atlantic slave trade, end of, 55, 58, 69; Blackness equated with,

57, 68; Columbus and, 55–56, 66; "coolie" system as replacement for, 70–71, 273; Indian, in New World, 55–56; Liberia, "founding" of, 177; Soviet Union, 112. *See also* "coolie" system
Smith, Chadwick, 259
socialism, 145
socialist republics, 17
social relations: authochthonous discourse and, 12–13; capitalist, 20, 29, 32, 66, 86, 122–23, 155, 161, 165, 201, 202, 271, 277, 281; indirect-rule colonialism's effect on, 45, 52; National-Nativeness and, 206; postcolonial, 123, 140–41, 243; post–World War II, 17–18
Soederberg, Susanne, 141
"soil," racialized ideas of, 164
solidarity: common purpose, sense of, 1–2; criminalization of, 202; as mobile politics, 35; rebuilding, 276–78
Somalia, 221
SOS Méditerranée (NGO), 238
South Africa, 177–80, 293n1 (chap. 7)
South East Asian Treaty Organization (SEATO), 140
Southern African Development Community member states, 179
Southern Poverty Law Center, 248
Southern Rhodesia (Zimbabwe), 180–81
South Korea, 173–74
South Sudan, 33, 222–24. *See also* Sudan
sovereignty. *See* national sovereignty (home rule); state sovereignty
Soviet Union, 17, 99, 158; Bretton Woods institutions and, 130–33; Cold War establishment and, 132–37; deportations, World War II, 111–12
Spanish Empire, 80–81, 83, 85, 260
Stalin, Joseph, 132, 133, 135
stasis: dependent on forced movement, 91; of Indigenous-Natives, 23, 41, 144; Native defined through, 88, 144;

normalized, 164; as origin of "state," 5; precolonial institutions, discourse of, 42–43. *See also* "people of a place"

state: as enclosed "society," 92; monopoly over legitimate movements, 60; nation form of, 5, 14–15, 22, 27; power of, 14–15, 22, 26, 60. *See also* imperial-state; nation-states; nation-state system

state capitalism, 135, 293n6

State Department (United States), 120

Stateless, 27, 107, 173, 226; passports for, 103–5. *See also* Refugees

state sovereignty, 2, 26, 65; nationalization of, 3, 5, 8, 20, 64, 113–14

state space, 3–4

Statute of Westminster (Britain, 1931), 77

sterilization, compulsory, 106

Strachey, John, 40

structure of feeling, 31, 154

subalterns, 20, 159

Sudan, 33, 43–44, 222–24; Black National-Natives, 43, 207; Darfur region, 9, 43, 223. *See also* South Sudan

Supreme Court (United States): *Chae Chan Ping v. United States*, 79; *Dred Scott* decision (1856), 49, 247

surveillance, 18, 19, 23, 104, 175, 276

Swaziland, 222

Swedish Democrats, 236

Swinton, Viscount, 190

Swiss People's Party, 237

Switzerland, 108, 237

Takaki, Ronald, 245–46

tariffs, 105, 127–28, 139

tax havens, 272

temporalities, racialization of, 41, 45

Temporary Law of Deportation (Turkey, 1915), 99

"temporary" restrictions made permanent, 91–92, 95–96, 186

terra nullius discourse, 58, 246, 296–97n13

territorialization, 22, 31–32, 34, 98, 121, 244, 254, 275; of consciousness, 114–15; of identity, 37–38, 40–41, 43, 123, 142, 203, 209–10; juridical, 123; racialized, 4, 37, 41, 45, 60, 94; state space, 3–4

Tevera, Daniel, 180–81

Thant, U, 146–47

Thatcher, Margaret, government, 193–94

Third Estate, 138

Third World, 17–18, 128, 138; bourgeoisie in, 18, 139–40, 152–55; capitalism, support for, 18, 156–57; conditional loans to, 30, 126–27, 153; as development target, 30, 143–47; land grabs, 31, 148; loss of political meaning, 146; neoliberalism in, 151–53; as net exporter of capital, 149–50; political project, 17–18, 138. *See also* national liberation states

Thompson, Dorothy, 104

Thornton, Russell, 56

Tigers, East Asian, 151–52

"timelessness," 26, 40–41, 53, 114; National-Native time, 221–25, 231

Tito, Josip Broz, 131, 132, 138

Toroczkai, Laszlo, 237

Torpey, John, 16, 60, 92, 104

Toussaint L'Ouverture, 85, 290n21

trade deficits, 127

"traditional" people, 18, 41–45; "protection" of by indirect rule, 25–26, 39, 44–45

transnational corporations, 153, 173

Trask, Haunani-Kay, 253–54

Treanor, Donna, 236

treaties, 79; with Indigenous-Natives, 46–47, 245, 250, 259–60; Minority Treaties, 16, 101–2, 233

Treaties of Tianjin (Tientsin) (China/United States, 1858), 78

Treaty of Kars, 99

Treaty of Wangxia/Wang-hiya (China/United States, 1844), 78

"tree logic," 41

Trefgarne, Lord, 194

Treuer, David, 48, 268

Tribals, 20

trickle-down theory of wealth redistribution, 139

True Levellers Standard Advanced: Or, The State of Community Opened, and Presented to the Sons of Men, 281–82

Truman, Harry, 134, 136, 141

Truman Doctrine, 133

Trump, Donald, 12, 248, 278

Turkey, 27, 95, 99–101, 103

Turner, Frederick Jackson, 246

Turpel, Mary Ellen, 255

Tutsis (Rwanda), 10, 222

Tydings, Millard, 97

Uganda, 215–16

uncanniness, 11, 33, 275

UN Convention on the Punishment and Prevention of the Crime of Genocide, 232

UN Declaration on the Rights of Indigenous People, 245

"underdevelopment," discourse of, 142, 146–47

"undesirable immigrants," 92, 96, 104, 109, 114; national sovereignty and, 76, 80, 84, 187

United Kingdom, 276; Commonwealth Immigrants Act (1962), 187, 190–91; entry into encouraged, 187–88; "integration" discourse, 241–42; labor vouchers, 190–91; patriality, 192–93, 195; prisoners of war in, 188; right of abode, 190, 193, 194; three citizenship categories, 1980s, 194. *See also* Britain; British Empire

United Kingdom Independence Party (UKIP), 242

United Nations (UN), 16–17, 119, 123–25, 179, 286n7; atrocity prevention as founding aim of, 232–33; conventions, 233; Development Decades, 146–47; General Assembly, 124–25, 147; Monetary and Financial Conference (1944), 125–26; Resolution 1514, the Declaration on the Granting of Independence to Colonial Countries and Peoples, 124; Special UN Fund for Economic Development (SUNFED) proposal, 146; veto-wielding members, 124–25; Working Group on Indigenous People (WGIP), 244

United Nations Charter, 17, 20, 29, 102, 117–18, 120, 123–24, 164, 286n7

United Nations Children's Emergency Fund (UNICEF), 147

United Nations Conference on International Organization (UNCIO, 1945), 120

United Nations Human Rights Commission (UNCHR), 231

United Nations Independent International Fact-Finding Mission on Myanmar, 233

United Nations Security Council, 124–25, 132

United States, 23–24, 45, 46–50, 60; "aliens," non-Whites and women as, 68–69; American Colonization Society, 177; anticommunism, 133–36; antimiscegenation laws, 48–49, 78; asylum refused to Nazi targets, 108–9; Atlantic slave trade outlawed, 1808, 55, 58; bottom decile, 21; Bretton Woods institutions and, 125–28; capitalism and, 126–32; capitalism and self-determination, 119–23, 128; Cherokee Indigenous-National Natives, 33, 256–60; Chinese Exclusion Act, 78–79; Constitution, 78, 79; developmentalism and, 146; European labor power needed, 55–57; European subsidiaries of companies, 129; expropriation by, 15–16,

121–22, 128–30; federal powers, 79; Fourteenth Amendment, 49; guest workers (Bracero Program), 200; immigration control, World War II, 110–11; immigration control of Chinese, 15, 63, 77–79, 289n15; immigration control of Europeans, 80; imperialism attributed to, 78, 81–82, 130, 155–56; Indian Rebellion, fears of, 38; Indian Tribal National-Natives, 207; interwar period, 96; Islamophobic U.S.-led war on terror, 9; key role in Postcolonial New World Order, 15, 118–20; Myanmar, support for, 234; nationalization of sovereignty, 78–80; national territories, 15; Natives, as "Indians," 46; Naturalization Law (1790), 247; "Open Door" policy, 119–20; Page Act, 15, 63, 77–78, 80, 93, 247, 289nn13–14; Pax Americana, 128–32; postcolonialism, influence on, 115–16; poverty rates, 271; Racial Integrity Act (Virginia, 1924)/"one drop" rule, 49, 50; racist immigration restrictions, 11, 26; "reserved" land/reservations, 46–47; self-determination as strategy power, 118–19; shift in form of, 78; slavery, 46, 79; Southern and Eastern European immigrants restricted, 96; treaties with Natives, 46–47, 259–60; U.S. Dollar Bloc, 121; as White Settler colony, 11; World War I-era immigration controls, 93–94

United States Naturalization Act of 1790, 69

Universal Declaration of Human Rights (United Nations, 1948), 120, 125, 233

urbanization, 18, 31

U.S. National Front, 248

U.S. National Security Act (1947), 135

"U.S. Policies and Programs in the Economic Field Which May Affect the War Potential of the Soviet Bloc" (Webb), 143

Valaskakis, Gail Guthrie, 255

Veit, Peter, 216

Victorian Half-Caste Act (Australia, 1886), 52

violence: autochthony produces, 33–34; in Balkans, 99; Bolivia, 262–64; European far right parties, 235–36; fascism encourages, 107; forced labor, 56; by Hindu nationalists, 213–14; massacres, 56, 95; of nation-building, 14–15, 26, 91, 99, 105, 181; of Native schools projects, 24, 53; normalization of, 27, 91, 157, 181, 229, 237; of population transfers, 101; reimagination of mobility as national security threat, 65; repression in national liberation states, 150–51; shared identification, destruction of, 86–87; U.S., against Natives/Indians, 47

Virginia, legal codification of slavery, 68

visas, 92, 93

Vishva Hindu Parishad (VHP), 213–14

Vlaams Belang party (Belgium), 239

Voigt, Udo, 236

Volta River Dam (Akosombo Dam) (Ghana), 157–58

Vyshinsky, Andrei, 131

wages: GCC states, 175; nationalization of, 32, 116, 165, 270, 276

Walters, William, 167

War Relocation Authority camps (United States), 110–11

Warrior, Robert, 259

Warsaw Ghetto (Poland), 110

Wartime Measures Act (United States, 1918), 94

Washington Consensus, 30–31, 148–51, 153

Watenpaugh, Keith David, 100

"we are all immigrants" narrative, 58

Webb, James, 143

welfare capitalism, 148–49, 264
Welles, Sumner, 119
"we-ness," 22
West Africa, French, 44
Western Africa, 225
Western Bloc, 131–33, 141
Westphalia, Treaty of (1648), 5
White National-Natives, 10–11, 24–25;
    American Dream and, 130; as com-
    munity, 24–25; Europe, 207, 211,
    235–43; as "first improvers" and "first
    sovereigns," 10, 244, 246; of former
    White Settler colonies, 207, 243–45;
    Migrant-Others of, 243–49; "we are
    all immigrants" narrative, 58
Whiteness: autochthonization of,
    24–25; of Canada, 77–78; invention
    of, 57–58, 68; as "possessive invest-
    ment," 57; of United States, 78
Whiteness, meaning of, 54
Whitening, of working class, 56–58
White Settler colonies, 10, 17, 23–25,
    45–53, 53–61; autochthon, claimants
    for the category of, 33, 54, 210; direct-
    and indirect-rule practices in, 23–24;
    distinctiveness of, 53–61; European
    labor power needed, 55–57; national-
    ization of sovereignty, 25, 76–80, 246;
    Whiteness historicized, 58. See also
    Australia; British White Dominions;
    Canada; New Zealand; United States
White Settler colonies, former: autoch-
    thonous discourses in, 210; "settler
    colonists," 11, 252–53; White National-
    Natives, 207, 243–45
White Supremacist National-Natives,
    46, 210–11, 247
Wildcat, Daniel, 255
Wilders, Geert, 239, 241
Wilson, Woodrow, 93, 118
Wilsonian doctrine of self-rule, 15–16,
    101, 118
Wimmer, Andreas, 255, 271
Win, Myo, 230, 234

Win, Ne, 226, 228
Wirathu, Ashin, 230
Wolfe, Patrick, 55–56
women: bodies of abstracted as
    national symbols, 10; patriarchy of
    the wage and, 265, 271; rape of, 10, 113,
    226; subordination of, 87, 271
working class: aliens barred from job
    actions, 95–96; American Dream
    and, 130; as autochthons, 123; citi-
    zenship and immigration controls
    as damaging to, 275; Third World,
    139–40; Whitening of portion of,
    56–58. See also labor
World Bank, 17, 20, 30, 126–27, 149–50
World Health Organization (WHO), 270
world system of nation-states, 8, 20
World Trade Organization (WTO), 20
World War I (1914–1918), 15, 26, 28, 88,
    186; immigration controls after, 63;
    immigration controls during, 91–95;
    nation-state form and, 81. See also
    interwar period
World War II (1939–1945), 15, 88, 110–13;
    "alien enemies," 110–11; immigration
    controls during, 27; Postcolonial New
    World Order established at end of,
    64. See also interwar period
worry, 244
Wyman, David S., 108–9

Yacimientos Petrolíferos Fiscales Boli-
    vianos (YPFB), 261
Yalta Conference (1945), 132
Young Turk Revolution (1908), 91, 99
Yugoslavia, 131, 132
Yugoslavia, former, 10, 14
Yugoslav Wars (1991–2002), 10, 136

Zarni, Maung, 226, 234
Zimbabwe (formerly "Southern Rhode-
    sia"), 180
Zolberg, Aristide, 92, 97–98
"Zomia," study of, 42–43, 286n2